In 1827 Emerson wrote in his journal: "It is said
singular." One could hardly ask for a more cc
program. In this book, *In Respect to Egotism: Stu*
Joel Porte offers a timely reassessment of ninetee
focusing on the general question of the American Romantic ego anu ito vaiymg
modalities of self-creation, self-display, self-projection, and self-concealment.
The book begins by exploring the status of the "text" in nineteenth-century
American writing, the relationship of "rhetorical" reading to historical context,
and the nature of "Romanticism" in an American setting. It then proceeds
through a series of chapters on the great authors of Romantic America individually – Brown, Irving, Parkman, Cooper, Poe, Emerson, Hawthorne, Thoreau,
Melville, Douglass, Stowe, Whitman, and Dickinson.

Throughout his important new study, Porte offers provocative reassessments
of familiar texts while at the same time casting an illuminating critical eye on less
well-known territory. Readers of this book will come away with increased respect for the achievement of American Romantic writers.

CAMBRIDGE STUDIES IN AMERICAN LITERATURE
AND CULTURE

In Respect to Egotism

Continued on pages following the Index

In Respect to Egotism

Studies in American Romantic Writing

JOEL PORTE
Cornell University

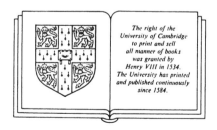

The right of the
University of Cambridge
to print and sell
all manner of books
was granted by
Henry VIII in 1534.
The University has printed
and published continuously
since 1584.

CAMBRIDGE UNIVERSITY PRESS

Cambridge

New York   Port Chester   Melbourne   Sydney

CAMBRIDGE UNIVERSITY PRESS
Cambridge, New York, Melbourne, Madrid, Cape Town, Singapore, São Paulo, Delhi

Cambridge University Press
The Edinburgh Building, Cambridge CB2 8RU, UK

Published in the United States of America by Cambridge University Press, New York

www.cambridge.org
Information on this title: www.cambridge.org/9780521110006

© Cambridge University Press 1991

First published 1991
This digitally printed version 2009

A catalogue record for this publication is available from the British Library

Library of Congress Cataloguing in Publication data
Porte, Joel.
In respect to egotism : studies in American Romantic writing / Joel Porte.
p.   cm. – (Cambridge studies in American literature and culture)
ISBN 0-521-36273-3 (hardback)
1. American literature – 19th century – History and criticism.
2. Romanticism – United States.   3. Egotism in literature.   4. Self in
literature.   I. Title.   II. Series.
PS217.R6P67   1991
810.9′145′09034 – dc20   90-29061
CIP

ISBN 978-0-521-36273-3 hardback
ISBN 978-0-521-11000-6 paperback

For Helene

"In most books, the *I*, or first person, is omitted; in this it will be retained; that, in respect to egotism, is the main difference."

–Thoreau, Walden

Contents

Preface

In 1982, when I produced the first draft of this book, I had in mind little more than a very loosely connected series of chapters on major American writers from Charles Brockden Brown to Emily Dickinson. Though I thought of them all as "Romantic" writers in some of the ways suggested in the Introduction, the book – perhaps with Matthiessen's *American Renaissance* as a model – was not intended to have a single overarching thesis. As I proceeded, however, I became aware of a persistent concern in the unfolding chapters, namely, an interest in modalities of self-display or self-concealment – ways of figuring and disfiguring the self – discernible among American authors in this period. If that interest was continuous from writer to writer, it probably had less to do with there being something exceptional about American writing as such than with concerns and anxieties shared from one author to the next.

Simply put, American writing became a community project because the artists involved tended to think of themselves as pioneers engaged in clearing a common provincial imaginative space.[1] As part of that project they individually and collectively kept one nervous eye on the culture and creations of England and western Europe, which provided both the impetus and the challenge for their own careers. In Harold Bloom's terms, they felt themselves to be both belated and empowered in respect to the antecedent culture. But, to repeat, those imperatives would be acted upon within a shared framework of new nationhood – implying new intellectual as well as new geographical territory.

The self, as Gertrude Stein reminds us, is radically responsive to its circumambient world:

> After all anybody is as their land and air is. Anybody is as the sky is low or high, the air heavy or clear and anybody is as there is wind or no wind there. It is that which makes them and the arts they make and the work they do and the way they eat and the way they drink and the way they learn and everything.[2]

If the problem of self-development and self-articulation was, so to speak, in the land and air in nineteenth-century America, it was as likely to

affect native-born authors as it was immigrants stepping off the boat at
the New World's ports of entry. Brash self-assertion alternating with
crippling self-doubt – advancement and retreat, aggressive neologism
giving way to shamed silence – were inescapable conditions of American
life during the nineteenth century and willy-nilly informed America's
first major burst of literary speech. These conditions could not be blinked
away by the New World's self-creating artistic makers as they worked to
appropriate their inherited language and the literary culture for which it
stood.

Thoreau's pseudoapology from the first page of *Walden* stands as my
epigraph to the whole project:

> In most books, the *I*, or first person, is omitted; in this it will be
> retained; that, in respect to egotism, is the main difference.

Polite gentlemanly tradition may demand lexical self-effacement, as it
frowns on one's putting oneself forward, but that will hardly serve as an
inducement to saying something new. The upstart will always be taught
to fear the too-frequent sound of his own voice, especially if he speaks in
a nonstandard way. For Thoreau, however, to omit the first person is to
wipe oneself off the literary map. "Most books" are written by other
people. In order to make a difference, one must respect one's own voice.

There are, of course, other things to respect, other differences to
make. But they all flow from the vitality of the articulating self as it fills
its cultural space with new speech. One is obliged, however, to assert the
claims of the first person, with a certain restraint and respect for others:
there is, after all, a community of readers to be addressed who have their
own stern claims and perfect circles. As Thoreau knew, John or Jonathan
may become impatient with overly importunate literary manners. So he
and his fellow American Romantic writers would learn to mask their
claims for absolute singularity in the guise of bragging for humanity.
Whether or not they succeeded in their claim to representativeness as
literary voices remains, of course, an open question. But there can be
little doubt that they did put themselves on the map, collectively helping
to establish an American identity that continues to sound its distinctive
notes among the competing egos of the modern world.

Acknowledgments

Since this book draws on a long experience of studying, teaching, and discussing American Romantic writing, any specific record of indebtedness is bound to be incomplete. The work and example of my own teacher, Perry Miller, has naturally cast a long shadow over my career. Many other friends and colleagues helped, advertently or inadvertently, with advice, encouragement, information, and criticism. Among these (in no special order) are Daniel Aaron, Werner Sollors, John McWilliams, Albert Gelpi, Morton Paley, Michael T. Gilmore, Andrew Delbanco, Barbara Johnson, M. H. Abrams, Jonathan Bishop, Dan McCall, Allan Emery, Cushing Strout, Sacvan Bercovitch, Saundra Morris, Michael Strelow, Maurice Gonnaud, Boris Ford, Robert D. Richardson, Jr., Philip Gura, Stuart Levine, James Engell, and Stanley Cavell. I am also indebted to students at Harvard in English 70 and 170 for allowing me to try out some of these chapters in the classroom. That is equally true of students at Cornell, particularly those in my seminars on Transcendentalism and Hawthorne and Melville. I am grateful to other audiences – at Harvard, Cornell, Rhode Island College, the Hawthorne Society, the University of Kansas at Lawrence, the University of Colorado at Boulder, and Willamette University – for their kind reception of, and valuable response to, my work. Andrew Brown deserves thanks for his infinite patience during the many revisions of this study. And I must thank Dianne Ferriss for her expert editorial help. Finally, my wife, Helene, has shared the experience of writing this book from the start – beginning with a delayed Thanksgiving in 1982 while I finished a draft of the Melville chapter and continuing on through many conversations later at breakfast and dinner and everywhere else. Her support has been the sine qua non of my completing this book.

An earlier, and briefer, version of the Emerson chapter appeared in *The New Pelican Guide to English Literature, 9: American Literature,* edited by Boris Ford.

In Respect to Egotism

Introduction: Writing, Reading, Romanticism

1

The question of "the text" has come increasingly to the center of attention in recent years and accordingly deserves some scrutiny here at the outset. In both their historical and technical aspects the major texts of the American literary tradition have come to be seen as somewhat problematic. In the first place, questions have quite properly been raised about the reliability of texts transmitted to us typically in surprisingly haphazard fashion. Quite literally, we have discovered that we did not know what we were reading – whether, for example, variations from edition to edition or from manuscript to first printing in periodicals or in pamphlet form and on to first book edition, could be ascribed to the author, to friends, relatives, or literary executors, or indeed to publishers and printers. In some cases manuscripts no longer exist or have not been found, and the same is true for galley and page proofs. Naturally, the problems vary from author to author.

James Fenimore Cooper, for example, was long considered a careless author who composed quickly and never bothered to revise, but recent textual scholarship suggests that this is not true.[1] Poe's literary estate was left, after his bizarre and premature death, in the hands of a malicious "executor" (Rufus Griswold) who altered some things to suit his own devious ends. Several of Emerson's most important pieces – "The American Scholar" and the Divinity School Address, in particular – were delivered orally only once for a specific audience from scripts that no longer exist. There is much evidence to suggest that Emerson altered these talks when he turned them into printed pamphlets, and we know that they were further changed when they were gathered into *Nature; Addresses, and Lectures* in 1849. Likewise, the seven states of *Walden*, like the seven layers of Troy, have been archaeologically exhumed.[2] Which versions, in both cases, should we study? To what extent, if any, was the composition of Frederick Douglass's *Narrative* influenced by his abolitionist mentors, Wendell Phillips and William Lloyd Garrison? It was

1

frequently charged, rightly or wrongly, that slave narratives were not entirely the work of their named authors.[3]

Whitman, as we know, was a notorious and tireless reviser, and *Leaves of Grass* grew and changed considerably in the course of Whitman's long career. To this day some critics prefer the 1855 *Leaves*, some the third edition of 1860, but most readers have gotten their Whitman from the so-called death-bed edition of 1891–2. It is true, in any case, that there is an enormous amount to be learned about Whitman's project from the early editions, especially from the 1855 *Leaves*, with its important prose preface and startling appearance. Later I shall draw attention to the significance of Whitman's first English edition in 1868. Of course, the most perplexing example of textual problems concerns Emily Dickinson who, as most readers are aware, published few of her poems in her lifetime and left the rest in a variety of manuscript forms – some on the backs of envelopes or on odd scraps of paper, others neatly copied and tied into packets or fascicles, but all notable for their bewildering word variants and odd punctuation and orthography. Her first editors, Thomas Wentworth Higginson and Mabel Loomis Todd, who selected material for the original slim volumes that appeared in the 1890s, have long been blamed for their emendations and intrusions, but their task was formidable, and their decisions were naturally guided by the standards and tastes of their time. Still, students of American literature breathed a collective sigh of relief when Thomas Johnson published the Harvard "variorum" edition in 1955. Subsequent investigation, however, raised serious questions about his procedures. And so the Harvard University Press was persuaded by R. W. Franklin to bring out in 1981 an expensive two-volume facsimile of the reconstituted fascicles, with little flaps of paper tipped in where Dickinson pinned them to her manuscript. In what amounts to a challenge to many of the now standard versions of Dickinson's poems, we can finally return to Dickinson's own original form of nonpublication as the "text" of most authority – or at least of greatest interest.

For more than a generation now, scholars of American literature have been busy reediting the major authors of the canon according to complex and sometimes contradictory principles of textual reconstruction. In the world of intellect at least, universities are known more for their scholarly editions than for their football teams (the Ohio State Hawthorne, the Northwestern Melville, the Harvard Emerson, the Yale Edwards, the Princeton Thoreau). I must admit that I do not root for all these editing teams with equal enthusiasm, for some of them play according to odd rules, though they are all *supposed* to be faithful to what is called – with varying degrees of disingenuousness – "final authorial intention." The trouble is that they manufacture eclectic "ideal" texts; that is, they do not as a rule reproduce any single contemporary edition such as an author or a reader could have laid hands on. Instead, starting with a manuscript or first edition as copy-text, they make emendations according to their own principles and critical judgments. Their aim is a "perfect" text, but it turns out in some cases to be perfect only in the sense in which the mad scientist Aylmer, in Hawthorne's "The Birth-mark," produces a "perfect" wife – a mortuary Georgiana, that is, replacing the real, breathing one, blemished as she may have been, loved or hated by her contemporaries.

One striking instance of this textual tampering occurs in the new Harvard edition of Emerson's works. The editor of Volume 1, *Nature, Addresses, and Lectures,* tells us that he decided to accept Emerson's subsequent revisions of the first printings of his work only when they expand the text, on the principle, presumably, that more is better. As a result Emerson is frequently denied that great gift of laconic wit or wisdom that strengthened with the years. In the famous "transparent eye-ball" passage in *Nature,* for example, Emerson wrote in 1836 concerning his spiritual exhilaration on crossing the bare common: "Almost I fear to think how glad I am." But by 1849 he had decided to say instead, marvelously: "I am glad to the brink of fear." Since the second version, which we have all known for years, contains one word fewer than the original one, it has been rejected in the Harvard edition. What is the difference? Consider the two sentences again: "Almost I fear to think how glad I am"; "I am glad to the brink of fear." Though it took Emerson thirteen fateful years to think how glad he was, he finally mustered the courage to realize it was "to the brink of fear." That kind of emotional brinksmanship – barely visible in the 1836 text of *Nature* – represents Emerson's own version of the Romantic agony. Keats had already written of Joy "whose hand is ever at his lips / Bidding adieu" and of "aching Pleasure . . . Turning to Poison while the bee-mouth sips," and Dickinson would refine the notion:

> For each ecstatic instant
> We must an anguish pay
> In keen and quivering ratio
> To the ecstasy.   (Poem 125)

This is, admittedly, a dramatic example of how much difference the choice of text can make, but others come to mind. For years I had students buy the Modern Library *Selected Writings* of Emerson because it was cheap and ample, but it was also amply supplied with mistakes – and the plates go uncorrected to the present.* So, for example, they print the last sentence of *Nature* as follows: "The kingdom of man over nature, which cometh not with observation – a kingdom such as now is beyond his dream of God – he shall enter without more wonder than the blind man feels who is gradually restored to sight." But that is wrong, for Emerson wrote: "who is gradually restored to *perfect* sight." We notice immediately the difference in cadence. But the word provides a crucial climax to *Nature* in other ways. Emerson begins his treatise by insisting that "we must trust the perfection of the creation" and goes on to exemplify that trust by describing his own "perfect exhilaration" on the bare common. Since the next sentence, as we have seen, tells us that Emerson is "glad to the brink of fear," we are implicitly invited to test, perhaps question, that concept of a perfect creation. How content can a man be with the restoration of "perfect sight" when he knows what it means to be blind? Paradise, Emerson would note later, "is under the shadow of swords."[4] In any case we see how the fate of our reading can hang on the omission – or possible misprinting – of a single word. In the admirable edition of Emerson prepared by Stephen Whicher for Houghton Mifflin in the 1950s and widely used since, Emerson can be heard in "The Poet" calling for a new American bard (and we are brought to a Whitmanian boil as we read) who will sing "our log-rolling, our stumps and their politics, our fisheries, our Negroes and Indians, our boats and our repudiations. . . ." Here an alert reader will stop and wonder: "our *boats* and our repudiations"? The pairing seems wrong, the logic off. And, indeed, another fine Emerson scholar, William Gilman, preparing his own Signet Classic Emerson in the 1960s, noticed the oddity and made a likely emendation that is now standard. He prints "our *boasts* and our repudiations," and that is undoubtedly what Emerson wrote, since especially in the Jacksonian period American *brag* was a household word. Thoreau would both ratify and refine that familiar native propensity in *Walden*: "If I seem to boast more than is becoming, my excuse is that I brag for humanity rather than for myself."[5]

Although there is no general agreement among Americanists regarding the "best" texts of our major authors (indeed I observe that most scholars cite the CEAA or CSE "approved" texts dutifully without considering the issues involved), informed opposition to the textual "scientists" has materialized in recent years. In particular, Jerome J. McGann, himself a textual scholar and distinguished student of English

---

* I was startled to notice recently that a new anthology of American literature, published by Harper, though claiming to use the Harvard Emerson text, has in fact been set from the Modern Library, with all the errors faithfully reproduced.

Romanticism, has argued for a conception of "the text" that avoids the pitfalls of the scientific model of an "ideal" text by favoring a model responsive to the status of every literary text as a cultural artifact.[6] Viewing an individual literary text as a nexus of "arrangements" among author, editor, printer, reader, and critic, McGann helps us to conceive of texts as cultural performances informed by all the conditions of their creation, production, and reception. To introduce a "new" version of a text that never existed in cultural space-time as if it were somehow superior to a particular existent text that was, in Stevens's phrase, "the cry of its occasion," is to misunderstand the nature of cultural exchange. Any first or subsequent edition that was read and discussed has the integrity and authority peculiar to every artifact that circulates in the social body. That process helps to define it as much as "authorial intention." In a Romantic context, in particular, the notion of a text as "organic" might equally be derived from its place in the social body as an inseparable element of the larger Gestalt. It derives its life from that setting and gives vitality back to the setting in turn. In addition, an individual text viewed as a performance might be said to have the Romantic virtue of immediacy – of being charged with the energy of specific utterance. Thus the original version of Frederick Douglass's *Narrative*, published in 1845, bristles with the abolitionist fervor of the period of the Mexican War and is equally energized by the terse, unsophisticated, even blunt power of Douglass's first appearances, in contrast to the flaccid expansions of his life story characteristic of the later, well-known public figure. It is a text that will always have its own "authority," though responsible opinion may decide in favor of other versions that answer to different cultural imperatives.

2

As is by now well known, even outside the academy, the question of "reading" has become a central issue in literary study, along with the equally vexed question of "writing." Phillipe Sollers noted some twenty years ago that "today the essential question is no longer that of the *writer* and the *work*, but that of *writing* and *reading*" – *écriture* and *lecture*.[7] These concepts have been brought to the fore, Jonathan Culler observes, "so as to divert attention from the author as source and the work as object and focus it instead on two correlated networks of convention: writing as an institution and reading as an activity." By "writing as an institution" is meant "a set of written texts printed in books," texts being viewed as semiological systems whose decoding is to be accomplished according to various linguistic structures and rules. Reading is seen as an activity, indeed, an unabashedly creative one, that is accomplished according to the competence of the reader in dealing not only with linguistic structures but also with the various traditions of literary writing antecedently available.[8]

This mode of interpretation, as Culler tells us, is "based on poetics itself, where the work is read against the conventions of discourse and where one's interpretation is an account of the ways in which the work complies with or undermines our procedures for making sense of things." Although such a mode of interpretation "does not, of course, replace ordinary thematic interpretations, it does avoid premature foreclosure – the unseemly rush from word to world – and stays within the literary system for as long as possible."[9] This way of focusing on the text differs from the so-called New Criticism in that it does not start from the premise that significant literary works are necessarily "harmonious totalities . . . complete in themselves and bearing a rich immanent meaning."[10] Meaning is not simply given, whether by authorial intention or otherwise, but is to be worked out "with respect to a system of conventions which the reader has assimilated." This *readerly* theory of writing, which insists, as Ferdinand de Saussure says, that literature is a "system that recognizes only its own order,"[11] is intended to function as a salutary corrective to some of the naive procedures of traditional literary history and biographical criticism and as such to send us back to our texts with renewed interest and confidence in our work as readers. "The absence of an ultimate meaning," as Jacques Derrida writes, "opens an unbounded space for the play of signification." In his view, each reader is invited to become a kind of Nietzschean superman reentering a semiological and semantic Garden of Eden where everything is possible and we are free to participate in "the joyous affirmation of the world's play and the innocence of becoming, the affirmation of a world of signs which has no truth, no origin, no nostalgic guilt and is presented simply for the activity of interpretation."[12]

It might be argued that this is Romantic reading par excellence – a realm of virginal texts perpetually teasing us out of thought in a Faustian quest that has no end because the pleasure of the text is infinite foreplay, free of any obligation to settle down and raise a family of determinate meanings. Let us, as Roland Barthes puts it, scatter, postpone, gear down, and finally discharge meaning. In our love affair with our texts we shall promise anything but deliver only the joys of literary dalliance. And if our pleasure is blocked by indifference or boredom, we shall find ways of enlivening the game of reading, for boredom can act as a provocation, enabling us "to make the text interesting by inquiring how and why it bores us." This sort of active involvement with the text can allow us to read in unconventional ways, to pay attention, citing Culler, to "the fragment, the incongruous detail, the charming excess of certain descriptions and elaborations, the well-constructed sentence whose elegance exceeds its function, or the flaws in a grand design."[13] These procedures, I am suggesting with only slight hyperbole, represent a romantic way of reading appropriate to Romantic texts, with their ambivalences, contradictions, open-endedness, ironies, ennuis, and peculiar gaieties of language.

But although we may allow ourselves to become excited by the possibility of unbounded freedom in interpretation, we ought not be entirely surprised to discover our Romantic saturnalia finally reined in by the invisible chain of necessity that always binds us. We cannot after all free ourselves entirely from meanings that are urged on us by historical considerations. We can, to follow Derrida again, only *imagine* escaping from the usual terms of literary discourse in order to allow other kinds of intellectual attention to operate.[14] We can resist history for the sake of our freedom, but we must finally reenter it for the sake of our sanity. So while we may willingly and happily grant the autonomy of the text as it opens before us in the mysterious silence of its absent presence, waiting to be uttered or read into being, we must also insist that it has a history – as personal expression, as part of the generic tradition to which it belongs, as cultural witness.[15]

Perhaps we can best analogize the status of the text to our sense of ourselves. Naturally, we exist most vividly for ourselves in the strong, though arguably specious, moment of our present experience. But, of course, we also have memories, and although it is frequently difficult for us to specify the mode or degree of reality to be ascribed to our past, we *know* that we have evolved as creatures of time and think as much about our lost worlds as we do about those we inhabit or hope to conquer. We are not content only to improvise the text of our present being. We need also to relive and reinterpret the texts we have already inscribed, and we tend to do so in terms of our historical moment (I was a child of the thirties or the forties or the fifties . . .). As Roy Harvey Pearce observes:

[At the center of our awareness of our humanity] we know ourselves to be, momentarily at least, neither conditioned nor contingent. But at the perimeter of that awareness, we know ourselves as in all things conditioned and contingent. On the one hand we are vital existences who may well be perverted or glorified, but nonetheless never deprived of our individual vitality, so long as we have at least the awareness that we exist. On the other hand, we are acculturated creatures whose least gesture can always be accounted for in someone's encyclopedic register of the life-style which obtains at our particular moment in history. We are both of these at once; so it has always been, so it must always be.[16]

Just as we can never fully realize or understand ourselves except in and through history, so, too, literature is "an expression *in* history"; it is thus not a question of history versus literature, but rather of "history (*our* history) via literature," and we must emphasize that *via*, for the means whereby history is transmitted is not easy to apprehend, since – as Pearce remarks – "a literary work carries the past into the present . . . not just as a monument endowed with the sort of factuality from which we may infer its previous mode of existence, but rather as a somehow 'living' thing from whose particularity of form we may apprehend that existence and to a significant degree share in it." Literature is not merely a "document," nor is reading a work of literature a matter of simple historical research (whatever that may be), but rather – Pearce again – "a transaction with persons in history, a continuing dialogue. Mastery of the theory of this dialogue – which would be a plenary theory of historical criticism – is a problem to be solved by a psycholinguistics and a poetics as yet beyond our ken." To reiterate, we would have to understand more not only about how we read but also about how our reading engages and reactivates the historical realities embedded or lurking in our texts.

The problems are superlatively exemplified, as Pearce notes, by a central cultural text like *The Scarlet Letter*. In our own time, Hawthorne himself has been investigated through this text by psychoanalytically inclined critics in terms of Oedipal difficulties or "a kind of libidinal timorousness." On the other hand, orthodox or neoorthodox critics have made much of the so-called *felix culpa* motif in the book, whereby sin or suffering is viewed as a mode of religious redemption. Now these approaches, as Pearce remarks,

> have yielded up valuable insights for us. But essentially they have not dealt with *The Scarlet Letter* so much as with its import and significance for the culture of its critics. They are deliberately ahistorical and must be accepted as such. I do not wish to dismiss such views but rather to suggest the possibility of another, superior to them at least in its attempt to make its center of interest the novel in relation at once to its historical situation and to ours, not just to ours. I should think that such an alternate view of *The Scarlet Letter* would fully grant that Hawthorne's culture had its constraining libidinal timorousness and its recusant Calvinism, but only to ask: what meanings could he create by evoking the possibilities for authentic human existence which that timorousness and that recusancy shaped and directed? What does it mean (not "how was it actually" – for these are different questions) to have existed in that Boston which Hawthorne's New England gave him the material to create? How was it possible to *live* then? How was it possible to live

in and through the forms (repressive and expressive) peculiar to *that* civilization? What sort of vital structure does Hawthorne create and how does its vitality partake of the vitality of his own culture and that earlier one which his own gave him to envisage?

We might rephrase and summarize the problem this way: *The Scarlet Letter* offers us a view of the seventeenth century in Boston from the perspective – from *a* perspective – of Boston in 1850; we, on the other hand, perceive both Hawthorne *and* the seventeenth century from our own perspective, but both views are mediated by the form of Hawthorne's fiction – as he used it, as we perceive it. It may seem impossible to read the book with all these perspectives actively engaged, but that only suggests how difficult is the task of responsible criticism. We are juggling a set of simultaneous equations, and an adequate response cannot afford to lose sight of any of these variables. To treat Hawthorne's book as nothing more than a system of encoded discourses available for certain operations of grammatical or rhetorical analysis is to leave it stranded as a cultural archive.

I have already referred to what I called "some of the naive procedures of traditional literary history and biographical criticism" in order to draw attention to the dangers involved in treating texts as determinate objects that are little more than direct transcriptions of their cultural moment and milieu or of their authors' lives and backgrounds. Like flowers that have escaped from human cultivation and struck out for the wild, literary texts can undergo strange transformations as they seek their fortunes with new readerships in different times and places. As Emerson says, "[O]ne must be an inventor to read well. . . . There is . . . creative reading as well as creative writing."[17] We must continue to cherish the opportunities for new life – in them, in us – inherent in our great books. From the point of view of our reading, we are invited to engage in that sort of archaeology described by Michel Foucault, which amounts to a kind of "rewriting" – or, in his phrase, "a regulated transformation of what has already been written."[18] But I am obliged to part company with Foucault when he denies validity to the history of ideas because, if I understand him, it tries to displace "discourse in its own volume" in favor of an account of how discourse comes into existence and to fruition through the operations of culture.[19]

If the history of ideas – which Foucault nicely defines as "the analysis of silent births, or distant correspondences, of permanences that persist beneath apparent changes, of slow formations that profit from innumerable blind complicities, of those total figures that gradually come together and suddenly condense into the fine point of the work" – if such history does violence to "the modalities of discourse," then it is rightly

suspect. But surely it ought to be possible to identify historical components and continuities in our literary "discourse-objects" without curtail-
ing our freedom as readers or removing them from the center of our
interest and attention, for indeed that interest and that attention are to a
large extent historically determined. We read our Irving and our Cooper
and our Hawthorne and our Dickinson not simply for the pleasures of
the text but in the belief that they are our veritable antecedents, indispensable elements in our collective self-definition. They are already in us
as we reenter them; in Eliot's phrase, we are "the present moment" of
their past. As we return to them with their work already in our bones, a
circuit is completed whereby history and individual consciousness con-
tinually inform and give birth to each other. At all events, whatever
historical frame we can invent in order to place our literary texts should
never be taken as an "explanation," but rather as a mode of clarifying the
terms of our knowledge. Such approaches must necessarily be tentative,
since we can never reconstruct the past, or the "history of ideas," in a
way that would adequately correspond to its presence or its passage for
those living and creating in that actual field of energy.

3

The particular field of energy that concerns me in this book is, of course,
American Romanticism. I am not content simply to denominate the
material I am studying as "American literature in the first half of the
nineteenth century"; rather, I believe it useful and possible to define a
Romantic movement in this country as a way of understanding our
literature from about 1820 to the Civil War (I shall treat Charles
Brockden Brown as a transitional figure). Now this is, to paraphrase
Melville, neither an uncontroversial nor an easy task, "the classification
of the constituents of a chaos." Since at least the 1920s, when Arthur O.
Lovejoy wrote a now famous essay on "The Discrimination of Romanti-
cisms,"[20] the rubric has often and justifiably been used in the plural. We
have arguments for "negative" and "positive" Romanticism as distinct
phenomena: Romantic agony and Romantic exaltation, the abyss and the
empyrean. We have debased Romanticism (sentimentality) and high, or
visionary, Romanticism: the man (or woman) of feeling versus the
prophet. We have Romantic sincerity and Romantic irony. The list can
be extended, but the central question remains: Can one speak intelligibly
of literary Romanticism *in general*?[21] Was there an international movement? If so, what were its characteristics, and do these apply mean-
ingfully to the American situation? Can or should we lump European
Romanticism together in opposing or comparing it to the American
variety? Are there no important differences, for example, among the
French, German, and English schools? Why do they occur at different

times? Are they genetically different, different in emphasis and theory, and finally of varying importance in the development of American Romanticism?

One can dispose of some of these problems, perhaps, by saying that Romanticism simply refers to the general cultural period after the French Revolution, that is, to the whole modern period. In fact, Friedrich Schlegel, writing of Shakespeare in 1800, uses the term in this sense.[22] There are indeed aspects of the so-called modern sensibility that seem to arise first, or to be given special weight, in the Romantic period: interest in the self, especially the divided self, as a psychological entity; self-consciousness; insistence on originality and creativity; interest in "organic form," and so on. It may in fact be unusefully polemical to stick with a term – "Romantic" – that was in common use at least by the mid-seventeenth century with the connotations of "romance-like," "extravagant," "absurd," "picturesque" (the word is employed with all these connotations in the writing of Charles Brockden Brown and Washington Irving) and would pick up many more, even contradictory meanings during the next two hundred years. We are concerned, after all, not so much with a term as with a new frame of mind, a new awareness, and this awareness, as René Wellek remarks, "may have existed without these terms, or these terms may have been introduced before the actual changes took place, merely as a program, as the expression of a wish, an incitement to change."[23] It was just such a desire for change that Emerson was describing when he spoke of Transcendental literature as being in the "optative mood." He was not himself much given to using the term "Romantic," perhaps because he had already been saddled with Transcendentalism (which he complained, in any case, was not a "fixed element" like salt or lime). Goethe was certainly a Romantic, but in a sour mood one day he said, "Classicism is health, Romanticism is disease"[24]; perhaps he was thinking nostalgically of a form of health that was simply no longer available to the nineteenth century. Stendhal in 1818 pronounced himself a "furious romantic, which is to say I am for Shakespeare and against Racine, for Lord Byron and against Boileau."[25] He was, of course, using the term "romantic" as a stick with which to beat the neoclassical tradition over the head, whereas a defender of the old school, at around the same time, scornfully defined *"romantique"* as

a term of sentimental jargon which certain writers have used to characterize a new school of literature under the direction of Professor Schlegel. The main principle drilled into the pupils of this school is that our Moliere, our Racine, our Voltaire are little more than minor talents bogged down in rules who never succeeded in reaching the level of some grand ideal, the pursuit of which is the object of *romantic activity*.[26]

The derogatory reference to "Professor Schlegel" here is by no means gratuitous, since both Schlegels – August Wilhelm and his brother Friedrich – had done much to advance the cause of Romanticism, and their theories and definitions would be widely disseminated among American intellectuals. The apostate Transcendentalist Orestes Brownson would declare in 1836, the year of Emerson's *Nature*, that the Schlegels were as important as Wordsworth and Byron in preaching the new spiritual gospel, Margaret Fuller would learn much about the new critical *Zeitgeist* from their writings, and even Poe, though he detested having to acknowledge any literary debt, would admit that his crucial notion of the "mystic" or "suggestive" undertone that characterizes all truly imaginative writing was borrowed from the Schlegels. It is probably fair to say that the most comprehensive program for Romantic writing was articulated by Friedrich Schlegel in 1798 in his journal, the *Atheneum*, when he called for a new form of writing that would be "*romantische*" not only, as he said, in having the character of "a progressive universal poetry," but also and more specifically in that it would provide a kind of "*noveau roman*" – a new genre of imaginative writing

> destined not merely to unite the separate genres of poetry and to link poetry to philosophy and rhetoric. It would and should also mingle and fuse poetry and prose, genius and criticism, artistic poetry and natural poetry, make poetry lively and sociable, and life and society poetic, poeticize wit, fill and saturate the forms of art with worthwhile subject-matter of every kind, animated by an upsurge of humor.[27]

Though Schlegel may have been thinking of Goethe's *Wilhelm Meister* as he wrote this passage,[28] we might justifiably look ahead to *Moby-Dick*. The kind of work Schlegel envisioned would be at once the full expression of the author's spirit and the modern equivalent/completion of the epic: "a mirror of the whole world, a picture of the age." At once subjective and objective, personal and universal, microcosm and macrocosm, it has, he goes on, "the potential of the highest, most manifold evolution, not only through outward expansion, but also through inward infiltration, for each thing destined to be a whole entity is organized uniformly in all its parts." We notice that Friedrich Schlegel here articulates a theory of organic form as part of his program for the *romantische Roman*. Its form will be characterized as much by growth toward inner meaning as by its building up a representation of the outer world, for both correspond and are part of the world's body. The Romantic – which is to say organic – work of art must move simultaneously toward the silent center of our being and outward to a world of shared discourse that is the sublimation or displacement of private experience. The link must never be broken, for the two compose one organic whole.

Here we might profitably pause and consider this single notion, organicism, as a possible key to Romantic thought or at least as one of the central concepts. As Alfred North Whitehead observed many years ago, "[T]he romantic revival was a protest on behalf of the organic view of nature."[29] Terms such as "organic" or "organicism" are everywhere to be found in the Romantic movement – in Rousseau, in Goethe, in the Schlegels, in Coleridge and Wordsworth, in Hazlitt, in Emerson and Fuller and Whitman. As James Engell tells us, Hazlitt's phrase for the "intuitive power that draws particulars into a purposeful whole" is "organic sensibility," and the agency of this sensibility is *gusto*, which is Hazlitt's way of talking about the organic imagination. For Hazlitt, the imagination is an "involuntary and even unnoticed" faculty that provides our vital link to experience, precisely that "*internal* principle of all thought" that Locke and other empiricists-mechanists of the seventeenth and eighteenth centuries overlooked. Gusto is "power or passion defining any object"; it recreates "the internal character, the living principle," of an object, and produces a "deep, sustained internal sentiment."[30]

We notice that the imagination and gusto have reference for Hazlitt to inner or internal experience and that in particular this experience is affective, passional, and calls the whole of our being into play. It would require the Freudian revolution – or at least the audacity of a Walt Whitman – for the full implications of this theory to be articulated less skittishly, though with all his talk about inner forces, secret motives, hidden conflict, the repression of desire, and (in M. H. Abrams's formulation) the "partial release of unconscious thought in sleep," Hazlitt comes very close to linking his "organic sensibility" with sexual impulse. As Abrams notes, "[I]n numerous passages, Hazlitt surrenders the poetic imagination, like the imagination of the dreamer, to the motive power of unrealized desires."[31] Hazlitt is in fact talking about creativity, the imagination, not simply as an intellectual force but as an almost physical impulse that draws on the deepest, perhaps most primitive sources of our being. As Whitman would put it waggishly in 1856, "shoats and geldings" could hardly be expected to produce a poetry adequate to modern expressive needs. Poetry must speak for *all* the modalities of the body.

It is interesting to note that organic theories of creation in the Romantic period almost invariably employ the language of sexual procreation as an analogy for the creative act and process – describe, that is, "inspired invention in terms of gestation and growth."[32] "From the first, or initiative Idea," Coleridge writes, "as from a seed, successive ideas germinate."[33] Although Dr. Johnson sniffed at the notion that Milton's poetic faculty was dependent upon "an *Impetus* or *oestrum*,"[34] Emerson would use precisely that word – "oestrum" – to describe the poetic impulse that precedes the "ejaculation" of thought,[35] and his outrageous disciple Whitman would make good on that description by speaking of his poems as "love spendings" and "amorous wet." The point at issue was the necessary *interiority* of both creation and appreciation, the coming together within an "organic sensibility" of both intellectual and instinctive components. "True genius," A. W. Schlegel noted, "is precisely the most intimate union of unconscious and self-conscious activity in the human spirit, of instinct and purpose, of freedom and necessity." Form must be an expression of the character, the total *Gestalt*, of the creator. Organic form, as Schlegel tells us, "is innate; it unfolds itself from within, and reaches its determination simultaneously with the fullest development of the seed."[36] It follows that true art is hardly to be expected from someone incapable of drawing from the deepest wellspring of being. Is it surprising that for the debased, or common, understanding, "Romantic" refers to "love"?[37]

An amusing example of how a too-constricted, or perhaps excessively sober, approach to this question can lead one to overlook the fullest implications of "organicism" is provided by an essay published in the early 1970s by the Yale critic William K. Wimsatt, who questioned the validity of the "organic metaphor" as applied to works of literary art, claiming that the analogy, so common in the Romantic period, between poems, say, and biological or botanical organisms was far-fetched and even absurd.[38] Goethe's notion that the total development of a tree could be traced to the metamorphosis of a single leaf should not be applied, Wimsatt argues, to poems; they are not necessarily organic wholes that flower mysteriously from a single germ whose character informs every part. If you carry home a bird's feather, you have not brought home the bird's spirit with it. "Ancient haruspicators," he goes on, "were bent on no aesthetic purpose," meaning that those priests who inspected the entrails of chickens were looking for prophetic signs and omens, not for the organic essence of chicken-ness. Wimsatt's point is that the inner or separate parts of an organism do not necessarily give us any poetic sense of the whole. So, Wimsatt continues, "when Humbert Humbert in Nabokov's *Lolita* longs in effect to eviscerate his nymphet, to kiss her insides, heart, liver, lungs, we . . . enjoy a dawning comprehension that he is a madman," and not a Romantic poet.

Wimsatt's example should be of particular interest in this context since so much of the inspiration for Nabokov's Humbert – and, indeed, for the book at large – is drawn from Edgar Allan Poe. It is worth noting, however, that Humbert Humbert does *not* long "in effect to eviscerate his nymphet." Here are Humbert's actual words:

> My only grudge against nature was that I could not turn my Lolita
> inside out and apply voracious lips to her young matrix, her un-
> known heart, her nacreous liver, the sea-grapes of her lungs, her
> comely twin kidneys.[39]

Wimsatt distorts the passage, and I think misses the point, by choosing
to overlook the comic, or insane, hyperbole with which Humbert masks
or dresses up his desire. Is it necessary to explain what Lolita's "young
matrix" refers to, or what a humorous displacement we have in "the sea-
grapes of her lungs"? Humbert says nothing about eviscerating his
nymphet. Rather, his intent (the true lover's desire) is to embrace, nay
devour, the interior essence of his love object, her "organic" center –
more specifically, her sexual organs. Thus, what is implied, as in the
theories of organicism we have been reviewing, is that every whole can
most intimately be experienced in a passionate attention to details that
themselves embody the spirit and quintessence of the whole. Lolita's
"young matrix" stands for – indeed, *is* – the center of her being for the
sexually obsessed Humbert, just as Whitman speaks of his "bare-stript
heart" as being the goal for his lover's eager tongue.

We might observe also that the spirit of Humbert Humbert's language, as Nabokov manages it (in such a phrase, for example, as
"nacreous liver"), argues a full awareness of similar language and situa-
tions in Poe. It was all very well for Poe, in his pose as rational critic, to
take the southern romancer William Gilmore Simms to task for his
"revolting images," in particular for the following passage from *Damsel
of Darien*:

> It was a pile of the oyster, which yielded the precious pearls of the
> South, and the artist had judiciously painted some with their lips
> parted, and showing within the large precious fruit in the attain-
> ment of which Spanish cupidity had already proved itself capable of
> every peril, as well as every crime.[40]

Poe's arch comment on this passage is "Body of Bacchus! – only think of
poetical beauty in the countenance of a gaping oyster!" Body of Bacchus
indeed. Poe was certainly well aware of what Simms was driving at with
his transparent talk about parted "lips," "precious fruit," and "Spanish
cupidity." This, after all, is the same Poe whose sexually obsessed
narrator Egaeus in "Berenice" would find more than "poetical beauty"
in the peculiar smile, gaping mouth, and glistening teeth of his cousin.
Driven to reach her "organic" center, he violates her body in a horrible
necrophiliac assault that represents a twisted version of the Romantic
quest, just as Hawthorne's Aylmer violates Georgiana in "The Birth-
mark" or Chillingworth gropes in Dimmesdale's breast in *The Scarlet*

Letter or Ahab thrusts his harpoon into Moby-Dick's deep heart (it is, presumably, in a very different spirit that Thoreau reaches for the bottom of the pond in *Walden*). For all of these Romantic questers, reality lies *within*, and "organic form" implies that there are inward organs from which the outward *expression* flowers. "America," after all, is an idea, a mere abstraction, but the living heart of the country, as Simms himself argues in an essay on Daniel Boone, lies within, in Kentucky, say, which in its Indian origins is supposed to mean the "Dark and bloody ground." That is the "organic" essence of the land that its pioneer-lover apparently intended to explore.[41]

4

Now that we have looked at the term *Romantic* and the related concept of organicism, it is time to adopt a more specifically historical frame to help in defining the American Romantic moment. As Jean Béranger and Maurice Gonnaud have observed in their excellent concise survey of American literature through the Civil War:

> It is a commonplace of criticism to point to the chronological lag that separates America's cultural emancipation from its political emancipation. It had taken scarcely eleven years (1776–1787) – years dotted with serious crises – for local concerns to be submerged in the unity of a secure federal republic. But this decade or so of political consolidation failed to bring forth that original literature whose function it would be to express the profoundest tendencies of a national community without precedent in human experience. The period stretching from the Declaration of Independence to the election of Monroe offers much evidence that this great ambition was on the minds of Americans now fully aware of their cultural imperatives (as early as 1800 the expression "American literature" had entered common speech). But there was also a fundamental uncertainty or lack of nerve. . . . We must remind ourselves of the gulf that existed around 1800 between the bourgeoning political confidence of the young nation and a corresponding sense of cultural autonomy. Over a period of many years, a group of audacious and determined souls would attempt, with praiseworthy singlemindedness, to remedy this failing. But despite some local successes, their work taken together would scarcely rise above the level of mediocrity. [Indeed, Emerson himself, looking back over this period, which constituted his father's generation, the generation that came to maturity between the signing of the Constitution and the War of 1812, would refer to "that early ignorant &

transitional *Month-of-March*, in our New England culture." – JP]
The collective character of that moment of cultural uncertainty
invites one to reflect: what particular obstacles prevented the emer-
gence of a national literature commensurate with the hopes and
efforts of its promoters? Why did the energy released by political
success fail to inform works of the imagination?[42]

Many answers suggest themselves and invite further reflection: the
lack of an immediate preceding tradition, that is, eighteenth-century
literature, to provide the basis for growth and response, the hegemony of
British writing, the lack of clear strategies for exploiting native language
and materials, the absence of a profession of letters in America, the
stranglehold exercised by religious orthodoxy on the mind of the nation,
and the inability to assimilate quickly enough the modern spirit in
literature as exemplified by and embodied in European Romanticism.[43]
One issue in particular deserves to be singled out here, namely, the
question of revolution and Romanticism.[44] It has often been observed
that the French Revolution provided a major impetus, especially for the
first wave of Romantics in England. As M. H. Abrams puts it, "[M]an
regenerate in a world made new: this was the theme of a multitude of
writers notable, forgotten, or anonymous," in the early 1790s, thanks to
the Revolution.[45] Vernon Parrington remarked many years ago that "the
first stage in the romanticization of American thought resulted from the
naturalization of French revolutionary theory."[46] Why *French* and not
American?[47] One quick response might be that although Americans were
determined to release themselves from English domination, *revolution*
itself as a theoretical program that would provide a rationale for sweeping changes in politics, law, social arrangements, religion, and literature
was never a popular notion.[48] Despite the fact that certain intellectuals,
such as William Ellery Channing and Emerson, would develop a kind of
Napoleon-mania, the French Revolution and its aftermath were generally regarded with great suspicion (witness the discussion in Chapter 14
of Cooper's *The Pioneers*).
But we must remind ourselves that the Romantic movement in
France, as in America, was in fact retarded by the Revolution, whatever
its effect on English writers. "The turmoil and proscriptions of twenty-
five years," as Geoffrey Hartman notes,[49] helped make the French Romantic movement one of the last in Europe. It is true in any case that it
would require almost a half century for the *idea* of Revolution, cleansed
of its regicides and bloodbaths and Terror, to be domesticated in America as part of a Romantic program.[50] It may be significant that Hazlitt's
The Spirit of the Age (published in England in 1825), which argued
precisely for the primacy of revolution in the new *Zeitgeist*, especially in

the work of Wordsworth, did not achieve a first American edition until 1846, when it became part of the Young America movement in New York, which caught Melville in its fervor. Along the way, Bryant could tentatively suggest (in lectures delivered in 1825–6 but not published until 1884) that "a literary reformation" in America might well require "some great moral or political revolution" in order to unsettle "old opinions" and familiarize "men to daring speculations," but he himself would not be part of that brave new literary world.

Emerson's battlecry – described by Oliver Wendell Holmes as America's literary Declaration of Independence – would not be uttered until 1837: "If there is any period one would desire to be born in," he asks rhetorically in "The American Scholar," "is it not the age of Revolution; when the old and the new stand side by side, and admit of being compared; when the energies of all men are searched by fear and by hope; when the historic glories of the old, can be compensated by the rich possibilities of the new era?"[51] Emerson's own revolutionary energies would be spent in struggling with a rational religion that itself had done battle with Calvinist orthodoxy, and, of course, slavery and women's rights loomed on the horizon. Otherwise he was content to internalize what he called "The Protest" as part of his personal spiritual quest. Thoreau, as we know, would initiate civil disobedience against the Commonwealth of Massachusetts over the Mexican War, but that revolution lasted one night, whereupon he was free to return to Walden Pond and continue struggling with himself. Hawthorne brooded over mobocracy in "My Kinsman Major Molineux" but otherwise placed his one truly great antinomian figure back in America's seventeenth century. Melville, in the 1850s, was content to portray a failed slave revolt led by a black Iago in "Benito Cereno" and a quietistic recusant in "Bartleby," whose protest amounts to a polite "I would prefer not to." Melville's two actual meditations on revolutionary times, *Israel Potter* and *Billy Budd*, would dissolve, respectively, in irony and psycho-theological mystery.

It was left to the redoubtable Margaret Fuller to witness at first hand the turmoil of 1848 in Europe and report the news exultantly to her countrymen and countrywomen:

> Whatever blood is to be shed, whatever altars cast down, those tremendous problems *must* be solved, whatever be the cost! That cost cannot fail to break many a bank, many a heart, in Europe, before the good can bud again out of a mighty corruption. To you, people of America, it may perhaps be given to look on and learn in time for a preventive wisdom. You may learn the real meaning of the words *Fraternity, Equality*: you may, despite the apes of the past

who strive to tutor you, learn the needs of a true democracy. You may in time learn to reverence, learn to guard, the true aristocracy of a nation, the only real nobles, – the *Laboring Classes*.[52]

Had they been paying attention, the mill owners of Massachusetts would have found such pronouncements hard to take. But there were harsher words to come:

> My friends . . . talk of our country as the land of the future. It is so, but that spirit which made it all it is of value in my eyes, which gave all of hope with which I can sympathize for that future, is more alive here at present than in America. My country is at present spoiled by prosperity, stupid with the lust of gain, soiled by crime in its willing perpetuation of slavery, shamed by an unjust war, noble sentiment much forgotten even by individuals, the aims of politicians selfish or petty, the literature frivolous and venal.[53]

Surely a prophetic utterance, and perhaps also a fair indictment of the American literary scene at large, for *The Scarlet Letter* and *Moby-Dick* and *Walden* and *Leaves of Grass* had not yet appeared. America's great Romantic flowering, a literary renaissance if not a revolution, was still to come, but Fuller would not live to see it. Yet she alone among her contemporaries had the wit and breadth of spirit to appreciate and publicly praise the whole sweep of America's new literature – from Brockden Brown through Emerson and Hawthorne and Poe and Melville and Douglass, though most of what she saw was only a beginning. So much, perhaps, had her "romantic sympathy" for the spirit of revolution done for Margaret Fuller.[54]

5

The ways in which I have already tried to characterize some of the forces and concepts, especially the foreign ones, responsible for stimulating America's nascent Romantic energies may seem rather general and even doctrinaire ways of accounting for a new impulse in American writing that probably came to individual writers in a more personal or it may be haphazard fashion – though we do in fact know that the Schlegels, Goethe, the English Romantics, Carlyle, and other "new wave" thinkers in Europe made a deep impression on the American literary scene in this period.[55] But it is possible to construct a picture that represents with greater particularity what the new *Zeitgeist* looked like to a developing young sensibility in America as the Romantic age was dawning. My example is Emerson because – to appropriate what he said about

Goethe – he was the cow from whom so many American writers drew their Romantic milk. More than any other literary figure of his time, Emerson eagerly exposed himself to the new winds of doctrine and made regular reports to his compatriots. For us, his journal provides a unique record of the contemporary intellectual ferment. Thus, for example, this journal entry in the year 1827, when Emerson was twenty-four, signals his active awareness that there *was* a new *Zeitgeist*. Under the heading "Peculiarities of the present Age," Emerson made these points, among others:

> It is said to be the age of the first person singular. . . . The reform
> of the Reformation. . . . Transcendentalism. Metaphysics & ethics
> look inwards – and France produces Mad. de Stael; England,
> Wordsworth; America, Sampson Reed; as well as Germany,
> Swedenborg.[56]

One could hardly ask for a more concise notation of the Romantic program or for a more interesting list – as eccentric as it may now seem – of the international cast of Romantic characters as they appeared to Emerson in the 1820s. Concern for the "first person singular" has, of course, long been recognized as a dominant issue in American Romanticism, as we remind ourselves whenever we recall some of the most famous opening lines in the writing of the period: "My name is Arthur Gordon Pym" or "It is a little remarkable, that – though disinclined to talk overmuch of myself and my affairs at the fireside, and to my personal friends – an autobiographical impulse should twice have taken possession of me, in addressing the public" or, again, "When I wrote the following pages . . . I lived alone in the woods" or "Call me Ishmael" or "I'm Nobody! Who are you?" or, most egregiously, "I celebrate myself, and sing myself." As Emerson himself would note many years later, looking back over his age, "[T]he mind had become aware of itself"[57] – hence the radical subjectiveness of much post-Kantian metaphysics, ethics, epistemology, and literature generally.

The "reform of the Reformation" implied that the Protestant Revolution, which centered religion, in Milton's phrase, in "the upright heart and pure," would continue to destabilize institutions in the name of individual conscience and inspiration. Consider simply Emerson's own magnificent conclusion to what begins as a reasoned, scholarly, and historically ordered attack on the institution of the Eucharist: "I am not interested in it."[58] For the sake of the individual, as Wallace Stevens would say,

> . . . exit lex,
> Rex and principium, exit the whole
> Shebang. Exeunt omnes.[59]

For good or ill, history comes to rest on a single point, namely, Whitman's simple separate person.

Emerson's list of names tends to circulate around the same issue. Emmanuel Swedenborg, for example, the great Swedish mystic who profoundly influenced writers as diverse as Blake, Balzac (who called him "the Buddha of the North"),[60] Baudelaire, Emerson himself, and Henry James, Senior, and whose disciples would found the Church of the New Jerusalem, was best known for his doctrine of "correspondence," as in this passage cited by Emerson in his own essay on Swedenborg:

> Man is a kind of very minute heaven, corresponding to the world of spirits and to heaven. Every particular idea of man, and every affection, yea, every smallest part of his affection, is an image and effigy of him. A spirit may be known from only a single thought. God is the grand man.[61]

Swedenborg's insistence on "the primary relation of mind to matter" was the fundamental principle that set Emerson aflame, especially in *Nature*:

> How can I have existed so long, I said to myself, outside Nature without identifying myself with her? Everything lives, everything acts, everything corresponds; the magnetic rays emanating from myself and others traverse unimpeded the infinite chain of created things; it is a transparent network which covers the world, and its fine threads communicate from one to another to the planets and the stars. I am now a captive on the earth, but I converse with choiring stars, who share my joys and sorrows![62]

That is not Emerson (though it might be) but rather another sometime-Swedenborgian, the mad French Romantic Gérard de Nerval. This passage from *Aurelia*, published in the same year as the first edition of *Leaves of Grass*, only demonstrates how widespread such notions had become, for Whitman himself would have found them consonant with his own.

As for Sampson Reed, though he has now pretty much dropped out of sight (except for scholars of Transcendentalism), this passionate Swedenborgian was touted by Emerson as a genius in the 1820s and 1830s, especially for his *Observations on the Growth of the Mind*, first published in 1826. A profoundly organicist document, it is provided in its original edition with an epigraph from Wordsworth's *Excursion* insisting that we build up our being by "deeply drinking-in the Soul of Things." It affirmed not only the new "powers of the mind" but also the necessary interpenetration of the mind and nature, for "the powers of the mind are

most intimately connected with the subjects by which they are occupied."[63] Explicitly rejecting Locke's *tabula rasa*, Reed argued that the
mind is not a blank sheet of paper waiting to be filled up but rather an
organism, "a most delicate germ whose husk is the body, planted in this
world that the light and heat of heaven may fall upon it with a gentle
radiance and call forth its energies."[64] Reed believed that the true incarnation was the descent of mind into matter – of the human spirit into the
garden of the world – and that the result of such an interpenetration of
mind and nature would be the modern equivalent of "apocalypse" – that
is, the withdrawing of the veil from the imagination.

Here, of course, Reed displays his thorough immersion in the writings
of Wordsworth, for Wordsworth had already declared, in the 1814
Prospectus to *The Recluse*:

> . . . Paradise, and groves
> Elysian, Fortunate Fields – like those of old
> Sought in the Atlantic Main, why should they be
> A history only of departed things,
> Or a mere fiction of what never was?
> For the discerning intellect of Man,
> When wedded to this goodly universe
> In love and holy passion, shall find these
> A simple produce of the common day.
> – I, long before the blissful hour arrives,
> Would chaunt, in lonely peace, the spousal verse
> Of this great consummation: – and, by words
> Which speak of nothing more than what we are,
> Would I arouse the sensual from their sleep
> Of Death, and win the vacant and the vain
> To noble raptures; while my voice proclaims
> How exquisitely the individual Mind
> (And the progressive powers perhaps no less
> Of the whole species) to the external World
> Is fitted: – and how exquisitely, too,
> Theme this but little heard of among Men,
> The external world is fitted to the Mind. . . .[65]

This passage, which, as M. H. Abrams notes, "stands as the manifesto
of a central Romantic enterprise," amounts to a prophetic *vision* (the
word is Wordsworth's own and is crucial to his writing) – a vision, again
in Abrams's words, "of the awesome depths and height of the human
mind, and of the power of that mind as in itself adequate, by consum-
mating a holy marriage with the external universe, to create out of the

world of all of us, in a quotidian and recurrent miracle, a new world which is the equivalent of paradise."[66] I shall have occasion later in this book, particularly in regard to Cooper and Emerson, to expatiate further on the "Vision," especially in its relation to nature in the new world. But for now it should suffice to note that the passage quoted above from Wordsworth's Prospectus would be cited in a lecture Emerson delivered in 1837.[67] His comment – "we divorce ourselves from nature" – summarizes the problem succinctly enough, and, of course, it was this problem to which Emerson principally addressed himself in his first book in 1836.

6

In many ways the most intriguing name on Emerson's little list in the 1827 journal entry is that of Madame de Staël. It requires a certain effort of the historical imagination to remind ourselves now that this extraordinary woman – hated and feared by Napoleon, beloved of Madame Récamier, consciously adopted by Margaret Fuller as her role-model – was considered, along with George Sand, Mrs. Browning, and George Eliot, one of the most distinguished female writers of the nineteenth century. Indeed, in his own annotations to a copy of Madame de Staël's *Germany*, Herman Melville remarks: "Who would one compare Madame de Stael too [*sic*] – Mrs. Browning – Mrs. Browning was a great woman, but Madame de Stael was a greater."[68] So far at least as her book on Germany was concerned, Melville was undoubtedly right, for as René Wellek observes, the "role of Madame de Staël was decisive" in purveying to the Latin and English-speaking worlds the essence of Romanticism as it had developed in Germany[69] – although, of course, her own tumultuous heart and soul went into it also.

The book was originally published in London in 1813 and immediately achieved a *succès de scandale* because it had been suppressed in Paris. So far as we know, Emerson first borrowed *Germany* from the Boston Library Society in 1822, though he probably had read reviews of it earlier. In any case references to Madame de Staël multiply after that date, and as we have observed she was considered worthy of a privileged place in Emerson's 1827 list. One can only speculate about which parts of Madame de Staël's exposition of Romantic art and thought most impressed the young Emerson, but there can be little doubt that the celebrated chapter on "Classic and Romantic Poetry" caught his eye. There, Emerson would have read, in a passage checked by Melville, that "in ancient times men attended to events alone, but among the moderns character is of greater importance; and that uneasy reflection, which, like the vulture of Prometheus, often internally devours us, would have been folly" in the clear atmosphere of the ancient world.[70]

This "constant habit of self-reflection"[71] characteristic of modern life Madame de Staël attributed to the Christian conscience – exacerbated, to be sure, by the subjective tendencies of modern philosophy. It was precisely such hypertrophied self-awareness that Emerson would point to later in reviewing his age: "The young men were born with knives in their brain, a tendency to introversion, self-dissection, anatomizing of motives."[72] The human mind, Madame de Staël remarked in 1813, was disposed to be most gratified

> by observations on what passes within the heart. This disposition is the consequence of those great intellectual changes that have taken place in man: he has in general a much greater tendency to fall back upon himself, and to seek religion, love, and sentiment, in the most inward recesses of his being.[73]

German literature in particular was given to referring "every thing to an interior existence," she went on, "and as that is the mystery of mysteries, it awakens an unbounded curiosity."[74]

Melville's Ishmael, in the first chapter of *Moby-Dick*, would also point to the narcissistic impulse as "the key to it all," but not without a characteristic caveat about the possibility of drowning in the unsounded depths of one's own being. "Heed it well, ye solipsists," he warns effectively. Some such danger also nagged at Madame de Staël, despite her great sympathy for Romantic self-absorption, for in her exposition of German thought she carefully notes that no man was more averse than Kant "to what is called the philosophy of the dreamers."[75] Although Kant was at pains to affirm "that there exists both a soul and an external nature, and that they act mutually one upon the other by such or such laws," his followers were less cautious.[76] Madame de Staël, too, clearly has strong leanings in the direction of absolute Idealism, for she cites the anecdote (much beloved of Emerson) wherein Luther says that the human mind "is like a drunken peasant on horseback; when we put it up on one side, it falls down on the other," noting that the varying claims of thought and sensation have alternated in authority, only to conclude:

> . . . the moment for a fixed doctrine has arrived. Metaphysics are about to undergo a revolution, like that which Copernicus has produced in the system of the world. They are about to replace the soul of man in the center, and to make it, in every respect, like the sun; round which external objects trace their circle.[77]

Here we have another prefiguration of an important Emersonian moment, namely, the opening of the great essay "Circles," with its assertion that "the eye is the first circle; the horizon which it forms is the second."[78] Such claims for the absolute creative power of the higher self were a prominent feature of the thought of Kant's pupil, J. G. Fichte, whom Madame de Staël openly admired. To the "immoveable soul," she reports, "Fichte attributes the gift of immortality, and the power of creating, or (to translate more exactly), of *drawing to a focus in itself the image of the universe*"[79] – another notion which, at least as the source of metaphor, would have strong appeal for Emerson. Despite her awareness, however, that Idealism has the advantage of "exciting, to the highest degree, the activity of the mind," Madame de Staël is brought up short by its greatest drawback, since "nature and love, by this system, lose all their charms; for, if the objects which we see, and the beings whom we love, are nothing but the works of our own ideas, it is man himself that may be considered as *the great coelibatary of the world*."[80] That last italicized phrase must have caught Emerson's eye, since he would himself in *Nature* come to criticize absolute Idealism because "it leaves me in the splendid labyrinth of my perceptions, to wander without end."[81] Ishmael would point more terrifyingly to the same problem when he described the "tormented spirit" that glared out of Ahab's eyes as "a ray of living light, to be sure, but without an object to color, and therefore a blankness in itself." But Madame de Staël was not about to abandon her German friends to solipsistic despair, for she goes on to claim that even when German philosophy penetrates "the deepest secrets of grief, and of faith, it enlightens and strengthens us."[82]

Madame de Staël concludes her book with a section on "enthusiasm," which she exposes as the great principle underlying the Romantic movement in Germany and the basis of German religion. Enthusiasm, she insists, has nothing to do with fanaticism, which concerns exclusive passions and opinions. Rather, it is "connected with the harmony of the universe: it is the love of the beautiful, elevation of soul, enjoyment of devotion, all united in one single feeling which combines grandeur and repose." It signifies "*God in us*."[83] That, of course, is why the Anglican establishment harried dissenters out of England in the time of Archbishop Laud, why the Puritan oligarchy in America drove Anne Hutchinson from the Bay Colony, and why the outspoken exponent of rational religion in eighteenth-century America, Charles Chauncy, condemned the adherents of the Great Awakening. Enthusiasm, indeed, became the great Romantic battlecry, but it could hardly shake off the legacy of extravagance and madness with which religious controversy had endowed it, especially in America.[84] It was all very well for William Cullen Bryant to say in 1825 that "enthusiasm is the parent of poetry," but Hester Prynne's wild freedom of speculation (which might, we learn in "Another View of Hester," have led her to attempt "to undermine the

foundations of the Puritan establishment") is also described as "enthusiasm." It was undoubtedly her "enthusiasm" that brought about her
sexual liaison with Dimmesdale, as it is pointedly her "enthusiasm" that
drives her to cry, "Up, and away!" to her confused and dispirited lover.
Hawthorne's sly manipulation of this loaded term also enables him to
describe Dimmesdale's final sermon as inspiring religious "enthusiasm"
in his audience, though we are told explicitly that the peculiar power of
his preaching derived from his personal fund of guilt and sorrow. Indeed, Madame de Staël herself had already created a famous Romantic
heroine – one might say *the* Romantic heroine – whose enthusiasm was at
once her glory and her tragedy.[85]

I am referring to the eponymous protagonist of *Corinne*, far more
famous and widely read even than *Germany*. The book was published in
1807, immediately translated into English, and, as Perry Miller remarks,
"promptly became a troubling intrusion into all Anglo-Saxon commu-
nities. It was perpetually denounced from middle-class pulpits and assid-
uously read by middle-class daughters in their chambers at night."[86] Not,
however, by daughters alone, for Emerson began reading the book, in
French, when he was seventeen and continued to browse in it for the
next two years. Perhaps when he listed Madame de Staël in 1827 as one
of the four major thinkers of the age, he had *Corinne* in mind as much as
Germany for, along with its sentimental bathos and high-minded attitudi-
nizing, the book is a veritable compendium of Romantic postures and
conventions.

It is the story of a great Italian beauty who is also a great intellectual
(Madame de Staël's fantasy version of herself) and whose genius lies in a
gift for improvisation. When she is crowned in Rome as, in effect, the
nation's literary Nobel laureate, she is seen by a melancholy English
lord – a kind of priggish Childe Harold *avant la lettre* – who immediately
falls in love with her. Now it turns out that this raven-haired, passionate,
and sensuous *improvvisatrice* is Italian only on her mother's side, for her
father is a Scottish lord (Lord Edgarmond) who remarried closer to
home after Corinne's mother's death and begot upon his frosty English
wife a blonde, blue-eyed wallflower named Lucy.

By chance – and a chance which provides, indeed, the necessary
scheme of the whole book and the large genre it inspired – the young
Lord Nevil had been promised to Lucy by his own father, now deceased
and therefore not available for consultation and special pleading. This is
effectively, therefore, the story of the Anglo-Saxon spirit torn between
duty and passion, chastity and sensuality, domestic dullness and socially
unmoored genius – between, finally (and this is the essential point),
northern prudence and southern Romanticism. This allegorical psychomachia, incidentally, would find its way into much American fiction of

the period, from Poe's "Ligeia" to Hawthorne's *Blithedale Romance* and *Marble Faun*, and most egregiously into Melville's *Pierre* (Melville procured a copy of *Corinne* in 1849, just prior to writing both *Moby-Dick* and *Pierre*). It is important to note the full title of Madame de Staël's novel, *Corinne; or, Italy*, for this metonomy represents Madame de Staël's most important contribution to Romantic mythology. Corinne *is* Italy – the wild, alluring, dangerous, soft Romantic antithesis to Anglo-Saxondom's rationality.[87] Well before *Corinne* was published, in fact, the antinomy between northern reason and southern romance had found its appropriate form in the *Italienische-Reise*, the obligatory journey south. J. J. Rousseau had said "that the southern languages were the daughters of pleasure, the northern of necessity," and Madame de Staël herself was to quote that sentence, in italics, in her book on Germany,[88] where she would also tell the paradigmatic story of the great German classical scholar, Winckelmann (both items, by the way, marked by Melville). Winckelmann, she writes,

> felt himself attracted with ardour towards the south; we still frequently find in German imagination some traces of that love of the sun, that weariness of the north, which formerly drew so many northern nations into the countries of the south. . . . When Winckelmann, after a long abode in Italy, returned to Germany, the sight of snow, of the pointed roofs which it covers, and of smoky houses, filled him with melancholy. He felt as if he could no longer enjoy the arts, when he no longer breathed the air which gave them birth.[89]

The anecdote would be amplified by Walter Pater in his chapter on Winckelmann in *Studies in the History of the Renaissance*, the tale considerably deepened by Pater's dark hints about Winckelmann's insatiable – finally fatal – attraction to Italian youths. And this perennial allegory would come to rest most magnificently, of course, in Thomas Mann's *Death in Venice*.

But we must return to Corinne and Lord Nevil in Rome. Inevitably drawn to her, as to the Romantic impulse itself, Nevil expresses surprise that the spirited *improvvisatrice* is also given to strong outbreaks of grief, whereupon Corinne responds passionately:

> "Hold . . . you know me not. Of all my faculties, the most powerful is that of suffering. I was formed for happiness; my nature is confiding and animated; but sorrow excites me to a degree that threatens my reason, nay, my life. Be careful of me! My gay versatility serves me but in appearance: within my soul is an abyss of despair."[90]

If Nevil is truly willing to "penetrate into the interior of the soul, with the torch of genius" (these phrases are from Madame de Staël's definition of Romanticism in *Germany*[91]), to plumb the "unknown soul," that is, with the aid of Corinne, he must be prepared for shocking sights – for a world at once alluring and appalling.

Such is precisely that Rome into which Corinne draws him as into her own unfathomed heart.[92] To study Rome, Madame de Staël avers, "is but to study the past in the present, to penetrate the secrets of all time,"[93] that is, to investigate the potentially disruptive element of temporality in the constitution of the self. Rome, she explains, "is not simply an assemblage of dwellings; it is a chronicle of the world, represented by figurative emblems." To learn to read Rome is to learn to decipher the palimpsestic hieroglyphics in and through which humanity figures itself. "Rome" thus stands for the history of consciousness. "The wondrous charm of Rome," we are told, "consists not only in the real beauty of her monuments, but in the interest they excite; the material for thinking they suggest." Roman nature, Corinne explains, "gives birth to reveries elsewhere unknown. She is as intimate with the heart of man as if the Creator made her the interpretess between his creatures and himself." Following Corinne's exposition, we may therefore say that *Rome-antique* is like herself quintessentially *Romantique* – an incitement to self-investigation, the *interpres cordis*. But it is not merely a neutral catalyst; the process being figured is seductive and perilous, a kind of Mephis-tophelean leading-on of the spirit that may be either a *gai science* or a provocation to despair. As symbolized by its famous *malaria*, Rome is duplex, at once delightful and deceitful: "Its malignant power is betrayed by no external sign: you respire an air that seems pure; the earth is fertile; a delicious freshness atones in the evening for the heat of the day; and all this is death!" Like that of Rappaccini's daughter, Rome's breath is both sweet and sickly: "fertile and pestilent at once," as Madame de Staël describes the Pontine marshes.

Such perhaps is the Janus-face of eros and thanatos that lies at the end of the Romantic quest – as when, introducing Corinne's translation of *Romeo and Juliet*, Madame de Staël describes the play as being endowed "with truly southern fancy . . . rushing from voluptuous felicity to despair and death."[94] Accordingly Nevil is impelled to exclaim in a letter to his beloved: "Corinne, Corinne! in loving you, it is impossible to avoid fearing and doubting too."[95] With such overpowering strains of the Romantic *Liebestod* playing perplexingly about his northern ears, Lord Nevil understandably begins to wonder about "his hopes for domestic tranquility." Which is to say that, faced with this enigmatic Moby-Dick of a woman, Nevil's eyes turn back longingly to the Spouter-Inn. Corinne agrees that her character is hard to fathom: "There is a savage wilderness," she explains, "beneath Italian cunning; it is that of a hunter lying in wait for his prey."[96] Perhaps the fact that one of Madame de Staël's principal models for Lord Nevil was actually an American archaeologist led her thus unexpectedly to shift her focus – figurally, at least – to the New World.[97] But the equations implicitly being proposed – Corinne equals Italy equals Romanticism equals wild nature equals the dangers and opportunities of the New World – could scarcely have surprised an ardent young American like Emerson in the 1820s, for whom like equations were being proposed in the fiction of Irving and Cooper (indeed, a fortiori had already been proposed by Brockden Brown, as we shall see).

What, after all, was in actual historical process if not a startling confrontation of the agonized Puritan conscience with both the real and imaginative possibilities of the American sublime – that daunting challenge to New World self-making? And how could Emerson know that within a decade he would come to be on intimate terms with a daughter of the Puritans turned enthusiast who consciously modeled herself on both Madame de Staël and her heroine? This "new Corinne," as Emerson himself would term Margaret Fuller, this "new Corinne" but "more variously gifted, wise, sportive, eloquent . . . magnificent, prophetic, reading my life at her will, and puzzling me with riddles,"[98] this passionately intellectual *improvvisatrice* with her yearning for all things Italian, her violent emotions, her desperate need for physical love, intrigued and terrified Emerson, who would say after her tragic death in 1850: "She remained inscrutable to me; her strength was not my strength, – her powers were a surprise."[99] He described her in fact as a "foreigner," and of course she had finally found her lovers and her greatest opportunities in Italy. But he also knew perfectly well that Margaret represented precisely what he and the rest of his cerebral circle hoped for as they emerged from the long Puritan chill into the *new* New World of Romantic America.

They needed expansion, expression, the loosening of "the knot of the heart," but they were constrained by their pinched New England instincts. "I miss in myself most of all, but also in my contemporaries," Emerson noted in his journal in 1847, a "style of manners & conversation . . . which . . . is equal to the needs of life, at once tender & bold, & with great arteries like Cleopatra & Corinne." But he knew, he went on, that his "fine souls" were "cautious & canny" and wished "to unite Corinth with Connecticutt."[100] *Their* Corinne understood the problem perfectly well but could find a solution only for herself. So far as her fellow would-be Romantics were concerned, she would have to content herself with goading them with mildly satiric letters, one of which – written to Emerson when he was being visited by a less enthusiastic friend – might serve as Margaret's epitaph: "Is —— there? Does water meet water? – no need of wine, sugar, spice, or even a *soupcon* of lemon to remind of a tropical climate? I fear me not. Yet, dear positives, believe me superlatively yours, Margaret."[101]

These playfully precise words of Fuller's help us to define the new consciousness in process of creation in American letters: a movement from the positive to the *superlative* degree, so as to induce a mood of Romantic exaltation that leads to the full articulation of the subject. This "enthusiastic" self – the self-as-divinity – is equivalent to Thoreau's own grammatical sublime: the impulse to write strongly "in respect to egotism" so that the water of ordinary discourse might be miraculously transformed into the wine of autocreating, self-stimulating speech. But it is important here to stress *grammatical* sublime, as distinct from the familiar "egotistical sublime" that Keats criticized in Wordsworth. Thoreau, as Geoffrey Hartman has observed, "perpetuates the ambiguity" inherent in a program of Romantic self-glorification that issues in self-transcendence – the "unconsciousness" productive of "a more communal power of vision."[102] The new subject thus achieved is "grammatical" in the sense of being the rhetorical sublation of what Emerson calls "mean egotism." This subject, as Thomas Pfau argues, "presents itself *as the referent* of expressive acts of a consciousness."[103] Brought into being by means of the act of writing ("believe me superlatively yours, Margaret"), it stands at once as the signature of the self ("believe *me* . . . Margaret") and as the willed translation of the self to the level of representativeness ("believe me superlatively *yours*"). In the formulation of Philippe Lacoue-Labarthe and Jean-Luc Nancy, this is Friedrich Schlegel's *mediatory* self: not an impossible moral pedagogue, but rather an *exemplary* subject, the artist "as example and figure at the very limit of exemplarity and figuration[;] . . . the Subject itself, in the possibility of its own infinitization or absolutization."[104] Here we have the gloriously difficult project, hedged about with dangers and anxieties that would enforce their own articulation, which became the work of Romanticism in the American epoch denominated by Emerson as "the age of the first person singular."[105]

Chapter 1

"Where . . . Is This Singular Career to Terminate?"

Bewildered Pilgrims in Early American Fiction

=========

1

Charles Brockden Brown's appearance as a serious novelist in 1798 may be understood both in terms of the felt need for a truly national literary expression in the decade after the Revolution and in the light of the nascent Romantic movement generally, with its emphasis on individualism, sensibility, psychological analysis, and a more direct relationship to the natural world. Brown clearly saw himself as writing distinctively *American* fiction, yet the impulse to begin his career seems to have come from European sources, notably from his reading of Godwin's *Caleb Williams*, which may be characterized, however qualifiedly, as a Gothic novel.[1] Brown's first significant publication, *Wieland*, now generally viewed as an American-Calvinist melodrama, represents the amalgamation of both nativist and imported elements in the service of a developing tradition that Hawthorne would later define as "psychological romance." It was precisely this tradition that Margaret Fuller pointed to in 1846 when she linked Godwin and Brown as "the dark masters, because they disclose the twilight recesses of the human heart."[2]

By 1798 there was, of course, a well-established body of English fiction with which Americans were familiar. One need name only Richardson, Fielding, Goldsmith, Smollett, Edgeworth, Burney. English Gothic fiction was an eccentric, though popular, spur off that main line. Why did Brown begin under its aegis, rather than as an imitator of Fielding? What were the English and American narrative modes and antecedents that influenced the primary direction his work would take? Such questions remind us that the appearance of Brown's novels exemplified the odd and perhaps fortuitous conjunction of some indigenous traditions and a minor but important strain in English writing. In partic-

31

ular, the use of the Gothic mode, especially by Godwin, as a medium for spiritual autobiography of a peculiarly Protestant sort may be said to have had its origins in the way in which John Bunyan, for example, appropriated and transformed picaresque fiction. "In the hands of middle-class Dissenters of the seventeenth century," as William Spengemann notes, "the wandering rogue became a guilt-laden pilgrim in search of the heavenly city, and the genre acquired a tone of religious exhortation."[3] The Bunyan tradition would continue as a strong note in American writing well into the nineteenth century, and I shall want to look at some of its ramifications. In addition, I want to devote some attention to European notions about the New World and the literature they inspired – the narrative of travel and exploration, as well as the Puritan Captivity and its gradual transformation into the wilderness tale. Throughout, as Roger Stein cautions us, we must maintain an open and flexible attitude toward what we call the novel, for in actuality it developed in America out of a manifestly mixed bag of literary forms, most of which – whatever currency they had in Europe – acquired special significance and greater intensity in the New World.[4]

It became clear to me some years ago that we really do need to continue reminding ourselves of the curious origins of prose narrative in America when I read a review, by an American scholar, of Peter Matthiessen's Snow Leopard – an account of a quasi-religious journey into the deepest recesses of the Himalayas between Nepal and Tibet.[5] "Villages are few, vegetation scant, trails are dangerous," notes Robert Adams; "all supplies must be carried in by animal or human porters. . . . [N]o medical attention is to be had for hundreds of miles in any direction. A severe frostbite, a major fracture, or an attack of appendicitis would almost certainly be fatal; sanitary conditions being what they are, dysentery is a constant possibility. Bandits are also a possibility," and so on. A student of the American past must already at this point have begun to entertain a sense of historical déjà vu that can only be increased by what the reviewer goes on to say: "The book Peter Matthiessen has written about this expedition is of a kind with which we are becoming familiar lately; it is part autobiography, part historical discourse, and predominantly lay sermon, in the shape of a quest narrative." It must surely have been only through inadvertence that Professor Adams allowed himself to speak about this as a kind of book "with which we are becoming familiar lately" – as if Edgar Huntly, Moby-Dick, and Walden had never been written! He goes on to mention Robert Pirsig's Zen and the Art of Motorcycle Maintenance, noting that these western pop-Buddhist tracts have proliferated endlessly and are to be found in every bookshop in America. He concludes, seemingly with unconscious irony, by wondering whether one needs to have "slogged through the snows of Nepal" to discover what Matthiessen has to offer, and we might respond most emphatically, no – nor to rediscover both the genre and the traditions of religious exploration that inform it.

With all deference to Nepal and Tibet, America was the land of mysterious adventure that beckoned to late-medieval, Renaissance, and post-Renaissance men, especially those with a religious bent. "Eschatological geography," to use John Kirtland Wright's memorable phrase, has been an American tradition since the earliest days, and "indeed, during Puritan times," as Wright puts it, "or, say, into the mid-third of the eighteenth century, American geographical understanding as manifested in print . . . absorbed piety from the surrounding intellectual atmosphere as a towel does moisture from a down-East fog."[6] By 1849 this American geomysticism was such a familiar notion that it could be spoofed by one of Melville's chief rivals for popular acclaim, Dr. William Starbuck Mayo, in a book called *Kaloolah*, where the archetypal American traveler (named Jonathan Romer) insists that his country is "bounded on the east by the rising sun, on the north by the aurora borealis, on the west by the precession of the equinoxes, and on the south by the Day of Judgment,"[7] turning America's religious destiny into a barely veiled pronouncement on the "domestic institution." In just a few years Harriet Beecher Stowe would make the Book of Revelation her proof-text in a much more serious fashion. But even as late as 1899 a now well-forgotten American author would continue to indulge in, and attempt to straighten out, this theo-geographic figuration by describing the United States of America as being "bounded on the north by the North Pole; on the South by the Antarctic Region; on the east by the first chapter of the Book of Genesis and on the west by the Day of Judgment."[8]

Was Mr. Arthur Bird aware, when he wrote that, of the language Columbus had used to describe his third voyage to the New World? "God made me the messenger of the new heaven and new earth," Columbus writes, "of which He spoke in the Apocalypse by St. John, after having spoken of it by the mouth of Isaiah; and He showed me the spot where to find it."[9] It was precisely Columbus's adherence to such concepts, as William Spengemann notes, that "elevated him above the secular world of science and politics, into a typically medieval realm of belief where geographical facts and cosmogonic legend are inextricably mingled." But "it also alienated him from the institutions of medieval authority by making him a direct instrument of God." Columbus's faith in himself as providentially chosen to lead a religious crusade into the heart of darkness not only "foreshadows the individualism of the Renaissance and the heresies of the Reformation,"[10] it also renders him the first American antinomian – blood brother to that Hester Prynne whom Hawthorne conflates with Anne Hutchinson, and to Whitman, with his self-apotheosis as the representative of an American earth saturated with incarnate divinity.

"Columbus's apocalyptic view of world geography," Spengemann continues,

> gave him the courage and the support he needed to cross the unknown, enabling him to persuade himself and his backers – most of whom believed that travel beyond the world perimeter led away from God into the regions of darkness – that these were really the seas of God. In effect, his interpretation of westward migration as an emblem of man's individual and collective progress toward salvation wrested the Ocean Sea from the grip of the demon and brought the dark side of the earth within the sanctified circle of divine dispensation.[11]

But with the decay of the traditional faith and the further development of Protestant individualism, the expectation of salvation in a reconstituted western earthly paradise would come to seem more problematic. That unknown world in the west, after all, had always "assumed two opposed guises in the European imagination: the isles of the blessed and the regions of chaos and death."[12] The Augustinian piety of the Puritans also had its dark obverse in a version of Augustine's Manicheanism, where the forces of darkness and light seemed locked in perpetual struggle, with the outcome uncertain. Shakespeare's "brave new world" of Mirandas and Prosperos also had its Calibans – and worse. It could be seen as "a *strange* New World," in Lowell's words,

> whose baby-bed
> Was prowled roun' by the Injun's cracklin' tread.

"The unpredictable, the abnormal, the inhuman, the cruel, the savage and the strange in terms of European experience were from the beginning part of the image of a land that was ours before we were the land's," notes Howard Mumford Jones. "The New World was filled with monsters animal and monsters human; it was a region of terrifying natural forces, of gigantic catastrophes, of unbearable heat and cold, an area where the laws of nature tidily governing Europe were transmogrified into something new and strange."[13]

Such notions suggested an uncertain fate for the New World adventurer – the dark side of Columbus's project, whereby Whitman could see the great admiral as a "sad shade," a "batter'd, wreck'd old man," thrown on a "savage shore," ending his life in perplexity and despair:

Is it the prophet's thought I speak, or am I raving?
What do I know of life? what of myself?[14]

Such a figure could easily change places with the desperate and deluded
Reverend Mr. Arthur Dimmesdale as he issues from the forest at the end
of Hawthorne's narrative, or with the Captain Ahab who can cry out,
"So far gone am I in the dark side of earth, that its other side, the
theoretic bright one, seems but uncertain twilight to me,"[15] or indeed
with Brockden Brown's Edgar Huntly, who returns from his initiation
in the American wilderness smeared with blood and acting like a maniac,
unable to decide himself whether he is a visionary or a lunatic and driven
to conclude that men have "little cognizance . . . over the actions and
motives of each other! How total is our blindness with regard to our own
performances!"[16] Perhaps America's true "eschatological geography"
would turn out to be a demonic one, with the south bounded by the
regions of the damned and the west – as in Poe's "Masque of the Red
Death" – holding out only an apocalypse of terror. Perhaps what had
seemed to be a New Canaan with its promise of spiritual rebirth and
salvation was really the heart of darkness, drawing the adventurer into a
kind of regressive primitivism and a confrontation with his own interior
horror. In *Edgar Huntly*, as Edwin Fussell notes, Brown "shows European emigrants and American natives penetrating the unknown future
and unwittingly going savage."[17] Brown's claim that the purpose of his
work is "to exhibit a series of adventures growing out of the condition of
our country"[18] finds ominous fulfillment in a nightmarish journey to
nowhere – the ultimate Utopia – representing an America beyond the
reaches of civilized experience. "No marks of habitation or culture, no
traces of the footsteps of men, were discernible," reports his hero. "I
scarcely knew in what region of the globe I was placed."[19] What indeed
can be the "condition" of such a place or of the men attempting to
explore it? Edgar realizes that his adventure has become a kind of
individual spiritual trial, for he is filled with a sense "of sanctity and awe"
by his "consciousness of absolute and utter loneliness." Having penetrated to an American soil never trod by human feet or seen by human
eyes, one even beyond the experience of the red man, he conceives of
himself as *the* New World pioneer: "Since the birth of this continent, I
was probably the first who had deviated thus remotely from the customary paths of men."[20] Those "customary paths," we might say, represent
ordinary adventure, but Edgar has strayed from the eighteenth century's
love of the "picturesque" into a land where the romance of travel has
taken on the dimensions of dark spiritual quest.[21] Moving toward a
perpetually receding "interior region" through "insuperable difficulties," an endless series of precipices and caverns measureless to ordinary

men, he comes to see that he is trapped in "a tedious maze and perpetual declivity"; his path leads inexorably to what seems a "bottomless pit."[22] Could a Jonathan Edwards go any further in describing the human condition?[23]

2

William Spengemann has remarked, rather shortsightedly it seems to me, that "when the novel came, belatedly, to America, travel-writing alone could claim any distinction as a native literary genre."[24] Such a view not only overlooks the sermon, which in fact deeply informed Brown's sense of literary discourse (and would continue to resonate for Cooper and Emerson and Hawthorne and Melville), but also and more particularly that curious kind of American adventure narrative that was effectively an extension of the Puritan sermon – the narrative of Indian captivity.[25] Spengemann goes on to argue that "novels written in America from 1789 to 1841 document an imaginative struggle between an imported form and native materials,"[26] basing his formulation on an idea of the "novel" that limits fictive narrative to a "poetics of domesticity," that conceives of the "novel," that is, in terms of the novel of manners, in the mode of Fielding or Smollett, where the action is completed with the restoration of order by means of marriage. But serious fiction in America can scarcely be assigned such a simple provenance. Brown, along with every other literate American of his time, was saturated with the quasi-sermonic literature of captivity (we notice how frequently the term is used in *Edgar Huntly*), whether John Williams's *The Redeemed Captive* or *The Narrative of the Captivity and Restauration of Mrs. Mary Rowlandson* or Cotton Mather's redaction of the Hannah Dustan captivity or – most especially – the pseudonymous Abraham Panther captivity published in Middletown, Connecticut, in 1787 and reprinted many times thereafter. All of these narratives, as Spengemann himself notes, "fed the [American] reader's appetite for moral melodrama and taught him how to define his own identity vis-à-vis the savage wilderness."[27] More pointedly, these were Calvinist mini-epics *as* melodrama, living sermons that lent themselves easily to elaboration in, and conflation with, fictive modes of discourse, particularly those in which the boundary between physical and metaphysical adventure blurs.

The Abraham Panther captivity, which, as Richard Slotkin points out, was "almost certainly" a source for *Edgar Huntly*, is "a blend of the sentimental romance, Hannah Dustin's captivity, *Sir Gawain and the Green Knight*, and archetypal motifs as ancient as human mythology (including the Indian myths of the sacrifice of the corn god). Like the Edwardsian revival sermon, it employs symbols drawn from the expe-

rience and traditions of its audience to evoke in that audience the sensations and emotions of a quasi-religious experience."[28] In Slotkin's useful
formulation:

> Indian captivity [or] victimization by the wilderness was the hard-
> est and most costly (and therefore the noblest) way of discovering
> the will of God in respect to one's soul, one's election or damna-
> tion. The captivity narratives were ideal for expressing this anxiety
> and for symbolically resolving it. They were based on an experi-
> ence which was a unique feature of the community's American
> experience but which was strongly reminiscent of older myths
> intrinsic to Christianity: the fall of man, the apocalypse, and divine
> judgment. The structure of the captivity narratives embodied, in
> symbolically heightened terms, the experience of personal conver-
> sion (as the Puritans conceived it), as well as the patterns of the
> traumatic experience of emigration that had brought the Puritans to
> New England in the beginning.[29]

In sum, the captivity narrative "reduced a complex of religious beliefs,
philosophical concepts, and historical experiences to a single, compelling, symbolic ritual-drama." But let us note additionally that it was one
in which, at least in Brown's hands, the outcome was by no means sure,
for although Edgar's trial leads to a certain degree of self-realization and
the formation of a chastened "higher" state of awareness, his alter-ego
Clithero is "delivered from captivity" only as a more totally confirmed
and thoroughly depraved moral madman. At all events, Slotkin concludes his exposition of the meaning of captivity narratives by observing
that "the trial is identical with that imposed on Bunyan's pilgrim,"[30]
linking this aspect of Brown's novel writing with a tradition of English
spiritual adventure narrative to which I have already made reference.

Here we must pay special attention to the curious confluence, in
America above all, of a seemingly disparate collection of prose genres
that contributed to the development of "psychological romance." The
centrality of Bunyan to this project is nowhere more tellingly suggested,
as Roger Stein points out, than in an engaging passage in Benjamin
Franklin's *Autobiography*, wherein he relates that during a sea voyage
from New York to Philadelphia in 1723 a "drunken Dutchman" fell
overboard in a storm:

> When he was sinking I reach'd thro' the Water to his shock Pate and
> drew him up so that we got him in again. His Ducking sober'd him
> a little, and he went to sleep, taking first out of his Pocket a Book
> which he desir'd I would dry for him. It prov'd to be my old

favourite Author Bunyan's Pilgrim's Progress in Dutch. . . . I have
since found that it has been translated into most of the Languages of
Europe, and suppose it has been more generally read than any other
book except perhaps the Bible.[31]

We may find it surprising that Franklin misses the opportunity to moral-
ize on how this dissolute European might well have gone to the bottom,
even with *the* Protestant manual of salvation in his pocket, had it not
been for the providential strong right arm of an American. At any rate,
he does go on to make an interesting point about Bunyan's book:

> Honest John was the first that I know of who mix'd Narration and
> Dialogue, a Method of Writing very engaging to the Reader, who
> in the most interesting Parts finds himself as it were brought into
> the Company, and present at the Discourse. Defoe in his Cruso, his
> Moll Flanders, Religious Courtship, Family Instructor, and other
> Pieces, has imitated it with Success. And Richardson has done the
> same in his Pamela, &c.

Stein remarks nicely of this passage "that we re-experience with Franklin
the birth of the novel as form," emphasizing that the concept of "fiction"
implicit in Franklin's comment is notably loose. Stein goes on to point
the significance of Franklin's associating Defoe's pure fictions with his
religious tracts. "He does not distinguish, as later categorizers of the
early American novel would distinguish retrospectively, between fiction
and nonfiction, between the novel of adventure, the love story (or the
seduction novel), and didactic, satirical or polemical works. His sense of
the boundaries of the new form is open and flexible." Even more
germane to our context here, Stein observes that behind all of these
narratives "for Franklin stands Bunyan's *Pilgrim's Progress*," underlining
a notion "that scholars have come to only recently: that *Crusoe* and the
novel in general, for all their sources in the rise of the middle class . . .
achieved their form through adapting the shapes of religious tradition to
new uses. The spiritual biography, the guide tradition, providential
narrative, and the structural possibilities inherent in type, emblem, and
allegory – all these Bunyan passes on to his eighteenth-century descendants." Of course, as we have noticed, such peculiarly American genres
as the captivity narrative bore an especially close relationship to Bunyan's
allegorical mode, and that relationship would strengthen throughout the
eighteenth century, and particularly toward the turn of the nineteenth
century, as these traditions were wedded, in a thoroughly reciprocal
fashion, with certain strains in Gothic fiction.

The link, in fact, between Bunyan and the Gothic-Romantic strain is made explicitly in an 1803 essay by Joseph Dennie, who, as a Harvard graduate and a staunch Federalist, preferred Augustan good sense to the "spectres, demons, Melancholy, Sorrow, black cares, and 'sights unholy' " of Gothic romance. "In the works of Mrs. Ratcliff, and of all her imitators," he complains,

> mournfull or horrible description predominates. The authors go out of the walks of Nature, to find some dreadful incident. Appalling noises must be created. Ghosts must be manufactured by dozens. A door is good for nothing, in the opinion of a romance writer, unless it creak. The value of a room is much enhanced by a few dismal groans. A chest full of human bones is twice as valuable as a casket of diamonds. Every grove must have its quiet disturbed, by the devil, in some shape or other. Not a bit of tapestry but must conceal a corpse; not an oak can grow, without sheltering banditti. Now, in real life, examined in any age, or in any country, we cannot find such a series, such a combination of horrible events, as the romance writers display in almost every page. All their knights are 'knights of the Doleful Countenance.' Fortunately for mortals, though there is much misfortune, and much evil here, yet every object is not covered with a pall. . . . It is a misrepresentation to state that the whole world resembles Bunyan's valley of the shadow of death. It is mischievous to exhibit such a false picture. It enfeebles the mind. It induces a habit of melancholy; it strengthens frantic fear. . . .[32]

Dennie's diatribe against the Gothic is presented as a "Lay" sermon. He is preaching the good tidings that the darkness has lifted, that the "mournfull" and the "horrible" are "out of the walks of Nature" (Brown would say, "Yes, out of the *customary* walks *in* or *of* nature"). It is worth noticing that in rejecting the Gothic mode, Dennie is not simply pouring scorn on a set of silly, faddish literary conventions but explicitly rejecting a tradition that descends from Bunyan and suggesting, perhaps inadvertently, that the Gothic is continuous with such a religious tradition – the Calvinist heritage. (I might observe here that Royall Tyler, in his 1797 preface to *The Algerine Captive*, seems to suggest the same linkage of tradition and taste when he tells us that American readers have given over "certain funeral discourses, the last words and dying speeches of Bryan Shaheen, and Levi Ames, and some dreary somebody's Day of Doom," in favor of contemporary fiction. They have forsaken "the sober sermons and Practical Pieties of their fathers. . . .

Bunyan's Pilgrim [climbing] up the 'hill of difficulty' or through the 'slough of despond,' " and turned to both sentimental novels *and* "the haunted houses and hobgoblins of Mrs. Ratcliffe."[33])

Unlike Dennie, however, Brockden Brown eschews "puerile superstition and . . . Gothic castles and chimeras"[34] because they are hackneyed and imported, not because the vision of life they portray is false or the passions and sympathies they evoke are unhealthy. Transformed in the hands of Godwin and Brown, as Margaret Fuller would note, the "darkest disclosures are not hobgoblin shows, but precious revelations."[35] Brown was domesticating the Gothic – Americanizing it – in order to point and deepen its moral implications. For him, the "walks of Nature," with their "incidents of Indian hostility and the perils of the Western wilderness," are sufficiently dreadful. For Brown, the American forest is haunted by real specters, the shadows of our rational humanity, and that view would be shared and explored further by such beneficiaries of Brown's fictive mode as Hawthorne and Melville. Although Dennie, speaking in 1803 as a modern rationalist and implicitly denying America's Calvinist heritage, could dismiss the notion that "every grove must have its quiet disturbed, by the devil, in some shape or other," Herman Melville, writing on Hawthorne almost a half-century later, would seem all but consciously to be replying to Dennie when, echoing his phrasing, he insists that Hawthorne's "great power of blackness . . . derives its force from its appeals to that Calvinistic sense of Innate Depravity and Original Sin, from whose visitations, in some shape or other, no deeply thinking mind is always and wholly free."[36]

3

Charles Brockden Brown could not have known, when he published *Edgar Huntly* in 1799, that he was providing a sourcebook of motifs and treatments for subsequent writers who would succeed in establishing a significant national literature, but he did know, as we have seen, that he was engaged in writing an American Gothic tale. Though his plot is highly improbable, indeed, almost impossible to follow in all its twistings and turnings, the elements of serious American Gothic are clearly marked. For one thing, Brown began the process of appropriating the ideology and jargon of Calvinism for more purely psychological purposes: Monstrous depravity, perverted will, inexpiable guilt, lively images of damnation – these redeployed categories of Calvinist theology have become part of the dialogue of an individual soul with and about itself.[37] Brown also makes highly imaginative use of the double motif as a way of exploring the notion of the duplex self, of dramatizing the debate between the rational daylight self and the maniacal sleepwalking *other* self.[38] It is as if Clithero draws Huntly into the midnight forest in order to exchange identities with him, to help transform Edgar into the savage hunter he becomes. Indeed, *transformation* – metamorphosis – not as part of the obligatory conventions of the fabulous associated with romance, but as a unique response to the bizarre conditions of life in the New World, is a central theme of the book (as it is of Brown's first novel, *Wieland; or, the Transformation*). "Few, perhaps, among mankind," Huntly claims, "have undergone vicissitudes of peril and wonder equal to mine. The miracles of poetry, the transitions of enchantment, are beggarly and mean compared with those which I had experienced. Passage into new forms, overleaping the bars of time and space, reversal of the laws of inanimate and intelligent existence, had been mine to perform and to witness."[39]

Edgar Huntly is the fable, in some ways inconclusive, of a callow and conventionally (that is, tamely) "romantic" youth who plunges into an eerie and threatening American wilderness almost for the purpose, we may say, of shedding his old identity and becoming a wilderness creature. The sublime American nature he enters is effectively a dark theater of self-discovery and self-realization, a phantasmagoric America of the divided and embattled mind.[40] As Hawthorne would note in *The Scarlet Letter*, the mysterious "primeval forest" in which Hester Prynne let down her hair "imaged not amiss the moral wilderness in which she had so long been wandering." Huntly's America, too, functions as the *image*, or representation, of his own moral confusion and struggle. It is a quasi-allegorical landscape, a problematical mental space, where frightening reversals and seemingly insurmountable obstacles not only impose new rules and call forth new powers but also enforce a new sense of self. As he sits down, on the first page of his narrative, to relate his fantastic adventures, Huntly is no longer what he was. He notes that he has exchanged his "ancient sobriety" for perturbing "headlong energies" and fears that the emotions attendant on that momentous *bouleversement* are in fact "incompatible with order and coherence" and cannot be recollected in tranquillity. His book may be contemporaneous with *Lyrical Ballads*, but Huntly seems as far from Wordsworth as the American wilderness was from Grasmere Vale. Wordsworth's central aim was to exemplify and embody what was *common* in the experiences and feelings of people; Brown is obsessively concerned with the "prodigious or the singular."[41]

I noted in my introduction that Brown is a "transitional figure," and I want now to amplify that observation. Though Brown would be an active presence for the writers of America's so-called Renaissance, his intellectual habits and indeed his vocabulary and style generally mark him as a man of the later eighteenth century, and he exhibits some of the contradictory impulses of that perplexing period.[42] Brown's two faces (or better, two voices), rationalist and romantic by turns, provide a rich discord in the very texture of his fiction. As the historian William Prescott noted, with a certain consternation, in his biographical sketch of Brown, the novelist's world seems principally to be one of "a troubled conscience, partial gleams of insanity, or bodings of imaginary evil which haunt the soul," and yet "in the midst of the fearful strife, we are coolly invited to investigate its causes and all the various phenomena which attend it; every contingency, probability, nay possibility, however remote, is discussed and nicely balanced." As a result, Prescott feared, "the heat of the reader" is in danger of evaporating "in this cold-blooded dissection. . . . We are constantly struck," he observed, "with the strange contrast of over-passion and over-reasoning."[43] If Prescott had had the opportunity to peruse the tales of Poe, he might have been struck by the same contrast and perhaps been led to consider these strange alternations as part of a conscious narrative strategy. But his observation does usefully point us back to the divided minds of many writers born in the second half of the eighteenth century. Like Godwin, whose own restless spirit moved between the bleak and terrible logic of Calvinism and what appear to be the more hopeful affirmations characteristic of his age, Brown was by day, so to speak, a rational progressivist who worked hard to better the conditions of associated life and believed generally in the possibility of amelioration through education and political and social change, but by night his Hamlet side took over, and he was haunted by bad dreams. That internal debate may be seen reflected in Brown's implicit critique of the eighteenth century's most glorious intellectual construction, the Argument from Design.

It is, of course, a commonplace of intellectual history that scientific rationalism was a principal element of Enlightenment thought. Whether we instance John Locke's belief that "the works of nature in every part of them sufficiently evidence a Deity,"[44] or Alexander Pope's insistence that the "mighty maze" is "not without a plan,"[45] or Dean Paley's comparison of nature to a great watch,[46] the fact is that the Argument from Design largely controlled views of God, nature, and man. The mechanical order and harmony of the universe were everywhere adduced as proof of the inherent rightness and fitness of things. It is against this prevailing eighteenth-century view that we may instructively set the manifestly darker vision of Charles Brockden Brown in his various versions of American Gothic. As Warner Berthoff has noted, "Brown's presentation of the ordinary contradictions of human behavior might reasonably be construed as a counterstatement to the rational optimism of Enlightenment psychology and ethics."[47] The world, Brown tells us, "is eternally producing what to our precipitate judgment, are prodigies, anomalies, monsters. Innate, dastardly, sordid wickedness frequently springs up where genial temperature and wise culture have promised us the most heavenly products."[48] Accordingly, Brown's Ormond is not only a cultured hyperrationalist; he is also a very monster of art and reason. And even Constantia Dudley, that seeming paragon of virtue whom Ormond tries relentlessly to seduce, is implicated by Brown's suggestion that dark forces are *everywhere* at work and that what we normally think of as virtue might be better conceived as a calculus of opportunity and motive:

> In no cases, perhaps, is the decision of a human being impartial, or totally uninfluenced by sinister and selfish motives. If Constantia surpassed others, it was not because her motives were pure, but because they possessed more of purity than those of others. Sinister considerations flow in upon us through imperceptible channels, and modify our thoughts in numberless ways, without our being truly conscious of their presence.[49]

In the new world of Brown's fiction, things are not what they seem (indeed, may be precisely the opposite of what they seem), and therefore not primal innocence but congenital caution is man's most valuable birthright. "I did not come into the world without my scruples and suspicions," Arthur Mervyn declares. "I was more apt to impute kindness to sinister and hidden than to obvious and laudable motives." Whereupon Mervyn pauses "to reflect upon the possible designs" of the persons with whom he has to deal, fearing that those designs are likely to prove eccentric.[50]

In line with the eighteenth-century philosopher Johann Georg Hamann's proto-Wittgensteinian observation that "the critique of systems of concepts is a critique, above all, of language,"[51] our attention may naturally be drawn to Brown's persistent use of certain terms that evidence his implicit rejection of Enlightenment Benevolism in favor of a nascent Gothic-Romantic interest in the unconscious as the sinister source of human behavior. One of Brown's favorite words, for example, appears to be *motive*, a term he repeatedly employs to suggest not only that human conduct must be carefully scrutinized but also that the prime impulse behind our conduct is a hidden force, a principle of *movement*, which lies embedded in the workings of the mind. "This little word," as Arthur Mervyn says in another context, "half whispered in a thoughtless mood . . . [can be] a key to unlock an extensive cabinet of secrets"[52] – namely, Brown's pervasive resort to a mechanical metaphor that appropriates the familiar Argument from Design and turns it to darker uses. In Brown's hands, the "machinery" of Enlightenment thought becomes the embodiment of Gothic deviltry.

The prefaces, or "Advertisements," to two of Brown's major works, the nearly contemporaneous *Wieland* and *Edgar Huntly*, point the reader in a useful direction. In the first, Brown supports his rendering of the bizarre conduct of the younger Wieland by appealing "to men conversant with the latent springs and occasional perversions of the human mind." And in the preface to *Edgar Huntly* Brown argues that "new springs of action and new motives to curiosity should operate" in the New World. Brown's figure, we notice, is primarily and persistently mechanical: His "springs of action . . . operate." Moreover, these devices are "latent" in the strict Latin sense of being hidden from view. And since Brown also insists, in the preface to *Huntly*, that the "Gothic castles and chimeras" of European literature will be replaced in his own book by "the perils of the Western wilderness," it is surely appropriate that Brown's hero finds himself immediately menaced from without as well as from within. The springs of action operative in American nature take the ferocious form of a panther, whose desperate "design" to reach Huntly by springing across an abyss is frustrated only by merest chance, leaving Brown's intrepid adventurer to be faced shortly thereafter by another beast. This one's deadly *spring* is countered by Huntly's own violent motion – the impulsive flinging of his deadly tomahawk. "No one knows the powers that are latent in his constitution," Huntly reflects, as he turns hungrily to the "yet warm blood and reeking fibers" of the brute.[53] If the workings of American nature, to cite Frost, are "but design of darkness to appall," Brown's hero discovers that a similar design governs the workings of his own human nature.

Like all of Brown's protagonists, Edgar Huntly is insatiably curious, forever probing into the dark or hidden places of experience. Himself a "mechanist" skilled in designing and constructing boxes and cabinets notable for their secret drawers and concealed springs, he turns "with the eye of an artist" to examining the mysterious box belonging to the maniacal Clithero, Huntly's somnambulistic alter-ego and Brown's prime example of human inscrutability and ambiguity. In this episode, loaded with the implications of a fatal Miltonic temptation and fall that readers of Brown's fiction come to find familiar, Huntly can be seen exploring, as if in a mechanical model, the obscure interior of his antagonist's slippery mind, with disastrous results:

> I surveyed it with the utmost attention. All its parts appeared equally solid and smooth. It could not be doubted that one of its sides served the purpose of a lid, and was possible to be raised. Mere strength could not be applied to raise it, because there was no projecture which might be firmly held by the hand, and by which force could be exerted. Some spring, therefore, secretly existed,

which might forever elude the senses, but on which the hand, by being moved over it in all directions, might accidentally light.

This process was effectual. A touch, casually applied at an angle, drove back the bolt, and a spring, at the same time, was set in action, by which the lid was raised above half an inch. No event could be supposed more fortuitous than this. A hundred hands might have sought in vain for this spring. The spot in which a certain degree of pressure was sufficient to produce the effect was, of all, the least likely to attract notice or awaken suspicion.[54]

Though Edgar believes that his discovery of the secret spring is owing to mere chance, it is clear that only a skilled hand such as his own could have been expected to do the trick, and that Clithero had counted on both Edgar's cleverness and his characteristic curiosity. The box has been designed with Edgar in mind. Opening it eagerly, Huntly is disappointed to discover only some tools and machinery, nothing "of moment." What turns out to be *of moment*, that which sets things in motion, however, is the very fact that Edgar has forced open the box:

My expectations being thus frustrated, I proceeded to restore things to their former state. I attempted to close the lid; but the spring which had raised it refused to bend. No measure that I could adopt enabled me to place the lid in the same situation in which I had found it. In my efforts to press down the lid, which were augmented in proportion to the resistance that I met with, the spring was broken. This obstacle being removed, the lid resumed its proper place; but no means, within the reach of my ingenuity to discover, enabled me to push forward the bolt, and thus to restore the fastening.

I now perceived that Clithero had provided not only against the opening of his cabinet, but likewise against the possibility of concealing that it had been opened. . . .

Edgar's ingenuity has overreached itself. The spring has indeed sprung; the trap has closed. Not the contents of the box but rather the *act* of rifling it has turned out to be significant. Things cannot be restored "to their former state": the Fall is irrevocable. Edgar "had been tempted," as he goes on to say, "by the belief that my action was without witnesses, and might be forever concealed." But the latent spring will remain as a permanent and patent witness to Edgar's hidden weakness, his propensity for meddlesome and clandestine behavior, and Clithero will never forgive him. Indeed, having discovered that Huntly is a useful tool whose curiosity and credulity can always be counted on,

Clithero will make Huntly the unwitting agent of his own mad fury. Thus Huntly's fatal mistake is his misguided belief that he can understand the mind and character of Clithero and therefore reform him. Like his box, Clithero is tricky and permanently deranged. The latent springs of his mind are sinister and dangerous ones. Edgar can find his way into the trap but not out of it, discovering in the course of his investigations that he, too, is a sleepwalker and consequently the source of his own confusion and distress.

Brown's tale suggests that the Enlightenment's comforting world-machine controlled by a benevolent deity had somehow, by the end of the eighteenth century and particularly in America, turned into a Gothic engine horribly shaped by nothing more than the inscrutable workings of the human mind.[55] "Disastrous and humiliating is the state of man!" Huntly concludes. "By his own hands is constructed the mass of misery and error in which his steps are forever involved."[56] The traps into which we fall are those we have ourselves set; the dark design that everywhere appalls is mainly of our own contrivance. Governed by such a view, Brown's book understandably concludes with this sober advice to Edgar from his friend and older mentor, Sarsefield: "Be more circumspect and more obsequious for the future."[57]

Given Brown's quasi-Calvinist attitude toward our fallen condition, perhaps caution and respect for the opinions of wiser heads represent the only reasonable conclusion. But it might be noted, by way both of a coda to Brown's tale and a glance forward to Melville, that a possible alternative to this gloomy view of experience is suggested in *Moby-Dick*. Though Ishmael, in the opening chapter, exhibits little more faith than do Brown's protagonists in the benevolence of "those stage managers, the Fates," he thinks he "can see a little into the springs and motives" which induced him to put himself in their hands. What impels him is not only a brash and perhaps unjustified fearlessness in the face of terror but a more positive desire to embrace and understand what appears to be a heartless and threatening universe. "Not ignoring what is good," he says, "I am quick to perceive a horror, and could still be social with it – would they let me – since it is well to be on friendly terms with all the inmates of the place one lodges in."

Since Ishmael is fundamentally motivated by a charitable impulse, it is not surprising that when he lodges in the Spouter-Inn he indeed embraces the initially frightening dark man he finds in his room. That friendship, of course, proves to be Ishmael's salvation, for it is Queequeg's coffin, that manifest extension of his own body, which is marked with hieroglyphics that contain "a complete theory of the heavens and the earth, and a mystical treatise on the art of attaining truth,"[58] that becomes Ishmael's lifebuoy. "Liberated by reason of its cunning spring, and, owing to its great buoyancy, rising with great force,"[59] it preserves Ishmael and demonstrates, presumably, that the only viable theory of the heavens and earth is one that includes love. Such is the "cunning spring" that symbolizes Queequeg's inner workings – not a trap but a great upward force capable of redeeming Ishmael's wolfish world.

4

It might seem difficult – indeed, impossible – to link the urbane and whimsical Irving, with his ironic poses and English affectations, to the haunted mind and phantasmagoric America of Charles Brockden Brown. As Richard Henry Dana, Sr., observed in an 1819 essay on *The Sketch Book* and Irving generally in the *North American Review*, "Mr. Irving has taken the lead . . . in the witty, humourous and playful cast of works – those suited to our happier feelings, – while Brown harasses us with anxiety and strange terror." But Dana also noted that Irving possessed "a power of mingling with his wit the wild, mysterious, and visionary," citing "Rip Van Winkle" as an example of this curious mixing of modes. "It is a very uncommon union of qualities," Dana concluded.[60]

Uncommon Irving was and is. As the first American writer in the nineteenth century to achieve international fame and a substantial measure of financial success, Irving was read by everyone, most of all by the American Romantic authors who followed in his footsteps, and his influence is widely diffused in their writings.[61] The Geoffrey Crayon who speaks to us in "The Author's Account of Himself" is a kind of armchair Ishmael – "a homeless man" (as he explains in "Stratford-on-Avon") "who has no spot on this wide world which he can truly call his own" – who nevertheless manages to find some version of the Spouter-Inn wherever he goes, replete with easy chair and fire. There he stretches himself out and travels, at least in imagination. Like Melville's sub-sublibrarian, he is something of an amateur scholar in the field of adventure; books of voyages and travels are his "passion." This connoisseur of wandering believes, with the English writer John Lyly, that travel is radically metamorphic, that, as Lyly puts it, the traveler who "stragleth from his owne country is in a short time transformed" into "monstrous" shapes; later (in "The Art of Bookmaking") he will advance a theory that books, too, in their migrations, "undergo a kind of metempsychosis and spring up under new forms," whence German fable (as in the two most famous pieces in *The Sketch Book*), transplanted to the "American woodlands," is revived as New World romance that attempts to fathom the deep and troubled heart of a nation itself in the process of radical metamorphosis.

Like Rip Van Winkle following his twenty years' sleep, our mental traveler, Geoffrey Crayon, feels himself to be an object of curiosity as he "finds himself writing in a strange land" ("L'Envoi") of an even stranger American past. Like Hawthorne after him, he has escaped "from the commonplace realities of the present" and lost himself "among the shadowy grandeurs of the past" – lost himself, that is, in the realm of romance. He believes, with Ishmael, that "water and meditation are wedded forever"; his sea voyage is thus a kind of folio whale, an opportunity to travel in the strangest and largest book of them all, for "the vast space of waters . . . is like a blank page in existence" that literally cries to be filled in. Again like Rip, he is "conscious of being cast loose from the secure anchorage of settled life and sent adrift upon a doubtful world" – the shifting world, that is, of his own dreaming imagination. "I had closed one volume of the world," he says, leaving himself free to enter the purely meditative space of daydream and revery. As he, like Ishmael, climbs the maintop on a calm summer's day, he sees almost nothing but what his musing mind creates, whether "fairy realms" in the clouds, waiting to be peopled with his own fantasy, or "silver volumes" in the "gently undulating billows" below. Here Irving comes perilously close to an actual anticipating and preempting of Melville's own romance world, for his Geoffrey Crayon looks down on the "monsters of the deep" and, absorbed by the shoals of porpoises, the huge grampus, and the specterlike "ravenous shark," is tempted to sketch the "watery world beneath," with its "fathomless valleys," "shapeless monsters that lurk among the very foundations of the earth," and other "wild phantasms that swell the tales of fishermen and sailors." But such, obviously, is not his métier. "I *might* fill a volume," he concludes, "with the reveries of a sea voyage," but he actually hastens "to get to shore."

The shore he gets to is presumably that of the Old World; but for Crayon it is really "our old home," as Hawthorne was to call England. Irving's main English, or British, characters (Roscoe, James the First of Scotland) are simply versions of his own dreamy, meditative romantic American self, lost in the rush and bustle of modern commercial England. Musing in Westminster Abbey, Crayon bethinks himself of those "military enthusiasts, who so strangely mingled religion and romance, and whose exploits form the connecting link between fact and fiction, between the history and the fairy tale." History, he tells us, "fades into fable; fact becomes clouded with doubt and controversy." The most celebrated "enthusiasts" (we need to remember the significance of this term) whom Irving conjures up, however, are the American Puritans and their literal or spiritual descendants, whose minds are dark closets of fear and superstition. We are circling back to the world of Brockden

Brown, those "dark and melancholy times," as Irving relates in his sketch of King Philip, when the "public mind" was in a "diseased state," when "the gloom of religious abstraction, and the wildness of their situation, among trackless forests and savage tribes, had disposed the colonists to superstitious fancies, and had filled their imaginations with the frightful chimeras of witchcraft and spectrology." The atmosphere seemed thick with omens, and strange sounds filled the air. Was it any different in the putative Dutch settlement of Rip Van Winkle? For Rip, too, appears to have the haunted mind of the seventeenth-century Puritans and is wont to tell the village children "long stories of ghosts, witches, and Indians." He is thought to have been "carried away by the Indians," a victim of captivity, and he returns to his village after two decades feeling "bewitched" and as "singularly metamorphosed" as the picture of King George that has turned into George Washington.

But Rip is neither tory nor patriot; he is rather a man who doubts his own identity and cannot tell, as he says, "who I am!" As a kind of American Ancient Mariner, Rip has left his most vital self in the wilderness along with his gun and can recapture his sense of himself only by endlessly repeating and embellishing the story of his captivity. He is thus a permanent hostage of that visionary interlude and remains, like King Philip, "a wanderer and a fugitive in his native land." The connection between the two is not entirely fanciful, for although Rip may simply be "out of his head," it is also suggested that the spirit of the land itself – this "region . . . of fable" – in the person of the Indians' shape-shifting Manitou has taken possession of our "bewildered hunter," with his irrepressible vagrant urge, who like Irving's aborigines and Brown's Huntly has slept "among the thunders of the cataract." Rip is precisely *bewildered*[62] in that his fateful straying into the American wilderness becomes *the* salient feature of his life, or rather, his death-in-life, for the years of what should have been his vigorous manhood have been dreamed away in the forest, and he returns as the ghost of himself to tell a tale that may be called (along with Huntly's) "Memoirs of a Sleepwalker." That ghost, however, continues to have an important function in this – alas, is it not? – ever-modernizing pre-Revolutionary village, just as the ghost of the vanishing Indian would continue not only to haunt but also to inspire an American mind that was already ashamed, at least in part, of having despoiled the magical wilderness and its own God-intoxicated settlements.[63] Some people may doubt the "reality" of Rip's story, but the "rising generation," in particular, loves to be reminded of another America where the quaint and quiet little inn had not yet been replaced by Jonathan Dolittle's wretched "large, ricketty, wooden building," with its "great gaping windows, some of them broken and mended with old hats and petticoats," where the tall, naked liberty pole had not yet usurped the place of the "great tree" of yore, and where the comfortable and humane "phlegm and drowsy tranquillity" of the prewar generation had not yet given way to the "busy, bustling, disputatious tone" of the new America. We notice especially that the once-holy spirit of New England is now represented, so it seems, by the at least aesthetically reprehensible Jonathan Dolittle (soon to migrate upstate into Cooper's *The Pioneers* under the name of Hiram, with notably sharpened features and the addition of "low cunning"); and even the much-maligned Dame Van Winkle has now fallen victim to a New England peddler. As Terence Martin remarks, the tale seems to dramatize, not only "Rip's loss of identity," but, "by inference, the loss of identity of the imaginative function"; "the magical, the marvelous, the imaginative" seem to have "no place in the founding of the new republic," as they appear to have lost their commanding place in the once nobly, if delusively, haunted New England mind.[64]

Irving's own narrator – this alienated wandering bachelor with his visionary and meditative habits – cannot help but be sympathetic with the Rip Van Winkles of his country, as he has nothing but love for that "drowsy, dreamy" Sleepy Hollow, filled with "witching power," whose people walk "in a continual reverie" and "are given to all kinds of marvellous beliefs . . . trances and visions" despite the fact that elsewhere their "restless country" is hell-bent on progress and change. It may be, as Irving suggests, that the "visionary propensity" that suffuses Sleepy Hollow is the legacy of "an old Indian chief, the prophet or wizard of his tribe," or perhaps, more sinisterly, the imaginative power enforced on all who reside in the region had its origins in the Teutonic black magic practiced by a certain German doctor in the early days. Sleepy Hollow is thus presented as a kind of spiritual backwater where the possibility of dreaming dreams and seeing apparitions is linked, on the one hand, to the rich traditions of the land's aboriginal inhabitants and, on the other, to the *pseudodoxia epidemica* imported to America along with the religious enthusiasm of its visionary settlers.

Ichabod Crane appears to be the test case, for he is introduced to us as a representative New Englander who brings to this already enchanted ground his own contradictory traditions. As "a native of Connecticut, a State which supplies the Union with pioneers for the mind as well as for the forest," Crane carries into the frontier settlement some very typical New England baggage: "Cotton Mather's History of Witchcraft, a New England Almanac, and a book of dreams and fortune-telling." We notice that it is pointedly not the high strain of New England's spiritual tradition that Ichabod is filled with – not the sermons of Hooker or Edwards or perhaps even the best of Mather's *Magnalia*[65] – but rather the witches' kitchen of the New England imagination, evidencing its sad decline from stern piety to fantastic credulity, rigid fanaticism, and cruelty. Even Crane's nasal psalm singing is described not so much as the expression of religious passion as it was another of those "make-shifts" whereby Crane made his way " 'by hook and by crook.' " From one angle, then, Crane seems to stand for the fag end of the Puritan tradition on the way to its becoming just one more disreputable seedy spiritualism. And Irving therefore chose his name with great care, for Ichabod, which means "inglorious," has stepped out as a monitory figure from the fourth chapter of the first Book of Samuel, wherein Israel is defeated by the Philistines, who carry off the ark of God, so that when Ichabod is born to his dying mother, she intones, "the glory is departed from Israel," as she despairingly names the child.[66]

This was an all too familiar text in the history of New England's spiritual declensions,[67] and a brief anecdote may help to illuminate Irving's intention. When Emerson, in 1841, recorded the death of his ninety-year-old step-grandfather, Ezra Ripley, the faithful Puritan patriarch of the Concord church, and celebrated that generation of "great, grim, earnest men," he told the story of the Reverend Mr. Ripley's confronting a ne'er-do-well son at the funeral of his father: "Sir, I knew your great grandfather," he told the dissolute young man; "When I came to this town, your great grandfather was a substantial farmer in this very place & an excellent citizen. Your grandfather followed him & was a virtuous man. Now your father has gone to his grave full of labors & virtues. There is none of that large family left, but you, and it rests with you to bear up the good name & usefulness of your ancestors. If you fail – Ichabod – the glory is departed."[68] Inferentially, even before Ichabod Crane's appearance the glory had indeed departed, for example, in New England's betrayal of its own true Christian faith as evidenced by the obscenities of the witchcraft delusion, and, as we have noted, it is precisely this decline that is represented in the unprepossessing person of Crane. Perhaps it is worth adding that this theme of betrayal of the true spirit of America is also given a political dimension in Irving's tale, for despite all the terrifying talk about the headless Hessian on horseback, it is the tragic agent of treason, Major André, whose specter more immediately presides over Ichabod's defeat.

But, of course, Crane is more properly self-defeated, done in by the superstitious credulity that has taken the place of piety in his craven soul. So much for Crane as a New England pioneer of the mind. But even his love of the land and its bounty as represented by the Van Tassel inheritance turns, not on its value as a spiritual resource or a natural or historical treasure, but on its cash value. "His imagination expanded," Irving tells us, as he conceived of marrying Katrina and selling the old estate in Sleepy Hollow so that he might invest the money "in immense tracts of wild land, and shingle palaces in the wilderness." He dreams of setting out for Kentucky or Tennessee, "or the Lord knows where," not for the love of the wild but for the sake of gain, and as Ichabod wanders ambiguously out of the pages of Irving's tale, we may infer that at least some of the New World's pioneers of the mind are leaving the realm of romance for the realm of land speculation and the great American jackpot. Or are we being unfair to poor Ichabod? For it is suggested that the story of his subsequent success is not likely to be true, that his poor shade, like some hapless version of Bunyan's Christian, still haunts the precincts of Sleepy Hollow, "chanting a melancholy psalm tune" – more, it would seem, in sorrow or perhaps penance for his spiritual failing than in disappointment over his missed opportunity.

Wherever Ichabod's wanderings may have carried him, it is true in any case that the singular careers of both Crane and Rip Van Winkle continued to engage the nineteenth-century American imagination, and nowhere more suggestively than in Herman Melville's "Rip Van Winkle's Lilac," an exquisite meditation on Irving's sketches that can be seen both as Melville's own last testament and as a critical reading of his predecessor's work.[69] It seems clear enough that Melville's young artist in the story, the "certain meditative vagabondo" who sets up his umbrella and easel in front of the ruins of Rip's house, is a kind of Geoffrey Crayon redivivus. And it should be equally clear that the "gaunt hatchet-faced stony-eyed individual, with a gray sort of salted complexion like that of a dried cod-fish, jogging by on a lank horse," is none other than the errant shade of Ichabod Crane, fancifully imaged by the artist as Death on a Pale Horse. Who but Melville could have conceived of having this sour-faced and primly desiccated remnant of New England's noble old-time religion confront both the genial Crayon and the flowering memento of Rip's lovable bohemianism?

Now the issues latent in Irving's tales are fully joined as Melville's mouthpiece, with his "paganish dream" of Greek temples crowning the hilltops of America, realizes how antipathetic are the Puritan tradition and the Romantic impulse (here is the place to recall Emerson's remark about his "cautious & canny" friends who wished "to unite Corinth with Connecticutt"). The glory that has departed is really the dream of Arcadia, not the impossible religious vision of a holy city on a hill. Melville's retouched Rip Van Winkle is poetic and sensual, as William Carlos Williams would reinvent a Daniel Boone who was "a great voluptuary born to the American settlements against the niggardliness of the damning puritanical tradition."[70] And in Melville's fantasy the Van Winkle house remains unfinished because the seductive bridegroom with his "sly magnetism" manifestly prefers amorous dalliance to wielding saw and hammer. Why *was* this garden in the west – America –

discovered if not to allow the finest and fullest impulses of the heart to flourish? Is Melville implicitly condemning Ichabod for thinking of making cash instead of love when faced with that "tempting . . . morsel" Katrina?

To such a flamboyant Romantic as Melville, religious hypocrisy and religious delusion might well have seemed lesser sins than the abstract mentality that lay behind them – that transcendentalizing habit of mind that could turn away from the pleasures and perfections of the particular, preferring the husks and shadows of experience to the substance. Perhaps the huge willow, called an "ancient Jeremiah," that weeps in traditional American fashion over the decaying Van Winkle house is lamenting not so much its incompletion as the departure from it of love's balm. That, in Melville's view at least, would represent a true spiritual declension; and here, it is pleasant to think, the "love-worthy" shade of Washington Irving might have felt inclined, even at the end of a successful career, to smile in rueful agreement and thank Melville for having provided so trenchant a commentary on his own bewildered pilgrims.

Chapter 2

"Where There Is No Vision, the People Perish. . . ."

Prophets and Pariahs in the Forest of the New World

===

1

When James Fenimore Cooper's daughter Susan looked back to the beginning of her father's career as an American romancer, she pointed to the publication of *The Last of the Mohicans* in 1826 as having produced "quite a startling effect" in Europe – especially in Europe – as well as in America because, she claimed, "the freshness of the subject" added "greatly to the vivid interest of the narrative."[1] The "subject" to which she was principally alluding was the American Indian, the one truly original subject available to American writers, particularly vis-à-vis European fiction. The romance of the New World could hardly be said to exist without the imaginative exploitation of the country's aborigines, and another notable American romancer, Hawthorne, would note ruefully that his own abhorrence of "an Indian story" had shut him out "from the most peculiar field of American fiction." No writer, he went on, "can be more secure of a permanent place in our literature, than the biographer of the Indian chiefs."[2] Susan Cooper was making her claim for the uniqueness of her father's work precisely on this point, and she was therefore obliged to deal with the prior claim of Brockden Brown. "As yet," she notes, "there had been but one American work of the imagination in which the red man was introduced with any prominence: 'Edgar Huntley,' by Brockden Brown, a writer of undoubted talent, but scarcely known in England" – an odd mistake, but we observe that she was simply trying to stake out her father's territory as securely as possible and was therefore brushing Brown aside. Thus she continues: "While alluding to his work, it may be well to remark that Mr. Cooper had not read 'Edgar Huntley' since his own boyhood, when his writing

54

an Indian romance himself would have seemed an event wildly improbable. . . . 'The Mohicans' would assuredly have been precisely the book it now is had 'Edgar Huntley' never been written."

Though the lady may seem to be protesting too much (and we may also wish to reflect on how lightly she passes over Cooper's own prior treatment of the Indian in *The Pioneers*), her claim about the influence of Brown is finally a fair one, for Brown's America, as we have seen, is a landscape of the mind, and *his* Indians, as opposed to Cooper's, are little more than projections of Huntly's fears and measures of his own prowess and transformation.[3] Though it is suggested that Huntly is on the way to becoming an Indian hater because of the extermination of his family, he murders reluctantly and only when pressed – *in extremis*. He has no programmatic or doctrinaire antipathy to Indians and becomes a version of the great American scourge only accidentally, as it were. In short, his "Indians" are shadows of himself, part of that symbolic nightmare world into which he sleepwalks. The "pest" is "consciousness," not the biracial character of the American forest or its sociopolitical stresses and polarities. Brown's world is that of Calvinist psychomachia, not of historical reality and political and social change. His view is bleak because it is the inevitable result of the Fall of Man: "Disastrous and humiliating is the state of man! By his own hands is constructed the mass of misery and error in which his steps are forever involved." *Design* is at fault, but we ourselves construct our own traps and mazes (the categories of "God" and the "Devil" have collapsed into our own heads; we are at odds with ourselves). Even our "benevolence" is a tainted impulse. All we can do is attempt to "be more circumspect."

Now Cooper's hero also learns to be wary, but mainly because the American wilderness is full of real dangers and pitfalls, not because his own spirit is divided. Though human character *is* duplex in Cooper's view (and the Indian, in certain regards, symbolizes that duplexity), his America has real coordinates in time and space, real social and political underpinnings and assumptions – as well, importantly, as spiritual ones. Cooper's mood is elegiac in the Leatherstocking Tales not mainly because he has a quasi-Calvinist view of what Brown calls "the condition of our country" but because his belief in the possibility of spiritual growth and self-realization is being undermined. His elegiac feeling is predicated on a sense of real potential once available to both whites and reds in the virgin forest of the New World.[4] He begins, in 1823, already with a strong sense of what has been lost (though he is willing to debate the opposed claims of the new and old systems of value), celebrates it tentatively, and then moves backward in his series further into myth and what Lawrence calls "wish-fulfillment." We have a "decrescendo of

Reality" and a crescendo of dream. But what must be stressed is that Cooper, unlike Brown, presents us with imaginative projections of the coordinates of an actual America, not an internalized spiritual struggle. Over and over, the country is shown to us in all its particularity as a true natural paradise. That "Vision" may still serve to correct error, guide conduct, and help construct the future. The myth of the dying red vegetation god and the waning Beowulfian hero is balanced by a strong awareness of an ongoing political and social entity. Thus Cooper's books, as we know, are typically split right down the middle between celebration of the passing heroic age and plots of reconciliation and social renewal (the repairing of ideological breaches or disjunction through marriage).

It should be noted that, quite apart from Brockden Brown, other treatments of the Indian in American writing predate Cooper's and in a number of interesting ways probably helped to shape his own practice. There are, of course, the two Indian chapters in Irving's *Sketch Book*, and though we may wish to dismiss his aborigines as sentimentalized copper-clad versions of his own meditative, wandering, romantic self, Irving does attempt to provide a kind of rudimentary ethnography. He insists, for example, on the Indians' attachment to the "native soil" and presents an account of a sachem's "vision," in which the spirit of his mother demands revenge on those "wild people" who have defaced Indian antiquities in their willful despoliation of the land. Irving's presentation of the white invader as a kind of savage imposing his thoughtless cruelty on tender-hearted redskins notable for their domestic affections and provoked to "sudden acts of hostility" only by the betrayal of their "generous motives" may not be very good history, and indeed it may tend to de-fang the Indian through an oversentimentalizing of his character. He portrays the Indian as a powerless victim, already on the wane and in the act of leaving the scene, not as an angry patriot still capable of enforcing his own position through strong and concerted action. But Irving's sketch at least has the virtue of underlining one important aspect of red–white relations in America, namely, that the enmity is largely to be ascribed to thwarted love.[5] In this regard it is a pity that Irving quotes, as his epigraph to "Traits of Indian Character," only the first sentence of the celebrated speech by Logan, second son of Shikellemus, a noted chief of the Cayuga nation.

The speech was first given wide currency by its inclusion in Jefferson's *Notes on the State of Virginia* in 1787 and ultimately found its way into McGuffey's *Reader* as a school recitation piece.[6] Perhaps its wide distribution was what led Irving to feel he needed to include no more than its opening sentence. But that sentence – "I appeal to any white man if ever he entered Logan's cabin hungry, and he gave him not to eat; if ever he

came cold and naked, and he clothed him not" – presents Logan only as a
kind of servant of the white man and not as a proud Indian who in fact
risked compromising his position among his own people through his
love for the usurpers. The speech continues:

> "During the course of the last long and bloody war, Logan re-
> mained idle in his cabin, an advocate for peace. Such was my love
> for the whites, that my countrymen pointed as they passed, and
> said, 'Logan is the friend of the white men.' I had even thought to
> have lived with you, but for the injuries of one man. Col. Cresap,
> the last spring, in cold blood, and unprovoked, murdered all the
> relations of Logan, not sparing even my women and children.
> There runs not a drop of my blood in the veins of any living
> creature. This called on me for revenge. I have sought it: I have
> killed many: I have fully glutted my vengeance. For my country, I
> rejoice at the beams of peace. But do not harbour a thought that
> mine is the joy of fear. Logan never felt fear."[7]

Logan's description of great love turned to undying hatred, of the dream
of a true mutual cohabitation soured by a betrayed faith and human
desolation, is a primary text in red–white relations and provides a bitterly
ironic commentary not only on the original Christian errand into the
wilderness, with its hope both of redemption for the whites and conversion for the pagans, but also – as one moves into a post-Puritan, indeed,
post-Christian, nineteenth century – on the Romantic dream of regeneration through immersion in the unspoiled garden-forest of the New
World.

   Indeed, early versions, whether history or myth, of white–red intercourse invariably concern an Indian maiden who exemplifies the possibility of mutual accommodation of the races *only* as a result of the
conversion of the pagan – as in the tale of the Algonquin-Iroquois
maiden Kateri Tekakwitha, Christianized by French Jesuits, whose holy
death is marked by the miraculous whitening of her face;[8] or in the
familiar story of Pocahontas, who not only saves a white man but presumably, and more significantly, saves herself by becoming Rebecca
Rolfe. In the formula Indian plays that had already proliferated widely by
Cooper's time "the Indian heroine's attraction to and sympathy for the
white European always involved a betrayal of her own race'"[9]; the sacrifice is all on one side, and the white fantasy is that of leading the Indian –
female, and therefore presumably docile – *out* of the forest and into the
church, rather than of being led the other way – toward the forest and a
kind of natural rebaptism. Cooper's developing myth of the love-feast

between Natty Bumppo and Chingachgook in the woods is Romantic both in its implicit rejection of the project of Christian conversion and in its glorification of the purely natural man. Though Natty is permitted, in ways not clearly definable, to hang on to his "whiteness," he in fact crosses the color-line in the direction of "redness," becoming, as Balzac remarked, a "magnificent moral hermaphrodite," an improbable representation of both civilization and the savage state.[10] It is worth emphasizing that whereas Natty's "conversion" to the wilderness strengthens him by adding purely natural piety to his already tenuously Christian virtues, the ineffectual conversion of Chingachgook to the white man's religion is portrayed as a degradation, the unfortunate transformation of a good Indian into a "Christian beast,"[11] rendering him not so much a moral hermaphrodite as a moral paradox. By thus portraying this failed conversion in such a pejorative light at the very beginning of the Leatherstocking series, Cooper, whether wittingly or not, provided a retrospectively grim but prospectively hopeful rewriting of the history of white–red relations, whereby his focus on the problems and paradoxes of conversion to Christianity progressively gives way as the series moves on to an idealization of man in the natural state. The red man is celebrated *as* a forest creature, and the white man is shown to be ennobled by his own measured accommodation to that creature. Of course, this is very much Cooper's version of the meeting of races in the forest. Other representations of what came of the Christian's errand into the wilderness were at best ambiguous and at worst dishearteningly bleak.

Every myth, of course, has its countermyth in the yin and yang of the imagination, night following day, and day night, in the endless dialectic of good and evil. So the myth of a possible Garden of Eden generates, through guilt or perversity, a fable of Paradise Lost. Such is R. M. Bird's *Nick of the Woods*, published in 1837, more or less in between the first three rather dour Leatherstocking books and the final two more hopeful exemplifications of Cooper's "yearning myth" (in Lawrence's familiar phrase). Bird's book is adorned with an epigraph from *Paradise Lost*, the final lines, describing Adam and Eve's uncertain entry into the unsanctified land of Eden. This, by obvious design, sets the stage for our entrance into Bird's Kentucky, a degenerate version of the seeming paradise encountered by Daniel Boone in the eighteenth century.[12] Kentucky is now truly the dark and bloody ground, the presumed garden-forest as charnel house, and the central figure of Bird's fable is an apparently mild-mannered Quaker ominously named Nathan Slaughter but called, "out of pure wantonness and derision," Bloody Nathan because, as everyone avers, "he's the only man in all Kentucky that *won't fight*."[13] Nathan Slaughter, however, proves sinisterly true to his oxymoronic name for he, far more than John Mohegan, is a veritable

"Christian beast": by day a meek and pious Nathan, by night the
Jibbenainosay, "the spirit that walks," a ubiquitous specter whose ferocious hatred of the Indian expresses itself in brutal murder. Though Bird
provides a feeble explanation for Nathan's night-wandering madness in
terms of epilepsy brought on by seeing his own family wiped out by
Indians, Nathan's work is presented as the almost necessary demonic
extreme of the spirit's work in the wilderness, for he marks his victims'
bodies with a bloody cross and is called Nick of the Woods. Effectively,
he is the devil as John the Baptist. This grotesque perversion of the
Christian mission partly grows out of Bird's dim view of human nature,
for he entertains a conviction "that there is something essentially demo-
niac in the human character and composition; as if, indeed, the earth of
which man is framed had been gathered only after it had been trodden by
the foot of the Prince of Darkness"[14]; but it is clearly the wilderness, with
its quasi-satanic denizens, that has twisted the mind and spirit of Bird's
demented backwoodsman. Nathan Slaughter, like Nathaniel Bumppo,
has gone native, become a species of white savage, not however for the
sake of perfecting his natural self but rather to figure forth in his own
body the red devil he has first imagined and then succeeded in acting out.
Nathan finally appears in "the countenance of an Indian . . . grimly and
hideously painted over with figures of snakes, lizards, skulls, and other
savage devices," the impersonation of his own nightmares.[15] Nathan
adopts one of the Indian's prime emblems, the snake, as his own personal
sign to mark his exchange of identities with this creature both admired
and hated. The Indian is little more than the mask of Nathan's own
darkest impulses; the death orgy almost the logical antitype of the
original myth and dream of love in the woods. The shape of Bird's fable,
especially in regard to the Christian project in the New World, seems to
prefigure Conrad's *The Heart of Darkness*, for these white enthusiasts,
initially bent on elevating the Indian and suppressing savage customs,
conclude as if with Kurtz's terrible words: "Exterminate all the brutes!"

Bird's fellow southern romancer, William Gilmore Simms, was not
the racist Bird appears to have been and in fact wrote a good deal in
defense of the Indian, unabashedly praising his robust beauty, grace, and
intelligence. "Properly diluted," he writes, "there was no better blood
than that of Cherokee and Natchez. It would have been a good infusion
into the paler fountain of Quaker and Puritan."[16] The whites' denigration
of the Indian's taste, judgment, and imagination, Simms argues, "is only
to be accounted for by reference to our blinding prejudices against the
race – prejudices which seem to have been fostered as necessary to justify
the reckless and unsparing hand with which we have smitten them in
their habitations, and expelled them from their country. We must prove
them unreasoning beings, to sustain our pretensions as human ones –

show them to have been irreclaimable, to maintain our own claims to the regards and respect of civilization."[17] If the Indian was *not* a beast, Simms argues, what then could the Christian destroyer call himself? But Simms's forthright view of the shabby underpinnings of the whites' pretensions to superiority did not protect him from ambivalent feelings about the wilderness and its aboriginal inhabitants. Its fascination was very real, but it was also, he feared, at base the fascination of the abomination.

In Simms's best and most celebrated romance of the forest, *The Yemassee*, he set down a very long purple passage (which was to become well known as a set piece for school recitation[18]) describing in highly colored language an encounter between the Anglo-Saxon heroine (named Elizabeth, as in Cooper's *The Pioneers*) and a most extraordinary rattlesnake. Simms's piece depends for its effect partly on the all but clichéd association of the rattlesnake and the Indian, and, indeed, Simms takes the trouble to inform any culturally benighted readers that "the gentleman, the nobleman – the very prince of snakes" is "devoutly esteemed" by the Indians, who derive "many of their own habits . . . from models furnished by his peculiarities."[19] This particular snake, in addition, has thirteen rattles, whereby Simms renders it – improbably – a symbol not only of the land's aborigines and the arch-deceiver but also of America's nascent political identity.

It is this preternatural snake that Bess, waiting in the forest for her white lover, finds herself enchanted with, at first unaware *what* it is. Its "star-like shining glance" sends a "fluid lustre" into her own, and as it fixes "with strange fondness" on Bess's terrified/fascinated eyes, becoming ever more "beautiful" as it dilates, "growing larger and more lustrous with every ray which it sent forth," a "dreaming sense that conjured up the wildest fancies, terribly beautiful," takes possession of her soul.[20] Bess longs "to pluck the gem-like thing from the bosom of the leaf in which it seemed to grow," and this glowing presence, on its side, seems "as if wooing her to seize." It appears to be the "very principle of light . . . a subtle, burning, piercing, fascinating gleam," which makes her dizzy and spellbinds her faculties and powers. Now she hears the rattle, announcing the true nature "of that splendid yet dangerous presence," but Bess is unable to move, riveted by terror. "The reptile all this while appeared to be conscious of, and to sport with, while seeking to excite her terrors." The horrible fangs display themselves while the serpent's "powerful eye shot forth glances of that fatal power of fascination, malignantly bright [a Miltonic oxymoron], which, by paralyzing, with a novel form of terror and of beauty, may readily account for the spell it possesses of binding the feet of the timid."

The creature meanwhile coils and uncoils, "its arching neck glittering like a ring of brazed copper, bright and lurid," and a strange silence descends on the forest. The "corded muscles" are now "all in coil. They have but to unclasp suddenly, and the dreadful folds will be upon her, its full length, and the fatal teeth will strike, and the deadly venom which they secrete will mingle with the life blood in her veins." Bess "cannot now mistake the horrid expression of its eye." It is pure nightmare, for she tries to scream and fails, but finally "a single wild cry" issues from her lips:

> She sinks down upon the grass before her enemy – her eyes, however, still open, and still looking upon those which he directs forever upon them. She sees him approach – now advancing, now receding – now swelling in every part with something of anger, while his neck is arched beautifully like that of a wild horse under the curb[;] . . . she sees the neck growing larger and becoming completely bronzed as about to strike – the huge jaws unclosing almost directly above her, the long tubulated fang, charged with venom, protruding from the cavernous mouth. . . .

and – she faints.

It is not entirely easy to measure Simms's intent here, for although the passage is blatantly and brazenly sexual – what we might call American forest-lore as soft pornography – and clearly designed to titillate a nineteenth-century readership that could expect to be gratified only in this oblique fashion, it is equally clear that Simms's tour de force contains much cultural mythology. The two intentions, in fact, are intimately interwoven. This is the same Simms, after all, who, in an otherwise sober essay entitled "Pocahontas: A Subject for the Historical Painter," was capable of saying, "We commend the study of this period, down to the date of English settlement in Virginia, to the peculiar care of the American student – satisfied, as we are, that he cannot fail to find among its chronicles a body of crude material, virgin and fertile, fresh and blooming with the beauty of its dawning youth, and susceptible to all the maternal uses which grow naturally from the embrace of the prolific genius."[21] Pocahontas, the historical material, the pristine American land – they are all one to this New World romancer, the appeal of whose subject is far more than merely intellectual. The wild forest of the west is a subject to embrace, and yet perhaps that embrace will prove fatal to a white identity equally devoted to protecting its presumed integrity. How would Simms have felt if his rhetorical appeal for the infusion of Cherokee and Natchez blood "into the paler fountain of Quaker and

Puritan" – and why not throw in the First Families of Virginia for good measure? – threatened to become a reality?

Bess, at all events, awakes from her swoon to find the evil snake-prince miraculously replaced by a handsome Indian brave, who in fact has killed the rattler and is now tenderly supporting the maiden's head; whereupon her white lover springs from the brush prepared to hatchet the red man for what appears to him to be an assault in progress: "What have you done to the maiden? Quickly speak or I strike." Explanations, of course, immediately follow, Occonestoga is exonerated and praised, and the maiden revives, uttering, with a shudder, "Oh, Gabriel, such a dream – such a horrible dream." That is the conscious voice, but we recall that when Bess was entranced by the creature of the forest her "dreaming sense . . . conjured up the wildest fancies" that were "terribly beautiful." There is, then, a call of the wild to which even the purest Anglo-Saxon breast responds – the wilderness dream of unbridled mating in the woods. Such a fantasy may prove in the end to be no better than death, but at issue was the possibility of freedom from all constraint and the hope of a kind of natural rebirth. It was sometimes difficult to tell whether that rough beast slouching out of the forests of the New World was a satanic snake, an Indian brave, or a wilderness-wise white hunter. Didn't those passionate revolutionaries, after all, proudly flaunt flags adorned with the rattler as the emblem of their nascent national identity ("Don't Tread On Me!")? And hadn't that rather indecorous tea-party in Boston been conducted in Indian dress? In such cases the slogan appeared to be, not "exterminate all the brutes," but rather *imitate them.*

There is no better example of the white Christian's dizzyingly contradictory attitudes toward the forest and the Indian than the first volume of Francis Parkman's monumental history of the French and English in the New World, *The Conspiracy of Pontiac.* Parkman himself, of course, was a passionate lover of unspoiled wilderness, and his elegiac purpose, as he says, was "to portray the American forest and the American Indian at the period when both received their final doom."[22] The two were destined to fall together, and Parkman could hardly celebrate the one without celebrating the other, however ambivalently. Pontiac is, by turns, "the savage hero of this dark forest tragedy" to whom "noble and generous thought was no stranger" and "the Satan of this forest paradise."[23] Indeed, that "paradise" itself is presented as perplexingly duplex. "With the opening of spring," Parkman writes, "when the forests are budding into leaf, and the prairies gemmed with flowers; when a warm, faint haze rests upon the landscape, – then heart and senses are inthralled with luxurious beauty."[24] *Inthralled with luxurious beauty* – the phrase is surely double edged and intended to be so, for Parkman knew that the link between *luxuria* and death was older than Milton's powerful treatment of it, as old, in fact, as the history of the race. And so, on the next page he warns:

> . . . this western paradise is not free from the primal curse. The beneficent sun, which kindles into life so many forms of loveliness and beauty, fails not to engender venom and death from the rank slime of pestilential swamp and marsh. In some stagnant pool, buried in the jungle-like depths of the forest, where the hot and lifeless water reeks with exhalations, the water-snake basks by the margin, or winds his checkered length of loathsome beauty across the sleepy surface. From beneath the rotten carcass of some fallen tree, the moccason thrusts his broad flat head, ready to dart on the intruder. On the dry, sun-scorched prairie, the rattlesnake, a more generous enemy, reposes in his spiral coil.

This garden of the west is replete, then, with rottenness and snakes, yet even so – and seemingly inexplicably – it exercises a fatal appeal over certain white settlers. Parkman takes pains to describe a class of so-called Christians, redeemed from Indian captivity, who had in fact to be "bound fast to prevent their escape" *back* to forest life.[25] These unwilling returnees would sit "sullen and scowling, angry that they were forced to abandon the wild license of the forest for the irksome restraints of society." This, Parkman goes on, "may appear to argue some strange perversity or moral malformation. Yet such has been the experience of many a sound and healthful mind. To him who has once tasted the reckless independence, the haughty self-reliance [Emersonianism!], the sense of irresponsible freedom, which the forest life engenders, civilization thenceforth seems flat and stale. Its pleasures are insipid, its pursuits wearisome, its conventionalities, duties, and mutual dependence alike tedious and disgusting. The entrapped wanderer grows fierce and restless" – like a caged Indian? – "and pants for breathing-room." Parkman concludes that "the wilderness, rough, harsh, and inexorable, has charms more potent in their seductive influence than all the lures of luxury and sloth. And often he on whom it has cast its magic finds no heart to dissolve the spell, and remains a wanderer and an Ishmaelite to the hour of his death." That may stand, perhaps, as a tolerably good description of Natty Bumppo, and we may note further that this portrait of the white pariah permanently seduced by the lure of the wild was published in the same year in which Melville's outcast hero found himself comfortably wedded to a savage.

One other, related aspect of Parkman's *Conspiracy of Pontiac* deserves attention before we turn to *The Pioneers*, namely, Parkman's investing of his fierce red protagonist with the robes of a religious prophet. Far from castigating the Indians for their benighted pagan beliefs, Parkman appears to praise them for holding an attitude toward the land and its significance that in many ways resembles his own. "To the Indian mind," he notes, "all nature was instinct with deity. A spirit was embodied in every mountain, lake, and cataract; every bird, beast, and reptile, every tree, shrub, or grassblade, was endued with a mystic influence; yet this untutored pantheism did not exclude the conception of certain divinities, of incongruous and ever shifting attributes."[26] And, Parkman continues, even "before the arrival of Europeans, the Indian recognized the existence of one, almighty, self-existent Being, The Great Spirit, the Lord of Heaven and Earth," although "the belief was so vague and dubious as scarcely to deserve the name." Parkman was not about to tell his Christian readership flat out that the Indians whom they tried to convert, and frequently spoiled in the process, in fact had an equally valid religion of their own, but he does call our attention to two important aspects of Indian belief: its natural piety and its recourse to a higher power in seeking to ratify that piety. It would have been altogether too easy, but finally disruptive of his own intent in the narrative, for Parkman to portray Pontiac as a brutal savage who led his conspiracy merely for the sake of revenge and blood-lust. What we are offered instead is a portrait of the native American impelled, as presumably were the white settlers themselves, by a sense of religious mission.

The historian accordingly devotes a good deal of space to describing a visionary legend related by Pontiac at the war council that preceded the great leader's campaign against the whites. The legend is presented as bearing "an allegoric significancy":

"A Delaware Indian," said Pontiac, "conceived an eager desire to learn wisdom from the Master of Life; but being ignorant where to find him, he had recourse to fasting, dreaming, and magical incantations. By these means it was revealed to him, that, by moving forward in a straight, undeviating course, he would reach the abode of the Great Spirit. . . . On the evening of the eighth day . . . he saw three large openings in the woods before him, and three well-beaten paths which entered them. . . . [H]e crossed the meadow, and entered the largest of the three openings. He had advanced but a short distance into the forest, when a bright flame sprang out of the ground before him, and arrested his steps. In great amazement, he turned back, and entered the second path, where the same wonderful phenomenon again encountered him; and now, in terror and bewilderment, yet still resolved to persevere, he took the last of the three paths. On this he journeyed a whole day without interruption, when at length, emerging from the forest, he saw before him a vast mountain, of dazzling whiteness. So precipitous was the ascent, that the Indian thought it hopeless to go farther, and looked around him in despair: at that moment, he saw, seated at some distance above, the figure of a beautiful woman arrayed in white, who arose as he looked upon her, and thus accosted him: 'How can you hope, encumbered as you are, to succeed in your design? Go down to the foot of the mountain, throw away your gun, your ammunition, your provisions, and your clothing; wash yourself in the stream which flows there, and you will then be prepared to stand before the Master of Life.' " . . .

The Indian obeys, and "after great toil and suffering" climbs the mountain and finds himself before the Great Spirit surrounded by "unspeakable splendor."

" 'I am the Maker of heaven and earth, the trees, lakes, rivers, and all things else. I am the Maker of mankind; and because I love you, you must do my will. The land on which you live I have made for you, and not for others. Why do you suffer the white men to dwell among you? My children, you have forgotten the customs and traditions of your forefathers. Why do you not clothe yourselves in skins, as they did, and use the bows and arrows, and the stone-pointed lances, which they used? You have bought guns, knives, kettles, and blankets, from the white men, until you can no longer do without them; and, what is worse, you have drunk the poison fire-water, which turns you into fools. Fling all these things away; live as your wise forefathers lived before you. . . .' "

The Great Spirit next gave his hearer various precepts of morality and religion, such as the prohibition to marry more than one wife; and warning against the practice of magic, which is worshipping the devil. A prayer, embodying the substance of all that he had heard, was then presented to the Delaware. It was cut in hieroglyphics upon a wooden stick, after the custom of his people; and he was directed to send copies of it to all the Indian villages.[27]

Since Parkman's sources for Pontiac's performance are notably vague, it is not clear to what extent this "Indian allegory" has been doctored up, or perhaps even unconsciously enriched, in the retelling and rewriting, with extraneous material, for there are many versions of this "visionquest," as it is usually termed. (Parkman may, in fact, have had in mind Irving's version of this fable in "Traits of Indian Character."[28]) What is especially interesting here, in any case, is that this redaction of the monitory and prophetic vision bears a general structural parallel to the story of Moses' going up to see the Lord in the book of Exodus (though Pontiac's version, conveniently enough, seems to collapse Moses' various interviews into one event): We have the equivalent of a burning bush, rites of purification and the putting off of clothes, the giving of the Law in suitably inscribed form, and most importantly of all, an injunction to return to a state of primitive purity. Pontiac's allegory, then, as Parkman chooses to represent it, seems to be invested with some of the grandeur of the Judaeo-Christian story itself, as if bearing a message of equal religious validity, though Parkman was obviously not inclined to draw such a conclusion explicitly and unequivocally.

Indeed he goes on to point out, in language that tends to look in two directions at once, that not Pontiac alone, "but many of the most notable men who have arisen among the Indians, have been opponents of civilization, and stanch advocates of primitive barbarism. Red Jacket and Tecumseh would gladly have brought back their people to the rude simplicity of their original condition."[29] Since the attractive notion of returning the great American forest and its natives to the "simplicity of their original condition" also implies rudeness and barbarism, Parkman's status as a progressive historian, in the mold of Bancroft and Prescott, who approves of the resistless march of white culture, appears to be uncompromised. He therefore concludes this discussion by noting that "there is nothing progressive in the rigid, inflexible nature of an Indian. He will not open his mind to the idea of improvement; and nearly every change that has been forced upon him has been a change for the worse." The crucial word here – again, a signal of Parkman's divided mind – is "forced," which appears to encapsulate that underlying elegiac mood of the book that to a large degree seems at odds with its official doctrine. Parkman clearly disapproves of the violence done to the Indian and his forest by the thoughtless agents of destiny. Indeed, in an earlier section entitled "The Forest" Parkman had already paused "to survey the grand arena of the strife, the goodly heritage which the wretched tribes of the forest struggled to retrieve from the hands of the spoiler."[30] Thus, unmistakably, if to an extent hard to measure, Parkman's heart would appear to be with Pontiac in his vision of a virgin land returned to the loving custodianship of its original inhabitants. "With us," Parkman notes, "the name of the savage is a byword of reproach. The Indian would look with equal scorn on those who . . . are blind and deaf to the great world of nature."[31]

2

As the spoliation of the Indian and the virgin forest continued relentlessly throughout the nineteenth century, America's most truly patriotic writers found themselves repeatedly in the mood that seized Emerson in

1841, when, in an address significantly but rather orphically entitled "The Method of Nature," he exhorted himself and his audience to forsake the trivialities and mendacities of society "and betake ourselves to some desert cliff of Mount Katahdin, some unvisited recess in Moosehead Lake, to bewail our innocency and to recover it."[32] Emerson signaled his belief that America had lost its original high sense of spiritual mission in a scramble for gain by citing, in his exordium, a powerful sentence from Proverbs: "Where there is no vision, the people perish."[33] It was just the text that Fenimore Cooper might have used as an epigraph to the first of his Leatherstocking books, *The Pioneers*, though he undoubtedly would have wanted to include the rest of the verse too: "But he that keepeth the Law, happy is he."[34] *The Pioneers*, I hope now to demonstrate, is informed by a deep sense of religious consecration, though – surprising as it may seem for at least a sometime Episcopalian like Cooper – not one that is fully circumscribed by the King James Bible and the Book of Common Prayer.[35] Lurking somewhere within the good manners and Christian civility of this enigmatic writer lay a powerful heretic, and even as he sat dutifully in the pew, Cooper's heart, it seems, frequently wandered back to the forest and the wigwam. Had not Chingachgook learned to his cost that the whites brought rum along with their religion? That was a far more dangerous weapon than the tomahawk and a more powerful agent of manifest destiny than the gospel – a key part, as D. H. Lawrence famously puts it, of "a specious little equation in providential mathematics: Rum + Savage = 0. Awfully nice!" He concludes: "You might add up the universe to nought, if you kept on. Rum plus savage may equal a dead savage. But is a dead savage nought? Can you make a land virgin by killing off its aborigines?"[36]

I have allowed myself somewhat fancifully to imagine Cooper in his pew meditating on the differences between Christianity and savagism because that is precisely where he puts us in Chapter 11 of *The Pioneers*, as he devotes several pages to reproducing a sermon by the Reverend Mr. Grant. The minister is presented as a good man, a deeply religious man, even a sometime evangelical despite his Anglican collar (though not quite the evangelical Melville would place in the pulpit in Chapters 8 and 9 of *Moby-Dick*). Mr. Grant is talking about diversity of creeds in the Christian community, and his conclusion, effectively, is that circumstances naturally alter the grounds and conditions of belief. (Query: Will Christianity actually suit a wilderness society?) Christianity is indeed a "revealed" religion, he argues, but the "revelations [have been] obscured by the lapse of ages." How far, we may wonder, has that "lapse" gone? Is it any longer possible to *see* a truth rendered opaque by thick layers of competing doctrine? Mr. Grant allows that there is a problem, but he still hopes for enlightenment, at least on that great day when "it may be humbly hoped, that the film, which has been spread by the subtleties of earthly arguments, will be dissipated by the spiritual light of heaven." Such a light, he believes, will finally make clear things that do indeed seem dark, such as the true nature of mercy, justice, and love.

But where now is one to look for guidance in such important matters? Mr. Grant stresses in particular the pitfalls awaiting any human being so arrogant as to judge another, noting that we are enjoined "to judge with lenity, all men," to put down self-righteousness and "be sparing of our condemnation of others, while our own salvation is not yet secure." To old John Mohegan, who is sitting among the congregation, these statements must seem, as Huck Finn says of Bunyan, "interesting but tough," for the white father of the village is called *Judge* Temple and has already been observed drawing innocent human blood. Prior to the sermon, indeed, Mohegan debated the question with Mr. Grant of whether the Judge should be judged guilty of that deed, whereupon the minister responded, "with much earnestness," that John should "remember the divine command of our Saviour, 'judge not, lest ye be judged.' What motive could Judge Temple have for injuring a youth like this . . . ?"[37] With so many permutations of that key word buzzing in his ear, it is little wonder that Mohegan backs down. This minister of a supposed higher law somehow is also an apologist for a lower one, and later, when Judge Temple does in fact judge Natty Bumppo, he speaks in defense of "the ministers of the law."[38] Which law? Which ministers? One of those so-called ministers demands a Bible of Natty for the swearing of an oath but receives only the trapper's cold response that he does not keep "such a Bible as the law needs."[39]

Perhaps it is not surprising, then, that after Mr. Grant's sermon about *justice* and *judging*, old John is seen with his blanket wrapped about his head as if in protection of his jangled wits. Nevertheless, he has the good manners to come forward, as any parishioner might, and compliment Mr. Grant on his performance:

> "Father, I thank you. The words that have been said, since the rising moon, have gone upward, and the Great Spirit is glad. What you have told your children, they will remember, and be good." He paused a moment, and then elevating himself to all the grandeur of an Indian chief, he added – "If Chingachgook lives to travel towards the setting sun, after his tribe, and the Great Spirit carries him over the lakes and mountains, with the breath in his body, he will tell his people the good talk he has heard; and they will believe him; for who can say that Mohegan has ever lied?"[40]

Mr. Grant's reply, despite his professionally enforced humility, does seem to betray a feeling of exasperation – must he really submit to being patronized by an Indian? "Let him place his dependence on the goodness of Divine mercy," Grant rather icily intones, and Cooper informs us that to the minister's ears "the proud consciousness of the Indian sounded a little heterodox." Natty Bumppo, also present at this edifying discourse, is now given his chance to speak, and what he says must in fact strike the minister as not only heterodox, but downright pert: "Heigh-ho!" Natty observes, "I never know'd preaching come into a settlement, but it made game scearce, and raised the price of gunpowder." That certainly must convince Mr. Grant that the woodsman and his savage companion are two peas in a pod. Neither one seems to have the proper respect for Christian doctrine and the institutions of the church. Both, obviously, would rather be off in the woods, sans sermon and the confusing revelations contained therein.

Cooper's evident ironies – the quibbles he enforces throughout the book on *justice* and *judge* and phrases like *ministers of the law* and *the sanctity of the laws* – tend unmistakably to decenter *The Pioneers* from the point of view of traditional Christian ethics. It is not so much a question of tilting away from Christianity as it is that of establishing a dialogue or debate between Christianity in its ordinary practices and results, on the one hand, and a wilderness view of things, on the other. Though it might be argued that Cooper's real objective is to demolish a purely Erastian position regarding the function of religion and the church, such an argument cannot deal adequately with the extraordinary imaginative weight Cooper gives to the wilderness view, especially as it is embodied in Chingachgook, ruined by Christianity in the person of the drunk and maundering old John Mohegan but progressively resurrected by Cooper as death approaches into his prophetic role as a truly noble savage. Chingachgook exemplifies what Simms calls the *genius loci* of America, the spirit that "makes place holy, and preserves it from degradation and decay." A national history, Simms insists, "preserved by a national poet, becomes, in fact, a national religion," and it is surely this heterodox *religion of the land* that the visionary red man is intended to represent.[41]

I use the word "visionary" advisedly, referring back at once to Parkman's presentation of Pontiac, to the text from Proverbs cited by Emerson, and to the principal symbolic element employed by Cooper in *The Pioneers*. It is Mount Vision that lies at the center of the book, as I read it.[42] The mount has been so named, the Judge tells his daughter, because when he first climbed there high above the Cherry Valley, the sight that met his eyes seemed to him "as the deceptions of a dream" (it is a question whether that is the sort of dream the Judge is willing to believe in):

I mounted a tree and sat for an hour looking on the silent wilderness. Not an opening was to be seen in the boundless forest, except where the lake lay, like a mirror of glass. The water was covered by myriads of the wild-fowl that migrate with the changes in the season; and while in my situation on the branch of the beech, I saw a bear, with her cubs, descend to the shore to drink. I had met many deer, gliding through the woods, in my journey; but not the vestige of a man could I trace, during my progress, nor from my elevated observatory. No clearing, no hut, none of the winding roads that are now to be seen, were there, nothing but mountains rising behind mountains, and the valley, with its surface of branches, enlivened here and there with the faded foliage of some tree. . . .[43]

The Judge looked on this magnificent scene, as he tells Bess, "with a mingled feeling of pleasure and desolation," for in truth he does not share Natty Bumppo's taste for the wild in "unimproved" condition.

Indeed when the latter, in the presence of Oliver Edwards, muses on his own memory of this sublimely solitary landscape, and the young man who is eventually to marry Bess remarks that "it must have been a sight of melancholy pleasure . . . to have roamed over these mountains, and along this sheet of beautiful water, without a living soul to speak to," Natty replies, with emphasis: "Haven't I said it was cheerful! . . . Yes, yes – when the trees began to be kivered with the leaves, and the ice was out of the lake, it was a second paradise."[44] In this description, and in one that immediately follows, setting forth a scene in the Catskills viewed by Natty from mountains even higher than the Vision, he expresses his enthusiasm for what he calls "creation": the woods in their pristine state. Marmaduke Temple, on the other hand, despite his good intentions and his hatred of waste, is seduced from this memory by the lure of progress. It may be that Cooper intended his readers to recall a passage in Book 11 of *Paradise Lost*, where Michael ascends with Adam:

> In the Visions of God: It was a Hill
> Of Paradise the highest, from whose top
> The Hemisphere of Earth in clearest Ken
> Stretcht out to the amplest reach of prospect lay.
> Not higher that Hill nor wider looking round,
> Whereon for different cause the Tempter set
> Our second *Adam* in the Wilderness,
> To show him all Earth's Kingdoms and thir Glory.[45]

Not the pure vision of God but the temptation to "Kingdoms and thir Glory" is what seems to compel Judge Temple in the wilderness of the New World. He had "a bias to look far into futurity," Cooper informs us, "in his speculations on the improvements that posterity were to make in his lands. . . . [W]here others saw nothing but a wilderness," he saw "towns, manufactories, bridges, canals, mines. . . . "[46] Chingachgook, too, when he ascends the Vision in his last hours, does so in a *speculative* mood, but not in the Judge's sense; he, too, has an eye that looks "into the womb of futurity,"[47] but what he sees is not the cheerful bustle of progress. Rather it is a land made desolate by the extermination of its natives: he sees the "many shapes / of Death" that Michael exposes to Adam's chastened new sight.[48]

There are, as Lawrence notes, "some of the loveliest, most glamorous pictures in all literature" contained in *The Pioneers*, and he instances "the raw village street, with woodfires blinking through the unglazed window-chinks, on a winter's night. The inn . . . the church, with the snowy congregation crowding to the fire. Then the lavish abundance of Christmas cheer, and turkey shooting in the snow. Spring coming, forests all green, maple-sugar taken from the trees: and clouds of pigeons flying from the south, myriads of pigeons, shot in heaps; and night-fishing on the teeming virgin lake; and deer hunting."[49] Even leaving aside, however, the gloomy aspect of what is happening to the pigeons, and the fish and the trees, as well as the ironies involved in what takes place in the church, a persistent dark stripe runs through these bright scenes: the grim, monitory presence of the ruined Indian. At the inn, for example, in Chapter 14, as hot rum makes the rounds, Natty is urged to join in the fun and sing with the others:

Then let us be jolly,
And cast away folly,
For grief turns a black head to gray.

But he declines, "with a melancholy shake of the head," adding: "I have lived to see what I thought eyes could never behold in these hills, and I have no heart left for singing." Natty had just been remembering his friend, the "Big Sarpent," before times became so "dreadfully altered": "Old John and Chingachgook were very different men to look on," he relates mournfully, going on to recall the Indian in his healthy manhood, "handsomely painted," his head brightly decorated with eagle's feathers, carrying thirteen scalps on his pole – the very emblem of the vigorous young nation.[50] Now Natty's sharp eye beholds a wretchedly intoxicated old John who has lost his strength and self-respect, not because of his seventy winters, but because "the white man brings old age with him,"[51] with his cupidity and its agent, the devil rum. Mohegan feels impotent to cast away the folly of having adopted the white man's ways, but neither can he add his voice to the jolly tune. So as the settlers carouse, Mohegan

provides his own counterpoint to their song, uttering in "dull, monotonous tones," much to the consternation of the party, "a wild, melancholy air" that celebrates his own departed glory, rising at times, as
Cooper tells us, "in sudden and quite elevated notes." Though his
Delaware chant grows louder "and soon [rises] to a height that [causes] a
general cessation in the discourse," Mohegan is too far gone in liquor to
sustain the height that his song has been competent to gain, and he finally
collapses in total inebriety.

I have purposely echoed Wordsworth in my last sentence – the lines
from *The Excursion* in which the Wanderer laments that it is "the most
difficult of tasks to *keep* / Heights which the soul is competent to gain"
(IV, 138–9) – because, as Emerson notes frequently, they provided a kind
of elegy on his times.[52] Nevertheless Wordsworth's lover of the wilderness goes on to insist that even when the human frame has drooped to the
dust

> . . . apparently, through weight
> Of anguish unrelieved, and lack of power
> An agonizing sorrow to transmute;
> Deem not that proof is here of hope withheld
> When wanted most; a confidence impaired
> So pitiably, that, having ceased to see
> With bodily eyes, they are borne down by love
> Of what is lost, and perish through regret.
> Oh! no, the innocent Sufferer often sees
> Too clearly; feels too vividly; and longs
> To realize the vision. . . .   (IV, 166–76)[53]

Perhaps Cooper had these lines in mind – or others from the same poem,
when the Wanderer remembers "what visionary powers of eye and soul"
were his in his youth as he watched the sunrise from "some huge hill"
(IV, 111–13)[54] – when he decided to climax *The Pioneers* by elevating
Chingachgook on the Vision in the posture of what can only be called
religious prophecy as a way of drawing together forcefully the principal
concerns of the book: law and justice, vengeance and mercy, despoliation
and renewal.

Elizabeth Temple comes upon the aged warrior seated "on the trunk
of a fallen oak," and his fierce and penetrating eyes fix on hers "with an
expression of wildness and fire."[55] This description is proleptic of the
actual fire that is about to involve the whole Vision, including
Chingachgook, whose log will soon burn in such a manner to make him
appear to be "surrounded with fire." Chingachgook is thus presented as

the very principle of "wildness and fire," the voice of the wilderness god speaking out of the burning bush in tones of reproach and resentment. When the Reverend Mr. Grant arrives to preach the predictable Christian homily, he describes the Indian as "the offspring of a race of heathens" who "has in truth been 'as a brand plucked from the burning.' "[56] But Natty will have none of such pious platitudes, insisting that the only burning that ails Chingachgook is "the burning of man's wicked thoughts for near fourscore years." Chingachgook's fiery speech serves as a judgment on the prodigality of white civilization and the pretensions of Christianity to superior ethical standards. His voice, we might say, is that of the country speaking to the nation, for he is not only arrayed in the full traditional regalia of an Indian warrior but also bears his cherished Washington medallion on his chest and therefore is invested with the authority of both nations (in Chapter 10 of *Moby-Dick* Ishmael will describe Queequeg as being "George Washington cannibalistically developed," suggesting the same conflation of natural and political power).

As Chingachgook reflects back on the happy days of his savage youth, Elizabeth replies, with notable insensitivity and unconscious irony, that his people have disappeared and "in place of chasing your enemies, you have learned to fear God and to live at peace."[57] Thus provoked, the Indian assumes the stance of the visionary, adopting a mode of speech designed to make Elizabeth *see* the truth:

> "Stand here, daughter, where you can see the great spring, the wigwams of your father, and the land on the crooked-river. John was yet young, when his tribe gave away the country, in council, from where the blue mountain stands above the water, to where the Susquehanna is hid by the trees. All this, and all that grew in it, and all that walked over it, and all that fed there, they gave to the Fire-eater – for they loved him. . . . Has John lived in peace! Daughter, since John was young, he has seen the white man from Frontinac come down on his white brothers at Albany, and fight. Did they fear God! He has seen his English and his American Fathers burying their tomahawks in each others' brains, for this very land. Did they fear God, and live in peace! He has seen the land pass away from the Fire-eater, and his children, and the child of his child, and a new chief set over the country. Did they live in peace who did this! did they fear God?"

Elizabeth, as Cooper notes, is "more embarrassed than she would own," but she nonetheless manages to reply that if Chingachgook knew white laws and customs better, he would "judge" differently. But the Indian has seen quite enough of white laws and customs and judgments. His eye is fixed on better things, and his expression now fills with a look "that might be supposed to border on the inspiration of a prophet."

What he sees is a vision of the place where "all just red-men shall live together as brothers,"[58] though that vision waxes and wanes, and Chingachgook returns to the mode of lamentation as Natty arrives to carry him off. " 'Why should Mohegan go?' returned the Indian, gloomily. 'He has seen the days of an eagle, and his eye grows dim. He looks on the valley; he looks on the water; he looks in the hunting-grounds – but he sees no Delawares. Every one has a white skin.' " Like Melville's paganish narrator in "Rip Van Winkle's Lilac," the Indian is distressed to see a whited sepulcher take the place of his ruddy arcadian America, and he dreams of traveling "to the land of the just," intoning the words in Delaware. The Reverend Mr. Grant asks Natty to translate ("what says he now? is he sensible of his lost state?"). Cooper's irony requires little comment, except perhaps for us to note that the paradisal "state" Chingachgook has lost at the hands of white Christians can hardly be returned to him by their minister. For him, the Christian revelation is truly too dark, and the final clarification of his sight that now follows, as the path becomes clear "and the eyes of Mohegan grow young," presents a world of "no white skins," only "just and brave Indians."

As Chingachgook's eyes fix in death on the distant hills, Cooper indulges in one more set of variations on the key terms of his book, providing a final ambiguous twist to the opposition of law and justice: "O Lord! how unsearchable are thy judgments," intones Mr. Grant; whereupon Natty replies, "He's to be judged by a righteous Judge, and by no laws that's made to suit times, and new ways." But perhaps what the thunder says is more significant, "seeming to shake the foundations of the earth to their centre." Chingachgook's own judgment and sacrificial death seem to prompt a ratifying voice from the creation itself, and the rain that now falls, diffusing itself over the dry rock, appears to promise relief, if only we can set our lands in order. This portentous scene, and its implied message, point forward eerily to Eliot's twentieth-century Wasteland and his own Sanskrit charge, whereby the American aborigine and the ancient East may be seen finally to join hands, intoning the sacred words as they complete the passage to more than India: *Da*; *Dayadhvam*; *Damyata* – give, sympathize, control. That might just do as a response to the Reverend Mr. Grant's sermon.

Chapter 3

Poe: Romantic Center, Critical Margin

In March 1850, about a half-year after Edgar Allan Poe's mysterious collapse and death in Baltimore at the age of forty, the *Southern Literary Messenger*, the journal Poe had edited in 1836, printed a long memorial notice in the form of a review of *The Works of Edgar Allan Poe*, edited by Nathaniel P. Willis, James Russell Lowell, and Rufus P. Griswold.[1] The author of the notice predictably spoke with great bitterness of this appropriation of his fellow southerner's work by the northern literary establishment (though born in Boston – indeed, his first book of poems, *Tamerlane*, was inscribed "by a Bostonian" – Poe grew up in Virginia and made common cause with southern writers, especially when it came to the hated abolitionists). Willis, a popular and fashionable magazinist of the time who had in fact befriended Poe, is cattily dismissed as "the man milliner of our literature"; Griswold, the self-important literary entrepreneur whom Poe inexplicably made his executor and who proceeded systematically both to calumniate Poe and to alter his work, is viewed sarcastically as that "great Apollo of our literary heavens" whose "eminent" name was trotted out by the publisher in order to confer respectability on the raffish genius now being celebrated; and Lowell, denominated a New England "literary insect" for his "transcendentalism, socialism, and abolition," is mockingly praised for having "found his sable sympathies sufficiently extensive to take in the distressed master of the Raven." The sectional spleen of this reviewer-eulogist is obvious enough and suggests graphically why the American literary establishment of the day, with its irreconcilable regional and political differences, was incapable of speaking with one voice before the world in the service of claiming preeminence for any single American author. Indeed, here was a prime illustration of the problem, for the *Literary Messenger* was in fact engaged in making a case for establishing Poe as "the greatest genius of the day" but could not resist the temptation to do so by flaying "these three horny-eyed dunces" of the North who had the effrontery to "come before the world as the patrons and literary vouchers" of an incomparable southern literary master.

The bias and bitterness of this southern reviewer are further apparent when he makes his most extravagant and sounding claim for the preeminence of Poe: "While the people of this day run after such authors as Prescott and Willis, speak with reverence of the Channings and the Adamses and Irvings, their children in referring back to our time in literary history, will say, 'this was the time of Poe.' " We notice, interestingly, that the one distinguished New England name pointedly omitted from this list is that of Emerson (Poe himself, for all his open scorn of "Transcendentalism," was very chary of attacking Emerson, except indirectly by saying that he was a writer of "true talent" and "real force" who betrayed his own genius by slavishly following Carlyle).[2] This reviewer indeed goes on to admit that Poe's single truly great poem, the one on whose "dusky wings he will sail securely over the gulf of oblivion to the eternal shore beyond," has but a sole rival to being considered the "first poem manufactured [sic] upon the American continent," namely, Emerson's "The Humble-Bee." (This may only be intended as a backhanded compliment, for how can a mere bee compete with a raven? But the seeming improbability of the comparison is dispelled a bit when one actually returns to Emerson's poem:

> Burly, dozing humble-bee,
> Where thou art is clime for me.
> Let them sail for Porto Rique,
> Far-off heats through seas to seek;
> I will follow thee alone,
> Thou animated torrid-zone!
> Zigzag steerer, desert cheerer,
> Let me chase thy waving lines;
> Keep me nearer, me thy hearer,
> Singing over shrubs and vines.

Emerson's insistent rhythms and internal rhymes demonstrate that he could be as tuneful a jingle-man as Poe when he wished, and it is hardly surprising that Poe himself was fond of "The Humble-Bee.") But the main point being made here, that this was indeed "the time of Poe," quite understandably takes shelter under the ample pinions of Poe's prodigious fowl (whether bird or devil) precisely because its litany of lamentation, that "stock and store / Caught from some unhappy master [who but Poe himself?] whom unmerciful disaster / Followed fast and followed faster till his songs one burden bore," chimed in perfectly with the dominant American mood of the period – the mood of morbid ideality.

The *Literary Messenger's* reviewer speaks scornfully of those "well educated people," still humming their Pope and Dryden and Milton (even "with a small sprinkling of Moore and Byron"), who were incapable of relishing "a poet tinged with the dyes" – the *dark* dyes, we should emphasize – "of the nineteenth century." In "The Raven" Poe finally succeeded in both exploiting and perfectly exemplifying a dominant strain and taste of his time and thus established his claim to wide acceptance, indeed, popularity. Poe was deeply and abidingly interested in the possibility of a serious writer's having a general appeal (witness his discussion of Hawthorne's *Twice-Told Tales*), and he shamelessly capitalized on his own success with "The Raven," not only by writing about its conception and execution in "The Philosophy of Composition" but also by participating vigorously in, if not actually instigating, discussions about possible plagiarism in the popular press. Poe plucked his ebon quills from sources as disparate as Coleridge's albatross, Richard Henry Dana Sr.'s "Dying Raven," a poem entitled "The Old Night Owl" by one James Rees, Dickens's *Barnaby Rudge*, and Elizabeth Barrett's "Lady Geraldine's Courtship," and he was not shy about employing his own pen in the service of puffing this poetic confection, which, he once told a friend, he wrote "to see how near to the absurd I could come without overstepping the dividing line."[3] Poe had a shrewd eye for the literary marketplace in his time, and it has never been easy to disentangle his own motives as a writer from the general exigencies enforced by a popular taste that relished the absurd as well as the sentimental, the bizarre along with the bathetic. In fact, with Poe as a test case, it is worth paying some attention to our now canonical authors and texts vis-à-vis the popular writings of their day. Though this has usually seemed to be only a tale of literary rivalry, whereby the books now considered classic were neglected in favor of less serious work that pandered to the vulgar tastes of the time, we may hope to discover something useful, at least insofar as Poe is concerned, about the relationship between these presumably disparate realms of discourse.[4]

It is hardly surprising that Poe's *Tamerlane and Other Poems* made no great splash when it appeared in 1827 (the same holds true for his fellow southerner William Gilmore Simms, who was also publishing his first volume of verse), since whatever attention American readers had to spare for native literary products was preempted by fiction – that of Cooper, for example, who had just published *The Last of the Mohicans* and was bringing out *The Prairie* and *The Red Rover*, or more importantly (since

Cooper, though he had a sizable audience, was in no sense a best-seller), that of Susanna Rowson, whose *Lucy Temple* (a sequel to the phenomenally popular *Charlotte Temple*) was eagerly awaited and would turn out to be the most successful novel before *Uncle Tom's Cabin*. One would hardly expect Emerson's *Nature* to have been on every breakfast table in 1836, but readers in any case had their eyes glued to Maria Monk's *Awful Disclosures* (a presumed exposé of life in a convent). Poe might have expected the sensational adventures recorded in *The Narrative of Arthur Gordon Pym* to bring him fame in 1838, but such was not the case – as it also pointedly failed to be with *Tales of the Grotesque and Arabesque*, published in a small edition in 1840 that "two years later had not earned enough to pay the printing."[5] Emerson's *Poems* of 1847 sold only 849 copies in the year of its publication, but Rufus Griswold's anthology *The Female Poets of America* was a great hit in 1849, the year when Thoreau's first book, *A Week on the Concord and Merrimack Rivers*, appeared and flopped. (Fours years later *A Week* had sold 219 copies, whereupon Thoreau's publisher returned to him what was left of the original printing of one thousand books, prompting the proud author to note in his journal: "I have now a library of nearly nine hundred volumes, over seven hundred of which I wrote myself."[6]) Thoreau should hardly have been surprised that *Walden* did little better in 1854, considering that it had to compete with Timothy Shay Arthur's smash-hit temperance novel, *Ten Nights in a Bar-Room*. As for *Moby-Dick*, in view of the unorthodox nature of that production (and Melville himself was perfectly well aware how oddly concocted the book was), we need not wonder that it failed to regain the audience that Melville had already lost with another manifestly strange brew, *Mardi*, in 1849. As one historian reports, "[O]nly sixty copies of . . . *Moby-Dick* survived the burning of Harper's warehouse in 1853, but these presumably satisfied the demand for ten years, since the book was not reissued until 1863. The reprint, even though it moved faster than an average of six copies a year, did not sell enough to warrant a third printing before 1892."[7]

In the fifties especially, popularity belonged mainly to female authors, whose books – alternately sentimental, pious, and sensational – went like hotcakes. Fanny Fern's *Fern Leaves from Fanny's Portfolio* sold seventy thousand copies in 1853, Maria Susanna Cummins the next year disposed of forty thousand copies of her pathetic-moralistic tale *The Lamplighter* in eight weeks, and, of course, *Uncle Tom's Cabin* reigned supreme. Hawthorne, who was modestly successful (in the manner of Cooper – four to six thousand copies a year at best[8]), vented his spleen in a now infamous letter to his publisher in 1855:

America is now wholly given over to a d——d mob of scribbling women, and I should have no chance of success while the public taste is occupied with their trash – and should be ashamed of myself if I did succeed. What is the mystery of these innumerable editions of the Lamplighter, and other books neither better nor worse? – worse they could not be, and better they need not be, when they sell by the 100,000.

Well, Hawthorne may have considered *The Lamplighter* beneath contempt, but he in fact apologized for his "vituperation" of female authors in his next letter, for he had in the meanwhile read Fanny Fern's bestselling novel *Ruth Hall* and confessed that he "enjoyed it a good deal. The woman writes as if the Devil was in her; and that is the only condition under which a woman ever writes anything worth reading."[9]

Though Poe generally preferred his lady authors when they were in the melting mood, he was usually more complimentary to the popular female writers of his time. He admired Mrs. Browning enormously, and she returned the compliment, praising "The Raven" extravagantly when it was published. Of a quartet of popular female poets, Poe exclaimed: "Hemans, Baillie, Landon, and, loveliest of all, Norton! . . . France with her gaiety; Italy with her splendid genius; even Greece with her passionate enthusiasm cannot rival such a galaxy. And this glory, too, belongs wholly to the present century; for though the harp of England has often been struck by female hands, it has heretofore only seldom given forth the rare, deep, prolonged harmony which now rolls from its chords."[10] When Emerson published his own copious anthology of favorite poems, *Parnassus*, in 1874, he did not scant on Mrs. Hemans or Mrs. Browning, but he made a special point of including American productions, especially, as he notes in his introduction, the recent "poems of a lady who contents herself with the initials H. H." (she turned out to be Emily Dickinson's friend Helen Hunt Jackson). But no room was found in his more than five hundred double-columned pages for either Poe or Whitman. By 1874, of course, Emerson had good reason to be ashamed of Whitman; his name was not often mentioned in polite society (and within seven years his book would be banned in Boston). But as for Poe, even though Emerson was said always cordially to have disliked him, his total omission from an anthology intended to have popular appeal is a little odd, for some of Poe's poetry at least was standard fare in almost every other such gathering.

The dominant mood of popular nineteenth-century American poetry was sentimental (darkening to grotesque) morbidity, and much of Poe's poetic production – not to mention his stories – was in perfect harmony with this prevailing taste. The central principle enunciated in Poe's "Philosophy of Composition," namely, that "the death . . . of a beautiful woman is, unquestionably, the most poetical topic in the world," so far from being esoteric, is the quintessence of the popular literature of the age, especially if that moribund female beauty happened to be a child. Writers beloved of the age, such as Dickens and Mrs. Stowe, understood this to a fault (as did Poe in "Annabel Lee," for example). The female poets in particular pumped dry the reservoir of mourners' tears – from Felicia Hemans's all-too-imitable gems, such as "Casabianca" ("The boy stood on the burning deck. . . ."), on through the American Mrs. Hemans, Lydia Sigourney, the "Sweet Singer of Hartford," her lesser avatar, Julia A. Moore, the "Sweet Singer of Michigan," and continuing down to Mark Twain's precocious poet-laureate of the tomb, Emmeline Grangerford, who, as Huck Finn records, before the age of fourteen wrote a splendid ode "about a boy name of Stephen Dowling Bots that fell down a well and was drownded."[11] Even so austere a figure as Andrews Norton, the hard-headed "Unitarian Pope" who was to be outraged by Emerson's Divinity School Address in 1838, found nothing to condemn in Mrs. Hemans's *Collected Poems*, which he consented to edit for a Boston publisher in 1827. Perhaps the literary tone of the age, in this regard, was set by Irving, who sang the pleasures of the morbid imagination in *The Sketch Book*:

> There is a voice from the tomb sweeter than song. There is a remembrance of the dead to which we turn even from the charms of the living. Oh the grave! – The grave! . . . The bed of death, with all its stifled griefs, its noiseless attendance, its mute, watchful assiduities – the last testimonies of expiring love – the feeble, fluttering, thrilling, oh! how thrilling! pressure of the hand – the faint, faltering accents struggling in death to give one more assurance of affection – the last fond look of the glazing eye, turning upon us even from the threshold of existence![12]

Surely an age nurtured on such stuff could hardly fail to find room in its wounded heart for the feeble, fluttering, thrilling accents of an Eddy Poe.

2

Late in life, looking back somewhat disappointedly over a career that had not realized his hopes of being acknowledged as *the* bard of the American people, Whitman, speaking of Poe, noted:

> By its popular poets the calibres of an age, the weak spots of its embankments, its sub-currents, (often more significant than the biggest surface ones), are unerringly indicated. The lush and the weird that have taken such extraordinary possession of Nineteenth

century verse-lovers – what mean they? The inevitable tendency of poetic culture to morbidity, abnormal beauty – the sickliness of all technical thought or refinement in itself – the abnegation of the perennial and democratic concretes at first hand, the body, the earth and sea, sex and the like – and the substitution of something for them at second or third hand – what bearings have they on current pathological study?[13]

Perhaps Whitman should not have wondered that a culture addicted from the beginning to receiving its instruction, entertainment, and consolation from literature (Irving had called America a "logocracy") was content to have its experience "at second or third hand," but his puzzlement over the general acceptance of Poe's sick genius with its superabundant "morbidity" can only strike us as a little odd in view of Whitman's own steady drift toward the "pathological," notwithstanding his presumed healthy-mindedness (we think, for example, of "Out of the Cradle Endlessly Rocking," where the sea whispers to the poet "the low and delicious word death, / And again death, death, death, death").

The truth is, of course, that far from being, as is so often said, totally disconnected from the contemporary American scene, much of Poe's work succeeds perfectly in representing its cultural ambience, even if only grotesquely or phantasmagorically or oneirically. It was truly, as *The Southern Literary Messenger* claimed, "the time of Poe," and interesting – indeed, amusing – examples of how widely the spirit of Poe diffused itself throughout the literature of the period are not hard to find, from Mrs. Stowe's description of her "poetical voluptuary" Augustine St. Clare and his home in *Uncle Tom's Cabin*, with its "Arabesque ornaments" and court "arranged to gratify a picturesque and voluptuous taste,"[14] to the hero of John W. De Forest's Civil War novel, *Miss Ravenel's Conversion*, who tries to console himself by reading the Bible when his tenderly beloved mother dies but finds instead that some perverse "inner, wayward self" forces him to repeat "over and over again these verses of the unhappy Poe":

Thank Heaven! the crisis,
   The danger is past,
And the lingering illness
   Is over at last,
And the fever called Living
   Is conquered at last.[15]

It might seem perverse indeed that one pious New Englander, Mrs. Stowe, portrays her redemptive white southern male as such a sickly and self-indulgent son of the raven and that another, De Forest's Colburne, finds stronger consolation in Poe than in the Bible, longing more for the grave than for the fulfillment of his mother's promise of a meeting in heaven. A third New Englander, reveling in the spooky evening sounds at Walden Pond, discovered a morbid pleasure in the screech owls, taking up their strain "like mourning women their ancient u-lu-lu."[16] Since Thoreau goes on to speak of "the mutual consolations of suicide lovers remembering the pangs and the delights of supernal love in the infernal groves," it is not difficult to guess which Poe poem he had in mind, representing "the dark and tearful side of music, the regrets and sighs that would fain be sung." This was the music

> of the low spirits and melancholy forebodings, of fallen souls that once in human shape night-walked the earth and did the deeds of darkness, now expiating their sins with their wailing hymns or threnodies . . . expressive of a mind which has reached the gelatinous mildewy stage in the mortification of all healthy and courageous thought.

Thoreau realized that the poetry of the American woods required owls as well as roosters, not just cheerful birds of the morning, but also mourning birds with an u-lu-lu capable of doing "the idiotic and maniacal hooting for men." Such were the pariah-poets of the American literary scene (the *Southern Literary Messenger* called Poe an "Ishmaelite"), expiating with their suffering the failings of those positivistic, go-getting republicans who, as Baudelaire argued in his 1852 piece on Poe, "are so proud of their youthful greatness . . . have such a naive faith in the omnipotence of industry . . . are so sure that it will succeed in devouring the Devil, that they . . . say, forward, and let us forget the dead."[17]

In the case of Poe, at least, it was hard to forget the dead, for the specter of this weird genius continued to haunt the mid-nineteenth-century imagination, inspiring portraits by turns tender and tendentious. Shortly after Poe's death, one of the lady poets whom he had befriended (*bewitched* would be closer to the truth) celebrated in very mournful numbers this ethereal though "earth-stained" master poet who seemed perversely bent on self-destruction:

> Had the prayers of those availed him,
> O'er whose path his shadow fell,
> Darkening with its raven pinions
> Life's dim way, it had been well.[18]

Such, alas, was not to be; the unfortunate Poe, as Baudelaire said, seemed to have the words "no luck" inscribed on his forehead. Mrs. Locke, intoning the requisite "nevermores," urged the world to "think not of his errors now" as she sang the incomparable bard to rest. Others, though, were less willing to put Poe's "errors," real or imagined, out of mind. A certain John Frankenstein, for example, a Cincinnati painter who believed Poe to have been the critic who savaged his work in the 1840s, composed some considerably less charitable funeral verses:

Come! be by searching truth's tribunal tried!
Come forth! if you've got sober since you died,
You, drunken mad-dog, EDGAR ALLAN POE –
Is it my fault that I must call you so?
Your works, like you, are born of alcohol;
Horrid monstrosities, distortions all. . . .
You, Poe, through all your nature most debased,
You pandered to this craving tiger-taste;
King Alcohol through you once ruled our realm
Of literature, you staggered at its helm. . . .
You, YOU, who all your life could not walk straight,
With swaggering ignorance my work berate?
When in the gutter the last time you lay,
When death, disgusted, almost turned away,
When you with rot-gut whisky dying stunk,
And thus into God's presence reeled DEAD-DRUNK –
I tell you, mad dog, when I heard all this,
I helped outraged humanity to hiss!

. . .

Avaunt! and *nevermore* to me come nigh –
I do believe you stink of whisky yet – good bye![19]

As the scholar who dug out this pungent antitribute appositely remarks, "[I]t seems altogether probable that Frankenstein blamed Poe for a criticism written by someone else and, like his fictional namesake, created a synthetic monster." Or was that monster rather the creation of a mid-nineteenth-century America (sometimes called the "rum republic"), whose popular mythology demanded a bestialized *poete maudit* whom it could at once lament and lambast (as it had both castigated and sentimentalized the figure of the drunken Indian)? America was the land of extremes par excellence, at once hard drinking and puritanical, and Poe was precisely the artistic paradox it needed as its emblem. One friend of Poe's insisted that "it was his excessive and at times marked sensibility which forced him into his 'frolics,' rather than any mere morbid appetite for drink, but if he took but one glass of wine or beer or cider, the Rubicon of the cup was passed with him, and it almost always ended in excess and sickness.''[20] So, it seems, Poe was not an alcoholic but a particularly high-strung genius, physically intolerant of drink, who was more the victim of his unaccountable moods than he was of madeira or port. Which version was true? A teetotaling poetaster named Thomas Dunn English, who had good reason to hate Poe (Poe had lampooned him in print, under the title "Thomas Dunn Brown," as an uneducated fool, pathetically trying to be a literary man despite his "deficiencies in English grammar" – "[A]n editor," Poe quipped, "should undoubtedly be able to write *his own name*"[21]), this same English produced a portrait of Poe, in his temperance novel *The Doom of the Drinkers; or Revel and Retribution* (published serially in *The Cold Water Magazine*), which described Poe at a wine party as

> a pale, gentlemanly-looking personage, with a quick, piercing, restless eye, and a very broad and peculiarly shaped forehead, [who] would occasionally under the excitement of the wine utter some brilliant jests, which fell all unheeded on the ears of the majority of the drinkers, for they could appreciate no witticisms that were not coarse and open. This man seemed hardly in his element, and no doubt wished himself away at least a dozen times during the evening. He was an extraordinary being, one of the few who arise among us with a power to steal judiciously. He was a writer of tact, which is of a higher order than ordinary genius. But he was better known as a critic, than as any thing else. His fine analytical powers, together with his bitter and apparently candid style, made him the terror of dunces and the evil spirit of wealthy blockheads, who create books without possessing brains. He made no ceremony though, in appropriating the ideas of others when it suited his turn; and as a man, was the very incarnation of treachery and falsehood.

This portrait has been termed "vicious" by William H. Gravely, Jr., who has written at length about English and his literary nemesis, but it strikes me as rather brilliantly confused in its effect. Poe is described at once as a literary thief and an "extraordinary being," less a probable alcoholic than the potential author of an American *Dunciad*, whose shrewd criticisms evidence both "fine analytical powers" and an only "apparently candid style." This man is a trickster ("the very incarnation of treachery and falsehood"), yet his guile seems to be the mask of genius. Melville, too, appears to have had some such notion in mind when, in a book appropriately entitled *The Confidence-Man*, he portrayed the puzzling Poe as an addled but possibly inspired (or is it inspired but possibly addled?) beggar trying to peddle his "rhapsodical tract" to an icy Yankee – semimystical, semishrewd – who refuses to buy because he considers the raven-haired "shatter-brain" a fraud: "I detected in him, sir," he tells his interlocutor, "a damning peep of sense – damning, I say; for sense in a seeming madman in scoundrelism. I take him for a cunning vagabond, who picks up a vagabond living by adroitly playing the madman."[22] "Poor Poe!" Melville seems to be saying, denounced at once for his sense and his screwiness, but especially damned for his cunning mixture of inspiration and insanity. Was he a Romantic genius or a Romantic fraud? But why choose, for Poe himself was perfectly aware that the essence of the modern – which is to say Romantic – temperament, as defined by A. W. Schlegel, was its *ironic* consciousness, its ability to delight "in indissoluble mixtures . . . nature and art, poetry and prose, seriousness and mirth," what Poe calls a "combination of antagonisms."[23]

Or, to put the matter in the nineteenth-century American terms that Poe himself capitalized on, art is "diddling considered as one of the exact sciences" – the expression, alternately comic or tragic, of humanity's essentially diddling nature: "A crow thieves; a fox cheats; a weasel outwits; [query: What does a raven do?] a man diddles."[24] Which is to say that man diddles consciously, and with malice prepense, for it is his nature to be serious about his intent to defraud. He perseveres in it, "he is not readily discouraged. . . . He steadily pursues his end, and . . . never lets go of his game. . . . Your diddler is audacious. He is a bold man. He carries the war into Africa. He conquers all by assault." He tries to be nonchalant, "not at all nervous." "Your diddler is original" (or so he says), "conscientiously so. His thoughts are his own. He would scorn to employ those of another" (except perhaps in a pinch). "Your diddler is impertinent. He swaggers" (except when he totters). "He sets his arms a-kimbo. He thrusts his hands in his trowsers' pockets" (and Whitman would add, "I cock my hat as I please indoors or out"; is the 1855 frontispiece a bit of diddling?). "He sneers in your face. He treads on your corns. He eats your dinner, he drinks your wine, he borrows your money, he pulls your nose, he kicks your poodle, and he kisses your wife." Finally, "your *true* diddler" – true, that is, to his ironic conscious-ness – "winds up all with a grin. But this nobody sees but himself." Why do we diddle? Why this outrageous propensity to lie in our sincerity and be sincere in our lying? Poe (or at least *this* voice of Poe) refers it "to the infancy of the Human Race. Perhaps the first diddler was Adam." Poe seems to redefine original sin as the human need to cheat, play-act, defraud, self-dramatize, and deceive.

Poe was the perfect spokesman for the diddling, confidence-gaming age and country into which he was born – a country and time at once

sentimental and savage, serious and silly, transcendental and descendental, puritanical and riotous, religious and irreverent. It was indeed "the
time of Poe," for in literary terms at least, as Edmund Clarence Stedman
noted many years ago, "Poe was the bantering monitor of his own
generation."[25] He was the greatest (and sometimes the quirkiest) critic of
his age in America, producing assessments both circumstantial and comprehensive (if often also gimlet-eyed and obsessive) of Hawthorne and
Bryant and Cooper and Longfellow and Simms and a host of other major
and minor characters, of American drama in general, of the craft of
poetry as well as fiction, and of a myriad other subjects, both significant
and trivial. Among the reviewers of his time, as Henry James noted,
"Edgar Poe perhaps held the scales the highest. He, at any rate, rattled
them loudest, and pretended, more than anyone else, to conduct the
weighing process on scientific principles." James goes on to pronounce
Poe's process "remarkable" and his principles "extraordinary," observing that he "had the advantage of being a man of genius" whose intelligence "was frequently great." But James found himself finally repelled
by the exercise of Poe's intelligence, for he thought it produced work
that was "probably the most complete and exquisite specimen of *provincialism* ever prepared for the edification of men," evincing a spirit "pretentious, spiteful, vulgar."[26] What James – surprisingly – seemed to
overlook was the element of willful freak and caprice in so much of
Poe's critical performance. To use Stedman's term, Poe's work frequently employs a conscious *bantering*; it is a teasing or mocking speech
conducted in a bewildering variety of voices, each of which seems to
enact a particular Poe mood. "He had the judicial mind," as Stedman
again notes, "but rarely was in the judicial state of mind."[27] Poe's freaks
of critical judgment and attitude appear to have arisen from an implicit
awareness that the critical activity itself is a *literary* one and thus not to be
conceived as innocent of the diddling that elsewhere defines the craft of
writing – as if in that very craft, or skill, lies the impulse to be *crafty*.
Poe's abiding concern everywhere is with the psychology of authorship
and readership, and his own performances are to be viewed accordingly
as exemplifications of that concern.[28] Poe's paragraphs in the "Marginalia," Stedman observes, "even in their posing . . . show phases of
the poet's temperament."[29] Should we not say *especially* in their posing?
Poe was as skilled in mocking himself, in whatever mode he adopted, as
he was in mocking others, but there is always something to be learned
about his craft in and through his banter.

The "Marginalia" represent an important case in point. The voice that
speaks in the introduction to the collection (is it Poe's? which Poe?)
appears at the outset to be genial and confidential:

In getting my books, I have been always solicitous of an ample margin; this not so much through any love of the thing in itself, however agreeable, as for the facility it affords me of pencilling suggested thoughts, agreements, and differences of opinion, or brief critical comments in general. Where what I have to note is too much to be included within the narrow limits of a margin, I commit it to a slip of paper, and deposit it between the leaves; taking care to secure it by an imperceptible portion of gum-tragacanth paste.[30]

That odd little detail about the "imperceptible portion" of paste calls attention to itself in an interesting way, suggesting a certain fussiness or even obsessiveness. This apparently open and good-natured voice that loves "an ample margin" also seems to be predisposed to secrecy, to hiding things. In fact, this character actually prefers a narrow margin because it enforces conciseness – which he defines, punningly, as "Tacitus-ism," meaning the art of being laconic, of saying less than one intends, "whatever diffuseness of idea we may clandestinely entertain." If you have a lot to say, he implies, keep it to yourself; and the best way to do that is to scribble it cryptically in the margin. Indeed, he describes marginalia as talk for oneself only. So this fellow is confidential in a Pickwickian sense, for he intends to confide nothing. The author of the margin, this marginal self – sly, confined to the corner, not easily noticed or deciphered – as opposed to the author of the text, is speaking out of whim and without definite purpose. He has little to say and he will say it in an abbreviated form.

Like certain seventeenth-century writers he names (Sir Thomas Browne, Burton), he is at least as much manner as matter; indeed, the "marginaliac" self is mostly manner, the matter being relegated to the main text. What the marginal comment is about is its own little performance, its cryptic dance. Our speaker accordingly worries that transferring his obiter scripta from the margin of his books to a text of their own, whereby the context will be lost, is likely to perplex the reader. And though he concludes, at length, "to put extensive faith in the acumen and imagination of the reader: – this as a general rule," in particular cases the reader is likely not to have "the ghost of a conception" what the marginalia are about unless they are remodeled so as to render them more self-contained. Thus the original marginalia, already rather shy of exposure, have performed a disappearing act in moving from the edge to center stage. They have become a new text in their own right, what can be called a marginal text: the frame transformed into a picture. But of what? What is "the ghost of a conception"? Writing itself, we might say, the frail spirit in which thought seeks to express itself. Is it to be trusted, does it *say* anything, this marginal writing? Here is our marginal narrator's conclusion to this frame for marginal scribblings:

> As for the multitudinous opinion expressed in the subjoined farrago – as for my present assent to all or dissent from any portion of it – as to the possibility of my having, in some instances, altered my mind – or as to the impossibility of my not having altered it often – these are points upon which I say nothing, because upon these there can be nothing cleverly said. It may be as well to observe, however, that just as the goodness of your true pun is in the direct ratio of its intolerability, so is nonsense the essential sense of the Marginal Note.

Your true pun is intolerable, your essential marginal note is nonsensical, and your humble author steps neatly from behind everything he has said – or rather, chooses in the end to say nothing, "nothing cleverly said." Only the reader is left holding the bag, so to speak, and the bag appears to be quite empty – unless, dear reader, you have enjoyed observing the author put himself *and* you through the paces.[31]

Anyhow, Poe seems to say, do you really believe or want to believe that literary constructs are anything more than verbal performances – that ravens in books are made of anything but papier-mâché? Poetry, Poe notes in his review of Longfellow's *Ballads*, may be defined as *"l'art d'exprimer les pensées par la fiction,"* the art of feigning.[32] Poe as critic is the Romantic ironist who enjoys deconstructing his own Romantic flights of fancy, as well as those of others, even though such a procedure deflates the frail balloons of fancy. "To see distinctly the machinery . . . of any work of Art," he writes in "Marginalia," "is, unquestionably, of itself, a pleasure, but one which we are able to enjoy only just in proportion as we do *not* enjoy the legitimate effect designed by the artist; and, in fact, it too often happens that to reflect analytically upon Art is to reflect after the fashion of the mirrors in the temple of Smyrna, which represent the fairest images as deformed."[33] Thought – reflection – deforms art because it forces art, so to speak, to examine itself critically, and in such a mirror every Snow White is in danger of looking like a witch – a stately raven, perhaps, being transformed into little more than a common crow. On the one hand, Poe wants to appear intoxicated with his own imaginative excesses; on the other, he delights in soberly examining that histrionic or fictive self. He both writes "The Raven" and unwrites it by writing *on* it:

> I have often thought how interesting a magazine paper might be written by any author who would – that is to say, who could –

detail, step by step, the processes by which any one of his composi-
tions attained its ultimate point of completion. Why such a paper
has never been given to the world, I am much at a loss to say; but,
perhaps, the authorial vanity has had more to do with the omission
than any one other cause. Most writers – poets in especial – prefer
having it understood that they compose by a species of fine frenzy –
an ecstatic intuition – and would positively shudder at letting the
public take a peep behind the scenes, at the elaborate and vacillating
crudities of thought – at the true purposes seized only at the last
moment – at the innumerable glimpses of idea that arrived not at
the maturity of full view, at the fully matured fancies discarded in
despair as unmanageable – at the cautious selections and rejections –
at the painful erasures and interpolations – in a word, at the wheels
and pinions – the tackle for scene-shifting – the step-ladders and
demon-traps – the cock's feathers, the red paint and the black
patches, which, in ninety-nine cases out of the hundred, constitute
the properties of the literary histrio.[34]

In this debunking account of his own performance, Poe's ominous raven
is seen as little more than a contrivance of "cock's feathers" and "black
patches," less a demon than a demon-trap, a trick to catch the unwary –
the pit of deception under the floor of illusion. "The Philosophy of
Composition" is a "marginaliac" effort because it shifts attention from
the center of the picture, from "The Raven" *as poem*, to the margin, that
is, to the scaffolding and constructive setting. "The Raven" as credible
imaginative event has been replaced by the voice of the critic, variously
ratiocinative, sarcastic, or humorous, and these "modes or inflections of
thought and expression," as Poe notes in his Hawthorne review, are
"antagonistical to the nature of the poem."[35] We, having read "The
Philosophy of Composition," and Poe, having written it, can return
naively to the illusions of "The Raven" – nevermore. "It is the curse of a
certain order of mind," he writes in "Marginalia," "that it can never rest
satisfied with the consciousness of its ability to do a thing. Still less is it
content with doing it. It must both know and show how it was done."[36]
   Much of Poe's critical effort has the curious effect not only of directing
our attention to the peculiarities of voice and manner in the critical
performance itself but also of casting new and often strange light on
Poe's own work as poet and taleteller. As Stedman notes, "that at which
he soonest took umbrage was a trick or fault which he detected the more
readily from having himself been guilty of it."[37] Poe's attacks, for example, on Hawthorne and Longfellow for plagiarism serve mainly to mark
his own sensitivity on the subject, for he knew perfectly well that he was
a literary magpie as well as a raven. The world – especially Poe's

nineteenth-century American scene – was awash in literature, and he was
not one to forget anything. The point of his most famous poem, he said,
was "*Never-ending Remembrance*"; that was the "emblematical" meaning
of a bird whose monotonous wisdom had been "learned by rote" from
an implied master. Perhaps that irrepressible bird will serve as an emblem also of Poe's own method as the collator of America's most popular
moods and messages.

It boggles the mind, for instance, to try to understand Poe's motives
in carrying on a protracted debate in 1845 in the New York newspapers
over the issue of plagiarism, especially as regards Longfellow, in the
course of which Poe responded at length to an attack on himself by a
certain "Outis" that now appears to have been written, in fact, by Poe.[38]
Thus, in one voice, Poe accuses himself of plagiarism, or "imitation,"
and in another defends himself vigorously and *ad taedium* – taking pains
also to demonstrate that Longfellow had shamelessly "imitated" Tennyson's "The Death of the Old Year" in his "Midnight Mass for the
Dying Year," as well as William Motherwell's "Bonnie George Campbell" in his poem "The Good George Campbell." In the latter case, Poe
prints both poems side by side, showing the reader that Motherwell's
refrain "But never cam he" is rendered by Longfellow "But he nevermore!" Since Longfellow's poem was published in 1843 and Poe's "Raven" in 1845, we must surely be expected to stare in amazement at a
presumed demonstration of Longfellow's plagiarism that in fact implicitly shows Poe to have been more seriously in debt. Thus we come to
suspect that this whole elaborate semihoax has been stage-managed by
Poe not only to keep his name and productions in the public eye, but
ultimately also to justify the interesting point that Poe makes in the final
section of his "Reply to 'Outis' ":

> It appears to me that what seems to be the gross inconsistency of
> plagiarism as perpetrated by a poet, is very easily thus resolved: –
> the poetic sentiment (even without reference to the poetic power)
> implies a peculiarly, perhaps an abnormally, keen appreciation of
> the beautiful, with a longing for its assimilation, or absorption, into
> the poetic identity. What the poet intensely admires, becomes thus,
> in very fact, although only partially, a portion of his own intellect.
> It has a secondary origination within his own soul – an origination
> altogether apart, although springing from its primary origination
> from without. The poet is thus possessed by another's thought, and
> cannot be said to take of it, possession. But, in either view, he
> thoroughly feels it as *his own* – and this feeling is counteracted only
> by the sensible presence of its true, palpable origin in the volume
> from which he has derived it – an origin which, in the long lapse of

years, it is almost impossible *not* to forget – for in the meantime the thought itself is forgotten. But the frailest association will regenerate it – it springs up with all the vigor of a new birth – its absolute originality is not even a matter of suspicion – and when the poet has written it and printed it, and on its account is charged with plagiarism, there will be no one in the world more entirely astounded than himself. Now from what I have said it will be evident that the liability to accidents of this character is in the direct ratio of the poetic sentiment – of the susceptibility to the poetic impression; and in fact all literary history demonstrates that, for the most frequent and palpable plagiarisms, we must search the works of the most eminent poets.

Here, in a conclusion worthy of T. S. Eliot, Poe demonstrates that his propensity for plagiarism, so called, is the mark of his "susceptibility to the poetic impression," thus verifying the clever gibe of "Outis" that his name should be written "EDGAR, A *Poet*, and then it is right to a *T*." Having in this odd manner proven himself to be one "of the most eminent poets," Poe succeeds in transforming the Nobody "Outis" into a very distinct Somebody, a literary hero capable of slaying the Giant Plagiarism, of subduing the many voices of imitation by assimilating them and forging them into one single, comprehensive "poetic identity." Poe's virtual obsession, in another mood, with "originality" (an especially Romantic failing, of course) often blinded him to the true character of his own poetic achievement, which was that of being the perfect if peculiar conduit of the "lush and the weird" voices that, as Whitman noted, had "taken such extraordinary possession of Nineteenth century verse-lovers." Another of Stedman's observations is pertinent here: Perhaps because of his curious vendetta, Poe "strangely failed to see that Longfellow's originality at times was strongest where he borrowed most; that it lay in the tone of his voice, – the individual key to which he set familiar thoughts and traditions."[39] Though we may justifiably be uneasy with applying that last phrase – suggestive of clichés and commonplaces – to the bizarre aura that surrounds Poe's Lenores or Annies or Ulalumes, the sentiment that informs the poetic settings in which we find such creatures is in fact only the age's "stock and store" (to pluck a plume from "The Raven"). Poe's poetic voice, in this sense, was surely not unique, but it was – to repeat – *peculiar*, and that is precisely how he himself defined true originality in his essay on Hawthorne. "True or commendable originality," he observes, "implies not the uniform, but the continuous peculiarity – a peculiarity springing from ever-active vigor of fancy – better still if from ever-present force of imagination, giving its own hue, its own character, to everything it touches, and, especially, *self-impelled to touch everything.*"⁴⁰ That last emphasized phrase is the veritable mark of Poe, the compulsion to put his hand on whatever he sees, to speak in every voice; to attempt every genre and subject, to be, in short, *the* spokesman for his time, to make it, finally, speak in the very accents of Poe.

When it would not, of course, Poe delighted in flaying it alive – perhaps flaying it *into* life, although he was also adept at flogging dead horses. Poe cared passionately about the state of letters in America and seemed to have appointed himself the principal arbiter of literary matters and manners. His criticism was propaedeutic, a way of clearing the ground of clutter in preparation for the better work (especially his own) that he envisioned. He also strongly resented the notion (much bruited about in England) that the amateurism of American poetry was to be tolerated because little else could be expected from such benighted provincials or was required in the face of English hegemony in letters. Knowing that bad literary currency would surely force out good in a country so raw in its standards, Poe laid about himself mercilessly to prick the cultural conscience of his fellow Americans. As literary gadfly, instigator, and instructor, there was to be no one quite like him until the time of Ezra Pound. And like Pound, he often allowed his own quirks, verbal virtuosity, and antic wit to get the upper hand. As Stedman notes, "[I]t was difficult for him to get through with one of his more serious essays without lowering its dignity by a side-snap or a passing jeer, at some harmless and sensitive votary of the craft"⁴¹ (we should add that no one had a thinner skin than Poe himself, whose sharpest thrusts were often designed to keep his enemies, real or imagined, at bay). Poe did enjoy sarcasm for its own sake (it was, after all, one of the masks of his genius), but at heart he believed the honor of American letters to be at stake.

So, for example, though he generally admired and had defended the much-maligned Margaret Fuller, his tone turned scornful when she published a piece entitled "American Literature; Its position in the present time, and Prospects for the Future," in which she had the effrontery, in Poe's words, "to speak of *Longfellow* as a booby, and of *Lowell* as so wretched a poetaster 'as to be disgusting even to his best friends.' "⁴² Never mind that Poe himself had raked Longfellow over the coals for his presumed "plagiarism" or was engaged in this very essay in roasting Lowell – it was ultimately a question of judging justly among America's claimants to literary distinction. "Messrs. Longfellow and Lowell," he went on, "so pointedly picked out for abuse as the worst of our poets, are, upon the whole, perhaps, our best – although Bryant, and one or two others, are scarcely inferior." Those "one or two others" might have included both Poe himself and the semisacrosanct Emerson, but this was scarcely the place (he certainly must have felt) for either puffing himself or putting forward a Transcendentalist. In fact, warming to his task, Poe now turned to Fuller's lavish praise for one of the Concord crowd's most persistent poetic pests, Ellery Channing, whom she had honored along with another minor-leaguer named Cornelius Matthews (author of a creation entitled "Wakondah" that Poe had already denominated "trumpery declamation . . . metaphor run-mad . . . twaddling verbiage . . . halting and doggerel rhythm . . . unintelligible rant and cant"[43]). As for Fuller's two favorites, Poe went on,

> it is really difficult to think of them, in connexion with poetry, without laughing. Mr. Mathews [sic] once wrote some sonnets "On Man," and Mr. Channing some lines on "A Tin Can," or something of that kind – and if the former gentleman be not the very worst poet that ever existed on the face of the earth, it is only because he is not quite so bad as the latter. To speak algebraically: – Mr. M. is *ex*ecrable, but Mr. C. is x + 1 - ecrable.[44]

Though it *is* Poe-ishly whimsical (the critic effectively provoking the laughter that the thought of these two is supposed to incite), this is not mere spite. Channing was really a remarkably bad poet whom Fuller and Emerson, presumably out of personal loyalty, never tired of praising, and perhaps it was the presence of Channing and his ilk in *The Dial*, rather than its sometimes insufferably high tone, which did the journal in.

Poe, at all events, continued with his calculus of execration, calling one Thomas Ward (pen-name "Flaccus") "a second-rate, or a third-rate, or perhaps a ninety-ninth rate, poetaster"[45]; but this reasonable and presumably dismissive judgment did not, in fact, prevent Poe from appreciating Ward's rather flaccid blank-verse tribute to the Passaic River, which concludes:

> Nor is your swelling prime, or green old age,
> Though calm, unlovely; still, where'er ye move,
> Your train is beauty; trees stand grouping by
> To mark your graceful progress; giddy flowers
> And vain, as beauties wont, stoop o'er the verge
> To greet their faces in your flattering glass:
> The thirsty herd are following at your side;
> And water-birds in clustering fleets convoy
> Your sea-bound tides; and jaded man, released
> From worldly thraldom, here his dwelling plants –
> Here pauses in your pleasant neighborhood,

Sure of repose along your tranquil shores;
And, when your end approaches, and ye blend
With the eternal ocean, ye shall fade
As placidly as when an infant dies,
And the Death-Angel shall your powers withdraw
Gently as twilight takes the parting day,
And, with a soft and gradual decline
That cheats the senses, lets it down to night.

Poe's comment ("There is nothing very *original* in all this; the general idea is, perhaps, the most absolutely trite in poetical literature; but the theme is not the less just on this account, while we must confess that it is admirably handled. . . . The seven final lines convey not only a novel but a highly appropriate and beautiful image") might very well strike us as at once to the point and odd: to the point because Poe himself, as we have seen, was perfectly adept at turning an "absolutely trite" idea into viable verse (that, indeed, was his stock in trade); but what could compel him to call the seven final lines "novel" when he knew as well as anyone that they were a close imitation of the conclusion to Bryant's "Thanatopsis"? He had, after all, already flayed Longfellow for plagiarizing Bryant's lines in a stanza that only vaguely resembled them. The truth would seem to be that Poe approved of Ward's lines because, imitative or not, with their eternal ocean and dying infant and "gradual decline . . . down to night," they chimed in perfectly with Poe's own voice and mood.

Like that celebrated hero of Niagara Falls, Sam Patch, whom Ward celebrated in another poem entitled "The Great Descender," Poe was addicted to the *descendant* mode, and his usual pleasure in scoring a point in the great plagiarism war was overwhelmed by the even stronger pleasure induced by these lulling lines on what he calls in *Eureka* the "Journey to the End." Poe blasted Longfellow, again, for writing – famously –

Art is long, and Time is fleeting,
And our hearts, though stout and brave,
Still like muffled drums are beating
Funeral marches to the grave. . . . [46]

because he claimed that was a steal from Henry King's "Exequy" on his dead wife ("But hark! *my pulse, like a soft drum, / Beats* my approach – tells thee I come! / And slow howe'er my *marches* be, / I shall at last sit down by thee"). But at the same time Poe could cite approvingly the Reverend Arthur Cleveland Coxe's lines,

March! march! march!
Making sounds as they tread,
Ho! ho! how they step,
Going down to the dead![47]

without a whisper about plagiarism, presumably because they sounded more like Poe himself, and that "going down to the dead" reminded him agreeably of his own midnight marches to the tomb, as in "Ulalume" ("I journeyed – I journeyed down here! / . . . I brought a dread burden down here"); or of the deliciously diabolical descent of the pendulum in his story ("Down – steadily down it crept. . . . Down – certainly, relentlessly down! . . . Down – still unceasingly – still inevitably down!"). Poe had little use for the Transcendental poet Christopher Cranch, but he admired Cranch's poem on Niagara Falls despite its "oddity of expression," citing as an example:

Down, down forever – down, down forever –
Something falling, falling, falling. . . . [48]

In all these cases, Poe's ostensibly objective standards as a literary judge somehow become intermeshed with, and even undermined by, his own private obsessions, so that the large body of Poe's critical writings finally seems to resemble a curious artistic and personal self-revelation. "Dante's praise," Emerson notes, "is, that he dared to write his autobiography in colossal cipher."[49] Poe effectively said as much about the encoding of the self in scripture:

The supposition that the book of an author is a thing apart from the author's self is, I think, ill-founded. The soul is a cipher, in the sense of a cryptograph; and the shorter a cryptograph is, the more difficulty there is in its comprehension – at a certain point of brevity it would bid defiance to an army of Champollions. And thus he who has written very little, may in that little either conceal his spirit or convey quite an erroneous idea of it – of his acquirements, talents, temper, manner, tenor, and depth (or shallowness) of thought – in a word, of character, of himself. But this is impossible with him who has written much. Of such a person we get, from his books, not merely a just, but the most just representation.[50]

We might add, though, that the very variety and spread of Poe's writing, its bewildering diversity of voice and posture, provide not so much more to go on as more to puzzle over.

3

"Poe remains an enigma, a stumbling-block for the critic," T. S. Eliot notes.[51] His work regarded as a whole, and not analytically, appears "a mass of unique shape and impressive size to which the eye constantly returns."[52] But "if we examine his work in detail," Eliot complained, "we seem to find in it nothing but slipshod writing, puerile thinking unsupported by wide reading or profound scholarship, haphazard experiments in various types of writing, chiefly under pressure of financial need, without perfection in any detail." Eliot himself was not satisfied with such a judgment, but hardly knew what to do with the "blemishes and imperfections of Poe's actual writing" in the face of the undeniable force and significance of the total oeuvre.[53] The poetry, for example – *such* poetry! (James had spoken of Poe's "valueless verses" in the original version of an essay on Baudelaire, then changed "valueless" to "superficial," and is finally quoted as saying to a friend, "I suppose I made a mistake."[54] But James had initially rejected Whitman, too, although later in his life he found special pleasure in crooning "Death, death, death, death. . . .") Perhaps, Eliot mused, it is only "very good *verse*" and not poetry, then caught himself for starting a hare he had no intention of following – "for it is, I am sure, 'poetry' and not 'verse.' "[55] But what *kind* of poetry? A kind whose "effect is immediate and undeveloping; it is probably much the same for the sensitive schoolboy and for the ripe mind and cultivated ear. . . . It has the effect of an incantation which, because of its very crudity, stirs the feelings at a deep and almost primitive level." But O O O O, Eliot goes on, those Edgarpoesquian gaffes when it comes to meaning. "Ulalume" is surely one of Poe's "most successful, as well as most typical, poems," but what in the name of Tennyson is one to do with "It was night, in the lonesome October / Of my most immemorial year"? *Immemorial* is supposed to mean "ancient beyond memory"; that is how Tennyson uses it in "The moan of doves in immemorial elms." But can we really read Poe, or any poetry, as Eliot is trying to do, with the Oxford English Dictionary open on our laps? Poe knew the ordinary meaning of *immemorial*; he uses, for example, the stock phrase "time immemorial." *Immemor*, in classical Latin, means *unmindful, not thinking, forgetful, regardless, negligent, heedless*; the adjective form, *immemorialis*, is medieval Latin, its meaning now lost in Gothic darkness. Why not most *thoughtless* or *heedless* year? George Saintsbury found *immemorial* "the most marvellous" of Poe's "marvellous single words,"[56] and Andrew Lang explained that although "it would puzzle the most adroit student of words to attach a distinct usual sense, authenticated by lexicons, to 'immemorial' . . . no one with an ear can fail to see that it is emphatically the right word, and supplies the necessary note of suggestion."[57]

Suggestion – that is one of Poe's central articles of faith, and even the possibility of being *suggestive* is not beyond his ken. Would Eliot's schoolboy know that Astarte is a rather wicked version of Venus and that Venus in Leo – in "the lair of the Lion" – signifies lust? That is the "sinfully *scin*tillant planet" that is leading the narrator and his soul on their wild goose chase this Halloween night. It is manifestly *not* Bryant's psalm-singing Waterfowl that guides the steps of these two to their love tryst among the tombs. If Poe's speaker has been endowed with a southern accent – and why not? – then we may notice a bit of welcome wit in his choice of the bediamonded eastern Venus over the life-chilling chaste goddess of the moon. We read: "And I said – 'She is warmer than Dian. . . .' " But are we not allowed perhaps to hear (particularly in view of the odd recessive stress on "D*ian*," calculated to rhyme with "dry on"): "An' ah said – 'She is warmer than Dyin'. . . .' "? Anything is warmer than *that*, even the "ghoul-haunted woodland of Weir" on a chilly October evening. We remember, in fact, that our speaker is recalling a time when his heart was "volcanic" and with his soothing manner and kisses he felt equal to the task of conquering the scruples of his Psyche and tempting her out of her gloom and down the misty forest path to the "legended tomb." Love is better than death, perhaps best, most thrilling, in the vicinity of death.

But why should one try to make sense of Poe's opulent fantasy? What enchants and deepens this night is the lush lullaby of words, the danse macabre of Poe's language. It *is* all suggestion: U-lu-la, u-lu-lare, U-lalume; gloom, tomb, *womb*; sere, year, fear, *weird*; titanic, volcanic, *panic*; morn, born, horn, *forlorn*; sighs, dies, *cries*; mistrust, dust, *lust*; light, night, *fright*; ghoul, *fool* . . . What we *hear* beneath the poem may be more important than what we read in it: the sounds of love and betrayal, terror and death, encapsulated in a few simple rhymes. Perhaps, however, "this is nothing but dreaming" – U-la-lume, All-alone (alone, alone, all all alone) . . . Ulalume. If Thoreau is right in catching throughout this nightmarish song of "supernal love in the infernal groves" the "ancient u-lu-lu" of the u-lu-la, the owl, then it may be sufficient to conclude that Poe has given us only a final version of his obsession with the frail intellect of humanity, now moaning in grief at its overthrow. The owl was once revered as the emblem of the Goddess of Reason, but the pallid bust of Pallas has been overspread by a ravening fowl that feeds on its host. A dark bird of night has entered the temple; the owl has descended to the infernal groves; Usher's palace is permanently haunted. Sense has indeed been overwhelmed by sound, and the sound that rings through Poe's world of words – never morrow, no more, no more, no more, nevermore – seems a nineteenth-century sentimental-morbid version of the old king's lament: "Thou'lt come no more, / Never, never, never, never. . . ." In Poe's hands, Shakespeare's weighty "promised end" is reevoked only as an apocalypse of sighs and tears.

Were such poetic whimpers an appropriate conclusion to the career of a writer who had hoped to decipher creation itself? Hardly. So as his last will and testament, Poe attempted to substitute "Eureka" for the cry of pain by which the world had mainly come to know him. It was to be his ultimate claim to having done an original thing, a strange incursion into the border-ground between truth and fiction, whereby he would hope to lay not only his own heart but also the universe bare.

4

Poe's final utterance, evidently intended as a triumphant cry of discovery to rival that of Archimedes, is designed to demonstrate that he had at last found a place to stand, as a writer, whence he could not only prod his disparate voices and theories into one unified utterance, but also move the very cosmos into his own mind. That *topos*, as he suggests in his Preface to *Eureka*, is the realm of "Romance," the "border-ground," as he had described it in "Marginalia," between "wakefulness and sleep," where "psychal impressions" or "fancies" flit like shadows before the mind's half-closed eye.[58] These "spiritual shadows," or "soul-reveries," as they are termed in *Eureka*, are the products not of ratiocination but of intuition, of a process *"so shadowy as to escape our consciousness, elude our reason, or defy our capacity of expression."*[59] To borrow a phrase from Cooper's brooding Romantic version of John Paul Jones, they are a "dream of reality,"[60] a dream that enables Poe to conceive of reality not only as a "plot of God" but also, and more significantly, as the design of his own inspired or moon-struck brain. Outer space, defined as "a shadowy and fluctuating domain, now shrinking, now swelling, with the vacillating energies of the imagination,"[61] blends with inner space, as the universe takes the shape of a master poet's supreme fiction. The antic Poe may take pleasure in writing the Transcendentalist Kant's name with a capital C, but his own epistemology is radically post-Kantian: reality can be known only as a reflex of the mind itself.

Poe's ultimate "Art-Product," variously defined as an "essay," a "romance," and a "poem," effectively breaks down the distinction between prose and poetry that had earlier been the basis of his aesthetic theory. "In enforcing a truth," Poe had previously argued, "we need severity rather than efflorescence of language."[62] Now Poe had come to understand that *all* discourse is essentially metaphoric, that there is no such thing as truth, or thought itself, without the "efflorescence of language." The Universe as Poe dreams of it is a "conception" of the divine, a "thought of God,"[63] and as such is subject to the vagaries of verbal imagination. The Logos creates by means of a *logos* that must be read and interpreted. As Poe himself begins "with that merest of words, 'Infinity,' " for example, he notices that

> this, like "God," "spirit," and some other expressions of which the equivalents exist in nearly all languages, is by no means the expression of an idea – but of an effort at one. It stands for the possible attempt at an impossible conception. Man needed a term by which to point out the *direction* of this effort – the cloud behind which lay, forever invisible, the *object* of this attempt.[64]

All objects remain shrouded in the unspeakable mystery of the Kantian *Ding an sich*, and language – symbolic gesture – continues to be our only method of pointing toward the objects of desire. "A word, in fine, was demanded," Poe continues, and the more *beautiful* our words, the more satisfying to the human imagination, the more they constitute the truth in our eyes. How can Poe hope to avoid the "efflorescence of language" when speaking of a universe in which a "parent body," the sun, *threw off* the planets like so many verbal articulations, so many "let there be's," of the prime mover? In presenting his truths about this fascinating "plot of God," Poe himself, repeating the divine work in his own, quite naturally says, "I throw them out."[65] His words, too, are little units of planetary force, minuscule reenactments of the infinite "I AM," which call the universe into being by articulating its fable.

Poe's attempt "to reconcile the obstinate oils and waters of Poetry and Truth"[66] turns on the notion of "symmetry" as both a physical and a metaphysical principle that defines the creation. Since the "poetical essence of the Universe" derives from the "supremeness of its symmetry," and "symmetry and consistency are convertible terms," the creation "designed" or "designated" in *Eureka* is both beautiful and true.[67] Effectively Poe enforces the idea that *his* figuration of the universe is true, since it is a consistent, perfect story of the origin, evolution, and destiny of creation, as well as an explanation of what appears to be "Divine injustice" or "Inexorable Fate." *Eureka* is thus a cosmogony, a cosmology, an apocalypse, and a theodicy, all in the form of a "prophetical and poetical rhapsody." Poe's romance proposes to decipher the mystery of creation precisely by imagining a creation in the process of *deciphering* itself, turning the complex codes of being back into the blissful plain text of nothingness. His universe begins in a primitive state of nonindividuation with an "absolute, irrelative particle," and it longs to return to the identical condition of empty unity. Thus Poe's Book of Genesis is the same as his Book of Revelation, for "in the beginning" and "in the end" are equivalent. The "initial sentence" of the tale, as Poe argued in his Hawthorne piece, necessarily tends toward the final effect – hence the perfect consistency and symmetry of his truth-telling fable.

The shape of this fable – a circle, a cipher, Ouroboros – suggests a cyclical process of unity, dispersion into the many, and return to unity, a kind of endless Paradise, Paradise Lost, Paradise Regained figuration. But that is not really what Poe has in mind. Though his fable seems to be one of constant new beginnings, it is finally "the great End" that concerns him, for each "new genesis," as he says, "can be but a very partial postponement" of that apocalypse.[68] Poe notes at the start, presumably speaking of his astronomical methodology, that "we many *a*scend or *de*scend," but his decision to commence "with a descent" gives the keynote of the whole. The traditional story of mankind, of course, also begins with an immediate descent from the primitive splendor of creation, but that story is ultimately a transcendent, not a descendent, one: In Adam's fall we sinned all, yet (as Thoreau insists) in the new Adam's rise we are to reach the skies. Poe's tale, though, is darker, for "gravity" is his primary and ultimate principle: The "state" of humanity is one of "progressive collapse." Thus entropy is Poe's theme, and *Eureka* is the necessary swan-song of both natural and human history. Poe's conception of social existence – the projected, dispersed, electrical, *repulsive* state in which many beings compete – is that it is "wrong" precisely because human relations are tragic: "That a thing may be wrong," he explains, "it is necessary that there be some other thing in *relation* to which it *is* wrong – some condition which it fails to satisfy; some law which it violates; some being whom it aggrieves."[69] Bliss in human relations can never be permanent, for we are intrinsically at odds with one another, seeking what we can never have or simply causing and finding pain in our mutual striving. Evil and sorrow are thus a necessary result of the blind impulse to be in *relation*, and the only solution lies in being released from the successive cycles of desire and repulsion. All things, Poe says, long to return to "their lost parent," that is "Unity,"[70] the mindless, primitive pleasure of asexual union with the mother in the womb or the relinquishing of the pain of consciousness in the final return to the bosom of Abraham. Poe's fable chooses *thanatos* over *eros*; death is viewed as the goal of life, not simply as its natural end.

This fable, in its basic structure, is an old one in the history of thought, though it found renewed currency in the Romantic period. In *Natural Supernaturalism* M. H. Abrams traces the putative origin of this mythos to Plotinus's notion that the source of all being is unity, the primal One or the Good, which produces the world through emanation, moving in stages from pure mind down to the most remote state, matter, which is "evil" only negatively (as both Poe and Emerson suggest) in that it is at the furthest remove from the Good and thereby separated from the unity of the All. To *real* being we must all revert if we wish to be happy. One analogy for the "epistrophe," or return, is that of the child seeking the lost father or home:

> . . . in this application Plotinus proposes an allegoric reading of Homer's epic narrative which was destined to have a long and prolific life in European thought. "But what must we do? How lies the path? How come to a vision of the inaccessible Beauty?" He cites the *Iliad*, II, 140:
>
>> "Let us flee then to the beloved Fatherland": this is the soundest counsel. But what is this flight? How are we to gain the open sea? For Odysseus is surely a parable to us when he commands the flight from the sorceries of Circe or Calypso – not content to linger for all the pleasure offered to his eyes and all the delight of sense filling his days.
>>
>> The Fatherland to us is There whence we have come, and there is the Father.

The course of all things is a "great circle," or process, as we have seen in *Eureka*, from unity to the many and back to unity (Good to Evil back to Good). In Dionysius the Areopagite, Abrams informs us, "Goodness" (like Poe's *gravity*, we may note) "draweth all things to Itself, and is the great Attractive Power which unites things that are sundered." This pagan Neoplatonic scheme of cyclical movement from unity to dispersion and back again, time without end, was echoed by a variety of Romantic writers who, as with Schelling in 1811, called for a new Homer, "the poet-prophet who will sing the greatest of all epics, of which the theme will be the journey back to the lost paradise, or golden age, which is the restoration of a lost unity of the human intellect with itself and with nature."[71]

Professor Abrams makes much of Wordsworth's similar call, in 1814, for a celebration of the new holy marriage between the mind of man and nature which would transform that old "history . . . of departed things," the ancient lost paradise, into a present reality. Poe, too, would seem to want to celebrate this momentous marriage of spirit and matter, soul and body, repulsion and attraction, but his brother and sister – as in "Ulalume" – march hand in hand not back to paradise, but to the grave. It is not the epistrophe to which Poe looks forward, but the final "catastrophe." His journey is ever downward, "to the end." Along the way, in a passage of extraordinary imaginative brilliance, Poe envisions a general precipitation "of the moons upon the planets, of the planets upon the suns, and of the suns upon the nuclei," resulting presumably in the formation of supernovas and black holes as "the myriad now-existing stars of the firmament" are gathered into "an almost infinitely less number of almost infinitely superior spheres," which, "being immeasurably fewer" than those we know, "will be immeasurably greater." Then, indeed, Poe notes terrifically, "amid unfathomable abysses, will be glaring unimaginable suns."[72]

But the language by means of which Poe figures "the great End" is finally less astronomically pseudoscientific and more personal. His ultimate "phonetical hieroglyphic" is the same one that resounds through much of Poe's major fiction, that ominous *rushing* noise that accompanies his descendental apocalypses. Lady Madeline of *Usher*, amid the "*rushing* gust*," bears down in death agony upon her brother, the *fissure* widens, and the walls are seen "*rushing* asunder" as the House collapses; the Lady Ligeia's raven black hair streams forth "into the *rushing* atmosphere of the chamber" to take possession of the obsessed narrator's brain; the victim in "The Pit and the Pendulum" is swallowed up "in a mad *rushing* descent as of the soul into Hades"; most spectacularly, Arthur Gordon Pym experiences both "the final bitterness of the *rushing* and headlong descent" into the arms of Dirk Peters and his more final "*rushed*" movement into the "embraces of the cataract" and its mysterious "shrouded human figure" of a perfect and perfectly terrifying whiteness. In *Eureka*, too, Poe describes his "system-atoms" as "*rushing* into consolidation in spheres." He envisions them:

> . . . *rushing* towards their own general centre . . . with a million-fold electric velocity, commensurate only with their material grandeur and with their spiritual passion for oneness, the majestic remnants of the tribe of Stars flash, at length, into a common embrace.[73]

Poe's universe, then, concludes its career in a wild acceleration of desire, a fearful haste to sate that seemingly insatiable need for union, to consume all in one last suicidal consummation. In this cosmos, the "big bang" comes not in the beginning but at the end in the form of a fatal *Liebestod*. It is a hostile embrace: the desire for annihilation wearing the mask of love, swift as it is savage, as if to say, "Let us be done with this once and for all." The frantic rushing together finishes in a "rushing asunder" that leaves everything uncreated.

Poe's extravagant attempt, in his final essay-romance, to produce something like a unified field theory of cosmic love and death in the guise of a scientific treatise has been ridiculed as often as it has been admired, but one must take it for what it is – Romantic mythmaking, not veritable gospel astrophysics. It may seem strange for literature to masquerade as science, or vice versa, but as we have seen, Poe himself finally called into question the distinction between one kind of discourse (call it scientific prose), designed to advance the truth by being simple, precise, and terse (his terms), and another kind (call it poetry), designed to express truth more deviously, or attractively, by means of fiction. Nor is Poe alone, even among scientists, in feeling the need to speculate on difficult or mysterious matters in modes of writing that approximate myth more than rational discourse. Reputable scientists have been known to indulge in science fiction that they and others were not prepared to dismiss as mere empty fantasy. But a more striking example of the confluence of mythmaking and scientific treatise occurs in a work that oddly resembles Poe's *Eureka* in its general drift and conclusions, namely, Sigmund Freud's *Beyond the Pleasure Principle*.[74] It has frequently been said that Poe anticipated or embodied many of Freud's insights into abnormal psychology (of course, not only his work but Poe himself has been analyzed as an *example* of psychosexual disorder). But it may be closer to the truth to say, not that Poe was a Freudian, but that Freud was Poesque, that is, a Romantic mythmaker in the manner of Poe. In any case, if Poe did anticipate some of Freud's views, it was precisely as Hawthorne did, by manipulating modes of symbolic discourse for the purposes of "psychological romance." It may be more useful, however, to observe that Poe, like Freud, began with an interest in psychological investigation and ended by trying to discover, or invent, more general myths of the soul and the universe. They were both sharply aware that the "design" of their scheme and its cogency depended radically on the power of words. All discourse, to repeat, is figurative; we must try to create metaphors to which we can give at least provisional assent.

Freud, in fact, concludes *Beyond the Pleasure Principle* with an intriguing discussion about the validity of his own terms of discourse. In the body of his essay Freud had developed the notion that human nature is fundamentally divided between "life instincts" – call them *erotic* – and "death instincts" – call them *thanatic*.[75] Moreover, Freud speculated that essentially "all instincts tend towards the restoration of an earlier state of things," and that that "*old* state of things" is death – "*the aim of all life*."[76] The libido, or erotic instinct, must then be viewed, paradoxically, as one of the "circuitous paths" by which all organic life strives to return to nonbeing – simply "a long way round to Nirvana," as Santayana phrased it in a review of Freud's book.[77] Freud writes:

> It is as though the life of the organism moved with a vacillating rhythm. One group of instincts rushes forward so as to reach the

final aim of life as swiftly as possible; but when a particular stage in the advance has been reached, the other group jerks back to a certain point to make a fresh start and so prolong the journey.

But that "new genesis," to use Poe's term, is but a "partial postponement" of the true goal of life. For as Freud notes, "union with the living substance of a different individual" serves to increase tension, "introducing what may be described as fresh 'vital differences' which must then be lived off," since "the dominating tendency of mental life, and perhaps of nervous life in general, is the effort to reduce . . . internal tension." The "most universal endeavour of all living substance" is "to return to the quiescence of the inorganic world."[78]

Having arrived at this conclusion, Freud reaches back both to join hands with the Romantic pessimism of Schopenhauer and to associate his own story about the *need to restore an earlier state of things* with the fable of original unity and division in Plato's *Symposium*. In doing so, Freud apologizes for introducing "fantastic" material – "a myth rather than a scientific explanation." But he really has no intention of making an invidious distinction between *myth* and *science*:

> It may be asked whether and how far I am myself convinced of the truth of the hypotheses that have been set out in these pages. My answer would be that I am not convinced myself and that I do not seek to persuade other people to believe in them. . . . [I]n any case it is impossible to pursue an idea of this kind except by repeatedly combining factual material with what is purely speculative and thus diverging widely from empirical observation. The more frequently this is done in the course of constructing a theory, the more untrustworthy, as we know, must be the final result. But the degree of uncertainty is not assignable. One may have made a lucky hit or one may have gone shamefully astray.[79]

The problem ultimately, Freud comes to see, is that language itself is, as Emerson had said, "fossil poetry," fundamentally metaphoric. His own "scientific terms" simply amount to "the figurative language peculiar to psychology," and without it he could not "describe the processes in question at all, and indeed . . . could not have become aware of them."

Of course, science dreams of a more precise system of signs – of the possibility of dispensing with poetry in the purer service of truth. "The deficiencies in our description," Freud goes on, "would probably vanish if we were already in a position to replace the psychological terms by physiological or chemical ones"; but such a hope is finally vain, for "they too are only part of a figurative language." All representation, Poe insists, is but "the *thought of a thought*."[80] Thus Santayana, who could read both Poe and Freud with pleasure, observes that "the chief terms employed in psycho-analysis have always been metaphorical: 'unconscious wishes,' 'the pleasure-principle,' 'the Oedipus complex,' 'Narcissism,' 'the censor'; nevertheless, interesting and profound vistas may be opened up, in such terms, into the tangle of events in a man's life." Myths, Santayana had noted earlier, "are not believed in, they are conceived and understood." Myths and metaphors may be said to be true "in the sense that, in terms drawn from moral predicaments or from literary psychology, they may report the general movement and the pertinent issue of material facts, and may inspire us with a wise sentiment in their presence."[81]

Why should we quarrel with Poe's fantastic haunted universe any more than with his haunted palace? Or, indeed, with Freud's? That famous hypostatization of mental space, which we may call the spooky House of Freud, with its relentless superego in the attic, its comfortable but fragile ego in the living quarters, and – *horribile dictu* – its still breathing corpse of the unconscious in the basement, may be no more substantial than the House of Usher, but most of us still hesitate to descend into that terrible cellar even for a particularly fine bottle of Amontillado. Both Poe and Freud made important discoveries about the mysterious hidden underpinnings of human experience, and both became mythmakers in order to bring those dark truths convincingly to our attention. Their Romantic dreams of reality continue to exist at the center of our collective cultural awareness despite the large amount of skeptical commentary which, not only others, but they themselves amply provide in the critical margins.

Chapter 4

Emerson: Experiments
in Self-Creation

"The history of the genesis," Emerson notes, is the "old mythology" that

> . . . repeats itself in the experience of every child. He too is a demon or god thrown into a particular chaos, where he strives ever to lead things from disorder into order. Each individual soul is such, in virtue of its being a power to translate the world into some particular language of its own.[1]

Emerson's description here of that poetic process whereby each youth seeks to inscribe his own fable of renewal is a fair portrayal of how a lapsed Unitarian minister in 1836 attempted to recuperate his powers by opening a literary discourse with the world. Emerson, Santayana notes, "was like a young god making experiments in creation."[2] *Nature*, accordingly, represents Emerson's initial effort at "restoring to the world original and eternal beauty" by redeeming and reconstituting his own soul in an imaginative apocalypse.[3]

Stephen Whicher remarks that Emerson's first book "might have exchanged titles with Poe's *Eureka*,"[4] That, however, is just about all these two odd treatises might be said to have in common. Poe's "apocalypse" is the revelation of a cosmos in decline, its stars dead or dying, burning on through light-time in paradoxical celebration of their fate. Coming at the end of Poe's painful career, it prophesies his own expiration by figuring that of the universe. But Emerson had no intention of singing a sad tale of the Conqueror Worm. *His* worm is mounting "through all the spires of form" on its triumphant way to becoming human. Emerson meditates on the "sepulchres of the fathers" in expectation not of joining them but of leaving them behind. We see him, in fact, "embosomed for a season in nature, whose floods of life stream around and through us," in preparation for spiritual rebirth. "Infancy is the perpetual Messiah," he announces, and it is precisely as a newborn bard of the Holy Ghost that he makes his own annunciation.[5]

It is not, however, without its discordant notes, for Emerson saw ruin where he hoped to see paradise. Unitarian Christianity, in his view, was "corpse-cold," burdened with formalistic rites that were creaking with age; greedy bankers had flooded the country with paper money insufficiently backed by real wealth, encouraging wild speculation; and Emerson saw little bullion in the vaults of language either. Diction was "rotten"; words needed to be reattached to real experience and to a revitalized inner life. Scholars were content to read old books – biographies, histories, criticism, the Bible itself – in accordance with received notions and not creatively with new eyes. Emerson's prime text, however, was nature itself, still gleaming with dew though violated by a "mean and squalid" propensity to treat the creation as little more than a commodity. He insisted that "a life in harmony with nature, the love of truth and of virtue," would "purge the eyes to understand her text." His own *Nature* – countertext and commentary to the creation – was designed to render the world "an open book" by helping to make the axis of his readers' vision "coincident with the axis of things." What Emerson understood by the word "revelation" was neither the Christian dispensation nor a Poesque unveiling of the arcane mysteries of the universe but rather a simple – or radical – purification of both the physical organ of sight and the mind's eye. He felt himself to be an "immortal pupil," deathless in his vision of the world's loveliness:

> I see the spectacle of morning from the hill-top over against my house, from day-break to sun-rise, with emotions which an angel might share. The long slender bars of cloud float like fishes in the sea of crimson light. From the earth, as a shore, I look out into that silent sea. I seem to partake its rapid transformations: the active enchantment reaches my dust, and I dilate and conspire with the morning wind.[6]

But this "immortal pupil" dilated most conspicuously and most famously elsewhere: on "a bare common, in snow puddles, at twilight, under a clouded sky," for example. This crepuscule provided a more mysterious, and perhaps more ambiguous, ecstasy than that of Emerson's Assyrian dawn – the *vespertina cognitio*, or "evening knowledge," appropriate to humans, rather than the *matutina cognitio*, or "morning knowledge," reserved for the divine. Could Emerson really hope to transcend the ordinary conditions of mortal being? Under that clouded sky in twilight, he writes, "I have enjoyed a perfect exhilaration. I am glad to the brink of fear." As we have noted before, a *perfect* exhilaration

would hardly seem consistent with being on the brink of such a disturbing emotion (and this, of course, is the 1849 text; in 1836 Emerson had
written, "[A]lmost I fear to think how glad I am," presumably realizing
– along with Keats – in the course of those crucial thirteen years that
gladness is a fragile state of being). So the word *perfect* shimmers with a
hint of its own dissolution, signaling with what is perhaps an unconscious equivocation that the mark of humankind's fallen state is on our
speaker, however lightly, even as he rhapsodically attempts to disown it.
In the woods, as opposed to the beclouded common, our death-defying
pupil seems to be promised "perpetual youth" – indeed, "a thousand
years," a millennium, of joy. He does not simply see the truth: He *is*
vision as he becomes a "transparent eyeball" through which "the currents of the Universal Being circulate" in apparently so perfect a circle of
divine energy that he is "part or particle of God." That seems closer to
matutina cognitio, but even here we find a slight anxiety because our
acolyte of apocalypse is worried about the security of his sight, either his
actual vision or the virtue it represents: "I feel that nothing can befall me
in life, – no disgrace, no calamity, (leaving me my eyes,) which nature
cannot repair."[7]

Emerson had intimated, at the beginning of his book, that he would
see "God and nature face to face," but he knew of the ancient injunction
against such an unmediated vision of the divine. In the "Over-Soul" he
would write of the "tendency to insanity" that "has always attended the
opening of the religious sense in men," as if they had been "blasted with
excess of light." So Emerson's fantasy in *Nature* of being taken up into
the "currents of the Universal Being" seems to be tinged with an
awareness that transcendental experience, the ultimate flight into the
intense inane, might well entail certain worldly dangers. He might find
that having dilated so sublimely, his eyes would never again be able to
focus in a merely normal way. Five years after the publication of *Nature*,
in one of his most orphic addresses, Emerson would tell a rather perplexed audience at Waterville College in Maine that a man capable of
exactly obeying the spirit would find himself adopted by it,

> so that he shall not any longer separate it from himself in his
> thought, he shall seem to be it, he shall be it. If he listen with
> insatiable ears, richer and greater wisdom is taught him, the sound
> swells to a ravishing music, he is borne away as with a flood, he
> becomes careless of his food and of his house, he is the fool of ideas,
> and leads a heavenly life.[8]

That was even a headier message than the injunction to spiritual
regeneration contained in *Nature*, and one delivered not in a book but in

person by the prophet himself. We ought to keep in mind that Emerson's greatest influence in his own time was achieved through his personal appearances. Those who flocked to hear him, as Santayana notes, went not so much for the meaning of his words (sufficiently startling, in any case, as we have observed), "as for the atmosphere of candour, purity, and serenity" that hung about them "as about a sort of sacred music. They felt themselves in the presence of a rare and beautiful spirit, who was in communion with a higher world.'" Emerson, the erstwhile minister turned Romantic rhapsode, demonstrated that public speech in America could be something more than mere oratory, far more moving even than pulpit eloquence. He was what he was not only by virtue of his power to translate the world into a particular language of his own but also by virtue of his *presence* as he delivered the word. That was a lesson not to be lost on such a fledgling Emersonian as Whitman, who would characteristically take the notion one step further and sing that the human body and its voice were themselves essentially the sublimest of poems.

2

Emerson's greatest orations, "The American Scholar" of 1837 and the Divinity School Address of 1838, are linked by their passionate concern for public speech, "the speech of man to men." They exhibit him in the act of forging a new vocation that resembled those of academic scholar and minister of the gospel in that he, too, was an expositor or interpreter, but not of written texts prepared by other hands. His new "text" was nature – material, human, divine. His new vocation was that of itinerant lecturer committed to expounding his own regenerated self in the idealized forms of Scholar or Preacher or Man of Letters. Emerson would spend his days in his "private observatory, cataloguing obscure and nebulous stars of the human mind," as he says in "The American Scholar." Then he would return to earth, stand on the platform, and sing of what he had seen. He would translate sublime observations into common speech.[10]

Emerson's central complaint in the Phi Beta Kappa address was that scholars had reversed the evolutionary process, descending the scale of being and becoming mere bookworms, "restorers of readings . . . emendators . . . bibliomaniacs," living and feeding between the pages of their moldy texts, unable to express themselves adequately or intelligibly. Their reclusive dedication to scholarship, and to scholarship alone, had warped them out of their own orbits – deprived them of an active sense of themselves – and made them satellites of other men's language. Emerson's nearly obsessive insistence on action in the address was not only a compensatory response to his own reclusive tendencies; it was also an attempt to argue the more general notion that the world outside the study is the true sounding-board of the self – the key to our thoughts, the means by which we become acquainted with ourselves. It is, he argues, the matrix of expression: "I run eagerly into this resounding tumult. I grasp the hands of those next me, and take my place in the ring to suffer and to work, taught by an instinct, that so shall the dumb abyss be vocal with speech." The circle of "Universal Being" has now been replaced by a human "ring" that produces enriching ordinary sound. This tumult of speech – "in country labors; in town; in . . . trades and manufactures; in frank intercourse with many men and women" – is the necessary source of our vocabulary, the way to wealth for an orator: "I learn immediately from any speaker how much he has already lived, through the poverty or the splendor of his speech."[11]

True speech, Emerson insists, is no more than the reflex of active life, and as a listener he expects to hear evidence of real experience; otherwise he feels "defrauded and disconsolate." This very issue lies, literally, at the center of the Divinity School Address and provides its most humanly effective moment. Emerson recalls a Sunday when he sat in his pew in Concord so bored with the droning tediosities of the minister that he resolved not to go to church again. He pictures his wandering thoughts, as his eye turns from the pulpit to the window. It was snowing and thus, we assume, rather a bleak alternative to what was taking place on the platform. But no, Emerson says: "The snow storm was real; the preacher merely spectral; and the eye felt the sad contrast in looking at him, and then out of the window behind him, into the beautiful meteor of the snow." *Cold preaching* (as the term then was) makes the snow seem positively hot. At least it is part of a real world filled with energy and motion. By contrast, the Reverend Barzillai Frost (for that was his self-troping name) had "lived in vain":

> He had no one word intimating that he had laughed or wept, was married or in love, had been commended, or cheated, or chagrined. If he had ever lived and acted, we were none the wiser for it. The capital secret of his profession, namely, to convert life into truth, he had not learned. Not one fact in all his experience, had he yet imported into his doctrine. This man had ploughed, and planted, and talked, and bought, and sold; he had read books; he had eaten and drunken; his head aches; his heart throbs; he smiles and suffers; yet was there not a surmise, a hint, in all the discourse, that he had ever lived at all. Not a line did he draw out of real history.[12]

The speaker has lived in vain, Emerson argues, if his life fails to inform his speech, if his human nature is not present on the platform.

Traditionally, of course, the minister is meant to be little more than the impersonal medium of divinity. But Emerson wants his divinity to coexist with love and marriage and eating and drinking and ploughing and planting. It was an audacious notion, and the fact that Emerson would say such things to an audience of theology students and their teachers is a measure not only of his determination to shock but also, and more crucially, of his desire to import the language of experience into his own discourse. "The true preacher can be known by this, that he deals out to the people his life." Such is Emerson's own practice on this occasion, and his words must have been delivered with the full force of conviction. His presence must surely have testified to the truth and sincerity of his speech, for the body speaks as well as the mouth. How can a man without conviction face an audience and not quake in his boots? They will know how to read him; they will see "fear in the face, form, and gait of the minister."[13]

This last phrase carries a special weight, for it echoes a famous passage in the Phi Beta Kappa address of the previous year. "What would we really know the meaning of?" Emerson had asked. "The meal in the firkin; the milk in the pan; the ballad in the street; the news of the boat; the glance of the eye; the form and the gait of the body." We need to know the meaning not just of the words we hear but of the body they issue from. Speech is symbolic action; but the body's movement is symbolic speech – life speaking through gesture. We get our experience twice, then, Emerson implies: from the orator's words and from the physical conviction that accompanies (indeed produces) them. The body is spirit incarnate, moving and breathing and giving a local habitation and a name to ideas. It was just such a living model of universal truth that Emerson hoped to be so that he might actually carry with him the feelings of his audience in stating his own belief. He would *stand* for them and thus represent their own dumb yearnings and strivings:

> The orator distrusts at first the fitness of his frank confessions, – his want of knowledge of the persons he addresses, – until he finds that he is the complement of his hearers; – that they drink his words because he fulfils for them their own nature; the deeper he dives into his privatest, secretest presentiment, to his wonder he finds, this is the most acceptable, most public, and universally true. The people delight in it; the better part of every man feels, This is my music; this is myself.[14]

Whether as sometime American preacher or lecturer or scholar, Emerson wanted to produce such sounds: not only the music of the spheres but also the ground bass of common humanity.

3

In some ways the 1830s were not a useful apprenticeship for Emerson the would-be essayist, for he had gotten used to the stimulus and excitement of the lecture engagement and found it hard to transfer that lively ambience to the printed page. He noted in his journal on October 7, 1840:

> I have been writing with some pains Essays on various subjects as a sort of apology to my country for my apparent idleness. But the poor work has looked poorer daily as I strove to end it. My genius seemed to quit me in such a mechanical work, a seeming wise – a cold exhibition of dead thoughts. When I write a letter to any one whom I love, I have no lack of words or thoughts: I am wiser than myself & read my paper with the pleasure of one who receives a letter, but what I write to fill up the gaps of a chapter is hard & cold, is grammar & logic; there is no magic in it; I do not wish to see it again.[15]

Emerson's concern here with the coldness of writing of course reminds us of his strong feelings on the issue of cold preaching, which we might now define as preaching devoid of intersubjectivity. Emerson himself could not bear not to be exciting, for in his lectures he had hoped, he said, to fire "the artillery of sympathy & emotion." Being *agitated* himself (his word), he wanted and needed to agitate his audience.[16] But he also needed to compose *for* an audience, to feel the presence of that other to whom he was presumably speaking, to write (as he says) as if writing a letter.

"Every man passes his life in the search after friendship," Emerson observes in his essay on that subject in the First Series, and he then actually wrote and published the letter that he seems always to have had in mind: "Dear Friend: – if I was sure of thee, sure of thy capacity, sure to match my mood with thine."[17] It is an engaging notion: the reader as actual or potential friend. How can we be sure of our readers, Emerson wonders, sure of their abilities and susceptibilities? The two crucial issues concern *capacity* and *mood*. On the first Emerson notes "that to a witness worse than myself & less intelligent, I should not willingly put a window into my breast, but to a witness more intelligent & virtuous than I, or to one precisely as intelligent & well-intentioned, I have no objection to uncover my heart."[18] Surely Emerson realized that it is impossible to achieve a precise calculus of intelligence and virtue on either side of the writing/reading transaction. As for mood, which fundamentally defines the work of essaying (a particular turn of mind), its very essence is changeability. The stability and matching of moods is not likely to be an accurate science, either. Thus we understand, as Emerson understood, that the essayist must take his or her chances, as we must take ours, in venturing to read so fluid a form. How can one put one's heart into such a chancy business? The answer would appear to be that one cannot, at least not all the time. In one place, accordingly (the great essay "Experience," the most personal-seeming of all Emerson's performances), he would write, "I have set my heart on honesty in this chapter," at once signaling and assuming an extraordinary degree of confidence for both writer and reader and yet casting doubt on the "honesty" of other chapters not marked by such a confidential tone. "I am always insincere, as always knowing there are other moods," he writes in another place, perhaps calling into question all avowals of "honesty" amid the shifting sands of literary subjectivity.[19]

"I am inclined to think," writes William H. Gass, "that it is just this lack of loyalty in Emerson, this moodiness of mind, the unfanatical hold he had on his hopes and ideals, despite the urgency of their expression, which appeals to us today."[20] To be sure, for the sake of an argument or an effect Emerson could carry the whole thing too far and sound wildly irresponsible, even brazen in his refusal to take the measure of his own trustworthiness as a guide:

> Lest I should mislead any when I have my own head and obey my whims, let me remind the reader that I am only an experimenter. Do not set the least value on what I do, or the least discredit on what I do not, as if I pretended to settle any thing as true or false. I unsettle all things. No facts are to me sacred; none are profane; I simply experiment, an endless seeker, with no Past at my back.

This is the voice of the devil's child, a truly unsettling voice that gives us no solid place to stand. An authorial voice that explicitly disclaims authority may seem flatly unworthy of any kind of credence unless we pay attention to Emerson's strategy as it unwinds throughout the whole course of "Circles." In that frame we come to see that the voice speaking here is not simply affirming its own right to experiment but authorizing ours as well. After asking why we value the poet, Emerson explains:

> . . . in my daily work I incline to repeat my old steps, and do not believe in remedial force, in the power of change and reform. But some Petrarch or Ariosto, filled with the new wine of his imagination, writes me an ode or a brisk romance, full of daring thought and action. He smites and arouses me with his shrill tones, breaks up my whole chain of habits, and I open my eye on my own possibilities.

Emerson's shrill tones, then, are intended to open up *our* eyes and encourage experimentation in turn. He has a right to cry "*Eureka!*" and we are equally empowered to echo it because he has discovered, and discovers to us, that writing can really provide the Archimedean moment: "Literature is a point outside of our hodiernal circle, through which a new one may be described. The use of literature is to afford us a platform whence we may command a view of our present life, a purchase by which we may move it."[21]

Standing on this platform, this essay that is racing so vertiginously away from the past, we may indeed find a perspective that will enable us to re-form our lives. But perhaps we are beginning to go too fast. There is always danger of falling if we rush too suddenly from "the centre to the verge of our orbit." Slow down, Emerson, we might feel impelled to say; we really cannot follow you. He gets there ahead of us; in fact he has already gotten there, admitting that sometimes, like his perplexed reader, he has trouble matching his own moods and acknowledging that he himself was actually the one who composed what he is now reviewing:

> Our moods do not believe in each other. To-day I am full of thoughts, and can write what I please. I see no reason why I should not have the same thought, the same power of expression, to-morrow. What I write, whilst I write it, seems the most natural thing in the world; but yesterday I saw a dreary vacuity in this direction in which now I see so much; and a month hence, I doubt not, I shall wonder who he was that wrote so many continuous pages. Alas for this infirm faith, this will not strenuous, this vast ebb of a vast flow! I am God in nature; I am a weed by the wall.

We may understandably feel that we have been abandoned on cloud nine while our erstwhile hectic guide collapses like a piece of limp vegetation by the side of the road. You told us to fly, to experiment, we complain, to *change*: "Nothing is secure but life, transition, the energizing spirit."[22] Now you have changed so drastically that the needful energy appears to have flagged and we must learn to deal with "vacuity" (the gap between successive circles?). "If anyone would make a mood into a metaphor, and a metaphor into a metaphysics," observes William Gass – watch out![23] But Emerson is honest enough. He has warned us about his moods (as he has worried about ours); he is warning us now. If we reread the essay, as he did, we see plenty of red lights flashing. This man sometimes feels full and sometimes vacuous, and we get both Emersons. He is a problematic cipher, at once an empty center and a circumference, and his essays follow these expanding and retracting curves, often in dismayingly rapid cycles. As Emerson notes in "Prudence": "In skating over thin ice, our safety is in our speed."[24] That is explicitly the shrewd Yankee voice of our slippery essayist all but explaining why he himself moves so nimbly from point to point and chapter to chapter. A shrewd reader will add that, in both cases, our "safety" is illusory.

The essay, Gass observes, "induces skepticism." It "is simply a watchful form. . . . Halfway between sermon and story, the essay interests itself in the narration of ideas – in their *unfolding* – and the conflict between philosophies or other points of view becomes a drama in its hands."[25] By committing himself to a form so unmoored in its methods, if not in its premises, Emerson agrees in effect to a public display of his own uncertainties. He speaks in "Circles" about being *unsettling*; that is his own posture and his claim to being on the way to truth. "God offers to every mind its choice between truth and repose," he writes in "Intellect":

> Take which you please, – you can never have both. Between these, as a pendulum, man oscillates. He in whom the love of repose predominates will accept the first creed, the first philosophy, the first political party he meets, – most likely his father's. He gets rest, commodity, and reputation; but he shuts the door of truth. He in whom the love of truth predominates will keep himself aloof from all moorings, and afloat. He will abstain from dogmatism, and recognize all the opposite negations between which, as walls, his being is swung. He submits to the inconvenience of suspense and imperfect opinion, but he is a candidate for truth, as the other is not. . . .[26]

Emerson the essayist is a dangling man, turning constantly in the turbulent winds of his own shifting doctrine. In particular we notice that he speaks of the "walls" between which he swings as "opposite negations." He likes the sayers of "no" better than the sayers of "yes" because to deny something requires a certain original energy; affirmation is so easy. He would come back to affirmation when it was a more difficult virtue, as after the death of his son.[27] Now he counsels patience ("patience, and still patience"), believing that he was destined to pass presently "into some new infinitude, out of this Iceland of negations." It would, of course, be wrong to suggest that Emerson's interest in the principle of negation turned him in the direction of pessimism. Quite the contrary. He was simply determined not to affirm things in any facile fashion. "We have yet to learn," he says, "that the thing uttered in words is not therefore affirmed. It must affirm itself, or no forms of logic or of oath can give it evidence." Negation, in fact, could be a mode of affirmation, allowing objections to have their day in court and then fall away in the face of contrary or superior evidence. At heart Emerson was a believer who allowed himself, for the sake of argument, frequently to play the devil's advocate. "Our philosophy is affirmative," he writes, "and readily accepts the testimony of negative facts, as every shadow points to the sun."[28]

4

That is the Emerson of the First Series of *Essays*, stepping confidently from the light to the shadow but always keeping his eye on the sun. The book is self-assured and almost manically agitated, despite Emerson's fears about producing a "cold exhibition of dead thoughts." His stress throughout is on the soul's *activity*, the thinking process that he had argued for so strenuously in "The American Scholar," and as a result we see him not so much displaying his thoughts as dancing among them in a wild play of intellectual energy. This is an Emerson determined not to sleep or pause, convinced that "all things renew, germinate, and spring." To the extent that he was also willing to accuse himself of "sloth and unprofitableness," it was only by way of advertising the soul's "enormous claim" to mastery; uneasiness and doubt were but the "fine inuendo" of hope. The heart, too, as Emerson points out, has its "systole and diastole," but it throbs on through its "tough fibre," casting its "flames and generosities" from the center to the suburbs of experience.[29]

Emerson's emphasis on the truth of the heart in his first collection of essays may seem surprising coming from such a presumably austere son of the Puritans, but the fact is that the book was completed – to adopt Emerson's own pun – in a highly *cordial* atmosphere. He was working closely with Margaret Fuller on *The Dial*, and between the two of them (as also between Emerson and some highly attractive and adoring female disciples) shared intellectual passion blossomed into exciting and troubling friendship. Emerson's Concord circle in this period became a kind of love-feast that helped considerably to warm his cold thoughts as he prepared his first book of essays. He was attempting, in fact, to get off his stilts and be more of a "stove" and less of a "photometer" (his terms in an apologetic letter written later to his wife). Emerson believed himself, at heart, to have more passion than he could ever express. Thus he noted in his journal on June 11, 1840:

> I finish this morning transcribing my old Essay on Love, but I see well its inadequateness. I cold because I am hot – cold at the surface

only as a sort of guard & compensation for the fluid tenderness of the core – have much more experience than I have written there, more than I will, more than I can write. In silence we must wrap much of our life, because it is too fine for speech, because also we cannot explain it to others, and because somewhat we cannot yet understand.[30]

Emerson seems perfectly divided between perplexity and reticence in this touching self-appraisal, and his own sense of the inadequateness of his essay as flowing from a fear of giving vent to the hot core at his center certainly helps to explain the curious evasiveness of the piece, the defensive and doctrinaire Platonism that shifts attention from the realities of physical passion to a theory of sublimation. But Emerson was not as completely in control of his feelings as his journal entry and the usual printed text of "Love" suggest. We normally read the 1847 revision of Emerson's first book of essays rather than the original version of 1841, and in the case of "Love" that is unfortunate because the essay began quite differently as originally published:

Every soul is a celestial Venus to every other soul. The heart has its sabbaths and jubilees, in which the world appears as a hymeneal feast, and all natural sounds and the circle of the seasons are erotic odes and dances. Love is omnipresent in nature as motive and reward. Love is our highest word, and the synonym of God.

These sentences were excised by the considerably more sober Emerson of 1847, and it is not difficult to see why. The notion that God is love is hardly shocking, but souls as Venuses, the world as "hymeneal feast," and natural sounds and seasons as "erotic odes and dances" – all this highly colored sexual language makes the heart's sabbath sound rather like a bacchanal and suggests how aroused, so to speak, Emerson was in 1840–1.

The truth is, however, that Emerson thought of the erotic impulse as the initiating motive behind all creation (he uses such words as *heat, passion, power,* and *force*), observing that "men have written good verses under the inspiration of passion who cannot write well under any other circumstances." Perhaps that also implied that men who ordinarily wrote well enough might do so even more powerfully when nourished by the "hymeneal feast." In fact, Emerson appears to have entertained a fantasy of himself as being sexually potent enough to wash away his audience in a veritable sea of erotic energy. He recorded the following in his 1840 journal:

A droll dream last night, whereat I ghastly laughed. A congregation assembled, like some of our late Conventions, to debate the
Institution of Marriage; & grave & alarming objections stated on all
hands to the usage; when one speaker at last rose & began to reply
to the arguments, but suddenly extended his hand & turned on the
audience the spout of an engine which was copiously supplied from
within the wall with water & whisking it vigorously about, up,
down, right, & left, he drove all the company in crowds hither &
thither & out of the house. Whilst I stood watching astonished &
amused at the malice and vigor of the orator, I saw the spout
lengthened by a supply of hose behind, & the man suddenly
brought it round a corner & drenched me as I gazed.[31]

Emerson would seem to be saying that the most appropriate response to
objections to marriage is not so much a lecture as a good drenching, a
demonstration of the orator's vigor as a man. The sources of his "art" (to
call it that) are "within" or "behind," a great fund of "amorous wet" (in
Whitman's phrase) that carries all before it. Emerson is both performer
and listener in this fantasy, which enacts some of his comments on
lecturing made the previous year. "It is an organ of sublime power," he
notes, going on to insist that it is successful only when the orator "is
himself agitated & is as much a hearer as any of the assembly."[32] He
might therefore be in a position to take the measure of his own force.
Emerson longed to fire his "artillery" thus effectively but took himself to
task for saying "fine things, pretty things, wise things" without "trans-
piercing" and "loving" and "enchantment." He complained about lacking sufficient "constitutional vigor" to lay himself out "utterly – large,
enormous, prodigal. . . . "[33] Such was his fantasy, and such were his not
so secret views (they would not be secret to Whitman) about the passional or sexual underpinnings of imaginative expression.

   "First we eat, then we beget," Emerson observes; "first we read, then
we write."[34] These simple equations (reading is eating and writing is
begetting), likening the creative process to the artist's physiological
subjectivity, might be said to inform Emerson's major statement about
the ideal or transcendental maker, the Poet. This universal figure is a
genius (and Emerson employs the word with the full force of its etymology) who "repairs the decays of things" by casting out his "seed," or
songs, which "ascend, and leap, and pierce into the deeps of infinite
time." He is the creation's "lover" and the prophet of its "new religion."
Emerson notes that "the religions of the world are the ejaculations of a
few imaginative men," and he seems to use that curious word with an
active sense of its two interchangeable meanings. The poet – or "the
painter, the sculptor, the composer, the epic rhapsodist, the orator" –

"all partake one desire, namely, to express themselves symmetrically and abundantly, not dwarfishly and fragmentarily." They feel hemmed in by demons, unnaturally contained, and cry out, "By God, it is in me and must go forth of me." Emerson conceives of speech and song as a "necessity," physically (male or female: In his journal the word is "oestrum"), for the poet must give vent to his pent-up emotions. Those "throbs and heart-beatings in the orator, at the door of the assembly," have one end, "namely, that thought may be ejaculated as Logos, or Word."[35] *Thought* here is not so much an intellectual construction as an organic impulse – "vegetation, the pullulation & universal budding of the plant man," as Emerson puts it in his journal.[36]

The poet must persist and say:

> "It is in me, and shall out." Stand there, baulked and dumb, stuttering and stammering, hissed and hooted, stand and strive, until, at last, rage draw out of thee that *dream*-power which every night shows thee is thine own; a power transcending all limit and privacy, and by virtue of which a man is the conductor of the whole river of electricity.[37]

Interestingly, the poet *transcends* privacy by *descending* into those secret parts of his being that tap the source of all creativity. It is the river of life, the universal dream-power that is the reservoir equally of love and rage, the vast undifferentiated pool of all primitive emotion, the volcano under the crust of consciousness (as in his own poem, "The Problem"). Emerson's malicious and vigorous speaker, the fantasy projection of himself as orator/poet, is at once fiend and fecundator, the demon-artist as flower and priest of Pan. As Harold Bloom observes, "the spirit that speaks in and through [Emerson] has the true Pythagorean and Orphic stink. . . . The ministerial Emerson . . . is full brother to the Dionysiac adept who may have torn living flesh with his inspired teeth."[38]

5

"The Poet" exhibits Emerson soaring into the empyrean of his thought from the shadowy realm of primitive instinct, turning from the shady groves of Bacchus to the sunny fields of Apollo. The transcendental and the descendental are linked in the voice of a bard who transforms dark impulse into bright song: "Every shadow points to the sun." In this mood his dreams were good ones, providing new perspectives in which "nations, times, systems, enter and disappear, like threads in tapestry of large figure and many colors."[39] He felt rich and intoxicated with a sense of power and procreativity, the world a mere ball in his hand. But he had once again, and more tragically, come to the brink of gladness, and over the edge was fear and a darker mood, the other side of the tapestry. Between "The Poet" and "Experience" falls the shadow of the death of Emerson's first-born, little Waldo, his namesake and brighter self. Now the subjectivity forged with so much difficulty was undone. There can be little doubt that the death of Emerson's son at the age of five – a major influence on the composition of this great meditation – wounded Emerson vitally, made him feel unmanned, less capable of creation. What before had been dreams of opulence and power decayed into mere illusions.

The essay begins with the speaker lost on a mysterious staircase, feeling drugged and dopey. Life is a series, like his book of essays, but it has no beginning, no end, and no apparent logic. He has drunk deeply of lethe and is "lethargic." It is noonday, but there seems to be no sun – indeed, there is no son. The shadows have deepened: "Sleep lingers all our lifetime about our eyes, as night hovers all day in the boughs of the fir-tree." Things swim, his perception is threatened, and he feels like a ghost (we are reminded of the Reverend Mr. Frost; has the speaker forgotten that he is married and has children?). Now he lacks "the affirmative principle" and has "no superfluity of spirit for new creation." He has barely enough energy to carry on his spectral existence but not enough "to impart or to invest." The question is, how can the artist go on writing in such a mood of deprivation and loss? How can he make a new essay, a further attempt, when the very ground on which he stands is shifting and all objects seem to slip through his fingers? His life looks trivial, and he shuns to record it. Perhaps the thing to do, always a good last resort for Emerson, is to try arguing with himself, as we pinch ourselves when we feel drowsy:

> But it is impossible that the creative power should exclude itself. Into every intelligence there is a door which is never closed, through which the creator passes. The intellect, seeker of absolute truth, or the heart, lover of absolute good, intervenes for our succor, and at one whisper of these high powers, we awake from ineffectual struggles with this nightmare. We hurl it into its own hell, and cannot again contract ourselves to so base a state.

These are brave words, but his moods are turning quickly, and he finds this momentary anchorage "quicksand." He still feels drowsy and de-energized and resorts to turning the pages of his books languidly. He tries to be "thankful for small mercies," but the world seems empty, and life itself "a bubble and a skepticism, and a sleep within a sleep."[40]

Emerson's problem as an artist deprived of his vital subjectivity – the hope of his future, the happy memory of his past – appears irremediable. He does indeed seem to be stuck on that ladder that figures the sliding scale of his consciousness, suspended somewhere between heaven and hell – his aspiration and his despair. How can he get moving? The truth is that he has never stopped, although he seems to be moving in circles. For the essence of the form Emerson is employing and enlarging is that it keeps on going: The essay is perpetually ongoing, a continuous talking with oneself that others are allowed to overhear. It may digress, change its stance and tone, break the monotony or stranglehold of one mind by citing others, pause to reflect on its own provisional conclusions, and then proceed once more to look for better ones. It has, precisely, the shape of experience. It will keep on going until it runs out of breath or expires, but even then it may start over, or we may choose to reread it. Though Emerson seems drained of belief, that will not stop him, for the essay is not designed, like a tract, simply to expound a faith. What interests Emerson is not what he or anyone else believes or does not believe; rather, as he says, it is *the universal impulse to believe*. That impulse will keep him and the essay moving. "Onward and onward!" he exclaims. "In liberated moments, we know that a new picture of life and duty is already possible." And even here, in the trap of temperament and mood, we may still begin to frame that new picture. "The elements already exist in many minds around you, of a doctrine of life which shall transcend any written record we have." *That* is Transcendentalism: the irrepressible hope, even from the bottom of the pit, that a new doctrine of life may carry us beyond the present written record, perhaps the very one we have been perusing:

> The new statement will comprise the skepticisms, as well as the faiths of society, and out of unbeliefs a creed shall be formed. For, skepticisms are not gratuitous or lawless, but are limitations of the affirmative statement, and the new philosophy must take them in, and make affirmations outside of them, just as much as it must include the oldest beliefs.[41]

Here, then, is the tougher theory of affirmation we were looking for – one that continues, even in the face of discouragement, to work through every negation to the new perspective beyond. But that will not guarantee a secure place to stand either. We must be prepared still to pack up and move on. "Every evil and every good thing is a shadow which we cast," Emerson goes on to say. The shadow, then, ultimately, is ourselves, and we can never hope to walk out of that shadow but must take it with us even as we continue to seek the sun. "In Flaxman's drawing of the Eumenides of Aeschylus," Emerson observes, "Orestes supplicates

Apollo, whilst the Furies sleep on the threshold. The face of the god
expresses a shade of regret and compassion, but is calm with the conviction of the irreconcilableness of the two spheres." In the guise of Apollo
the sun has returned, but with a "shade" that acknowledges the dark
presence of the human. Emerson's description of the drawing renders it
as an emblem of our condition, caught as we are somewhere between the
Eumenides and Apollo. Though the Furies will continue to sleep on our
doorstep, we must not cease to supplicate the god. Emerson will have
nothing to do with the despair that "prejudges the law by a paltry
empiricism." And once again he counsels patience: What else have we to
fall back on?

> Patience and patience, we shall win at the last. We must be very
> suspicious of the deceptions of the element of time. It takes a good
> deal of time to eat or to sleep, or to earn a hundred dollars, and a
> very little time to entertain a hope and an insight which becomes
> the light of our life.[42]

We note that Emerson is somewhat sly here, for though he says we shall
win "at the last," he does not mean that we will have to wait, necessarily,
until the end of time. It may happen in a flash. In the midst of our loss we
may catch sight of a possible gain. That is not a facile optimism but
rather a tentative vote of confidence in the spirit's recuperative powers,
in its ability to leap to a new quantum level of energy. Here is what
Emerson had to say in his journal barely three months after the death of
his beloved boy:

> . . . there ought to be no such thing as Fate. As long as we use this
> word, it is a sign of our impotence & that we are not yet ourselves.
> There is now a sublime revelation in each of us which makes us so
> strangely aware & certain of our riches that although I have never
> since I was born for so much as one moment expressed the truth,
> and although I have never heard the expression of it from any
> other, I know that the whole is here – the wealth of the Universe is
> for me. Every thing is explicable & practicable for me. And yet
> whilst I adore this ineffable life which is at my heart, it will not
> condescend to gossip with me, it will not announce to me any
> particulars of science, it will not enter into the details of my
> biography, & say to me why I have a son & daughters born to me,
> or why my son dies in his sixth year of joy. Herein then I have this
> latent omniscience coexistent with omnignorance. Moreover,
> whilst this Deity glows at the heart, & by his unlimited presenti-
> ments gives me all power, I know that tomorrow will be as this

day, I am a dwarf, & I remain a dwarf. That is to say, I believe in
Fate. As long as I am weak, I shall talk of Fate; whenever the God
fills me with his fulness, I shall see the disappearance of Fate.
  I am *Defeated* all the time; yet to Victory I am born.[43]

This remarkable passage links Emerson's faith in his recuperative
powers to the modalities of speech. If he uses the word "Fate" it will at
once "sign" his impotence and his failure to complete the articulation of
his self in language. "Fate" is in fact the sign that he is spoken for (*fatus*)
by an alien power; it is the word, or decree, of another. The "sublime
revelation" that represents the sublation of the self into its superlative
form is "ineffable"; it has not yet been spoken at all. So long as Emerson
is unable to speak this crucial word and weakly allows himself to substitute "Fate" as an explanation for his condition, he remains an empty
signifier. But when he is filled with the "fulness" of his own self-
divinity, he is granted an extraordinary vision. The evil word is withdrawn, and he sees, we might say, as on a scroll written in the heavens
the magic formula of his renewal: "I am *Defeated* all the time, yet to
Victory I am born." Which is to say, I am perpetually unmade, yet I
cannot fail ultimately to remake myself. This "young god," in Santayana's phrase, was indeed "making experiments in creation," but they
had less to do with the cosmos than with his power to "translate the
world" into the language of his own self-renewal.

Chapter 5

Hawthorne: "The Obscurest Man of Letters in America"

On May 24, 1864, Emerson set down in his journal an account of Hawthorne's funeral, held the previous day in Concord, and reflected at large on the perplexing character of this reticent friend whom he had never really gotten to know. Emerson remembered a fine September day some twenty years earlier, when he and Hawthorne had set out on a long walk, "in excellent spirits," and conversed easily, "for we were both old collectors who had never had opportunity before to show each other our cabinets"; however, his dominant recollection was not one of such genial and free interchange of confidence. Hawthorne's life and death, Emerson opined, were endured in a "painful solitude" that was not easily penetrated, even by a sympathetic friend. Emerson found "unwillingness and caprice" where he looked for "unreserved intercourse," and one odd little detail of the ceremony that he notes – "the corpse was unwillingly shown" – seems intended to serve as an emblem of Hawthorne's unconquerable reserve. The day was "a pomp of sunshine" but Hawthorne remained in the shade – to which, indeed, in a larger sense, the preacher noted, he "had done more justice than any other."[1]

Emerson's inability to read his friend's character clearly may not have been owing simply to Hawthorne's self-concealing nature, however, but rather to the Transcendentalist's impatience with Hawthorne's fiction. For Hawthorne had noted explicitly in the preface to *The Snow-Image, and Other Twice-Told Tales* that the direct confessions of a romancer were not to be trusted: "[T]hese things hide the man instead of displaying him." If you really wish "to detect any of his essential traits," Hawthorne observed, "you must make quite another kind of inquest," the kind Emerson was incapable of; namely, "you must look through the whole range of his fictitious characters, good and evil." Hawthorne's character was in his *characters*, and the one, he insisted, could hardly be read without a reading of the others. Hawthorne had inscribed himself in his books, and he was therefore available only to a kind of semiological analysis, to a close inspection of his fictive signs. He had made himself master of such analysis, for his art was invested in modes of discourse in which the self ciphers and deciphers itself, and he clearly believed that Emerson, for all his insistence that "we are symbols and inhabit symbols," had never perfected these skills. "In truth, the heart of many an ordinary man," Hawthorne writes of Emerson, "had, perchance, inscriptions which he could not read."

This remark, interestingly enough, is to be found in one of those whimsical and capricious introductions in which Hawthorne amused himself by doing a deceptive little dance designed to pass for personal confession. In this case (the introduction to *Mosses from an Old Manse*), Hawthorne was actually, and literally, on Emerson's home territory, an appropriate place for contrasting his own all but nonexistent literary reputation with that of his already illustrious contemporary. "These fitful sketches," as Hawthorne terms them, "so reserved, even while they sometimes seem so frank – often but half in earnest, and never, even when most so, expressing satisfactorily the thoughts which they profess to image," amount to an ambiguous autobiography, and none more so than the exquisitely delicate "The Old Manse," in which Hawthorne deviously inscribes his own heart in the process of attempting to read Emerson's inscriptions. Written, as Hawthorne tells us, in the very place where Emerson wrote *Nature*, the introduction to *Mosses* is in large measure a meditation on Emerson's premises.[2] Hidden in the "transparent obscurity" of his mosses, Hawthorne peeps out at Emerson's "intellectual fire" burning like a "beacon . . . on a hill-top" as at the antipode of his own shady self, for this "great original Thinker," he notes, "had his earthly abode at the opposite extremity of our village." Thus positioned, Hawthorne writes himself into existence by commenting critically on *Nature* – perhaps with the hope, at least partially, that Emerson might come to understand something about his romancer friend by perusing *his* text.[3]

Hawthorne presents himself, at the outset, in the posture of an intellectual lightweight, "a writer of idle stories," who ventures to hope that with the example and spirit of Emerson and his sober ministerial forebears surrounding him in the Manse, wisdom might descend upon him and inspire "profound treatises of morality," or the expression of some "unprejudiced views of religion" or perhaps histories "bright with picture" but weighted with "a depth of philosophic thought." At least he looks forward to achieving "a novel, that should evolve some deep lesson." With such a serious goal in mind, Hawthorne appears willing to turn himself into a kind of Transcendentalist, to subordinate his "animal eye," as Emerson had urged in *Nature*, to the "eye of Reason," so that "grace and expression" might succeed "outline and surface"; nay, more, so that outlines and surfaces might become "transparent" and give way to "causes and spirits." Emerson insisted that "culture inverts the vulgar views of nature, and brings the mind to call that apparent which it uses to call real, and that real which it uses to call visionary."[4] Presumably putting such a theory to the test, Hawthorne observes that the "slumbering" Concord River "has a dream picture in its bosom" of the sky above that amounts to an imaginative transformation of reality. "Which, after all, was the most real," he asks, "the picture, or the original? – the objects palpable to our grosser senses, or their apotheosis in the stream beneath?" Hawthorne's provisional conclusion seems appropriately Emersonian: "Surely the disembodied images stand in closer relation to the soul." However, Hawthorne is not willing to let go of the *palpable* so easily: "But, both the original and the reflection had here an ideal charm." Somehow, the actual world seems real *and* ideal at the same time, and one's epistemological bias, so to speak, might tip in either direction. Reflection *is* a blessing, but a writer of fiction might be excused for reflecting that the figures of the imagination stand in greater need of being *realized* than of being idealized. Are the things of this world nothing more than transcendental toys to be etherealized by a facile moralizing? Another passage about the river puts the Emersonian case to a severer test as Hawthorne exercises the craftiest part of his craft – that subtle and ambiguous manipulation of detail and tone that is his hallmark.

Emerson had argued, of course, that nature is the symbol of spirit and therefore malleable and plastic to the transcendentalizing eye. "The sordor and filths of nature,"[5] he insisted, will dry up and blow away before the renewed sight of the visionary. Hawthorne, however, found the natural environment of the river somewhat of a puzzle as he meditated on the relationship between the actual and the ideal, or the body and the spirit. Focusing on the "fragrant white pond-lily," he wonders over its arising from a natural base that he presents as all but disgusting: "It is a marvel whence this perfect flower derives its loveliness and perfume, springing, as it does, from the black mud over which the river sleeps, and where lurk the slimy eel, and speckled frog, and the mud turtle, whom continual washing cannot cleanse. It is the very same black mud out of which the yellow lily sucks its obscene life and noisome odor." One ought not, he goes on, contract a distaste for the river because of such disturbing contradictions, for there are after all still those lovely reflections in the bosom of the stream in which each natural object, "however unsightly in reality, assumes ideal beauty." Then, too, whatever lurks beneath, the river still reproduces an image of the heavens on its surface. How can one "malign our river as gross and impure, while it can glorify itself with so adequate a picture of the heaven that broods above it; or, if we remember its tawny hue and the muddiness of its bed, let it be a symbol that the earthliest human soul has an infinite spiritual capacity, and may contain the better world within its depths." Let it be a symbol indeed, but will it remain one – a convincing one – with that darker reality lurking beneath? Hawthorne concludes: "But, indeed, the same lesson might be drawn out of any mud puddle in the streets of a city; and, being taught us everywhere, it must be true." So we have not only sermons in streams, but parables in mud puddles. Wasn't it, after all, while walking through snow puddles that Emerson experienced his "perfect exhilaration"? This much had been taught in *Nature*, and Hawthorne *seems* disposed to believe it. But even if we do not go on to notice that the next paragraph begins with an apology for the "somewhat devious track" along which Hawthorne has taken us in this odd nature walk (this odd walk through *Nature*), we may pause to consider his last phrase: "being taught us everywhere, it must be true." Everything turns on the tone. How *does* one read Hawthorne? "The earthliest human soul has an infinite spiritual capacity, and may contain the better world within its depths." It may indeed, or it *may* contain a worse one. What lies within the depths of the Reverend Mr. Hooper or the scientist Aylmer or old Roger Chillingworth? Arthur Dimmesdale seems a saint to some, to many, but to at least one sharp eye he is an arrant hypocrite whose depths contain a "strong animal nature."

Though Emerson's *Nature* works its way up to a full-blown theory of transcendental second-sight, it begins on a different note, with a strong condemnation of reliance on past authority and the mind of "the fathers." Emerson, as we know, turns away from their sepulchers, insisting instead on beholding "God and nature face to face." He seems to reject an historical approach to experience: "Why should we grope among the dry bones of the past, or put the living generation into masquerade out of its faded wardrobe?"[6] In principle, at least, or by way of hypothesis, Hawthorne would once again appear to be in agreement with Emerson, for he describes in his introduction how on gloomy days, when the rain kept him indoors, he passed the time in the dimly lit garret of the Manse rummaging among the dry bones of New England's spiritual past, without, it seems, much profit:

> I burrowed among these venerable books, in search of any living thought, which should burn like a coal of fire, or glow like an inextinguishable gem, beneath the dead trumpery that had long hidden it. But I found no such treasure; all was dead alike; and I could not but muse deeply and wonderingly upon the humiliating fact that the works of man's intellect decay like those of his hands. Thought grows mouldy. What was good and nourishing food for the spirits of one generation, affords no sustenance for the next.

That last sentence amounts almost to a precis of the opening paragraph of *Nature*. But as usual, Hawthorne has not had his last word on the subject; indeed, it might be taken as axiomatic in reading Hawthorne that whenever he offers us a sounding sentence that appears to close off debate in its didactic certainty, he is slyly preparing (or has already prepared) to sow the seeds of *un*certainty. Hawthorne's familiar, and irresistible, compulsion to burrow in that very moldy past that also repels him is all the while digging away at the foundation of his confident assertion. For although, on the one hand, he seems to be echoing both Emerson's thought and language in rejecting the past, on the other, he displays a curious interest in dramatizing, to quite different effect, Emerson's phrase about beholding the oracles of truth "face to face." While the "young visionaries" of the day are engaged, at one end of Concord, in seeking release from the "labyrinth" of their "self-involved bewilderment" by speaking with Emerson "face to face," another sort of confrontation is in progress at the Manse. Hawthorne, we might say, finds himself torn between Emerson's new premises and the older ones contained in the ancestral Emerson house in which he happens to be living. Somehow Hawthorne is led to feel that the "stately edifice," with its "gray, homely aspect," serves to "rebuke the speculative extravagances of the day": "It had grown sacred, in connection with the artificial life against which we inveighed; it had been a home, for many years, in spite of all; it was my home, too: – and, with these thoughts, it seemed to me that all the artifice and conventionalism of life was but an impalpable thinness upon its surface, and that the depth below was none the worse for it." In such a mood, he feels like praying for the protection of "the institutions that had grown out of the heart of mankind," for the artificial constraints and conventional expectations that so enraged Emerson strike Hawthorne as being as insubstantial as the reflections that play over the surface of the Concord River – *merely* a masquerade covering the troubling and durable human concerns below.

Why tilt at the windmills of history, Hawthorne might be saying, when the grain of human experience may still be grinding inside? The romancer, with his sharp eye for perceiving dramatic substance even in the trash and trumpery of time's accumulations, is almost inevitably, if unwillingly, drawn to the past. But the exquisite irony of Hawthorne's situation was that even while agreeing with Emerson's call for a prospective view, he discovered himself domesticated in the very "sepulchres of the fathers" so resoundingly rejected in the opening paragraph of *Nature*. What *was* the Old Manse if not the tomb of the patriarchs? They were once young men themselves, Hawthorne notes, filled with "solemn enthusiasm and . . . saintly dreams." As if archly filling out the drama implicit in the initial sentences of *Nature* and turning Emerson's own words against him, Hawthorne describes how he discovered an old scroll in the Emerson homestead

> which, on inspection, proved to be the forcibly wrought picture of a clergyman, in wig, band, and gown, holding a Bible in his hand. As I turned his face towards the light he eyed me with an air of authority such as men of his profession seldom assume, in our days. The original had been pastor of the parish more than a century ago, a friend of Whitefield, and almost his equal in fervid eloquence. I bowed before the effigy of the dignified divine, and felt as if I had now met face to face with the ghost, by whom, as there was reason to apprehend, the Manse was haunted.

We should pay attention to the careful calculation, and implicit humor, with which Hawthorne has constructed this contrast between his own situation and Emerson's. In his prominent new house, all too easily accessible at the juncture of the Cambridge and Lexington turnpikes, Emerson – at the spiritual vanguard of his times – is engaged, if not in an original relation to the universe, at least in relations with some curious originals, as Hawthorne views them, "hobgoblins of flesh and blood" who have arrived in Concord to ask "this prophet the master word" that might solve "the riddle of the universe." Hawthorne, however, at his end of town, immured in a kind of spiritual backwater, presents himself face to face with a pictorial ghost whose "air of authority" suggests a very different kind of inquisition. This "dignified divine," as we might surmise, was the author of a great many theological dissertations and wanders restlessly through the corridors of the Manse not for his sins but for his sermons, still lacking the substantiality of print and therefore a perpetual trial to their equally insubstantial author. "Not improbably," Hawthorne infers, "he wished me to edit and publish a selection from a chest full of manuscript discourses that stood in the garret." But Hawthorne has no intention of putting his own literary reputation in the faded wardrobe of this defunct Puritan father. What Hawthorne wants from this patriarchal poltergeist is the answer to a question about literary *authority* in general, for he nourishes a "superstitious reverence for literature of all kinds"and needs to know why the works of these "mighty Puritan divines," impressively bound in "black leather" and seeming to be "books of enchantment," "earnestly written" and once warm with spiritual meaning, had now "cooled down even to the freezing point."

Emerson seemed content simply to wave these productions aside, but Hawthorne was intrigued. What gives an author continuing authority? To say that old books are dead to us only because they *are* old is surely a superficial and even dangerous proposition, for do we not thereby prepare for and predict our own oblivion? Hawthorne himself refused to accept the notion that the writing of the past was, ipso facto, corpse-cold. Perhaps the problem with the Puritan divines was that their writings lacked reality even in their own day because they failed to tap and embody the human energy and interest of their age. It was not the Puritan world and its religion per se that were dead, but rather accounts of them that hovered insubstantially over the compelling realities that underlay them, presenting the *ideas* of the time and not the living essence. Hawthorne notes that what retained sap was not the pamphlets and books filled with theological and philosophical abstractions, and therefore supposed to be of lasting significance, but rather

> what had been written for the passing day and year without the remotest pretension or idea of permanence. There were a few old newspapers, and still older almanacs, which reproduced, to my mental eye, the epochs when they had issued from the press, with a distinctness that was altogether unaccountable. It was as if I had found bits of magic looking-glass among the books, with the images of a vanished century in them.

Hawthorne appears to have moved closer to grasping the key to his puzzle in focusing on the *images* of the past as opposed merely to ideas. Really to look through the eyes of the foregoing generations, rather than through their brains, to see what they saw, rather than what they reflected, would provide a true window on their world. Hawthorne wants a pellucid observer, not a profound thinker, and accordingly he confronts anew this seemingly impressive old effigy on canvas with only a rhetorical question on his lips, since that mute ghost, with its abstract and decaying authority, can hardly be expected to respond appropriately:

> I turned my eyes towards the tattered picture, above mentioned, and asked of the austere divine, wherefore it was that he and his brethren, after the most painful rummaging and groping into their minds, had been able to produce nothing half so real, as these newspaper scribblers and almanac makers had thrown off, in the effervescence of a moment. The portrait responded not; so I sought an answer for myself. It is the Age itself that writes newspapers and almanacs, which, therefore, have a distinct purpose and meaning at the time, and a kind of intelligible truth for all times; whereas most other works – being written by men who, in the very act, set themselves apart from their age – are likely to possess little significance when new, and none at all, when old. Genius, indeed, melts many ages into one, and thus effects something permanent, yet still

with a similarity of office to that of the more ephemeral writer. A work of genius is but the newspaper of a century, or perchance of a hundred centuries.

Making due allowance, as always, for the element of calculated whimsy in Hawthorne's theory, we may nonetheless observe him working toward a serious point. Newspapers and almanacs amount to the spontaneous and unselfconscious chronicles of their age, providing the raw data – information, sensation, sentiment, human interest and concern – that are perennially engaging to readers. Moreover, they are virtually anonymous, suggesting an ideal of self-effacing authorship – authorship without authority – that had a strong appeal for Hawthorne. He would have agreed with Flaubert that "an author in his book must be like God in the universe, present everywhere and visible nowhere."[7] Hawthorne was Romantic in his interests and in the peculiar form he chose for his major works of fiction, not in any desire to wear his heart upon his sleeve. "I want to write the moral history of the men of my generation – or, more accurately, the history of their *feelings*,"[8] Flaubert noted in the year of Hawthorne's death: "their" feelings, not his own – and Hawthorne's goal was similar. Commenting on Turgenev's preference for lingering among the shadows of human experience, James observes that "dusky subjects" may be treated quite "innocently" by an artist, and his example is Hawthorne: "innocently, because with that delightfully unconscious genius it [the taste for the somber] remained imaginative, sportive, inconclusive, to the end."[9]

Hawthorne offers us no opinions or conclusions of his own. Undoubtedly he has them, but he does not choose to share them precisely because such an act would shift attention from his subject to himself. He carries on his researches, as he terms them, in the "dusky region" of psychological romance in the hope of illuminating "our common nature," not his own. Thus he insists in his introduction to *Mosses* that he tells almost nothing that is "tinctured with any quality that makes it exclusively my own! . . . I have appealed to no sentiment or sensibilities save such as are diffused among us all. So far as I am a man of really individual attributes, I veil my face." The gently ironic voice that speaks with subtly shifting tones in virtually all of Hawthorne's writing is calculatedly inconclusive; it is not a personal voice but a set of perspectives. It lacks authority because its conclusions are intended to be provisional, nothing more than points of view set to words. Hawthorne (or at least the Hawthorne voice that speaks in the Preface to *Twice-Told Tales*) professes or pretends to be amused by the attempts of his readers to fashion a Romantic personality for him "on the internal evidence of his sketches," to imagine him "as a mild, shy, gentle, melancholic, exceedingly sensitive, and not very forcible man"; and he further admits that he has not been above playing to that expectation: "He is by no means certain," he opines, "that some of his subsequent productions have not been influenced and modified by a natural desire to fill up so amiable an outline, and to act in accordance with the character assigned to him; nor, even now, could he forfeit it without a few tears of tender sensibility." His character indeed can only be *assigned*, for it exists only in a reading of the signs or characters in his books. And Hawthorne himself, shedding his crocodile tears along with his putative identity as a man of feeling, ducks back nimbly into the shadows where Emerson found him and left him.

As a writer of fiction, Hawthorne refused to set himself apart from his age, or to stand out *in* his age, either by exhibiting a strong extraliterary personality or by consenting to be associated with a particular set of opinions. He was content to be the connoisseur of its moods – psychological, moral, historical – and to leave to others the task of articulating the age's ideas. (Hawthorne puckishly observes in "The Old Manse" that if he *had* been disposed "to adopt a pet idea, as so many people do, and fondle it in my embraces to the exclusion of all others, it would be that the great want which mankind labors under, at this present period, is sleep! The world should recline its vast head on the first convenient pillow, and take an age-long nap. It has gone distracted, through a morbid activity, and, while preternaturally wide-awake, is nevertheless tormented by visions, that seem real to it now, but would assume their true aspect and character, were all things once set right by an interval of sound repose." Since Hawthorne goes on directly to speak sarcastically of the harebrained "young visionaries" and "gray-headed theorists" who were flocking feverishly to Emerson's beacon-fire, it seems clear that he is offering the slumber-inducing atmosphere of the Manse as a kind of blissfully mindless antidote to the relentlessly un-blinking transparent eyeball. In *Nature*, after all, Emerson had recom-mended that that "little drudge," the ant, be taken as a symbol and "monitor" to man because of the "sublime" fact "that it never sleeps."[10])

Hawthorne took a dim view of works, whether by Puritan theo-logians or by their nineteenth-century avatars, explicitly designed to solve "the riddle of the universe" because, in passing over the pressing human concerns of their time in order to reach for a spurious profundity, he believed them likely to prove stillborn. The problem with the "aus-tere divine" of the Old Manse and his brethren was precisely their "pain-ful rummaging and groping into their own minds" – or, to cite Emer-son's phrase from *Nature*, their descent into the "splendid labyrinth" of their perceptions. Hawthorne preferred to have them cast their learned eyes objectively on the *mortalia* of the larger world in which they lived.

He was interested in writing that speaks from and to its age in language that can be understood by all. Profundity, as such, was not a quality he appeared to value, though he might himself, as Melville noted, be as "deep as Dante" while offering himself as a supplement to Goody Two-Shoes. Hawthorne would undoubtedly have assented to Wittgenstein's observation that "all the facts that concern us lie open before us," and "ordinary language is all right."[11] The sketches in *Twice-Told Tales*, Hawthorne tells us,

> are not, it is hardly necessary to say, profound; but it is rather more remarkable that they so seldom, if ever, show any design on the writer's part to make them so. They have none of the abstruseness of idea, or obscurity of expression, which mark the written communications of a solitary mind with itself. They never need translation. It is, in fact, the style of a man of society. Every sentence, so far as it embodies thought or sensibility, may be understood and felt by anybody, who will give himself the trouble to read it, and will take up the book in a proper mood.

Although Hawthorne's suggestion here that his tales might be characterized as easy reading is, as usual, more than slightly deceptive, his fundamental premise is fair enough. His gift, as he understood it, lay in the clarity with which the surfaces of experience are perceived and the depths merely adumbrated, as well as in the limpidity of the expression. He is a master of description, not explanation, and in his best work the world and its inhabitants are allowed to make their own case for themselves.

Hawthorne's quarrel with Emerson, such as it was, lay in the philosopher's dogged search, as he said on the opening page of *Nature*, for a "true theory" that would "explain all phenomena." Undoubtedly, Emerson had insisted, "we have no questions to ask which are unanswerable." But Hawthorne professed himself no longer interested in such an interrogation. "For myself," he observes in the introduction to *Mosses*, "there had been epochs of my life, when I, too, might have asked of this prophet the master word that should solve me the riddle of the universe; but now, being happy, I felt as if there were no question to be put, and therefore admired Emerson as a poet of deep beauty and austere tenderness, but sought nothing from him as a philosopher." Hawthorne must have found himself somewhat perplexed by, or at least of two minds about, the thrust of Emerson's first book, since that restless search for a true theory and ultimate explanation which so repelled Hawthorne could seem to coexist with another, more congenial, view of experience. "Every man's condition," Emerson writes, "is a solution in hieroglyphic to those inquiries he would put. He acts it as life, before he apprehends it as truth."[12] If that *was* Emerson's premise, Hawthorne would have been happy to share it but not to go beyond it, since his deepest impulse as an observer and writer was to allow his eye to linger on the hieroglyphics through which each individual being acts out its meanings. The *condition* of men and women – the forms and gestures of the body, movements, expressions, nervous tics, choices of clothing, habits of posture and speech, outbursts, cadences, and silences – these are the signs of the self that Hawthorne never tired of recording.

One of the sketches in *Mosses*, "The Old Apple Dealer," seems little more than an exercise in patient observation and argues, as Melville noted, "a boundless sympathy with all forms of being" in Hawthorne. This apparently nondescript old man, "this almost hueless object," as the author himself puts it, becomes "a naturalized citizen of [Hawthorne's] inner world" by means of a scrutiny so self-effacing that, quite literally, in Wallace Stevens's words, it "beholds / Nothing that is not there and the nothing that is."[13] Hawthorne allows himself to have a mind of old age in order to enter this colorless figure without preconception or cliché. He begins with physical description – "a small man, with gray hair and gray stubble beard . . . invariably clad in a shabby surtout of snuff color, closely buttoned, and half concealing a pair of gray pantaloons" – that amounts to a study in gray and snuff, the emblems of a characterless antiquity. The old man's face ("thin, withered, fur-rowed") has "features which even age has failed to render impressive" and, coupled with his aspect ("patient, long-suffering, quiet, hopeless, shivering"), suggests not a clichéd desperation, but a starker and more terrible emptiness. "He is not desperate, – that, though its etymology implies no more, would be too positive an expression, – but merely devoid of hope." Hawthorne's insistent negatives move this implicit definition of old age in the direction of Dante's Inferno. The ultimate horror is that the poverty, perpetual coldness, and discomfort of this hopeless gerontion have become "a matter of course: he thinks it the definition of existence," though we may think it the definition of nonex-istence. Hawthorne does not allow us to content ourselves with comfort-able chestnuts about the dignity and venerability of senior citizens. "Time has not thrown dignity, as a mantle, over the old man's figure; there is nothing venerable about him." His last years are not peaceful: "A slight observer would speak of the old man's quietude; but, on a closer scrutiny, you discover that there is a continual unrest within him, which somewhat resembles the fluttering action of the nerves in a corpse from which life has recently departed." These are the motions only of life anticipating death – life in the grip of death. When the old man sighs, it seems to be "gentle," but our pitiless observer notes that "this sigh, so faint as to be hardly perceptible, and not expressive of any definite emotion, is the accompaniment and conclusion of all his actions. It is the symbol of the chillness and torpid melancholy of his old age, which only make themselves felt sensibly, when his repose is slightly disturbed."

Hawthorne's aim – to *embody* a body that is all but empty, to present the hieroglyphics of a being whose inscriptions are rapidly fading – requires not only patient observation but the ability to introject dissolution and to find a way of speaking credibly of its pale negations. Thus the exquisite subtlety of his own mode of describing his method: "To confess the truth, it is not the easiest matter in the world to define and individualize a character like this which we are now handling. The portrait must be so generally negative that the most delicate pencil is likely to spoil it by introducing some too positive tint. Every touch must be kept down, or else you destroy the subdued tone which is absolutely essential to the whole effect." Hawthorne does not speak *about* old age, he speaks *in* its tones, allowing its utter grayness to tint all his pages. Though Hawthorne does seem to make a gesture, in his final paragraph, toward what we might call not only a "theory" of old age but an Emersonian one (he says, "[T]here is a spiritual essence in this gray and lean old shape that shall flit upward too"), it amounts not just to a deception but to the last twist of the knife. "Yes," he continues and concludes, "doubtless there is a region where the life-long shiver will pass away from his being, and that quiet sigh, which it has taken him so many years to breathe, will be brought to a close for good and all." Where *is* that region? we are undoubtedly intended to ask, and Poe might supply the answer. Hawthorne has stuck with old age right to the end, doing "more justice than any other," as James Freeman Clarke said, "to the shades of life."[14]

It is not a performance that Emerson could have been expected to appreciate, insisting as he does, in *Nature*, that "every natural fact is a symbol of some spiritual fact," for Hawthorne has managed to pursue his natural fact so doggedly that it seems to negate the spiritual promise. His reality is so unsightly that it fails to assume "ideal beauty." Perhaps the reason why Emerson, as Hawthorne viewed him, was incapable of reading those inscriptions in "the heart of many an ordinary man" was that they were not sufficiently transcendental. "My destiny is linked with the realities of earth," says Hawthorne's Virtuoso on the last page of *Mosses*. "You are welcome to your visions and shadows of a future state, but give me what I can see, and touch, and understand, and I ask no more." The author's narrator pretends to be horrified by this stark expression of what, after all, is a fair statement of Hawthorne's own position vis-à-vis Emerson, and extends only a tentative hand to receive the Virtuoso's icy shake, for he does not feel, he tells us, "a single heart-throb of human brotherhood." But Hawthorne knew better. He knew, along with Melville, that "genius, all over the world, stands hand in hand, and one shock of recognition runs the whole circle round," though some speak predominantly from the sunshine and others from the shade.

2

Along with other readers of his time, Hawthorne would have had no trouble identifying Emerson as a secular prophet engaged in translating the traditional language of religious apocalypse into that of immediate epistemological reality. The call in the opening paragraph of *Nature* for a confrontation with "God and nature face to face" implied the possibility of unmediated vision, and that exciting prospect was most appropriately embodied in a figural language everywhere stressing *transparency*. Emerson hoped to "behold unveiled the nature of Justice and Truth," as well as the nature of Nature. *Perfect sight* was his principal goal. Like Christ, as he described him in the Divinity School Address, Emerson intended to see "with open eye the mystery of the soul," and he urged the young ministers to "dare to love God without mediator or veil." The Christian promise of ultimate revelation was to be realized now, both in spiritual affairs and in the affairs of the heart. "Revelation is the disclosure of the soul," Emerson teaches, "and by the same fire, vital, consecrating, celestial, which burns until it shall dissolve all things into the waves and surges of an ocean of light, we see and know each other, and what spirit each is of." Emerson would have us all speak "from within the veil, where the word is one with that it tells of," cast aside our trappings and deal "man to man in naked truth, plain confession, and omniscient affirmation."[15]

By the time he published his second series of *Essays* in 1844, however, Emerson had been to school in experience and had learned that threats to perception, the inescapable subjectivity of knowledge, and fear of exposure threatened to shatter the integrity of the transparent eyeball and impede the search for union with all being. The most effective response Emerson could muster turned out to be the wry humor of his mature style:

> Every body we know surrounds himself with a fine house, fine books, conservatory, gardens, equipage and all manner of toys, as screens to interpose between himself and his guest. Does it not seem as if man was of a very sly, elusive nature, and dreaded nothing so much as a full rencontre front to front with his fellow?

It would be unmerciful, he now argues, "quite to abolish the use of these screens, which are of eminent convenience," for "if, perchance, a searching realist comes to our gate, before whose eye we have no care to stand, then again we run to our curtain, and hide ourselves as Adam at the voice of the Lord God in the garden."[16]

The impulse to self-concealment, then, is universal, the mark of our fallen state, and hardly to be dissipated even by Emerson's eloquent exhortations to apocalyptic openness. Is "naked truth" possible for such guilt-ridden creatures as the sons and daughters of Adam? We are indeed symbols, living in symbols, speaking in symbols, but do we dare interpret them? Are they adequate to our expression, and can they be read with clarity? Perhaps the Reverend Mr. Frost, that spectral minister so mercilessly pilloried in the Divinity School Address, longed to speak himself into real being but lacked a vocabulary equal to the task of converting his life into truth. Perhaps he simply feared to "deal out to the people his life." He may well have wondered if that sort of preaching could succeed in forwarding the work of redemption. By 1850 Mr. Frost would have learned in *The Scarlet Letter*, if he needed to be taught, that some men "are kept silent by the very constitution of their nature." And ministers, in particular, "guilty as they may be, retaining, nevertheless, a zeal for God's glory and man's welfare," may "shrink from displaying themselves black and filthy in the view of men . . . because, thenceforward, no good can be achieved by them; no evil of the past be redeemed by better service."[17] That, at least, is the opinion of the Reverend Mr. Arthur Dimmesdale. Are his words merely a screen?

Nathaniel Hawthorne was by nature a reticent man, and the language of veils and screens is his most familiar idiom. His instinct, as we have seen in the preface to *Mosses*, is to veil his face. Yet he observes in "The Custom-House" that despite his disinclination to speak of himself and his affairs, he was nevertheless sometimes seized with "an autobiographical impulse." There are writers, he notes, who "indulge themselves in such confidential depths of revelation as could fittingly be addressed, only and exclusively, to the one heart and mind of perfect sympathy" in a laudable desire to complete the circle of their existence by communing with others. Hawthorne, apparently so solitary a man by nature or choice, was born on the Fourth of July and understood that the need to declare one's independence could coexist with – indeed, be the necessary prelude to – a more perfect union. "As thoughts are frozen and utterance benumbed," he continues, "unless the speaker stand in some true relation with his audience – it may be pardonable to imagine that a friend, a kind and apprehensive, though not the closest friend, is listening to our talk." In that case we may speak freely, "but still keep the inmost Me behind its veil." This instinctive determination to offer his cake and have it too, as F. O. Matthiessen remarks in another context, is "as American as the strip-tease, of which it forms the spiritual counterpart."[18]

But there *is* justification for Hawthorne's procedure. As we have seen, his reticence about putting himself forward has something to do with Hawthorne's desire to maintain the purity of his stance as an objective observer. The "I" of the prefaces, like the narrative voice of his sketches and stories, represents a mode of positioning himself in relation to his material, and that mode would be compromised by true confession. But how, in any case, can Hawthorne be expected to speak without a veil? His voice itself is the garment that simultaneously conceals and reveals, as his symbols and emblems typically are placed on the surface of the body in order to mediate between inside and outside. They may be obstructive or expressive or both together, for they are at once hard material facts and mere concretions in discourse. They stand for meanings but are not those meanings. They function both to invite interpretation and to thwart it. "We must interpret, we must find meanings in things," writes Jung, "otherwise we would be quite unable to think about them."[19] But our need to find meaning and our way of thinking about things do not guarantee accuracy or truth to experience. They may be merely modes of exploration, exposing only the contours of the epistemological process. Hawthorne knew himself, as a writer, possessed of a medium capable of producing no more than ambiguous or imperfect revelations. "I have felt a thousand times," he wrote Sophia Peabody in 1840, "that words may be a thick and darksome veil of mystery between the soul and the truth which it seeks."[20]

Thus Hawthorne's persistent smile, in his prefaces, at the imputation of egotism to him "in virtue of a little preliminary talk about his external habits, his abode, his casual associates, and other matters entirely upon the surface."[21] His language is indeed *preliminary* in that it stands only upon the doorstep of his inner sanctum, as all language necessarily does. His symbols, too, stand in the same place, tipping alternately toward the real and the ideal as we, by turns, fix on their substance or attempt to strike through them. Hawthorne's words, like "the glimmering shadows that lay half asleep between the door [of the Manse] and the public highway," are "a kind of spiritual medium, seen through which" his edifice has "not quite the aspect of belonging to the material world." They both idealize the real and realize the ideal, and thus exist in "a neutral territory . . . where the Actual and the Imaginary may meet, and each imbue itself with the nature of the other." Hawthorne, in fact, likes this spot, in its oxymoronic "near retirement and accessible seclusion," since it allows him to maintain his privacy and a vital link to his inner life while continuing to sustain a tentative intercourse with the world. His prefaces and introductions, Hawthorne observes, are designed "to pave the reader's way into the interior edifice of a book,"[22] but they may lead the unwary astray. As Melville noted in a letter to his friend, "this man

of Mosses . . . takes great delight in hoodwinking the world"; even
when we arrive at the inner chamber with its "rich hangings" and
comfortable appointments, we find "in one corner . . . a dark little
black-letter volume in gold clasps, entitled 'Hawthorne: A Problem.' "[23]
Here is Hawthorne's own formulation:

> A cloudy veil stretches over the abyss of my nature. I have, how-
> ever, no love of secrecy and darkness. I am glad to think that God
> sees through my heart, and, if any angel has power to penetrate
> into it, he is welcome to know everything that is there. Yes, and so
> may any mortal who is capable of full sympathy, and therefore
> worthy to come into my depths. But he must find his own way
> there. I can neither guide nor enlighten him. It is this involuntary
> reserve, I suppose, that has given the objectivity to my writings;
> and when people think that I am pouring myself out in a tale or
> essay, I am merely telling what is common to human nature, not
> what is peculiar to myself. I sympathize with them, not they with
> me.[24]

Hawthorne's "problem," then, what Arthur Dimmesdale calls "the
dark problem of this life," concerns the possibility or desirability of self-
exposure. Hawthorne's shifting point of view neatly balances apocalypse
against antiapocalypse, revelation against velation, in his most powerful
early treatment of this question, "The Minister's Black Veil," published
in the year of Emerson's *Nature*, 1836. With a marvelous economy of
means, Hawthorne dramatizes the very issue of unmediated vision abstracted by Emerson from the Pauline promise in I Corinthians but
complicates its purely secular and humanistic import by providing a
theological frame of reference.[25] We are dealing not simply with a human
"screen" but with a veil on the face of a minister. Though the religious
question may be a mere obfuscation, a trick to throw us off the human
scent, it is what presents itself most immediately. Hawthorne's tale, as its
subtitle indicates, is "a parable." We are, accordingly, placed back in the
world of the gospels, where the America of Hawthorne's historical time
still felt itself largely to be. Such a setting does not simply suggest a Bible
text or texts; it enforces the notion that the veil is literally a text interposed between the minister and his parishioners, in two senses at once.
Hawthorne's full title, "The Minister's Black Veil: A Parable," suggests,
with rich ambiguity, that the veil is *itself* a parable, carrying its own
religious lesson.

The tale it tells most directly is that of postponed apocalypse. "There
is an hour to come," Mr. Hooper informs his fiancée, "when all of us
shall cast aside our veils. Take it not amiss, beloved friend, if I wear this

piece of crape till then."[26] The veil thus preaches the necessity of velation. "For now," says Paul, "we see through a glass, darkly; but then face to face." Hawthorne, however, might well have expected his readers to set this text from I Corinthians against another one from II Corinthians even more powerful in its historical implications for God's chosen New Englanders newly gathered in Zion:

> Seeing that we have such hope, we use great plainness of speech, and not as Moses, which put a veil over his face, that the children of Israel could not stedfastly look to the end of that which is abolished: but their minds were blinded: for until this day remaineth the same veil untaken away in the reading of the old testament; which veil is done away in Christ. But even unto this day, when Moses is read, the veil is upon their heart. Nevertheless when it shall turn to the Lord, the veil shall be taken away.

The Reverend Mr. Hooper manifestly does not "use great plainness of speech," not in the eyes of his fiancée: " 'Your words are a mystery too,' returned the young lady. 'Take away the veil from them, at least.' " Allowing Elizabeth implicitly to equate the veiled words of the minister with the veil of Moses, Hawthorne presents him as a parable of nonconversion, of the Christian who has not truly accepted Christ. The veil, in Hooper's own terminology, is a "type" whose antitype, or fulfillment, as Paul figures it, is the inability to read the Old Testament *as* an old testament, to read it, that is, typologically as a foreshadowing of the new gospel in Christ. Mr. Hooper's assumption of the veil, then, is all but explicitly retrogressive in Christian terms. Here is how Hawthorne presents the minister:

> Mr. Hooper . . . ascended the stairs, and showed himself in the pulpit, face to face with his congregation, except for the black veil. That mysterious emblem was never once withdrawn. It shook with his measured breath as he gave out the psalm; it threw its obscurity between him and the holy page, as he read the Scriptures; and while he prayed, the veil lay heavily on his uplifted countenance. Did he seek to hide it from the dread Being whom he was addressing?

Since the minister prays with his veil on, he has *not*, in Paul's terms, turned to the Lord, and Hawthorne's quiet irony couples this nonconverted state with Hooper's postlapsarian terror of being exposed. Since he shows himself in the pulpit only with a veil, he does *not* show himself; since he is "face to face with his congregation, except for the black veil," he is *not* face to face. Hooper reads his Bible *obscurely*, in the darkness of an unregenerate soul. His veil is a somber old testament interposed between his parishioners and himself. He does not bring the new dispensation of love and mystic union.

Hawthorne's own subtle manipulations of tone and meaning are significant. Preaching the election sermon "once, during Governor Belcher's administration" (and *once* would seem to have been enough for the pious but optimistic Jonathan Belcher), Hooper "wrought so deep an impression, that the legislative measures of that year were characterized by all the gloom and piety of our earliest ancestral sway." *Gloom* would not appear to be Hawthorne's most commendatory characterization of the seventeenth-century Puritans' religious intensity. More telling is Hawthorne's description of Hooper's interview with his "plighted wife." Elizabeth is "unappalled by the awe with which the black veil had impressed all beside herself," perhaps because she has the confidence of a true faith. Hawthorne pointedly allows her exhortation to Hooper to sound the traditional double-entendre of Christian homiletics: "Come, good sir, let the sun shine from behind the cloud." But Hooper's veil does not permit the triumphant light of Christ to irradiate his face or comfort others. Rather, it shades "him from the sunshine of eternity." The minister's veil appears to be an emblem of benightedness, and thus the act of assuming it cannot represent an *imitatio Christi*, since Christ is the son/sun who came to remove the veil. If Hooper had been granted the privilege to read Preparatory Meditation I.4 by his fellow New England minister the Reverend Mr. Edward Taylor, he might have been enlightened on this point:

> Shall not thy golden gleams run through this gloom?
> Shall my black Velvet mask thy fair face Vaile?
> Pass o'er my faults; shine forth, bright sun: arise
> Enthrone thy Rosy-selfe within my Eyes.

Hawthorne does indeed suggest that the veil had the "one desirable effect, of making its wearer a very efficient clergyman" in the work of saving souls from sin, but his own calculated ambiguity undercuts even this hint of grace: "His converts always regarded him with a dread peculiar to themselves, affirming, though but figuratively, that, before he brought them to celestial light, they had been with him behind the black veil." It is perfectly impossible to determine whether that *figuratively* applies to their being behind the veil, to being brought to "celestial light," or to both. Ultimately, Hooper is characterized as a "dark old man" by the "young and zealous divine" who officiates at his deathbed – characterized, that is, as a minister of antirevelation, whose soul is as black as his piece of crape. Borne to his grave a veiled corpse, Hooper molders under that same obstruction to vision, implying perhaps that his eyes are not to be blessed with their promised reward. Even his tombstone is "moss-grown," an emblem, it may be, of the obscurity of his spiritual mission. Hawthorne, to be sure, inspissates the mystery by employing language taut with ambiguity and unresolved innuendo. The words of this "mossy" writer are also veiled. How can he after all pretend to pronounce on whether or not an individual soul impedes or furthers redemption, or is itself saved or damned? The possibility or impossibility of revelation is his subject, not his conviction, and he simply presents the case that he sees.

Of course, what Hawthorne sees and shows is not merely a religious parable. Hooper is presented, by his own confession, as a frightened and lonely man whose decision to assume the veil effectively confirms and ensures his inability to overcome these infirmities. The veil announces how he feels; it is an emblem of his terror and his solitude, and he understandably "never willingly passed before a mirror, nor stooped to drink at a still fountain, lest, in its peaceful bosom, he should be affrighted by himself." Hooper's bosom, in contrast, is not peaceful, and it would seem to be a measure of the extremity of his terror that even a shrouded view of himself is so fearful. It is not the veil that affrights him but the impossibility of concealing himself adequately from his own tortured sight. Such a reading of Hooper's condition is reinforced by the village physician, in conversation with his wife, who affirms that men sometimes *are* afraid to be alone with themselves. The townspeople gossip about the veil in terms of the "mystery concealed *behind* it" as if that mystery were somehow separable from the minister's existential condition. What is behind the veil, however, is *Hooper*.

Edgar Allan Poe, trying to be clever but not being quite clever enough, suggested that the "exquisite skill" of the tale would be caviar to the general because they would fail to perceive "the *true* import of the narrative . . . that a crime of dark dye (having reference to the 'young lady') has been committed."[27] That is only one of the easier traps Hawthorne has set for the reader's imagination, for although Poe's reading is not necessarily wrong, it is surely inadequate and might well have provoked Hawthorne's smile from beneath his own veil. If the minister were, indeed, punishing himself so rigorously and unremittingly for the crime of fornication (or did Poe characteristically think of murder rather than sex?), it would be hard to understand why that odd little smile so frequently plays about Hooper's mouth. What he did, if he did it, is scarcely funny, and his fearful act of contrition, if that is what it is, does not suggest that he takes it so. Hooper, in fact, flashes his dotty smirk three times during the visit in which Elizabeth tries to wrest his secret from him – once after she, in manifest embarrassment, wonders whether it is "secret sin" and not "innocent sorrow" that is plaguing her betrothed. Does his grin suggest that, in the perpetual privacy in which he has involved himself, he is all the while saying, "Elizabeth, if only you knew!" Perhaps she, too, would smile if she did know, but he will not share the joke.[28]

Hooper, after all, has taken the veil and made a "vow" – concepts that hint at his having turned himself into a kind of Puritan nun ("a simple black veil, such as any woman might wear on her bonnet," notes the physician's wife). Is the veil an emblem of his having unmanned himself? How has he done so? Has he been immodest? Has he polluted himself? Why would he feel obliged to symbolize such things? But, of course, the veil is not only a symbol but also an article of apparel that covers part of Hooper's body. Is he attempting to say, with Adam, "I was afraid, because I was naked"? He cannot bear to look his sweetheart in the face and offers her a marriage in which the veil will always lie between them as an obstruction to the union of their flesh. Does she understand, in that "one long, shuddering gaze, that seemed almost to penetrate the mystery of the black veil," that Hooper is offering a marriage without consummation, a marriage in which he will never uncover his nakedness? Hooper *is* behind the veil, and he evidently intends to remain there, *virgo intacta*. "Mr. Hooper smiled to think that only a material emblem had separated him from happiness, though the horrors which it shadowed forth, must be drawn darkly between the fondest of lovers." Of course, it is not simply a material *emblem* but a material *fact* that separates him from happiness – his inability, perhaps, to accept the realities of sexual love. Are those the "horrors" shadowed forth by the veil, in a kind of fearful typology of defloration, that "must be drawn darkly between the fondest of lovers"?

"The darkness which conventionally covers this passion is one of the saddest consequences of Adam's fall," notes Santayana in a passage that sounds as if it might have come from the hand of Hawthorne:

> It was a terrible misfortune in man's development that he should
> not have been able to acquire the higher functions without deranging the lower. Why should the depths of his being be thus polluted
> and the most delightful of nature's mysteries be an occasion not for
> communion with her, as it should have remained, but for depravity
> and sorrow?[29]

Though Santayana's speaking here of "man's development" may be only a gesture of courtesy, it is not amiss in the context of this discussion, since it is typically Hawthorne's men, not his women, who are presented as being so agonized over the question of sexuality. It is Arthur Dimmesdale who shrinks from displaying himself, as he says, "black and filthy in the view of men," as a result of his liaison with Hester Prynne; but she, despite her suffering and ostracism, is still willing to assert that what she and Arthur did without benefit of sacrament "had a consecration of its own." Though it may not be that Mr. Hooper's tortured fantasy of sin or sorrow – "so dark a fantasy," in Elizabeth's eyes – is in fact sexual in its etiology, the effect of his assuming the veil is to render impossible the marriage that he seems at once to long for and to reject.[30] The minister's black veil, as the physician's wife observes, "makes him ghost-like from head to foot," and that finally may express Hooper's desire, conscious or not – to spiritualize himself in punishment for or in flight from his animal body. He renders himself insubstantial, the merest shadow of an idea, a walking abstraction – a "type," an "emblem," a "symbol" – where once stood a man.

Had Hooper lived in the time of Emerson and become one of those unchurched seekers whom Hawthorne describes in the Preface to *Mosses* as "hobgoblins of flesh and blood" lost in their "self-involved bewilderment," "theorists" imprisoned in an "iron framework" of ideas, he, too, might have darkened the clear morning light of the master's new revelation with his "dusky wings." By 1846, when he published *Mosses*, Hawthorne no longer felt disposed to be overly sympathetic with the fears and abstract croakings of these "night birds" because he had married Sophia in 1842 and was, as he said, "happy." He understood their problem, however – knew them simply to be lost in the dark coils of their own fantasy and thus cut off from redemptive human contact. As he had written to Sophia: "Indeed, we are but shadows; we are not endowed with real life, all that seems most real about us is but the thinnest substance of a dream, – till the heart be touched. That touch creates us, – then we begin to be – thereby we are beings of reality and inheritors of eternity."[31] The apocalypse of the heart, then, was the true revelation. As Melville's Pierre would exclaim in just a few years: "The heart! the heart! 'tis God's anointed!"[32]

Now Hawthorne certainly believed that, though one ought not underestimate his continuing sense of the problematic nature of human relations – the difficulty of mutual exposure and of accepting one's own physical body and the bodies of others as the actual condition of human love. It is surely a matter of some significance, or at least of great interest, that only about six months after his marriage Hawthorne published his darkest meditation on male–female relations. "The Birth-mark," which could have been entitled "The Scarlet Hand," looks forward directly to his greatest work in that it, too, focuses the attention of the community – Hawthorne's community of readers – on the material realities of the female body and the state of being female. One must be especially careful, in reading this compelling but carefully controlled and calculated fable, not to push off too quickly into that region of high-minded abstraction that Hawthorne himself gives much evidence of distrusting. "It is not difficult, in fact," notes a Hawthorne scholar highly regarded in his lifetime, "to read 'The Birthmark' as an allegory of mankind's desperate striving for perfection" – not difficult, though highly misleading, unless we underline "desperate." That was not, however, Arlin Turner's intent: he claims that in "The Birth-mark" Hawthorne "applauded Aylmer's noble pursuit of perfection, in contrast to Aminadab's ready acceptance of earthiness. . . ."[33]

As we have seen, it was not normally Hawthorne's practice to "applaud" – indeed, to be present at all – in his fictions. He is an observer. What catches his eye is the image of a woman – described as "beautiful" – whose left cheek is marked (her husband, but not the narrator, would say *marred*) by a crimson figure in the shape of a human hand, "though of the smallest pigmy size." Georgiana's husband Aylmer, a scientist whose work, we are told, rivaled "the love of woman, in its depth and absorbing energy," reveals himself "very soon after their marriage" to be deeply disturbed by this mark. He then suggests the possibility of having it removed. Georgiana, blushing deeply (and thus, as we soon learn, effectively if temporarily removing the mark), is surprised. "To tell you the truth, it has been so often called a charm, that I was simple enough to imagine it might be so." It might be, but not to Aylmer, who finds his wife "nearly perfect" and longs to complete the job. This mark that, he says, "we hesitate whether to term a defect or a beauty" shocks him "as being the visible mark of earthly imperfection." Georgiana is "deeply hurt" to hear this from her husband and after "first reddening with momentary anger," bursts into tears, exclaiming, pregnantly: "Then why did you take me from my mother's side? You cannot love what shocks you!" Here is the heart of the matter. Did Aylmer take Georgiana from her mother's side, as God took Eve from Adam's, without wanting to cleave unto her and become one flesh? What *is* it that shocks Aylmer? *Can* one love where one is *shocked*?

In a paragraph rich with innuendo and double meaning, the narrator goes on "to explain this conversation":

> [In the usual state of Georgiana's] complexion, – a healthy, though delicate bloom, – the mark wore a tint of deeper crimson, which imperfectly defined its shape amid the surrounding rosiness. When she blushed, it gradually became more indistinct, and finally vanished amid the triumphant rush of blood, that bathed the whole cheek with its brilliant glow.

This description, obviously not offered from Aylmer's point of view, suggests that Georgiana is a lusty beauty in whose normal state of health (i.e., when Aylmer is not around) the mark scarcely appears at all. When she is excited, it disappears entirely – which is to say that in a state of pleasure Georgiana is *perfectly* beautiful. What *is* this mark, then? "Georgiana's lovers were wont to say, that some fairy, at her birth-hour, had laid her tiny hand upon the infant's cheek, and left this impress there, in token of the magic endowments that were to give her such sway over all hearts." This tiny red hand, coincident with Georgiana's birth, is the "token" of her "magic endowments" as a woman – that is, to use the word not available to Hawthorne, of her female sexuality. It marks, at once, her own birth as a female and her capacity to *give* birth – hence its virtual description as an infant's hand (whose "tiny grasp," we are later told in Aylmer's wildly hostile dream, "appeared to have caught hold of Georgiana's heart"). There are a large number of men who find Georgiana's "mark" extremely attractive: "Many a desperate swain would have risked life for the privilege of pressing his lips to the mysterious hand." But reactions to the mark "varied exceedingly, according to the difference of temperament in the beholders. Some fastidious persons – but they were exclusively of her own sex – affirmed that the Bloody Hand, as they chose to call it, quite destroyed the effect of Georgiana's beauty, and rendered her countenance even hideous."

We might well marvel that Hawthorne was allowed to print that sentence in 1843 (though as much might be said of the whole tale, as of *The Scarlet Letter* to follow). Does one have to explain why "fastidious persons" of Georgiana's own sex chose to call it "the Bloody Hand"? The mark makes manifest to their own eyes, and broadcasts to the world, the condition of woman – the periodic shedding of blood that, though apparently viewed by the fastidious ladies as a mark of the primal curse, is involved with the deepest mysteries of creation and in typological terms is the token of redemption. The "stains" upon the figure of Eve, Hawthorne suggests, depict her not as a "monster" but rather as the mother of us all. Georgiana, true enough, is not perfect; the "fatal flaw of humanity" is upon her. The angels are neither given nor received in marriage. We are sexual beings as well as spiritual ones – "such gods or demigods," in Thoreau's formulation, "only as fauns and satyrs, the divine allied to beasts, the creatures of appetite."[34] But the divine *not* allied to beasts is cold and distant, inhumanly perfect, an abstract design traced by the transcendentalizing imagination. Hawthorne's tale may actually have been intended as a devastating gloss on a frigidly high-minded passage in Emerson's "Love" (1841), wherein a husband,

> in the particular society of his mate . . . attains a clearer sight of any
> spot, any taint, which her beauty has contracted from this world,
> and is able to point it out, and this with mutual joy that they are

now able, without offence, to indicate blemishes and hindrances in each other, and give to each all help and comfort in curing the same.

The "cure" prescribed by Emerson transforms the loved one into a "Divinity" by moving her up the platonic ladder of being away from the "subterranean prudence which presides at marriages." In Aylmer's case, the higher "prudence" paradoxically leads to an equally "subterranean" interment.[35]

Blindly fixing his gaze on a fantasy of disembodied perfection that masks the naked aggressiveness of his so-called scientific project, Aylmer disables himself from seeing what is obvious to other men, namely, that Georgiana's "crimson hand" is the token of her capacity for pleasure, procreation, and new life. Aylmer, in contrast, willfully "selects" it "as the symbol of his wife's liability to sin, sorrow, decay, and death." His aversion is blood; his obsession is with the actual female body in its menstruous condition. He feels compelled to drain it, to reverse the myth of Pygmalion, who turned his statue into a breathing and fecund incarnation of Aphrodite, and decree Georgiana in the form of a lifeless and unthreatening statue. He is enraged by that mysterious interior ebb and flow of Georgiana's body that both controls his relationship to her and mocks his own creative efforts in the laboratory. Aylmer, we are told, "had studied the wonders of the human frame, and attempted to fathom the very process by which Nature assimilates all her precious influences from earth and air, and from the spiritual world, to create and foster Man, her masterpiece." But Aylmer is utterly thwarted and forced to recognize

> that our great creative Mother, while she amuses us with apparently working in the broadest sunshine, is yet severely careful to keep her own secrets, and, in spite of her pretended openness, shows us nothing but results. She permits us indeed, to mar, but seldom to mend, and, like a jealous patentee, on no account to make.

Georgiana, obviously enough, is that "great creative Mother" shoved near Aylmer, indeed, occupying his very bed. The organic *secrecy* of the female body is what maddens him – its containing an interior power that he can serve only as a kind of unwilling tool. Georgiana's sexual attractiveness seems to be a threat to him personally as well as professionally, a way of drawing him into a process over which he has no control. And, of course, the fact that something in Aylmer (call it his own sexuality, the rival of his intellectual activity) is tempted by this very threat reinforces his compulsion to do away with it. We remember that while working on his sleeping wife in the laboratory Aylmer "failed not to gaze often at the fatal Hand, and not without a shudder. Yet once, by a strange and unaccountable impulse, he pressed it with his lips."

Sexual impulse can manifest itself in Aylmer only as necrophilia, the love of the disanimated and de-energized. His project amounts to a "veiling," or putting-away, of that female body, warm with life, which remains refractory to his fantasy of self-contained omnipotence and requires that he define himself in terms of a female other. The birthmark is the sign of Aylmer's own infant self, inscribed in a woman's face, which forces him to acknowledge his debt to the female body.[36] Hawthorne's fable amounts to a rewriting of Mary Shelley's *Frankenstein* (the pre-text of "The Birth-mark," virtually quoted in the tale), for Aylmer perfectly fits Robert Kiely's description of Victor Frankenstein as a man who "seeks to combine the role of both parents in one, to eliminate the need for woman in the creative act, to make sex unnecessary."[37] Let us remember that Frankenstein's monster himself desires a mate (the expression of Frankenstein's own unacceptable wishes), and when denied this gratification, he kills Frankenstein's fiancée Elizabeth, acting out in manifest aggression the veiled aggression contained and expressed by the scientific project.

Aylmer is involved in rooting out the potential child in Georgiana's body, in nullifying her procreative force. He is a negative image of the lover: His laboratory, now called a "boudoir," becomes the "secluded abode of a lovely woman" who is about to be rendered invisible; he feels "rapture" in attempting his "abortive" experiments that, alas, are no better than "mortifying failures"; he exhibits chemicals capable of "impregnating all the breezes" while searching for a universal solvent whose "potency" will reside in its power of destroying Georgiana; the birthmark casts a fatal blight over his "labors," for his "highest and deepest conception" is not the blessing of fatherhood but rather a fantasy of anticreation, and he achieves his dark goal by forcing Georgiana to drink a colorless liquor that is effectively an antisperm, the antagonist of her menstrual blood (the alchemical *menstruum* or *alkahest*) and the agent of her destruction. It may also be viewed as the instrument of antiapocalypse, the means of veiling forever the female other whom Aylmer cannot bear to face. His project is the negation of that marriage of flesh and spirit traditionally promised at the end of time but reconceived by the Romantics as a present possibility for regenerated men and women capable of believing that their mortal selves are, in fact, to use Hawthorne's language, "woven . . . of the self-same texture with the celestial."

3

Ludwig Wittgenstein begins one of his notebooks with the momentous question, "What is the meaning of a word?"[38] Hawthorne's inveterately modest and self-deprecating manner suggested a more attenuated question: What is the meaning of a letter? It seems perfectly appropriate that "Monsieur Aubepine," as he calls himself in the mock preface to "Rappaccini's Daughter," should have made a name for himself by exploring the obscurities of that primary letter, a word and a world in itself, the letter *A*. It is a natural and ideal place to begin, the *incipit* of all dictionaries, encyclopedias, and directories, our introduction to the alphabet and thus to language – the primary medium of our social existence. History, presumably, began with Adam; America, so to speak, with Amerigo Vespucci; a study of Latin begins with *amo, amas, amat . . .* The story of Hester Prynne begins with an act called adultery. *A* is, par excellence, *initial* – it must be elaborated. *The Scarlet Letter* is our primary American horn-book, in which we may learn the lessons of dozens of crucial *A*-words. What follows is a partial Lexicon of the Letter – alphabits, drawn from the book, which we may regard as fragments of Hawthorne's writing personality.

Alchemy.[39] One of Hawthorne's favorite figures. In the medieval analogy, the female womb, or *vas*, is the crucible in which the base metal, sperm or *homunculus*, is transformed into a higher state through the action of the menstrual blood, the *menstruum* or universal solvent. Sexual love and procreation and the alchemical process are thus interchangeable figures. When Hester casts off her stigma in the forest and lets down her magnificent hair, the "crimson flush" of sexuality "glowing on her cheek" replaces the letter as curse and the natural world responds: "All at once, as with a sudden smile of heaven, forth burst the sunshine, pouring a very flood into the obscure forest, gladdening each green leaf, transmuting the yellow fallen ones to gold. . . ." In this heretical re-creation myth, sexual love reverses the Fall, transforming waste into precious substance. Hester views her physical conjunction with Dimmesdale as a consecrated act, whence issues the Pearl of great price, "the oneness of their being," symbolizing the mystic union of body and spirit. Hawthorne suggests, rather whimsically, in the last chapter that earthly "hatred and antipathy" may be "transmuted into golden love" in the world to come by a species of cosmic compensation. Since he is referring to the diabolical relationship of Dimmesdale and Chillingworth, readers may be excused if they feel that is little more than alchemical pie in the sky. Hester, on the contrary, has already demonstrated that there is no need to wait, for sexual love may mint heaven's own coin here below.

Ann. There are two opposed figures bearing this name in *The Scarlet Letter*: Ann Hutchinson and Ann Turner. The first, putative saint and prophetess of a personal indwelling of the spirit that abrogates the Law, has as her token the rose ("Far-off, most secret, and inviolate Rose," in Yeats's fine phrase), the token of passion sublimed. Ann Turner, on the other hand, linked in the narrative with the witch, Mistress Hibbens, is the physician's widow who poisoned Sir Thomas Overbury in 1613 and whose emblem is the yellow ruff, the token of deceit and of a fallen spirit. Hester, neither angel nor devil, is set between these two in the unstable equilibrium of ordinary human aspiration and desire.

Able. Hawthorne tells us in Chapter 5 that the world had set a mark upon Hester "more intolerable to a woman's heart than that which branded the brow of Cain." We may be excused, then, for hearing a homophonic pun in the chapter designed to balance this one – Chapter 13 – when we are informed that the world finally came round to a different interpretation of the *A*: "They said it meant Able; so strong was Hester Prynne, with a woman's strength." Cain and Abel: vengeance and strength, anger and faith – the first- and second-born of this indomitable Eve.

Accountable, Accountability, Account. "Woman, woman, thou art accountable for this!" Twisting in the net of his own ambivalence and anguish, filled alternately with shame and anger, Dimmesdale bursts out thus at Hester in the forest. What is Hester "accountable" for here? What is *this*? surely not simply that she has allowed her lover to expose himself to Chillingworth's cruelty. Dimmesdale seems really to be blaming Hester for his passional life – his impulses, his desires, the mess they have gotten him into. It is the cry of Adam against Eve. But Hawthorne may expect us to recall Dimmesdale's words in Chapter 3, when he is enjoined by the Reverend Mr. Wilson to extract a confession from his refractory parishioner. "Hester Prynne . . . thou hearest what this good man says, and seest the accountability under which I labor." Hester has already labored, the minister is now laboring fearfully. Terrified that Hester will reveal him as her lover and thus bring him to the reckoning he cannot face, he speaks with a forked tongue, alluding to an "accountability" he will not acknowledge. It is hard indeed to settle accounts when conflicting emotions and conflicting versions of experience are brought into confrontation. Hawthorne seems to have the same problem, as we observe by the way in which he begins his concluding chapter: "After many days, when time sufficed for the people to arrange their thoughts in reference to the foregoing scene, there was more than one account of what had been witnessed on the scaffold." Precisely. How can we get a clear view of that which is fundamentally murky –

men and women struggling equally with themselves and with each other. Can Hawthorne possibly choose sides? Literary accounts can never be balanced.

Author, Authorize, Authority, Authenticated, Authenticity. Whose book is this, and is it true? Hawthorne tells us that during his tenure in the Salem custom-house he "had ceased to be a writer of tolerably poor tales and essays, and had become a tolerably good Surveyor of the Customs." But his release from that dulling thralldom to Uncle Sam's business does not appear unequivocally to have returned him to authorship, since the main facts of his story "are authorized and authenticated by the document of Mr. Surveyor Pue." Hawthorne is thus a secondary author (he calls himself an editor), who has, however, elaborated his predecessor's work with so much license that he might have invented the whole thing. It is unlikely that Mr. Pue would have authorized such tampering, for his own contribution has thereby been nullified. But Hawthorne still insists on invoking Pue's manuscript, contending on that basis for the "authenticity of the outline." That outline, of course, is in the shape of an *A* that Hawthorne has filled in. The outline is true, the filling possibly false. That sounds like Arthur Dimmesdale, whose secret shame and consequent hypocrisy have emptied out his insides while the outward shell of ministerial authority alone remains. Or we may be reminded, as always, of Hester's letter (and the letter *is* the book), which is surely an *A* externally but otherwise only a provocation to meaning – a husk without a solid core, authentic in outline but authorizing nothing. Under the pressure of Hester's mysteriously multivalent sign, authority seems to be crumbling – as her own antinomian tendencies threatened to call the whole Puritan establishment into question. Can a book be authentic that gropes its way in parabolic darkness rather than in the steady light of clear assertion?

The author himself makes such a distinction – between parabolic fable and authentic truth – in describing an interview between Hester and Mistress Hibbens. And that distinction is underlined when Dimmesdale's shocking words on the scaffold are called mere "parable" – a fiction – by those admirers who claim that they were not true because they contradicted the familiar contours and public history of his apparently blameless life. Can Hawthorne be blamed for such confusion? No, for he is an author whose own authority is derived from others: "The authority which we have chiefly followed," he asserts in the final chapter,

> – a manuscript of old date, drawn up from the verbal testimony of individuals, some of whom had known Hester Prynne, while others had heard the tale from contemporary witnesses – fully confirms the view taken in the foregoing pages.

Which view? There are so many! Hawthorne has followed a manuscript based on verbal testimony and second-hand repetitions of a tale. Are such procedures any different from his own? How can they finally authenticate a narrative put together with so much license that the whole might reasonably be considered mere fabrication? Well, the author assures us, if you doubt the authenticity of what he has related, "the original papers, together with the scarlet letter itself, – a most curious relic," are still in his possession and will be "freely exhibited" to curious persons. You might just want to bring along your own copy of *The Scarlet Letter* for purposes of comparison . . .

Adultery.[40] A term not used in the book, for obvious reasons. *Adultery* the word was almost as taboo in the American nineteenth century as the act for which it stands. But Hawthorne, in any case, avoids a term so loaded with pejorative association that it would immediately compromise and short-circuit the rich ambiguities of his argument. A curious word: *ad-ul (al) terium*, in Latin, a movement of one person toward another – as a word, the very type of human need and human sympathy. The sunshine, in the third chapter, is described, curiously, as "unadulterated." Presumably the sun and other things in nature, being inhuman, have no awareness of needing something outside themselves. There is no sorrow in nature; it seems cruelly indifferent to the human condition. " 'Mother,' said little Pearl, 'the sunshine does not love you. It runs away and hides itself, because it is afraid of something on your bosom' ": unadulterated sunshine versus the adulterous bosom. Pearl goes on to say that she will catch the sun: "I am but a child. It will not flee from me; for I wear nothing on my bosom yet." Pearl scarcely has a bosom yet. Only fully sexual adults can commit adultery – feel the need to do so. Hester hopes that Pearl will *never* wear the *A* on her bosom. "And why not mother?" asks the child. "Will it not come of its own accord, when I am a woman grown?" What will surely come is not this specific transgression but the desire to reach out ad-ulterium, to another, in sorrow if not in sunshine. It is the fear of being alone – unloved, untouched, unmated – that leads to adultery. Hester had been left alone by Chillingworth for two years. Dimmesdale, undoubtedly, was a lonely bachelor, and he tells Hester in the forest that he has not the strength "to venture into the wide, strange, difficult world, alone!" He repeats the word, in a cry that seems the primal definition of why they have done what they have done: "Alone, Hester!" Whereupon Hester responds, "in a deep whisper," with a sentence that defines her heresy in a form that is startling. It is her eleventh commandment, her counterstatement to the seventh: "Thou shalt not go alone!"

Animal. Dimmesdale, "this man," Chillingworth observes, "pure as they deem him, – all spiritual as he seems, – hath inherited a strong animal nature from his father or his mother. Let us dig a little deeper in this vein." What *is* the relationship between Dimmesdale's strong but severely repressed instincts and his religious power? It is odd that the word *animal* is derived from the Latin *anima*, "breath" or "spirit." Dimmesdale's "crime," the "hot passion of his heart," has

> . . . kept him down, on a level with the lowest; him, the man of ethereal attributes, whose voice the angels might else have listened to and answered! But this very burden it was, that gave him sympathies so intimate with the sinful brotherhood of mankind; so that his heart vibrated in unison with theirs, and received their pain into itself, and sent its own throb of pain through a thousand other hearts, in gushes of sad, persuasive eloquence. Oftenest persuasive, but sometimes terrible! The people knew not the power that moved them thus. They deemed the young clergyman a miracle of holiness. They fancied him the mouth-piece of Heaven's messages of wisdom and rebuke, and love. In their eyes, the very ground on which he trod was sanctified. The virgins of his church grew pale around him, victims of a passion so imbued with religious sentiment that they imagined it to be all religion, and brought it openly, in their white bosoms, as their most acceptable sacrifice before the altar.

So the "virgins" of the parish, too, are the "victims" of this passion that masquerades as "religious sentiment" and drives them to church to sit at Dimmesdale's feet, adoring the "mouth-piece" of heaven above but ignoring, perhaps, the cod-piece of the devil below. This terrible power "that moved them thus" also moves Dimmesdale to inscribe his most inspired sermon, written after his rousing interview with Hester in the forest, when, having sated his "ravenous appetite," he returns to his desk and gives vent to "an impulsive flow of thought and emotions." How can it be that heaven sees fit "to transmit the grand and solemn music of its oracles" through the "foul . . . organ-pipe" of man? Moreover, just as positive animal impulse may flower in religious expression, so, too, may "bodily disease," as Chillingworth notes, "be but a symptom of some ailment in the spiritual part." Dimmesdale is a living symbol of the mysterious relationship between the animal and the anima. "You, Sir, of all men I have known," Chillingworth goes on, "are he whose body is the closest conjoined, and imbued, and identified, so to speak, with the spirit whereof it is the instrument." So to speak. But *which* is tenor, and which vehicle? Body and spirit – an odd marriage, an even more terrible divorce.

Apocalypse. Hawthorne does not use this term as such, preferring the more familiar Latin *revelation*, which is everywhere in the book, most

notably in the title of Chapter 23, "The Revelation of the Scarlet Letter."
Here the irony is striking, since Dimmesdale's final performance on the
scaffold is a kind of striptease – exposing and not exposing. It is not at all
clear, since there are conflicting accounts, that Dimmesdale in fact exhibited either a mark on his chest or a stain on his otherwise spotless
reputation. He is the expert concealer, a man who lives in desperate fear
of being unveiled, though, as he admits to Chillingworth, such an
outpouring of the hidden self might provide a great relief. Dimmesdale
holds, however, that "the dark problem of this life" can be made plain
only on that promised day "when all hidden things shall be revealed."

But to his agitated imagination that moment actually seems to arrive
during the weird night when he ascends the scaffold and finds the
heavens and the earth so powerfully illuminated by a meteor that the
"strange and solemn splendor" produced appears to be "the light that is
to reveal all secrets." To his "disordered mental state" Revelation is
imminent and is so indicated by the immense letter *A* glowing redly in
the sky as a sign, so he fears, of both apocalypse and his own name.
Apocalypse finally is no more than the moment when his name will be
universally known as the true key to deciphering the enigmatic emblem
on Hester's bosom. But Dimmesdale is mistaken, that moment is not at
hand, and the cosmic letter is taken as betokening the translation of
Governor Winthrop into an angel. Of course, the apocalypse has been
walking around Boston all along in the shape of Hester's badge of shame,
but she will not spell it out, and others lack the wit to catch on. Is Hester,
then, guilty of prolonging Arthur's agony by consenting, through her
silence, to become the agent of his concealment? Has she, like Calypso,
kept this failed Ulysses buried in the middle of his psychic ocean for
those requisite seven years, an indentured servant to his own diabolical
contract? The answer would seem to be no, for Dimmesdale has *calypsoed*
himself, kept himself hidden out of fear of exposing his identity as lover
and father. For him there will be no return to Ithaka and Penelope at the
end of the line, merely an obscure grave in the King's Chapel burial-
ground marked by a tombstone as ambiguously apocalyptic as the letter
on Hester's bosom: "one ever-glowing point of light gloomier than the
shadow."

Act, Acts, Actor. Despite Hawthorne's playful talk about his sources and
documents, *The Scarlet Letter* is a performance, an "act" of the "imaginative faculty" elaborating the merest fragment of a historical conception
into a full-blown romance of the moral life. Hawthorne's characters are
carefully and self-consciously placed on stage. Indeed, the neatly balanced Aristotelian scaffolding of the book, as has frequently been noticed, provides at the beginning, middle, and end – first, twelfth, and

twenty-third/-fourth chapters – an actual stage on which the principal action takes place. In the first instance, with the groundlings down below and the clergy in the balcony, Hester is cast in the role of the Fallen Woman, though she *acts* like something quite different, impersonating or embodying by turns the figures of a healthy natural woman in full bloom and of Divine Maternity. It is an "exhibition," and what Hester is expected to exhibit, apart from the "sinful" splendor of her female body, is a contrite adulteress prepared to disclose her lover's identity. She consents to neither role, speaking only of her determination not to speak.

There are, of course, other players: principally, Chillingworth in the crowd, choosing to play the part of a stranger and wanderer recently brought out of Indian captivity so as not to play the part of the cuckolded husband, and Dimmesdale, mouthing the lines of a pious minister concerned only for the safety and salvation of his misguided parishioner so as not to have to speak as the partner of her shame. These, then, are our three players, with their ambiguous and shifting roles. In the interview backstage (i.e., in the prison) that follows, masks are dropped between Hester and her husband, and she speaks with rich double-meaning of the terrible disparity between his false role-playing and his plain speech to her: "Thy acts are like mercy . . . [b]ut thy words interpret thee as a terror!" Chillingworth has no intention of remaining a spectator but rather obtains a part as "chief actor . . . in the minister's interior world" so as to force Dimmesdale to act out his true meaning. Indeed, Chillingworth unfolds to Hester a theory of the work in which they function simply as players. "Ye that have wronged me are not sinful, save in a kind of typical illusion; neither am I fiend-like, who have snatched a fiend's office from his hands." How can one speak of sinners and fiends when they are all only playing their preordained parts in this Puritan Morality? All the world is indeed a stage, especially when these characters in a romance by Nathaniel Hawthorne are conceived as members of a society that explains everything that is done and suffered in terms of a divine drama.

Precisely in the middle of this drama Dimmesdale himself climbs the stage and stands "where Hester Prynne had stood" in a mock reprise of Hester's performance by day, for it is night and nothing is disclosed. Hester freely acted out her shame but said nothing to incriminate her lover. Dimmesdale seems to shriek involuntarily but is not heard, speaks without uttering a sound, goes through the motions of an Everyman torn between Remorse and Cowardice; but all remains a "vain show of expiation" because, as is suggested, this is no more than sleepwalking, a fantasy of public disclosure rather than the dramatic reality. Of course, it finally is seen to be a private dress rehearsal for the theatrical denouement in Chapter 23, when Dimmesdale stands with Hester and Pearl on a stage fully lighted by the noonday sun. We recall that in the forest where Dimmesdale and Hester re-create for *us* the love scene that had been played out offstage before the portion of the drama we see had begun, Hester exhorts her dispirited paramour to "Preach! Write! Act!" He does in fact proceed to do all three things, inditing the election sermon, preaching it with ambiguous religious intensity, and finally playing out on the scaffold the final catastrophe of this "drama of guilt and sorrow in which they had all been actors."

Dimmesdale's confession, however, is *so* theatrically conceived and executed that it does indeed amount to an act, for many members of the audience insist on viewing his last performance as no more than "a parable" designed "to impress on his admirers the mighty and mournful lesson, that, in the view of infinite Purity, we are all sinners alike." Dimmesdale, we might say, has become so expert in hypocrisy (taking the word in its root sense of playing a part on stage) that he is no longer capable of stepping out in front of the footlights and will not be accepted in such a role, as an actor at last trying to speak without his mask. The narrator advises us all to be true, to "show freely to the world, if not [our] worst, yet some trait whereby the worst may be inferred," while fixing one of his principal characters in a posture of such inveterate and consummate histrionic duplicity that his *best* is inferred from his worst, his worst being taken as simply another part acted out for public edification. Perhaps the true problem being exposed here is that of the clergyman – any clergyman, but especially one in the American seventeenth century – forced to adopt the role of saint in a world composed, finally, of mere flesh and blood. That was precisely the reason why, almost two hundred years after Dimmesdale's demise, another minister named Waldo Emerson prepared to step down from the pulpit because, as he said, he rejected the notion that any man should "try to angel it thro' the world."[41]

Analysis. Hawthorne reports that when he discovered the "rag of scarlet cloth" in the unfinished second story of the Custom-House, he "suspected some deep meaning in it, most worthy of interpretation," that evaded the "analysis" of his mind while communicating itself to his sensibilities. Placed on his own breast, it made its peculiar power felt. Sympathetic identification, then, and not analysis is the primary desideratum. The romancer wants not so much to interpret the dreams of the past as to redream them, making them part of his own fantasy life.

"Analysis" is not normally a praiseworthy term in Hawthorne's vocabulary, suggesting as it does the breaking down of an organism into its component parts in cold scientific fashion. It is, of course, the mode of Dr. Chillingworth, who devotes himself "to the constant analysis of a heart full of torture . . . deriving his enjoyment thence, and adding fuel to those fiery tortures which he analyzed and gloated over." Effectively, Dimmesdale is *in* analysis with this flawed protopsychiatrist,[42] who combines a theory of psychosomatic disease with the art of talking through his patient's problems. Unfortunately, however, though "he had begun [his] investigation, as he imagined, with the severe and equal integrity of a judge, desirous only of truth," his project is compromised by his own terrible involvement in the psychoanalytic process. Hawthorne presents a fully formed and perfectly lucid model of the ideal analyst-therapist to which, it is suggested, Chillingworth may only partially conform: He must possess

> native sagacity, and a nameless something more, – let us call it intuition; if he show no intrusive egotism, nor disagreeably prominent characteristics of his own; if he have the power, which must be born with him, to bring his mind into such affinity with his patient's, that this last shall unawares have spoken what he imagines himself only to have thought; if such revelations be received without tumult, and acknowledged not so often by an uttered sympathy, as by silence, an inarticulate breath, and here and there a word, to indicate that all is understood; if, to these qualifications of a confidant be joined the advantages afforded by his recognized character as a physician; – then, at some inevitable moment, will the soul of the sufferer be dissolved, and flow forth in a dark, but transparent stream, bringing all its mysteries into the daylight.

True analysis is apocalyptic, removing the veil that lies between the unconscious and the conscious. As such, it represents a mode of personal redemption.

Dimmesdale, however, has put himself, not in the hands of a neutral agent of this process, but in the clutches, as it were, of an enraged Oedipal father – the cuckolded aged parent/husband of Dimmesdale's maternal lover. In a further striking anticipation of Freud, Hawthorne provides another model – of a *bad* analytic procedure in which transference is distorted and countertransference vicious. First, the transference. Dimmesdale reacts to Chillingworth through alternating moods of submission and rebellion that reflect his reenactment of the father–son relationship in the analytic process. On one occasion in particular, when Chillingworth has kept at Dimmesdale relentlessly, attempting to prod him into laying open the "wound or trouble" in his soul, Dimmesdale turns on the doctor in wild anger, as if facing down the avenging father who has driven the nasty little boy into a corner:

"No! – not to thee! – not to an earthly physician!" cried Mr. Dimmesdale, passionately, and turning his eyes, full and bright, and with a kind of fierceness, on old Roger Chillingworth. "Not to thee! But, if it be the soul's disease, then do I commit myself to the one Physician of the soul! He, if it stand with his good pleasure, can cure; or he can kill! Let him do with me as, in justice and wisdom, he shall see good. But who art thou, that meddlest in this matter? – that dares thrust himself between the sufferer and his God?" With a frantic gesture, he rushed out of the room.

Dimmesdale's violent reaction to the demands of this father-analyst effectively would displace the Oedipal struggle to the level of a theological debate with an abstract and noncorporeal God whose presence and punishment are deferred. He is a surrogate father who, in Dimmesdale's fantasy, makes no immediate demands for confession. "Do you think you are God?" is essentially Dimmesdale's taunt, as he tries to cut the doctor-parent down to size, to disarm him. But Chillingworth maintains his composure in the face of this negative transference, believing that his procedure is correct. " 'It is well to have made this step,' said Chillingworth to himself, looking after the minister with a grave smile. 'There is nothing lost. We shall be friends again anon.' " Chillingworth understands that Dimmesdale's overreaction is a measure of the force of other, repressed material: " 'But see, now, how passion takes hold upon this man, and hurrieth him out of himself! As with one passion, so with another! He hath done a wild thing ere now, this pious Master Dimmesdale, in the hot passion of his heart!' "

As Chillingworth expects,

> it proved not difficult to reestablish the intimacy of the two companions, on the same footing and in the same degree as heretofore. The young clergyman, after a few hours of privacy, was sensible that the disorder of his nerves had hurried him into an unseemly outbreak of temper, which there had been nothing in the physician's words to excuse or palliate. He marvelled, indeed, at the violence with which he had thrust back the kind old man, when merely proffering the advice which it was his duty to bestow, and which the minister himself had expressly sought. With these remorseful feelings, he lost no time in making the amplest apologies, and besought his friend still to continue the care. . . .

Good little boy – an appropriate response! But his analyst is a devil, and he has been tricked, for the cycle of anger/remorse represents not a true analytic transference but a mockery of one. Dimmesdale's anger, though

he does not know it, is justified, since the old man's provocation is fueled
by hatred, malice, and a desire for revenge. This "analysis" is intended to
break down the patient, not to reintegrate him.

Dr. Chillingworth's posture toward Dimmesdale involves a bad case
of unhealthy countertransference. He becomes, "not a spectator only,
but a chief actor, in the poor minister's interior world." Since Chillingworth has already admitted that he committed the first wrong by betray-
ing Hester's "budding youth into a false and unnatural relation" with his
"decay," he is bound to approach Dimmesdale with a large fund of guilt
for which he will scapegoat the minister. There is a strong identification
between the two, because Dimmesdale has succeeded in completing the
sexual act that Chillingworth was manifestly incapable of performing.
Chillingworth's own impotent rage, then, is invested in the exercise of
negative healing, of deepening Dimmesdale's guilt and further unmanning him. The analysis represents a source of narcissistic gratification for
the doctor, who sees himself as omnipotent in his power to hurt:

> He could play upon [Dimmesdale] as he chose. Would he arouse
> him with a throb of agony? The victim was forever on the rack;
> it needed only to know the spring that controlled the engine; –
> and the physician knew it well! Would he startle him with
> sudden fear? As at the waving of a magician's wand, uprose a
> grisly phantom, – uprose a thousand phantoms, – in many
> shapes, of death, or more awful shame, all flocking roundabout
> the clergyman, and pointing with their fingers at his breast!

Chillingworth's desire to "arouse [Dimmesdale] with a throb of agony"
reveals the source of his personal gratification, in this parody of the
analytic situation, as a sexually cathected aggressive impulse. His power
to release the phantoms of Dimmesdale's unconscious is placed in the
service of the Oedipal father's need to torture the disobedient son/
cuckolder.

But what can the poor patient do to protect himself? This process
whereby hostility masquerades as healing is "accomplished with a subtlety so perfect, that the minister, though he had constantly a dim
perception of some evil influence watching over him, could never gain a
knowledge of its actual nature." True, he has vague feelings of doubt,
fear, and even hatred of this deformed old figure, this demonic misrepre-
sentation of a father/doctor. But Dimmesdale is in a bad way, needs help
so badly that he is unable to acknowledge to himself the objective basis
for his antipathy. He has been initiated only too well into the psychoanalytic trap, the carefully nurtured habit of distrusting his own motives
and not those of the physician: "He took himself to task for his bad
sympathies in reference to Roger Chillingworth." Where, after all, can

Dimmesdale turn? Chillingworth is the only psychiatrist in Boston – a situation hardly to be conceived in the last decade of the twentieth century.

As Hawthorne tells us in the concluding chapter of *The Scarlet Letter*, the old physician and the minister were not so much doctor and patient as "mutual victims," bound by a fundamental hatred that the author ventures to suggest may have been "transmuted into golden love" in those realms where analysis has no place. We have already observed that Hawthorne's alchemical flourish here may be viewed as little more than ironic whimsy, since the resolution of opposites is not something that takes place easily between the covers of this sad book. Still, the narrator seems to be insisting on a crucial point: The ultimate injunction of the Letter is not antipathy and the impulse to analyze but a more durable, powerful, integrative force . . .

Amor. The word is present by implication only, but that implication is clear and strong. "The scarlet letter," we are told,

> had the effect of the cross on a nun's bosom. It imparted to the wearer a kind of sacredness, which enabled her to walk securely amid all peril. Had she fallen among thieves, it would have kept her safe. It was reported, and believed by many, that an Indian had drawn his arrow against the badge, and that the missile struck it, but fell harmless to the ground.

Hawthorne's description of a supposed badge of shame that functions as the sacred talisman of Christ immediately invites comparison with a well-known figure in *The Canterbury Tales* (Chaucer, of course, is mentioned in Hawthorne's introductory essay; they are both surveyors of the customs of their culture): the nun in the General Prologue, whose arm displays a brooch with a "crowned *A*" and a motto filched from Virgil's tenth Eclogue, *Amor vincit omnia*. The nun displays a religious emblem that is ambiguously pious, whereas the fallen woman displays a profane one that develops a sacred function.

What we have, in effect, is a suggestion that the two modes of love cannot be kept apart – or only artificially and at our peril. Though Hester, with her infamous emblem, is moralized upon "as the figure, the body, the reality of sin," she appears magnificently as the figure, body, and reality of maternal femininity, the fruit of which nestles crowned in her ample bosom. Though Hester adopts an austere and even ascetic mode of dress and demeanor, so "that there seemed to be no longer any thing in Hester's face for Love to dwell upon; nothing in Hester's form . . . that Passion would ever dream of clasping in its embrace; nothing in Hester's bosom, to make it ever again the pillow of Affection," all three faces of Amor are mystically linked together in her fancifully embroidered emblem, and all three are aroused together in the tender, erotic, and nurturing figure she presents to Dimmesdale in the forest. Amor is Hester's emblem alone, for no one else in the community is prepared to conceive of her synthesis of spiritual and bodily love. The "red ignominy" seemed to be "so deeply scorched into [Hester's] brain, that all her conceptions assumed its form," and whether with her needle or her warm nature, she is forever forging analogies between the "emblem of her guilt" and the objects of her affection, forcing the ignominious A to transform itself into a triumphant one.

Dimmesdale, on the other hand, is incapable of such conceptions. Like so many of his Puritan brethren, he has an imagination capable of seeing his soul's fate terrifyingly emblazoned on the very face of heaven. What he lacks, to use Henry James's fine phrase, is "the imagination of loving"[43] – an imagination capable of conceiving of a world framed not in terror, but in love. Dimmesdale sees the token that burns on Hester's bosom as a personal indictment, not as a possible pledge of his redemption. ("What we did," Hester says passionately to her minister-lover, trying to teach him a new kind of theology, "had a consecration of its own.") He and most members of the community tend to read Hester's emblem in a pejorative fashion. They see Adultery, Anguish, Agony, Antinomianism – not Affection, never Amor. *That* is Hester's secret and her salvation. In that sign she conquers and continues to live in our imagination as a model of endurance and charity. Though Hawthorne obviously honors the Puritans' stern dedication to ideal virtue and their seriousness of purpose, he does not share their faith. As a man of the nineteenth century he seems to have been certain of nothing, in Keats's words, but "the holiness of the Heart's affections and the truth of Imagination."[44] Hester's sentence about the consecration inherent in her union with Dimmesdale would have been arch-heresy in 1649. But recreated by Hawthorne two hundred years later, it suggests a startling shift of values, whereby the imagination of loving has been apotheosized.

A. Reality is the beginning not the end,
   Naked Alpha . . .
   It is the infant A standing on infant legs,
   Not twisted, stooping, polymathic Z. . . . [45]

A stands at the beginning of the alphabet, whence all meanings flow: an all-but-voiceless sound (*aaah* – a breath), thus infant, unspeaking, merely initial, the letter most resembling a small person ("by an accurate measurement," Hawthorne observes, "each limb proved to be precisely three inches and a quarter in length"), the first glimmering in the womb of thought. The book grows from that small beginning, like little Pearl, the acrid fruit of the archetypal forbidden tree of carnal knowledge. Hawthorne's narrative in fact issues from the naked Alpha – infant *A* set against the multitudinous clamor of many letters, "A throng . . ." – as Hester issues from the prison, the place of gestation, with her letter and her child to stand before the crowd, virtually saying, "I am *A*." Literal self-definition is the narrative's first gesture.

The book's penultimate word is also the letter *A*, though the final word, *gules*, despite its sounding fiendish, is but the color red, and so we conclude with the title reversed, "The Letter (*A*), Scarlet," as if to suggest that we may begin *A*-gain, or endlessly circulate, through the permutations of Hawthorne's fertile emblem. If Hawthorne's narrative were in the form of a medieval manuscript (and it sometimes resembles a medieval morality play with its personified majuscular virtues and vices – Remorse, Cowardice, Love, Passion, Affection), its first letter would be illuminated as a rubric, an elaborated red *A* (the whole title in 1850 was indeed printed in red). But, of course, Hawthorne's *A* in fact is illuminated, brought out of the dark, winking, like Pearl, "in the un-adulterated sunshine" of Puritan Boston. "Iniquity is dragged out into the sunshine," cries the grim beadle, but, strange to observe, its initial appearance is strikingly beautiful: "on the breast of [Hester's] gown, in fine red cloth, surrounded with an elaborate embroidery and fantastic flourishes of gold thread . . . so artistically done, and with so much fertility and gorgeous luxuriance of fancy," that it seems the very queen of letters. How can Hester be degraded when her letter stands at the top of the scale?

Polymathic *Z*, on the other hand, lies at the bottom and *is* twisted and stooping, the "deformed old figure" of the physician, whose beard almost touches the ground as he creeps along. He is all head and no heart: a learned "whoreson zed," in Shakespearean language, an unnecessary letter that dries up and blows away at the end as if it were a metaphysical nullity, the negation of being, cold to the touch (Chillingworth), un-procreative; a Mephistopheles figure, the spirit that denies. Why does Hawthorne's magnificent first lady – the Eve of this fallen New World – marry (though she does not mate with) such decrepitude? Perhaps it is a type of her destiny, since youth must finally marry age. But Hester's age is only an elaboration of her infant *A*. ("There is no virtue which is final," notes Emerson; "all are initial."[46]) Hester in age represents indi-vidual sexual passion transformed into something more mellow and universally diffused. When she takes up her letter at the end, it is no longer "a stigma which attracted the world's scorn and bitterness," but a sign of increasing sympathetic human awareness, the first token of something to come, the revelation of a "new truth" that would "establish the whole relation between man and woman on a surer ground of mutual happiness." Thus the infant alpha of seventeenth-century American female individualism and egotism grows into the new woman of nineteenth-century and later feminism, and perhaps – why not? – into the fully achieved omega of "mutual happiness" envisioned by Hawthorne for some ultimate America of the spirit.

Chapter 6

Thoreau's Self-Perpetuating Artifacts

1

Henry Thoreau had a horror of ending things, perhaps because it felt like death. His great theme, of course, was renewal, the Romantic myth of infinite self-possibility and self-extension. In the second chapter of *Walden,* for example, he makes much of the ritual of morning ablutions because it represented his principal "religious" exercise in the Thoreauvian cult of regeneration. He cites with pleasure words supposed to have been "engraven on the bathing tub of King Tching-thang" as if to appropriate them for his own motto: "Renew thyself completely each day; do it again, and again, and forever again."¹ Doing things again was to become Thoreau's only stock in trade: another walk in Concord or further excursions elsewhere, another bath in Walden Pond, a tireless reiteration in his journal of the year's natural phenomena. Thoreau believed that his pilgrimages, no matter how trivial or repetitive, presented fresh opportunities for renewal and thus constituted religious exercises; the traveler, he tells us in the "Thursday" section of *A Week,* must expect to be "born again on the road." His favorite journeys, accordingly, were westerly ones – not for the usual American reasons (a chance to start over in the Western Reserve or in the gold-laced foothills of the Sierras), but for the sake of a geographico-spiritual paradox that engaged him as much as it would Whitman after him. Noting that "there is an orientalism in the most restless pioneer," Thoreau concludes that "the farthest west is but the farthest east." His typical journey was circular: he would travel west to reach the east, reorient himself, so to speak, and then continue on – or back – with a refreshened sense of purpose and meaning, having recovered the Sanskrit in his own brain.

Thoreau especially delighted in the Hindu scriptures, and particularly in the Laws of Menu, because they seemed " 'to have been promulged in the beginning of time'. . . uttered from some eastern summit, with a sober morning prescience." They thus provided the kind of original and preliminary knowledge he needed to help him start his life over. The Laws of Menu, he says, "conveys a new gloss to the meadows and the depths of the wood. . . . While we are reading these sentences, this fair modern world seems only a reprint of the Laws of Menu." The puns here are *typical* in more than just the sense of being familiarly Thoreauvian: His Hindu bible casts a new light on the text of nature so that the world seems to exist in a reciprocal relationship with that scripture, reinscribing and fulfilling its truth with fresh illustrations. As Thoreau reads and rereads this book, nature – including his own body – appears to be miraculously recreated, for he feels himself "dabbling" (literally *bathing*) "in the very elements of our present conventional and actual life." It is like that tub of King Tching-thang, only filled with the currents of his own regenerated being. Its sentences are sentences "which no intelligence can understand" because they are thoughts that the body thought, not just the brain. There is "a kind of life and palpitation to it, and under its words a kind of blood" circulates, reflecting the circulations of vital fluid and thought that nourish his own life. It is a book that never ends because its theory of creation is infinitely regressive, describing a world which, though it appears to exist, is only forever about to be. "It hardly allows the reader to rest in any supreme first cause," Thoreau observes, "but directly it hints at a supremer still which created the last, and the Creator is still behind increate."

Such a theory is all forethought and no afterthought, forever Prometheus and never Epimetheus, a perpetual planning for new creation that transcends time, as in Thoreau's parable of the artist of Kouroo in *Walden*. Thoreau's ideal book, one that he would never tire of rereading, would be a book proposing an endless series of new beginnings and therefore one that "would be more salutary than the morning or the spring to our lives, and possibly put a new aspect on the face of things for us" ("Reading"). Of course, he hoped that his own books might be scriptures of this sort – circular journeys of body and spirit capable of inspiring new eras in the lives of their readers. The mythus of rebirth, he knew, was the most ancient and persistent hope of humankind, a fable that had migrated "from east to west, and again from west to east," and that he himself was engaged in reiterating and retouching. Though the myths persist, the particular *epos* or *epea*, the symbols or words themselves, needed to be reinvented and reinscribed for each new age and culture. Carlyle's *Sartor Resartus,* which Thoreau had read in college, argues precisely for the necessity of retailoring the old symbols. "Homer's Epos has not ceased to be true," Carlyle concedes – and Thoreau dearly loved his Homer – "yet it is no longer *our* Epos, but shines in the distance, if clearer and clearer, yet also smaller and smaller, like a receding Star. It needs a scientific telescope, it needs to be rein-terpreted and artificially brought near to us, before we can so much as know that it *was* a Sun. So likewise a day comes when the Runic Thor, with his Eddas, must withdraw into dimness." Carlyle accordingly called for a new "hierarch" or "Pontiff of the World," a "Poet and inspired Maker . . . who, Prometheus-like, can shape new Symbols, and bring new Fire from Heaven."[2] That must have seemed a direct challenge to Thoreau, who would take the place of Runic Thor for America and shape his own magic symbols of creation.

"The poet is he who can write some pure mythology to-day without the aid of posterity," Thoreau wrote in his first book, articulating his own hope. He wanted not simply to collect "materials to serve for a mythology" but to shape the enduring fable himself that would cause his name "to shine in some corner of the firmament." His desire was to make at least one book that posterity would read and reread as the story of its own aspirations. He realized, of course, that he had stiff competi-tion, for New England, at least, had its own Bible, which it claimed to know by heart and to accept as the fable of its origin and destiny. With an audacity that was a measure both of the enormousness of his ambitions and of the calculated innocence with which he set out to fulfill them, Thoreau took the whole New England religious tradition and establish-ment on in the "Sunday" section of *A Week,* somewhat as Emerson had done in the Divinity School Address. Thoreau's stance, however, was much more aggressively cheeky than Emerson's had been ("he did not feel himself except in opposition," Emerson was to write). It was a gesture of pure Romantic rebellion.

Fresh from his excited reading in pagan literature, and especially in the eastern scriptures (definitely not on the Harvard syllabus in the 1830s), Thoreau declared himself a follower of Pan and Buddha rather than of the pale Galilean and apologized for his tastes with bland insolence: "I know that some will have hard thoughts of me, when they hear their Christ named beside my Buddha, yet I am sure that I am willing they should love their Christ more than my Buddha, for the love is the main thing, and I like him too." Thoreau's posture was that of a young scholar who has been reading up on the latest theories – comparative religion or comparative mythology, for example. He declared himself tolerant of "all philosophies, Atomists, Pneumatologists, Atheists, Theists, – Plato, Aristotle, Leucippus, Democritus, Pythagoras, Zoroaster, and Con-fucius." Noting the endless dispute "between them and their commenta-tors," he reasonably concluded that when "you compare notes, then you are all wrong." These competing fables simply canceled each other out leaving, perhaps, his own "pure mythology" to take their place.

Thoreau had also developed a taste for Ossian, the bard of James Macpherson's pseudo-Celtic legends, and warned his readers:

. . . it will not avail to call him a heathen, because he personifies the sun and addresses it; and what if his heroes did "worship the ghosts of their fathers," their thin, airy, and unsubstantial forms? we worship but the ghosts of our fathers in more substantial forms. We cannot but respect the vigorous faith of those heathen, who sternly believed somewhat, and are inclined to say to the critics, who are offended by their superstitious rites, – Don't interrupt these men's prayers. As if we knew more about human life and a God, than the heathen and the ancients. Does English theology contain the recent discoveries!

That was another direct challenge, this time based on the new science of paleontology, for when Thoreau blasted the mythology of "Father, Son, and Holy Ghost, and the like," in the "Sunday" section of his book, he argued that although they seemed "like the everlasting hills" to believers, he – in his "wanderings" – had never come across "the least vestige of authority for these things. They have not left so distinct a trace as the delicate flower of a remote geological period on the coal in my grate." Thoreau's impudent allusion was to Robert Chambers's *Vestiges of the Natural History of Creation,* published in 1844, which appeared to call into question orthodox theories of creation. But Thoreau was not in fact preaching a doctrine, scientific or otherwise; rather, he was arguing against a literal reading of writing that was essentially fabulous – pregnant myth, not gospel truth. That trace of a delicate flower on the coal in his grate was not proof of a particular theory of the earth's age and thus a refutation of calculations supposedly based on the Bible, but rather a repudiation of all such calculated readings of mythology. For Thoreau it was a sign that the true natural history of creation was endless, as old as the hills, as young as the latest flower in the fields around Concord.

His own reading of the New Testament, Thoreau tells us, was radically different from the traditional one, and he got to it late because he had been prejudiced against the book "by the church and the Sabbath school, so that it seemed, before I read it, to be the yellowest book in the catalogue." It seemed, that is, to be a collection of yellow leaves and not fresh ones because of a fixation on past events that ran counter to Thoreau's own views of creation and redemption. He insists that he loves to read scriptures, but not so much the Judeo-Christian writings as "those of the Hindoos, the Chinese, and the Persians. . . . Give me one of these Bibles and you have silenced me for a while." Silenced him, presumably, because they have taken the words right out of his mouth, said what he would say. What he has learned from these books, what he *would* say (and what his neighbors do not find very witty), is that life is to be lived; he is not overly interested in "spiritual affairs" yet because he is not yet ready to die. Christ, Thoreau notes, "taught mankind but imperfectly to live; his thoughts were all directed toward another world. There is another kind of success than his. Even here we have a sort of living to get, and must buffet it somewhat longer. There are various tough problems yet to solve, and we must make shift to live, betwixt spirit and matter, such a human life as we can."

Thoreau's insistence on *humanistic* scriptures – on scriptures that teach and preach the perfection and regeneration of our lives as creatures of the earth earthy as well as of the spirit spiritual – leads him to propose a strategy of reading the New Testament which provides a model for all such reading and is couched in one of his tightest paradoxes: "I have not yet got to the crucifixion, I have read it over so many times." Of course, if he has been going through the Gospels as he says he has, he must certainly have "got to the crucifixion," for that is where each of them gets. How could one read them over so many times and not get there? In two ways, perhaps: first, by skipping *over* the story of the crucifixion (reading *over* it); second, by refusing to stop there, by going right back to the beginning. Thoreau is proposing a circular reading of the Bible rather than a linear one, in which the end is tightly linked to the beginning. He would read, perpetually, "in the beginning" and not "in the end." Thoreau balks at the fact that the principal emblem of Christianity is a bloody crucifix and not a budding tree; though it speaks of redemption, it focuses on death. "It has hung its harp on the willows, and cannot sing a song in a strange land," he goes on; "it has dreamed a sad dream, and does not yet welcome the morning with joy." The "strange land" of Christianity is what this life becomes when viewed as an exile; but, in Thoreau's eyes, the "other world" is a mere realm of shadows. How can the joyless welcome the morning with a joyful noise? Thoreau considers psalm singing to be simply mournful: "Our hymn-books resound with a melodious cursing of God and enduring Him forever. One would say that even the prophets and redeemers had rather consoled the fears than confirmed the hopes of man."[3]

Poetry, for Thoreau, is fundamentally "the simplest relation of phenomena, and describes the commonest sensations." It is the expression of life's circulations: "The poet sings how the blood flows in his veins." He would have men and women live a *"natural* life, round which the vine clings, and which the elm willingly shadows," a life rooted in nature and its endless cycles of creation. He would not "fable of the ineffable," try to speak of the unspeakable things that no one has experienced, but rather sing of the heaven that lies about us like an image of paradise. (Here Thoreau directly anticipates Rilke: *"Preise dem Engel die Welt, nicht die unsägliche. . . ."*)[4] Thoreau is prepared to *"see* God," not "to be put off and amused in this life, as it were with a mere allegory[.] Is not Nature, rightly read, that of which she is commonly taken to be the symbol merely?" In the reading of allegory we assume that meaning lies elsewhere, not in the substance of what we are reading but in its shadow. Thoreau, however, proposes that nature is its own meaning, standing for itself, both type and antitype, the fulfillment of its own prophecy, a true creation story. He is now disposed to read that story in every natural object and to read it over in the procession of all things, from birth through life to death, world without end. Why should we give nature a bad name? "When the common man looks into the sky," Thoreau notes, "which he has not so much profaned, he thinks it less gross than the earth, and with reverence speaks of 'the Heavens,' but the seer will in the same sense speak of 'the Earths,' and his Father who is in them." The father is in the mother, spirit in body, not as a crucifixion but as a promise of union and rebirth. Why bewail our descent into life as a loss and punishment, looking back on a former state we can never hope to recover? "Everywhere 'good men' sound a retreat," Thoreau observes, "and the word has gone forth to fall back on innocence. Fall forward rather on to whatever there is there." Thoreau's own "word," then, is a counterstatement to what he considers to be a mournful gospel that tells that the battle was over before we began, that keeps the end so much in sight that even the brave live in terror.

There is, to be sure, enough to be mournful about. As the self-appointed inspector of the condition of the New World, or at least of New England, Thoreau finds his country in a rather seedy condition – the Indian killed or driven out, the whites grown gray, the farms mortgaged or exhausted. Here, for example, was a village:

> . . . Billerica, settled not long ago, and the children still bear the names of the first settlers in this late 'howling wilderness'; yet to all intents and purposes it is as old as Fernay or as Mantua, an old gray town where men grow old and sleep already under moss-grown monuments, – outgrow their usefulness. This is ancient Billerica, (Villa-rica?) now in its dotage, named from the English Billericay, and whose Indian name was Shawshine. I never heard that it was young. See, is not nature here gone to decay, farms all run out, meeting-house grown gray and racked with age? If you would know of its early youth, ask those old gray rocks in the pasture.

Thoreau will not forget those old gray rocks; he stores them away, as it were, for future reference. But here, in the "Sunday" section of his book, he wonders, as Stevens would later, why "the wind whimpers oldly of old age / In the western night."[5]

Thoreau's mild parenthetical query about the derivation of Billerica – "(Villa-rica?)" – simply brackets that ancient hope of finding El Dorado in the west and would be echoed by William Carlos Williams in his chapter on Ponce de Leon and "The Fountain of Eternal Youth" in *In the American Grain*: "Puerto Rico, *rico!* all ruined."[6] It is the same question that perplexes Hester Prynne as she confronts the disheartened Arthur Dimmesdale in the garden-forest of the New World: "Alas, what a ruin has befallen thee! . . .Wilt thou die for very weakness?" Dimmesdale explains that the "judgment of God" is on him, that the "boundless forest" appears to him no more than a harvest of "fallen leaves."[7] And that is precisely what Thoreau had observed and was determined to examine in his first book: the obsession, especially in New England, with the Fall, the nearly universal acceptance of a myth of *lapsing*. He and his brother had set out on their heroic voyage up the Merrimack in 1839 to explore the history of that myth. And as Thoreau shaped his book over the following decade as a kind of compensation for the death of John, he saw that journey up the river and back in time as a way of refuting the old fable of loss that he found still current in his own day.

It is true that some sort of primal curse seems to lie on the land, for "our brave forefathers have exterminated all the Indians," and now, Thoreau observes, their children are "degenerate." The old settlers journeyed "on foot and on horseback through the wilderness, to preach the Gospel to these minks and muskrats," but they also brought their firewater and their swords. They planted the apple tree and all were compelled to eat its bitter fruit. Thoreau understands that, of course, for he had commenced his voyage with his eye on the "lapse of the current" and seen that it was "an emblem of all progress," of the relentless march of all that is made toward the melancholy fulfillment of its fate. Death had surely come into the world with the forbidden fruit of that appealing tree. But Thoreau pauses to reflect on whether that fruit is *only* bitter. He has a notion, introduced early in the book, that "in the lapse of ages, Nature will recover and indemnify herself" – nature, and perhaps not man, but he is engaged in testing the proposition that we may become truly *naturalized* and therefore share in that recovery.

Thoreau seems to take as a kind of personal challenge a remark quoted from the New Hampshire historian Jeremy Belknap to the effect that although people in the state profess the Christian religion, there are "a sort of *wise men* who pretend to reject it; but they have not yet been able to substitute a better in its place." So, as he sits in the shade of a maple or a willow tree, munching on a melon (Thoreau was fond of noting that the word *melon* means "apple" in Greek), he contemplates "the lapse of the river and of human life" and ventures to observe that that very *lapse* may be a kind of illusion since "as things flow they circulate, and the ebb always balances the flow." Thoreau is not prepared to concede that the human race, in the Christian era, is in any greater need of reform, or more capable of effecting it, than in any other period of history. "I come out into the streets," he goes on, "and meet men who declare that the time is near at hand for the redemption of the race"; but when precisely is the time, and whose chronometer should we trust? Thoreau observes that while the reformers in Marlboro Chapel are singing, "There's a good time coming, boys," someone in the audience asks, "in good faith, 'Can you fix the date?' " and Thoreau himself adds, "Will you help it along?"

He is certainly trying, for as he eats his melon and spits out the seeds Thoreau turns and reproaches himself: "He who eats the fruit, should at least plant the seed; aye, if possible, a better seed than that whose fruit he has enjoyed. Seeds! there are seeds enough which need only to be stirred in with the soil where they lie, by an inspired voice or pen, to bear fruit of a divine flavor." What Thoreau, as a myth-making author, has to put in place of the mournful Christianity of his time is a fable of dissemination that will, he hopes, supplant the fable of decay. He will be the wastrel Henry Thoreau no longer but rather Henry Appleseed, preaching a gospel of pomology that is also a gospel of natural regeneration. Yet Thoreau is no simpleminded Pollyanna in the manner of many hyperliberal religionists of his day. He will not deny the Fall but rather assimilate it into a more comprehensive fable of rebirth. Why should we be so shy of eating apples because of that putatively painful first experience? Is knowledge bad? Is there no nourishment in it? Perhaps it contains the "seeds of a better life," as he says in *Walden*.

Thoreau acknowledges, in retelling the story of Hannah Dustan's captivity, that "she had seen her infant's brains dashed out against an apple-tree," justifying, it may be, her own brutal scalping of her captives. The reds and whites were mutual victims in this dark tale of fatal antipathy and blood lust in the forest of the New World. If awareness of the human condition is only painful and corrosive, then Hannah Dustan's baby might have been better off in suffering that single violent stroke that precluded both life and knowledge at once. It might have grown up to be an adult whose brains would be dashed out in other ways. Thoreau does not blink at the violence and cruelty inherent in human relations. Indeed, he concludes the story by reminding us that the Dustan family's reunion took place minus "the infant whose brains were dashed out against the apple-tree" and goes on to report that "there have been many who in later times have lived to say that they had eaten of the fruit of that apple-tree." He hardly needs to add, though he does, that all this "happened since Milton wrote his Paradise Lost"; we *know* that this is the sort of thing that happens post–paradise lost. We notice, however, the double-edge of Thoreau's wit: Many have lived to eat of the fruit of that apple-tree in the Miltonic sense, but they have also *lived* to eat the fruit in a simpler sense. It *is* good fruit. The infant died, alas, but others have been nourished. Shall we blame the tree for dealing out death without praising it for helping life along? God himself acknowledged that the creation was good; why should we insist that he has gone back on his word?

A passage from the "Wednesday" section of the book provides a cognate view of this issue, allowing the most serious concerns to arise colloquially and with seeming artlessness from ordinary observation:

> It is soothing to be reminded that wild nature produces anything ready for the use of man. Men know that *something* is good. One says that it is yellow-dock, another that it is bitter-sweet, another that it is slippery-elm bark, burdock, catnip, calamint, elicampane, thoroughwort, or pennyroyal. A man may esteem himself happy when that which is his food is also his medicine. There is no kind of herb, but somebody or other says that it is good. I am very glad to hear it. It reminds me of the first chapter of Genesis. But how should they know that it is good? That is the mystery to me. I am always agreeably disappointed; it is incredible that they should have found it out. Since all things are good, men fail at last to distinguish which is the bane, and which the antidote. There are sure to be two prescriptions diametrically opposite.

We may be reminded here of Genesis in more ways than one, for God pronounced the creation good and we have found that out, mainly through trial and error, by tasting the fruits of the earth. Is knowledge bad, then? Is it really useful to try to distinguish between a natural fruit that is supposed to be a "bane" and a supernatural one, perhaps like the Eucharist, that is supposedly the "antidote"? It may be that the prescription that insists that we take our medicine before we have clearly ascertained that we have a disease is not worth following. If we treat all natural things as food, we may find ourselves in better health at last, ceasing to keep our hands on our pulses in anticipation of disasters that have been predicted.

Thoreau, at all events, is content to munch his fruit, bittersweet as it may be, getting what nourishment he can and laying the seeds aside for another season, thus helping to keep things in circulation. As Thoreau prepares to return to Concord in the "Friday" section of his book (that day marked darkly in the Christian calendar), he notes the change of season, summer to autumn, but is cheered by the sound of the river endlessly running. "He who hears the rippling of rivers in these degenerate days," he observes, "will not utterly despair." But as his boat rapidly descends the Merrimack, the shores appear to be lined with grave men whose faces announce "that the Fall had commenced." Thoreau, however, is determined not to be discouraged. Things do, it is true, go to seed, but "the constant abrasion and decay of our lives makes the soil of our future growth." He allows himself to fall into an autumnal mood, noting, for instance, that "the banks and the distant meadows wore a sober and deepened tinge," as does this chapter; but the disease and the antidote, we recall, are one and the same. Getting ready to reenter Concord, Thoreau holds "in one hand half of a tart country apple-pie . . . purchased to celebrate our return" and devours it with relish and "a devil-may-care look" on his face. He will enjoy the crisp autumnal weather but defy the Fall, for sometimes – perhaps most of the time – an apple is simply an apple, and the devils we most fear are the ones we ourselves have conjured up.

Thoreau is in a mood to attend to the "literal" rather than the "metaphorical sense" of words and the things for which they stand. "They are already *supernatural* philosophy," but he wants to savor their natural meaning, believing as he does that "the laws of Nature are the purest morality." Of course, Thoreau understands that "the Tree of Knowledge is a Tree of Knowledge of good and evil"; that is precisely why he refuses to separate out the notion of the Fall as simply representing irreparable disaster. He has undertaken to make his own experiments, for true knowledge can be acquired in no other way. He must eat his own apple, tart as it may be. "How can we *know* what we are *told* merely?" he asks.

Each man can interpret another's experience only by his own. We read that Newton discovered the law of gravitation, but how many who have heard of his famous discovery have recognized the same truth that he did? It may be not one. The revelation which was then made to him has not been superseded by the revelation made to any successor.

> We see the *planet* fall,
> And that is all.

We see in our mind's eye that little cosmos, Newton's apple, descending onto his head, but how many of us have been touched in a similar way? It may be that, with Newton, we see the *planet* fall, but do we see or feel ourselves falling with it? Perhaps from the standpoint of an individual human life the Fall is merely an illusion, for the ground still seems solid under our feet. Though Thoreau's mood is undeniably fallish (the days are shorter and the chill is increasing), he finds himself, as he rows homeward, thinking of "some autumnal work to do" that may "help on the revolution of the seasons," thus keeping things in circulation, rather than bringing them to an end. Even if his own seeds fail to take root, he may hope to be the unwitting agent of future dissemination: "Perhaps Nature would condescend to make use of us even without our knowledge, as when we help to scatter her seeds in our walks, and carry burrs and cockles on our clothes from field to field."

But Thoreau does realize that he is a marked man in one important respect, at least, for he is about to conclude his book. "The most excellent speech," he must admit, "finally falls into Silence." And so silence becomes his subject, briefly, as a means of forestalling the end and filling the void. One typically Thoreauvian approach is humor. "Silence," he notes, "is the universal refuge, the sequel to all dull discourses," implying that we may be content to have him stop talking. Another equally Thoreauvian strategy is paradox: Why not argue that the best part of the book is the one we have not yet succeeded in composing? "We not unfrequently refer the interest which belongs to our own unwritten sequel, to the written and comparatively lifeless body of the work. Of all books this sequel is the most indispensable part." The rest may be silence, Thoreau implies, but it is a pregnant silence, promising to fulfill what has not yet been accomplished. Books, then, are endless, representing only the spoken part of a further creation that we are not yet in a position to hear. But Thoreau realizes that he is only temporizing, postponing an inevitable conclusion that he must soon face. Silence *is* a tough nut to crack: "A man may run on confidently for a time, thinking he has her under his thumb, and shall one day exhaust her, but he too must at last be silent, and men remark only how brave a beginning he made." Has the lapse of time finally done Thoreau in? Is his book only a brave beginning leading to a rather shaky finish? How can he recover himself from this imminent threat of extinction – which is, after all, the very negation of his boast that experience is circular, linking every end to a new beginning?

One answer lies in the fact that Thoreau's courageous little essay on silence is not his last word in *A Week*. He concludes rather, and more appropriately, by tying up the loose ends of his narrative of discovery:

> We had made about fifty miles this day with sail and oar, and now, far in the evening, our boat was grating against the bulrushes of its native port, and its keel recognized the Concord mud, where some semblance of its outline was still preserved in the flattened flags which had scarce yet erected themselves since our departure; and we leaped gladly on shore, drawing it up, and fastening it to the wild apple-tree, whose stem still bore the mark which its chain had worn in the chafing of the spring freshets.

"O Joy!" Thoreau might exclaim with Wordsworth,

> . . . that in our embers
> Is something that doth live,
> That nature yet remembers
> What was so fugitive!

Thoreau and his boat *have* been fugitives – from Concord and that receding springtime – as all our experience is steadily fleeing down the corridors of time in a ceaseless flow that may be considered the emblem of our ephemerality and lapse. But nature does remember – and *we* remember. That wild apple tree, with its spring-inflicted gash, is as much the promise of what is to come as it is the reminder of an ancient affliction. The gash is a high-water mark that sustains Thoreau at the low point of the year's cycle, evidence that nature will recoup its own losses.

But there is another passage in the "Friday" section of *A Week* that embodies, with less self-conscious myth making, Thoreau's unshakable belief in the possibility of renewal. It is a good example of Thoreau's real strength as a writer: unforced description and exposition that opens out to larger implication without rhetorical exaggeration, strained wit, or the flashy paradoxes of his more metaphysical displays:

> When I visit again some haunt of my youth, I am glad to find that nature wears so well. The landscape is indeed something real, and solid, and sincere, and I have not put my foot through it yet. There is a pleasant tract on the bank of the Concord, called Conantum, which I have in my mind: – the old deserted farm-house, the desolate pasture with its bleak cliff, the open wood, the river-reach, the green meadow in the midst, and the moss-grown wild-apple orchard, – places where one may have many thoughts and not decide anything. It is a scene which I can not only remember, as I might a vision, but when I will can bodily revisit, and find it even so, unaccountable, yet unpretending in its pleasant dreariness. When my thoughts are sensible of change, I love to see and sit on rocks which I *have* known, and pry into their moss, and see unchangeableness so established. I not yet gray on rocks forever gray, I no longer green under the evergreens. There is something even in the lapse of time by which time recovers itself.

This passage is clearly meant to respond to the one on Billerica from the "Monday" section of the book, for the "old gray rocks in the pasture" of the earlier description that are the sole witness to the town's youth reappear here as the memorial of nature's stability. Thoreau, "not yet gray" but "no longer green," caught for a moment somewhere between youth and age, confronts a nature that is at once "forever gray" and "evergreen." The landscape is real, solid, and sincere – a dependable world, not a façade one can fall through. It is a world both ideal and real, a *real* vision, for Thoreau can have it in his mind as a permanent possession of the imagination *and* return to sit with his body as a way of verifying its stability. It enables him also to recapture the past, his lost youth, because the scene is *haunted* by his younger self, still inhabited by the spirit of Thoreau's earlier time. He *has* known these rocks and knows them still in an epistemological continuity that annuls the passage of time. When Thoreau sits on these familiar rocks it is as if he had never left them, and he is thus enabled to feel the stability of his existence. Memory is made concrete, a real presence and not the ghost of experience. It is worth noting that the scene as described has no definable links to a particular season but instead represents that "unimaginable point of time," mentioned earlier in the chapter, in which summer turns into autumn, or any season into any other.[8] It is a scene in which all the seasons are rolled into one, whereby time does not stand still but rather transcends itself. We know time by its effects, but time knows itself not at all; Thoreau has managed to create an image of pure duration: time in its own endless present.[9] *That* is the "something even in the lapse of time by which time recovers itself."

The principle of "unchangeableness" is the one Thoreau wrote his book to establish as a credible response to the Fall, and by inserting himself into the scene he attempts to procure the only kind of immortality a writer can hope for. Thoreau is now, in fact, "no longer green under the evergreens" in Concord's Sleepy Hollow cemetery, but in our mind's eye we can still see him sitting on that pleasantly dreary rock whenever we revisit *A Week on the Concord and Merrimack Rivers.*

2

We may get some idea of the long foreground that preceded the composition of *Walden* by noting this entry in Emerson's journal for September 8, 1838: "Henry Thoreau told a good story of Deacon Parkman, who lived in the house he now occupies, & kept a store close by. He hung out a salt fish for a sign, & it hung so long & grew so hard, black & deformed, that the deacon forgot what thing it was, & nobody in town knew, but being examined chemically it proved to be salt fish. But duly every morning the deacon hung it on its peg."[10] In good Emersonian fashion the story suggests, perhaps, how symbols decay, becoming detached from the things for which they originally stood. If Deacon Parkman was a good Christian, as we may suppose, the black and deformed fish might be imagined as a kind of satire on the pretensions of his faith to be a living one. Indeed, the grotesquely indurated fish seems almost to satirize Deacon Parkman himself, for it is his sign and he hangs it on its peg out of sheer habit, despite what time has done to it, apparently unaware that it is no longer a good advertisement for his business.

When Thoreau retold his own story sixteen years later in *Walden,* he pointed the moral somewhat differently:

> Who has not seen a salt fish, thoroughly cured for this world, so that nothing can spoil it, and putting the perseverance of the saints to the blush? with which you may sweep or pave the streets, and split your kindlings, and the teamster shelter himself and his lading against sun wind and rain behind it, – and the trader, as a Concord trader once did, hang it up by his door for a sign when he commences business, until at last his oldest customer cannot tell surely whether it be animal, vegetable, or mineral, and yet it shall be as pure as a snowflake, and if it be put into a pot and boiled, will come out an excellent dun fish for a Saturday's dinner. ("Sounds")

That may not be the kind of New England boiled dinner many would want to sit down to, but Thoreau, of course, has other fish to fry. In its incredible metamorphosis, this magical object does indeed run through the cycle of animal, vegetable, and mineral, becoming by turns a broom, a paving stone, an axe, a shelter, a sign, and finally – once again – a fish, more nourishing in the lesson it teaches about the durability of life than are the persevering saints themselves. The cure for disbelief, Thoreau implies, is the *cured* fish itself, which functions here as a symbol of the possibility of rebirth that we may find more credible, in its humor, than the better-known and rather labored parable of the resurrected bug at the end of *Walden.* At least one contemporary reader of Thoreau's book – namely, Herman Melville – thought that bug parable so fantastic and overinflated that he took the trouble to parody it in his own sketch, "The Apple-Tree Table," in which the newly risen bug, beautiful as "a sparkle of a glorious sunset," enjoys its perfect summer life for only a day before expiring. We are free to assume that Melville found Thoreau's good fish-story more to his taste.[11]

It appears, at all events, that the trope of rebirth, whether embodied in Deacon Parkman's cured fish or the bug parable or the resounding sentence announcing that "Walden was dead and is alive again," represents Thoreau's earliest conception for his book. Why, we may ask, was Thoreau so attracted to the notion of defunct things *returning* to life as opposed to the story of birth itself? His favorite myths are those of re-

creation or pre-creation rather than of procreation, which, as in the
"Spring" chapter of *Walden,* is described with fascinated horror in terms
of "excrements of all kinds," with "no end to the heaps of liver lights and
bowels, as if the globe were turned wrong side outward." The human
being – "a mass of thawing clay" – is born, in Thoreau's fantasy, in a
great splash of filth. Though Thoreau's overarching theme is the endless
cycle of the seasons, the cycle of human procreation seems to have filled
him with the sort of existential disgust that laces Sweeney's words in
Eliot's "Fragment of an Agon":

> Birth, and copulation, and death.
> That's all the facts when you come to brass tacks:
> Birth, and copulation, and death.
> I've been born, and once is enough.
> You don't remember, but I remember,
> Once is enough.[12]

Thoreau appears to have remembered only too well the welter of
blood, guts, urine, and excrement out of which we all issue, so his re-
creation fable tells of new life proceeding from a state of dryness rather
than of wetness: the hard salt-fish, the dry ice, so to speak, of Walden
frozen, the "dry leaf" of the apple tree table. The very insistence on re-
creation instead of creation marks the central mood of Walden: Thoreau's sharp sense of the Fall, of the introduction of death and sex into the
world, of his having *lapsed* into life (that is his term in "Spring") from the
messy body of nature. The Golden Age he truly fancies is one when
"punishment and fear were not," when "there was eternal spring, and
placid zephyrs with warm / Blasts soothed the flowers born without
seed." The world after the Fall, which enforces the familiar conditions of
birth, copulation, and death, was repugnant to Thoreau's imagination
and thus drove him into a kind of Romantic prelapsarianism, a glorification of pre-Adamic life, or at least of Adam and Eve in their first state,
when, as he says, they "wore the bower before other clothes." He hopes
to nullify the effects of the Fall, insisting that "it is not necessary that a
man should earn his living by the sweat of his brow, unless he sweats
easier than I do." Thoreau refuses to sweat at all: He pretends there is no
labor in his reconstituted world. He loves Walden and its woods because
he believes they were "already in existence" before "Adam and Eve were
driven out of Eden" and were "covered with myriads of ducks and
geese, which had not heard of the fall." Thoreau's unwillingness to enter
into the world's work, to *rise* in the world, anticipates a fall and deflects
it. "It is best," he says, "to avoid the beginnings of evil." He makes his
bread without yeast, for this principle of expansion and growth, "first

brought over in the Mayflower, did the business for America, and its influence is still rising, swelling, spreading, in cerealian billows over the land." It represents the "seed" of aggressiveness in the American spirit. Thoreau used to carry a bottleful of it in his pocket until it popped and discharged its contents, to his "discomfiture," proving him to be no better than any other fallen creature.

"I care not how obscene my *words* are," Thoreau insists, and he makes good on that promise to speak frankly, discoursing on the functions of the body and exhibiting himself urinating on trees to keep them from withering and squatting on the land to enhance its value. He is, as he says, "elevating what is mean." Particularly concerned to preserve his "generative energy," Thoreau is openly disgusted by the phallic aggressiveness and wastefulness of American business, whether embodied in the new Fitchburg Railroad, plowing "a furrow from the mountains to the seaboard, in which the cars, like a following drill-barrow, sprinkle all the restless men and floating merchandise in the country for seed," or in the ravishing of Walden Pond. In the latter case a hundred men, "with many car-loads of ungainly-looking farming tools, sleds, plows, drill-barrows, turf-knives, spades, saws, rakes, and each man . . . armed with a double-pointed pike-staff," go to work "plowing, harrowing, rolling, furrowing . . . as if they were bent on making this a model farm; but when I was looking sharp to see what kind of seed they dropped into the furrow, a gang of fellows by my side suddenly began to hook up the virgin mould itself, with a peculiar jerk" (Thoreau is happy to report that "sometimes Squaw Walden had her revenge, and a hired man, walking behind his team, slipped through a crack in the ground down toward Tartarus . . . or sometimes the frozen soil took a piece of steel out of a ploughshare, or a plow got set in the furrow and had to be cut out"). This is the sexual battle of the modern world, rendered in proto-technological terms, whereby not even insemination but only brutal appropriation is accomplished, and Thoreau wants no part of it.

His disgust, finally, is with sexuality itself, as in one of the strangest of Thoreau's journal entries, a description of the stinkhorn, or *phallus impudicus,* which shows Thoreau fully involved in the fascination of the abomination. Bringing this offensive object home, he watches it "melting and defiling what it touched with a fetid, olivaceous, semiliquid matter," filling the house with the odor of dead rat. "Pray," he asks, "what was Nature thinking of when she made this? She almost puts herself on a level with those who draw in privies."[13] Since Thoreau actually made a drawing of this shameless phallic fungus in the privacy of his journal,[14] his own complicity is manifest. Among other things, nature was undoubtedly "thinking" of Henry Thoreau himself, a male animal who also had a sexual organ that must have seemed to him to deliquesce, like the *phallus impudicus,* after depositing its spores. Thoreau feared to become what, he suggested in "Economy," most men were, "the tools of their tools" – little more than sexual instruments in nature's postlapsarian plan. Better to be a piece of dried cod, miraculously transformed into good edible fish, than a cod-piece ingloriously detumesced into a pool of fetid "semiliquid matter."

Thoreau felt that most men were content to be merely sexual animals, "busy about their beans," ploughing and sowing and finally incapable of transcending the physical conditions of their lives. "We would not deal with man thus plodding ever," he writes in "The Bean-Field" chapter, "leaning on a hoe or a spade as a staff between his work, not as a mushroom, but partially risen out of the earth, something more than erect. . . ." This is a persistent figure in Thoreau's writings, one he had already used in the "Friday" section of *A Week,* where he quotes two lines, often described as among his favorites, from Samuel Daniel's "Epistle to the Lady Margaret, Countess of Cumberland":

> Unless above himself he can
> Erect himself, how poor a thing is man!

Then Thoreau comments: "With our music we would fain challenge transiently another and finer sort of intercourse than our daily toil permits. . . . Why have they so painted the fruits, and freighted them with such fragrance as to satisfy a more than animal appetite?" Daily toil – the curse of Adam – permits and encourages little more than sexual intercourse, in Thoreau's eyes. By erecting himself above himself, becoming "something more than erect," he hoped to challenge traditional definitions of masculine virtue and rekindle a spark of divinity in his fellows. He would "brag as lustily as chanticleer in the morning" not to prove that he was cock-of-the-walk but to awaken his neighbors to his own peculiar mode of secular redemption. Thus he imagines himself, at the end of the "Higher Laws" chapter, playing his flute, like Orpheus, to charm John Farmer out of thinking of his labor and help him to "recreate his intellectual man." The notes of Thoreau's flute

> came home to his ears out of a different sphere from that he worked in, and suggested work for certain faculties which slumbered in him. They gently did away with the street, and the village, and the state in which he lived. A voice said to him, – Why do you stay here and live this mean moiling life, when a glorious existence is possible for you? Those same stars twinkle over other fields than these. – But how to come out of this condition and actually migrate thither? All that he could think of was to practise some new

austerity, to let his mind descend into his body and redeem it, and treat himself with ever increasing respect.

That is an inspiriting message, but Thoreau's austerities are undeniably a bit severe, suggesting why, as Emerson reports, one of Thoreau's friends said "I love Henry . . . but I cannot like him; and as for taking his arm, I should as soon think of taking the arm of an elm-tree."[15] If the cure for the human condition is to turn yourself into a hard object, to become so thoroughly cured of physical appetite and desire that nothing can spoil or touch you, it might seem too high a price to pay for perfection, at least in terms of human relations – as when Thoreau articulates a view of friendship in the "Wednesday" section of *A Week* that insists that it "is not so kind as is imagined; it has not much human blood in it, but consists with a certain disregard for men and their erections, the Christian duties and humanities, while it purifies the air like electricity." That desire to purify the air may be said to mark Thoreau as the true Romantic-Puritan ("a protestant *à outrance*," as Emerson called him), whose protest against the messy nature of ordinary life led him to Walden in the hope of reducing it to its simplest essence. His aim was "to drive life into a corner," as if it were a trapped rat, perhaps just as he had cornered the *phallus impudicus* – to "reduce it to its lowest terms, and, if it proved to be mean, why then to get the whole and genuine meanness of it, and publish its meanness to the world." If, on the other hand, it proved finally to be "sublime," Thoreau would know that, too, "by experience," so as to be able to give "a true account of it."

The essential point here is Thoreau's function as a writer – his consuming desire to *publish* life, to give an *account* of it. We may say that such a procedure dehumanizes experience, in Ortega y Gasset's language, but it also redeems it, saves it from the natural processes that are devouring it. Thoreau's project turns Walden Pond into *Walden* the book[16]; to appropriate his own figures, it turns the *liber,* or inner bark of the tree, into an intellectual *liber,* or garment of words; it dries nature out, as if nature were a drunkard in need of reform, translating the squishy, wet innards of the world into pressed and dried letters, so that life may transcend itself and express itself "outwardly in leaves." The only way to get life permanently to reform, to "turn over a new leaf at last," is to force it to flower into language. Thoreau's true staff of life is his writing implement. He erects himself above himself by making his pencil his tool, or his tool his pencil (let us remember that he defines himself in *A Week* as "a pencil-maker"), whereby he works in his bean-field "only for the sake of tropes and expression, to serve a parable-maker one day." He had already made the same point in *A Week*: "What have I to do with ploughs? I cut another furrow than you see." The proposition is reversible, of course, in the sense that the writer's actual work in the bean-field gives vigor, vitality, and a base of reality to his craft:

> A sentence should read as if its author, had he held a plough instead of a pen, could have drawn a furrow deep and straight to the end. The scholar requires hard and serious labor to give an impetus to his thought. He will learn to grasp the pen firmly so, and wield it gracefully and effectively, as an axe or a sword.

Thoreau had in fact held the plow himself, but the *as if* is important here, for the staff that Thoreau shapes so lovingly and wields so deliberately, as in the artist of Kouroo parable, is finally, as we have noted, a pencil, the instrument with which he helps "to clothe that fabulous landscape of [his] infant dreams" (as he calls Walden Woods) in a decent shift of words.

"This world is but canvas to our imaginations," Thoreau observes in *A Week*. "I see men with infinite pains endeavoring to realize to their bodies, what I, with at least equal pains, would realize to my imagination, – its capacities; for certainly there is a life of the mind above the wants of the body, and independent of it." Thoreau's need to erect himself above his body marks him as an artist who miraculously retards "the waste and decay of physical life" by removing it to the silent death-in-life of his page, as if he had scrawled on the wall of nature's privy, "Gone, but returning soon." He appropriates Deacon Parkman's fish as his emblem because it represents nature dried and hardened and transformed into a tool of expression. The Deacon's "sign" is Thoreau's book – a signifier without a signified, a seed not yet sown but eternally ready for fertilization, like the Egyptian wheat he speaks of in "Economy," which "was handed down to us by a mummy." We the readers must soak that petrified *Walden* in our own fluid imaginations, as in King Tching-thang's tub, in order to bring it back to life whereby, as Thoreau says of himself and his journal, we get our "labor" for our "pains."

That is the point of Thoreau's submerged figure of parturition in the "Reading" chapter of *Walden*. The best books "will always be in a language dead to degenerate times; and we must laboriously seek the meaning of each word and line, conjecturing a larger sense than common use permits out of what wisdom and valor and generosity we have." A written word is no more than a relic, though it may be "the choicest of relics." Only through our labors can "the symbol of an ancient man's thought [become] a modern man's speech." Thoreau's *Walden,* which was dead before (*nature morte,* a collection of silent, dried leaves), is thus reborn as living flesh and good nourishment. Signing his own process,

Thoreau promises that the "throes" of that new birth "will heave our exuviae from their graves." The landscape of Walden as we have it in Thoreau's book is indeed a dreamscape, a world capable of being realized only through the agency of a reader's imagination. And the composition of *Walden* is endless because it is only preliminary, the prolegomenon to all future interpretations. The regenerated life it prophesies lies wholly within us, waiting to come forth, and Thoreau seems, like Whitman, to "recline by the sills of the exquisite flexible doors" in this metaphysical *accouchement*, to "mark the outlet, and mark the relief and escape."[17]

In fact Thoreau is preeminently the man of the doorsill who sits musing in the margins of ordinary experience, reluctant to cross over into a fallen world of things accomplished and life consumed. A crucial passage in the "Sounds" chapter of *Walden* defines his peculiar posture:

I did not read books the first summer; I hoed beans. Nay, I often did better than this. There were times when I could not afford to sacrifice the bloom of the present moment to any work, whether of the head or hands. I love a broad margin to my life. Sometimes, in a summer morning, having taken my accustomed bath, I sat in my sunny doorway from sunrise till noon, rapt in a revery, amidst the pines and hickories and sumacs, in undisturbed solitude and still- ness, while the birds sang around or flitted noiseless through the house, until by the sun falling in at my west window, or the noise of some traveller's wagon on the distant highway, I was reminded of the lapse of time. I grew in those seasons like corn in the night, and they were far better than any work of the hands would have been. They were not time subtracted from my life, but so much over and above my usual allowance. I realized what the Orientals mean by contemplation and the forsaking of works. For the most part, I minded not how the hours went. The day advanced as if to light some work of mine; it was morning, and lo, now it is evening, and nothing memorable is accomplished. Instead of sing- ing like the birds, I silently smiled at my incessant good fortune. As the sparrow had its trill, sitting on the hickory before my door, so had I my chuckle or suppressed warble which he might hear out of my nest. My days were not days of the week, bearing the stamp of any heathen deity, nor were they minced into hours and fretted by the ticking of a clock. . . . This was sheer idleness to my fellow- townsmen, no doubt; but if the birds and flowers had tried me by their standard, I should not have been found wanting. A man must find his occasions in himself, it is true. The natural day is very calm, and will hardly reprove his indolence.

Presumably the usual order of our existence is to rise early, perform our ablutions (perhaps mainly by force of habit), and then proceed to our tasks. Thoreau, by contrast, refuses "to sacrifice the bloom of the present moment," as he puts it, "to any work." The sacred ritual of the bath is an act of physical and spiritual renewal that leads, not to work, but rather to a calculated abstention from work. It is preliminary, one might say, to nothing; for Thoreau proceeds simply to sit in the "sunny doorway" and let time and the world pass by and away. "I love a broad margin to my life," he says. And we might add: He loves to live *in* the margins of life, just to one side of the ordinary occupations and concerns that engage most people. Thoreau prefers to sit in the doorway (*limen,* in Latin). His position in the world can thus be called *liminary.* He lives perpetually in the threshold, in the place of anticipation and entrance, and imagines that he can thereby transcend human time and become one with the un-selfconscious birds and flowers who never know that they were born to die. To live in the margin, to rest in preliminaries, Thoreau seems to suggest, is to achieve a sense of eternity, for there is always something more to expect. If we refuse to begin, we may not be forced to end. We may be able to say at the end of our book that "there is more day to dawn."

Anthropologists tell us that the so-called *rites de passage,* namely, the "rites which accompany every change of place, state, social position and age," are "marked by three phases: separation, margin (or *limen,* signifying 'threshold' in Latin), and aggregation. The first phase (of separation)," as Victor Turner explains, "comprises symbolic behavior signifying the detachment of the individual . . . from an earlier fixed point in the social structure, from a set of cultural conditions (a 'state'), or from both." We may recognize here a description of Thoreau's decision to leave his "restless, nervous, bustling, trivial Nineteenth Century" and live alone, in a kind of holy solitude, at Walden Pond. Our neophyte then enters the "liminal" stage and becomes a "passenger." According to Turner, "the attributes of liminality or of liminal *personae* ('threshold people')"

> are necessarily ambiguous, since this condition and these persons elude or slip through the network of classifications that normally locate states and positions in cultural space. Liminal entities are neither here nor there; they are betwixt and between the positions assigned and arrayed by law, custom, convention, and ceremonial.

This ambiguous condition may be likened "to death, to being in the womb, to invisibility, to darkness, to bisexuality, to the wilderness. . . ."[18] Having relinquished his social identity and his place in society, Thoreau has retired to Walden Woods in the hope of preparing himself for spiritual rebirth in a "more perfect and glorious State." But, like some medieval monk in his monastery, Thoreau discovers that this liminal or withdrawn condition, this life of preparation for or transition toward a higher state, becomes more or less permanent: not because he believes, as does the monk, that the New Jerusalem is to be found only on the other side of every earthly Jordan, but rather because he discovers he loves to linger in the margins of experience, unburdened by the responsibilities and expectations normally associated with life in society. Thoreau could say, with Whitman:

> Beginning my studies the first step pleas'd me so much,
> The mere fact consciousness, these forms, the power of motion,
> The least insect or animal, the senses, eyesight, love,
> The first step I say awed me and pleas'd me so much,
> I have hardly gone and hardly wish'd to go any farther,
> But stop and loiter all the time to sing it in ecstatic songs.[19]

At this point common sense may wish to enter and complain that Thoreau in fact *did* leave his doorstep in the woods and return, as he puts it, to "civilized life again." The best response would be that that is precisely the illusion Thoreau attempts to create in his book, the illusion that he has performed the whole cycle of separation, liminality, and return, only in order that he might become a good citizen again at the end: Huckleberry Finn, so to speak, capitulating to the world of Tom Sawyer after his escapade with Jim on the raft. But I shall undertake to demonstrate shortly that Thoreau is an incorrigible rascal and never intended to relinquish his marginal existence as "self-appointed inspector of snow storms and rain storms." He was a professional loiterer whose vocation it was to "anticipate, not the sunrise and the dawn merely, but, if possible, Nature herself!" – meaning, presumably, that Thoreau was determined to catch nature herself in the very act of crossing the threshold of existence.

Thoreau wants to be in at the beginning, not at the end of things. He discovered the peculiar pleasures of lingering over preliminaries. Thoreau insists that Walden Pond "is a good port and a good foundation," but he never took the time to drive his piles. His business, as he notes, was "entered into without the usual capital." As a result, and thanks to strict accounting procedures, he never suffered bankruptcy. "The cart before the horse," he says, "is neither beautiful nor useful"; however, avoiding both, he was never forced to go to market. What he did, in fact, was to borrow an axe in March, 1845, and begin to cut down trees. Thoreau's description of that period makes it clear that he took time to linger over his work, enjoying both the labor and the metamorphoses of nature in that spring season. "I made no haste in my work," he writes, "but rather made the most of it." Thoreau's little joke, as always, is instructive. We make the "most" of our work not by hurrying through it but rather by savoring its every detail. "The truly efficient laborer," he notes in *A Week,* "will not crowd his day with work but will saunter to his task surrounded by a wide halo [a margin] of ease and leisure, and then do but what he loves best." The point of making something lies in the pleasure of the activity and not in the proposed end. Thoreau himself worked so slowly that his tiny house was still not quite done when he moved in on the Fourth of July. Lacking a chimney, he had to cook outdoors (which he seemed to prefer in any case). Indeed, the work of construction is suspended, imaginatively at least, until Chapter 13, when we finally learn in detail about the building of the chimney. "I lingered most about the fireplace," he tells us, as he dwells lovingly over the scraping of each second-hand brick. The work was done in true Thoreauvian fashion – "deliberately," as he says. "I was pleased to see my work rising so square and solid by degrees, and reflected, that, if it proceeded slowly, it was calculated to endure a long time." We may take that as a commentary on the book as well. And we shall see that Thoreau's impulse was in fact to proceed so slowly and deliberately that neither the book nor his experience at the pond would ever end. Thus, presumably, would he be certain to have made the most enduring work of art.

What Thoreau has to say, at all events, about his method of construction is that "it would be worth the while to build still more deliberately than I did, considering, for instance, what foundation a door, a window, a cellar, a garret, have in the nature of man, and perchance never raising any superstructure until we found a better reason for it than our temporal necessities even." We may think we need a superstructure, he suggests, but our time would be better spent thinking about fundamentals – the premises of our premises. The door, for example, is the entrance to our premises. How can we hope to give birth to any solid ideas until we have thoroughly examined the point of entrance, our assumptions and aims? "The mode of founding a college," Thoreau says,

> is, commonly, to get up a subscription of dollars and cents, and then following blindly the principles of a division of labor to its extreme, a principle which should never be followed but with circumspection, – to call in a contractor who makes this a subject of speculation, and he employs Irishmen or other operatives actually to lay the foundations, while the students that are to be are said to be fitting themselves for it; and for these oversights successive

generations have to pay. I think it would be *better than this,* for the students, or those who desire to be benefited by it, even to lay the foundation themselves. ("Economy")

By "laying the foundation" Thoreau clearly means that students should prepare the ground for their own education, taking care not to separate themselves from those first steps, which are not antecedent to college and living, but the very thing itself, the preliminary phase of an experiment for which it may serve as the perfect model of deliberate activity. If you live this beginning earnestly enough, Thoreau suggests, you may find yourself never quite leaving the threshold, discovering an end in that beginning. "With a little more deliberation in the choice of their pursuits," he writes, "all men would perhaps become essentially students and observers, for certainly their nature and destiny are interesting to all alike." Why rush forward hastily to meet that destiny before you have dwelt sufficiently on the preliminaries? Thoreau's parable of the artist of Kouroo promises that life can become a kind of eternal present for the dedicated searcher after truth and perfection.

I have been arguing that Thoreau is par excellence the artist of the eternal present whose belief in doing the work before him with full intention and devotion helped him to feel that he had transcended time, that his beginnings would never end. He started his house in the spring and finished his book in the same place; or if we wish to consider the "Conclusion" as the end, he leaves us in the margins of an ever-dawning day that has nothing to do with the lapse of time. How do we square that unconcluded conclusion with the obvious fact that the very opening of the book announces that Thoreau's Walden life ended after two years and two months? We are everywhere in *Walden* promised an endless beginning but the book begins with a clear-cut ending and return, as if Thoreau had actually abandoned the posture of the liminal man and completed the third stage of the *rites de passage* in a reconciliation with "civilized life." Notice, however, one small equivocation right here: He says, at the end of the first paragraph, "[A]t present I am a sojourner in civilized life again." A *sojourner* is not a dweller, but rather a traveler. Where is our pilgrim off to now?

The most amusing and instructive answer is to be found in the book itself. The "bulk" of it, we are told (another sly equivocation: did he add the *sense* later?), was assembled during the two years and two months. That is in fact untrue, but we do not need to know anything about the history of the composition of *Walden* to see that Thoreau is not telling the whole truth. Though he reports at the end of the "Spring" chapter that he left the pond on September 6, 1847, because it seemed to him that he "had several more lives to live, and could not spare any more time for that one," this very chapter opens with a note on the pond in the winter of 1852–3 and goes on to list similar data right up to 1854, when *Walden* was published. Thoreau's "leisure and opportunity to see the Spring come in" thus stretched well beyond the official date of withdrawal from his hermitage because his principal occupation continued to be that of observing his beloved pond cross the threshold from winter to spring. Thoreau was drawn back to that beginning – that "memorable crisis" – for as long as his feet would carry him, indeed, until he himself suffered the last crisis of his health and crossed his final threshold in the spring of 1862. His actual book, *Walden*, reports on the pond's transition from winter to spring as long as possible – until the printer locked up his forms in the late spring of 1854. But Thoreau's *ideal* book, the *Walden* he never ceased writing in his head and his journals, goes on forever recording new beginnings. The actual *Walden* may be considered a mere paradigm of that self-perpetuating account of the liminal life. How can a work of art endure forever if it is incapable of renewing itself with the regeneration of nature in the spring? We ourselves, of course, and the endless procession of readers to follow, are invited to fill in the dates as *Walden* comes alive again in successive springs.

So we come to understand Thoreau's little joke. The "several more lives" he had to live were in fact no different from the one he immortalized in the book. "More of the same" might have been Thoreau's motto.[20] How could a man who loved to loiter and linger in the broad margins of existence really worry about sparing "any more time" for the only life he had and the only occupations he believed in? The next life, which we are in such haste to get to, Thoreau might be suggesting, is likely to be only a poor imitation of the one we now have. A bird in the hand . . . Thus Thoreau preferred to return to Walden, sitting in the doorsill even after the superstructure had collapsed, as he sat on the gray rocks in *A Week,* having "many thoughts and not [deciding] anything," forever meditating on his premises and anticipating "that morrow which mere lapse of time can never make to dawn." Such, he must have thought, was the only way to end; for he understood that it was also the perfect threshold to endless new beginnings and a perpetually resurrecting self.

Chapter 7

Melville: Romantic Cock-and-Bull; or, The Great Art of Telling the Truth

―――――――

1

Chapter 99 of *Moby-Dick*, "The Doubloon."[1] Ahab is pacing his quarter-deck, as always, and stops to meditate on the sixteen-dollar gold piece that he has nailed to the mainmast as "the White Whale's talisman" and reward to whosoever raises Moby-Dick. Ahab, of course, will collect his own reward, since he is the one fated to discover the preternatural creature he has effectively conjured up, but now he pauses, before the payoff, to read his horoscope in this "equatorial coin" with its three Andes summits, tower, "crowing cock," and cabalistic zodiac:

> "There's something ever egotistical in mountain-tops and towers, and all other grand and lofty things; look here, – three peaks as proud as Lucifer. The firm tower, that is Ahab; the volcano, that is Ahab, the courageous, the undaunted, and victorious fowl, that, too, is Ahab; all are Ahab; and this round gold is but the image of the rounder globe, which, like a magician's glass, to each and every man in turn but mirrors back his own mysterious self. . . . [T]his coined sun wears a ruddy face; but see! aye, he enters the sign of storms, the equinox! and but six months before he wheeled out of a former equinox at Aries! From storm to storm! So be it, then. Born in throes, 'tis fit that man should live in pains and die in pangs! So be it, then! Here's stout stuff for woe to work on. So be it, then."

As has often been observed, Ahab's reading of the coin is narcissistic or solipsistic – the Emersonian "noble doubt" run wild. Ahab, we are not surprised to learn, sees the world and its contents as mere mirrors of himself – more specifically, of his manly strength. Though his reading of the life cycle, from the throes of birth to the pangs of death, is tragic, that woeful destiny has "stout stuff" to work on, for he is confident of his

189

hell-fired force. The proud peaks, the firm tower, the internal flame, and most especially "the courageous, the undaunted, and victorious fowl" seem to him clear representations of his own almost superhuman virtue. To use the terms that Thoreau borrows from the poet Samuel Daniel, Ahab erects himself above himself by positing a hyperphallic ferocity capable of facing down the great sperm whale itself. But, of course, as we know, the coin remains "the White Whale's talisman," a symbol of the powers inherent in the creation that will give final victory to Moby-Dick. Ahab merely pockets his own doom. As Ishmael says, "however baby man may brag of his science and skill, and however much, in a flattering future, that science and skill may augment; yet for ever and for ever, to the crack of doom, the sea will insult and murder him, and pulverize the stateliest, stiffest frigate he can make." Ishmael has little faith in the "small erections" of man; or rather, he believes that the only truly grand erections are those, like the cathedral of Cologne or his own "Cetological System," that are the endless work of a humbler spirit and "leave the copestone to posterity."

That Melville himself came to subscribe to Ishmael's modest view of the durability of unreconstructed man and his erections is not difficult to demonstrate, since he published in 1853 a bizarre sketch, entitled "Cock-A-Doodle-Doo! Or the Crowing of the Noble Cock Beneventano," that puts Ahab's "stout stuff" to the test and finds it sadly wanting. Melville's phallic joking in this piece is so extreme that it has both fascinated and horrified critics; one of the latter, Newton Arvin, thought it was "taste-less" to do more than glance at what he felt to be such a "painfully concocted" exercise.[2] But the more intrepid reader may notice that "Cock-A-Doodle-Doo!" bears an interesting structural, as well as the-matic, resemblance to *Moby-Dick* and thus makes a valuable comment on it. The narrator is recognizably Ishmaelian and begins this way: "In all parts of the world many high-spirited revolts from rascally despotisms had of late been knocked on the head; many dreadful casualties, by locomotive and steamer, had likewise knocked hundreds of high-spirited travelers on the head (I lost a dear friend in one of them); my own private affairs were also full of despotisms, casualties, and knockings on the head, when early one morning in Spring, being too full of hypoes to sleep, I sallied out to walk on my hill-side pasture."[3]

Though the tone here is more easy and confidential than Ishmael's, the parallels to the opening of *Moby-Dick* are obvious. This man, like Ish-mael, is suffering from "hypoes" (feeling depressed and nervous); the world and he have been so knocked on the head (by the force of revolution and reaction) that he is not even inclined, as Ishmael was, to do any knocking of his own. But he does need a change of scene on this misty and disagreeable spring morning, as Ishmael did in the damp and drizzly November of his soul. Venturing out, he encounters a country version of Ahab's crowing cock that is "full of pluck, full of fire," and seems to shout "*Never say die!*" He is at once caught up in the excitement of it all but also assailed by second thoughts:

> Bless me – it makes my blood bound – I feel wild. What? Jumping on this rotten old log here, to flap my elbows and crow too? And just now in the doleful dumps. And all this from the simple crow of a cock. Marvelous cock! But soft – this fellow now crows most lustily; but it's only morning; let's see how he'll crow about noon, and toward night-fall. Come to think of it, cocks crow mostly in the beginning of the day. Their pluck ain't lasting, after all. Yes, yes; even cocks have to succumb to the universal spell of tribulation: jubilant in the beginning, but down in the mouth at the end.

> ". . . of fine mornings,
> We fine lusty cocks begin our crows in gladness;
> But when eve does come we don't crow quite so much,
> For then cometh despondency and madness."

Warner Berthoff quite properly speaks of Melville's "alarming parody-reference" to Wordsworth's "Resolution and Independence" here,[4] but even more alarming is the near-obscenity of Melville's puns ("tribulation," "down in the mouth," the joke about Eve's coming). Barely three years after the publication of *Moby-Dick*, Melville-Ishmael's dubious fascination with Ahab's proud phallic bragging seems to come to a dead end in disgust and bitter sarcasm. The cock's owner, a pastoral-pathetic reduction of the Ahabian spirit named Merrymusk who has returned from the sea to eke out a life of poverty with his wife and four children, puts a brave face on his misery and brags about his seemingly invincible cock, but before long he and his brood are dead and the cock itself follows suit after celebrating their demise and sounding one final "supernatural note." The narrator, who buries them all, pretends to be inspired by this experience, and concludes by announcing that he has never since "felt the doleful dumps, but under all circumstances crow[s] late and early with a continual crow." Melville's last line, however ("C O C K - A - D O O D L E - D O O! - O O! - O O! - O O! - O O!"), sounds more than one note. Pride dribbles off into pain as Ahab's victorious fowl continues to celebrate only a Pyrrhic success.

It has been suggested with some cogency by a variety of Melville scholars that "Cock-A-Doodle-Doo!" was largely intended as a parody of Thoreau's pretensions to being an optimistic chanticleer in *Walden* and elsewhere,[5] and in view of Melville's response to Thoreau's resurrected bug at the end of *Walden* the claim certainly has merit, even though it assumes a rather shallow reading of Thoreau by Melville. It is equally plausible, one might argue, to trace both Thoreau's use of this motif and Melville's critical appropriation of it back to Emerson's second series of *Essays,* where he notes: "[W]e think our civilization near its meridian, but we are yet only at the cock-crowing and the morning-star."[6] That is, however, only an example of Emerson's optative mood, for he more frequently complained that America's performance had not yet matched its boast and expectation. Three years later, in 1847, Emerson sounded a much more monitory note while introducing Theodore Parker's new *Massachusetts Quarterly Review* to the public: "We see that reckless and destructive fury which characterizes the lower classes of American society, and which is pampered by hundreds of profligate presses. The young intriguers who drive in bar-rooms and town-meetings the trade of politics, sagacious only to seize the victorious side, have put the country into the position of an overgrown bully. . . . We have a bad war, many victories – each of which converts the country into an immense chanticleer. . . ."[7]

This passage (which Melville could very well have seen), with its allusion to the Mexican War, reminds us that Emerson, Thoreau, *and* Melville were in fact united in their opposition to the sort of bragging jingoism, tragically exemplified by the incursion into Mexico, which was already a familiar strain in American folklore and literature. In R. M. Bird's *Nick of the Woods* (1837), for example, Roaring Ralph Stackpole provides the American daylight rant that balances Nathan Slaughter's sinisterly silent bloody work in the dark, as he crows "Ar'n't I a ring-tailed squealer? Can go down Salt on my back, and swim up the Ohio! Whar's the man to fight Roaring Ralph Stackpole? . . . Show me the critter, and let me fly! Cock-a-doodle-doo!"[8] Similar language is to be found in newspapers, almanacs, and more artful creations, from Mike Fink down through Mark Twain's raftsmen in *Huckleberry Finn*; it is the sheerest commonplace of Southwestern humor and one of the most venerable of American postures. The "cock-a-doodle-doo" of the ring-tailed roarer is simply a version of the New World's Yankee Doodle dandyism, and Melville hardly needed to find his examples of such grandiose strutting in the writings of Emerson and Thoreau when he had more commonplace evidence that many a brutalized and brutalizing Yankee Doodle was energetically engaged in plucking feathers from the Indian's war-bonnet and sticking them in his own cap. One of Melville's most enduring concerns – from the go-getting missionaries of *Typee* to the slick snake-oil salesmen and soul-merchants of *The Confidence Man* – was the American's propensity to erect his own success on the backs and miseries of others. Ahab was to be only the most egregious, and arguably the most heroic, exemplification of a tendency toward self-inflation and self-aggrandizement as vicious in American politics as in American business and metaphysics. The dark underside of America's golden promise was its greedy self-promotion. And so when Melville came to allegorize his country as Vivenza in *Mardi,* he carefully balanced his hope that "Vivenza might be likened to St. John, feeding on locusts and wild honey, and with prophetic voice, crying to the nations from the wilderness,'" or to a child-Christ discoursing with the bearded rabbis, against his fear that it might be no better than the Devil's child bragging its way to a spurious greatness. Ahab was clearly already looming on the horizon when Melville observed in 1849 that although Vivenza seemed a "Young Messiah" in its "better aspect," it was also "a braggadocio in Mardi; the only brave one ever known. As an army of spurred and crested roosters, her people chanticleered at the resplendent rising of their sun. For shame, Vivenza! . . . Oh, Vivenza! know that true grandeur is too big for a boast; and nations, as well as men, may be too clever to be great."

When Melville's friend and fellow worker in the Young America movement, Evert Duyckinck, reviewed *Mardi* in *The Literary World* on April 21, 1849, he cited precisely this passage and then ventured to ask whether this was not "sign of true manhood, when an American author lifts his voice boldly to tell the truth to his country people? There has been a time when the land could not bear this strong meat, but forsooth must be fed on windy adulation. As she grows stronger, and girts herself for stouter enterprises, she appears less afraid to look at her own faults. This is a good sign!" True manhood, then, was not the bragging chanticleer, but the bold voice of truth willing to undercut such empty ejaculations. There is a grandeur that does not deign to be clever, that shies away from putting itself forward, and this is as true in literary matters as in political ones. Duyckinck goes on to note that "Mardi probes yet deeper" than its madcap national satire might suggest:

> States and kingdoms . . . do not touch the whole matter yet. The individual world of man, the microcosm, is to be explored and navigated. To this must all true literature come at the last. The Poets but begin
>
> > in gladness
> > Whereof in the end comes despondency and sadness.
>
> There is no such thing as trifling in a genuine book.

Duyckinck may have intended these last remarks as much by way of warning to Melville as by way of directing the reader of *Mardi* to a level of seriousness beneath its satiric thrusts, for Melville's tendency to do some crowing of his own – to display his own fine literary feathers while complaining about strutting – was obvious enough, and Duyckinck's citation of Wordsworth's lines seems to urge Melville to move on from youthful sportiveness to the sad wisdom of maturity. Duyckinck has, however, misquoted the lines in such a way as to blunt their harsher meaning: Wordsworth, as we have seen, wrote "madness" and not "sadness" in the last line. When Melville developed his argument about crowing and picked up Duyckinck's allusion in "Cock-A-Doodle-Doo!" he himself pointed the moral differently and more seriously – indeed, more alarmingly: Literary mania – boast and braggadocio – could lead not simply to depression, the "hypoes," but to the undermining of reason itself. If Melville intended all this as a reminder that Ahab's egotistical sublime was not only delusive and humanly cruel but potentially self-destructive, it was a lesson he hardly needed to repeat to himself, since he was well on the way to mastering the art of diminished things. Bartleby the Scrivener – a creation coeval with "Cock-A-Doodle-Doo!" – prefers finally not to speak at all and represents only the most extreme case of Melville's quieter voices in the period following the publication of *Pierre* (the apostrophe to Silence in that book may thus be taken as premonitory). But when he produced *Moby-Dick* Melville seems to have been rather delicately balanced between phallic aggressiveness and the more diffused erotic claims of sperm-squeezing – balanced, that is, between the opposed modes of Ahabian fustian and Ishmaelian homespun. It was equally a literary and a human question.

2

Ever since Charles Olson and F. O. Matthiessen made their excited discoveries in the late 1930s in Melville's Shakespeare marginalia, it has been the custom generally to locate the seeming grandeur of Melville's concept of Ahab and of his most extravagant speeches in Shakespeare. Olson led off by likening the whaling chapters – Ishmael's "Cetology," for example – to "the comic plot of an Elizabethan play" and then ascribing the more serious dramatic structure of *Moby-Dick* to Shakespearean tragedy, especially in terms of soliloquy:

> Within the device of the soliloquy the most subtle presence of Elizabethan speech is felt. In fact, it is precisely in the soliloquy, especially as Ahab uses it, that the too frequent and facile comparison of Melville's prose to blank verse has some point. Too often, when the comparison is made general, it arises from a dislike of Melville's prose. In fact, the remark denies Melville his prose which

is rhetoric in its widest and best sense. Such rhetoric subsumes both the cadences and acclivities of Melville's prose. Ahab's "nervous, lofty" language is integrally used by Melville in his novel. In the soliloquies it is staggered and broken speech, fractured like that of Shakespeare's tragic hero whose speech like his heart often cracks in the agony of the fourth and fifth act.[10]

Olson glides rather easily over objections to Melville's high-poetic prose in the Ahab soliloquies by assuming that they represent simply a resistance to Melville's prose generally. For him, the best of Melville's rhetoric is in those nearly scannable moments.

Matthiessen, however, took up the challenge in a more critically comprehensive fashion and with more subtlety.[11] Agreeing with Olson that the mode of Shakespearean soliloquy "became Melville's most effective means of expressing Ahab's development," Matthiessen avoided the question of whether or not Ahab may be said to develop at all as a character and proceeded to test the virtue of Ahab's flights into near blank verse. Providing his own reasonably accurate scansion, Matthiessen prints Ahab's speech in "The Quarter Deck" as dramatic poetry:

"But look ye, Starbuck, what is said in heat,
That thing unsays itself. There are men
From whom warm words are small indignity.
I meant not to incense thee. Let it go.
Look! see yonder Turkish cheeks of spotted tawn –
Living, breathing pictures painted by the sun.
The pagan leopards – the unrecking and
Unworshipping things, that live; and seek and give
No reasons for the torrid life they feel!"

To be sure, Matthiessen notes fairly that "the danger of such unconsciously compelled verse is always evident. As it wavers and breaks down again into ejaculatory prose, it seems never to have belonged to the speaker, to have been at best a ventriloquist's trick." And he cites an 1838 journal entry in which Emerson argued that if he had tried to match a scene in *Lear* or *Hamlet,* he would "instantly depart into mouthing rhetoric." Matthiessen admits "that Melville so departed on many occasions" and in his first attempts at appropriating Shakespeare's language "started to write high-flown speeches entirely under the dramatist's spell." However, he concludes, "they did not remain mere posturing." Matthiessen insists that Melville rediscovered "what the Elizabethan dramatists had known, that rhetoric did not necessarily involve a mere barren formalism, but that it could be so constructed as to carry a full freight of emotion. But his possession by Shakespeare went far beyond all other influences, and, if Melville had been a man of less vigor, would have served to reduce him to the ranks of the dozens of stagey nineteenth-century imitators of the dramatist's stylistic mannerisms."

Here, then, is the crucial question: Do Melville's redactions of Shakespearean soliloquy in Ahab's speeches in fact rise above the level of imitation? And what did Melville intend in producing such near-pastiche? Matthiessen claims that "Melville had learned under Shakespeare's tutelage to master, at times, a dramatic speech that does not encroach upon verse, but draws upon a magnificent variety and flow of language," and his example is Ahab's defiance of fire in Chapter 119. The passage, however, can be scanned as easily as any other such speech:

"Oh! thou clear spirit of clear fire, whom on
These seas I as Persian once did worship, till
In the sacramental act so burned by thee,
That to this hour I bear the scar; I now
Know thee, thou clear spirit, and I now know
That thy right worship is defiance.
To neither love nor reverence will thou
Be kind; and e'en for hate thou canst but kill;
And all are killed. No fearless fool now fronts thee.
I own thy speechless, placeless power; but
To the last gasp of my earthquake life will dispute
Its unconditional, unintegral mastery
In me. . . ."

It is difficult, I think, to understand how Matthiessen could have allowed himself to believe that this passage is "proof that the dialect of mid-nineteenth-century America could rise to dramatic heights." Despite his own caveat ("that does not mean that any American ever spoke like this, any more than Elizabethans talked like Lear"), Matthiessen must be challenged when he insists "that the progressions of Melville's prose are now based on a sense of speech rhythm, and not on anybody else's verse." Quite the contrary: Ahab's heroic speeches are mere tinsel Shakespeare and could be matched by a dozen passages in the flamboyant pseudo-Elizabethan style that reigned in so-called serious drama in America at the time. Perhaps the most instructive example is Poe's unfinished play *Politian,* which adds to Shakespearean pastiche – as Melville manifestly does – more than a touch of Byron. Here are some lines from Politian's speech in the Colosseum:

Type of the antique Rome – rich reliquary
Of lofty contemplation left to Time

By buried centuries of pomp and power!
At length at length after so many days
Of weary pilgrimage, and burning thirst
(Thirst for the springs of lore that in thee lie)
I stand, an altered and an humble man
Amid thy shadows, and so drink within
My very soul thy grandeur, gloom, and glory!
She comes not, and the spirit of the place
Oppresses me!
Vastness and Age and Memories of Eld
Silence and Desolation and dim Night
Gaunt vestibules, and phantom-peopled aisles
I feel ye now – I feel ye in your strength![12]

The rhetorical overopulence of both passages – with an insistent alliteration pressed into the service of supercharged apostrophes to unseen powers – turns them in the direction of pure bombast and confers, it seems to me, just about an equal amount of mock-dignity on the inflated stalking horses who serve essentially as mouthpieces for their utterance. Ahab manifestly invests himself in very majestic robes of rhetoric, but Melville has other fish to fry as well. It is hard to believe that he was not himself aware of how fraudulent, almost to the point of ludicrousness, much of this pompous boilerplate frequently becomes. Indeed, Melville's fooling with the high heroic mode in Chapter 40, "Midnight, Forecastle," when a Tahitian sailor improbably appropriates a familiar Miltonic turn in the service of sexual apostrophe ("Hail, holy nakedness of our dancing girls!"), suggests that Melville throughout is perilously close to open revolt against the great tradition.

Despite Olson's and Matthiessen's easy and even uncritical acceptance of Ahab's fustian, and the tradition that has grown out of that acceptance, dissenting opinions have been heard more recently, as in a monograph on *Moby-Dick* by an English scholar, Brian Way, who looks askance at the book's most obvious Shakespearizing: "The chapters which are written as dramatic scenes," he notes, "complete with stage directions, are among the least successful in the novel. Some of the Shakespearean set-piece speeches, too, which hover uneasily between prose and blank verse, seem strained and obtrusive. I do not share F. O. Matthiessen's admiration for Ahab's speech apostrophizing the 'clear spirit' of fire . . . with its unmistakable echoes from the storm scenes in *Lear*."[13] In the face of this sort of a demurral, we are forced to ask if Melville's own critical faculty faltered in the production of such obvious extravaganzas; the crucial question, again, is that of the singlemindedness of Melville's intent. What contrary evidence is there? One obvious place to look, and it has not been overlooked, though it may well deserve

further consideration, is, of course, Melville's celebrated essay on Hawthorne, "Hawthorne and His Mosses," written while he himself was
working on *Moby-Dick*. Explicitly rejecting imitation in favor of originality ("it is better to fail in originality, than to succeed in imitation"),
Melville disdains those who allow themselves to believe that the great
American "literary genius" can credibly appear "in the costume of
Queen Elizabeth's day." The Shakespeare he admires is not the popular
Shakespeare of theatrical "rant" – the "mere man of Richard-the-Third
humps and Macbeth daggers" – who has been debased "on the tricky
stage, (which alone made, and is still making him his mere mob re-
known)." Melville especially praises Shakespeare for his restraint, "for
what he did not do, or refrained from doing," more than for what he
did, and *his* Hawthorne equally "refrains from all the popularizing noise
and show of broad farce, and blood-besmeared tragedy." Melville claims
to have discovered a secret Shakespeare, almost an unwritten one, whose
"deep far-away things[,] . . . occasional flashings-forth of the intuitive
Truth[,] . . . short, quick probings at the very axis of reality," demand a
meditative, inner reading rather than flamboyant speech and action.
Which Shakespeare does Ahab represent?

The question cannot be answered with absolute certainty and indeed
brings the whole of *Moby-Dick* into our lap, since Melville's propensity
for melodrama is not only exhibited in Ahab. Is there much advance in
substituting the white whale's "hump" for Richard the Third's? or
Ahab's violent desire to strike through the mask for Macbeth's dagger?
There is no lack of "blood-besmeared tragedy" throughout Melville's
book. But Ahab and his mode of discourse are the test case. Is he
Shakespeare's Lear or Coleridge's Lear or Lear the Old Pretender?
Melville speaks approvingly of Lear "the frantic king" who "tears off the
mask, and speaks the sane madness of vital truth." Is Ahab that? There is
no doubt that he is mad, but is he *sanely* mad? Ahab speaks freely and
energetically about tearing off Moby-Dick's pasteboard mask to reveal
the "inscrutable" thing behind, whether "agent" or "principal," though
it may, horribly, be "naught." What lies behind his own histrionic mask?
Just as he keeps his purposes dark, away from center stage ("the full
terror of the voyage must be kept withdrawn into the obscure background"), because, as Ishmael hints in Chapter 45, they may be "remote
and blank," he seems to avoid showing, even to himself, the emptiness
that yawns within. He is his own pasteboard mask with "naught beyond," Ishmael suggests in Chapter 44: "Crazy Ahab, the scheming,
unappeasedly steadfast hunter of the White Whale," is *not* the "living
principle or soul in him" that causes him to burst in horror from his
sleep; his conscious "characterizing mind," the histrio, is simply a mask
("outer vehicle or agent") for the "principle" within. But what is *that*?

Precisely, Ishmael reports, "a vacated thing, a formless somnambulistic being, a ray of living light, to be sure, but without an object to color, and therefore a blankness in itself." Ahab without his mask, Ahab offstage, is simply nothing – or rather, the "colorless, all-color of atheism" from which Ishmael shrinks in the chapter on the whale's whiteness.

What are we to make of the curious observation, in "The Specksynder" (Chapter 33), touching Ahab's observation "of the paramount forms and usages of the sea"? It will be "eventually perceived," Ishmael informs us, that "behind those forms and usages, as it were," Ahab "sometimes masked himself; incidentally making use of them for other and more private ends than they were legitimately intended to subserve." Those ends, we may venture, do not represent *legitimate* theater because, as we have seen, they are "remote and blank." What Ishmael now goes on to say deserves the closest attention, and not least to the language of the stage it employs:

> For be a man's intellectual superiority what it will, it can never assume the practical, available supremacy over other men, without the aid of some sort of external arts and entrenchments, always, in themselves, more or less paltry and base. This it is, that for ever keeps God's true princes of the Empire from the world's hustings; and leaves the highest honors that this air can give, to those men who become famous more through their infinite inferiority to the choice hidden handful of the Divine Inert, than through their undoubted superiority over the dead level of the mass.

That is a difficult passage, but there is none more important in the book. The players of this world, Ishmael suggests, are the ones who hold sway. The unperforming intellect is powerless. But, alas, the "arts and entrenchments" of the histrio are always "more or less paltry and base," and as a result "God's true princes" (and Shakespeare's, we might add) simply do not deign to perform. Thus "the highest honors" go to those who *do* perform and thereby exhibit themselves as infinitely inferior "to the choice hidden handful of the Divine Inert."

There can be no doubt about Ahab's "superiority over the dead level of the mass," but does that make him a true prince or simply another strutting player? For Ahab, let us keep in mind, does *not* keep away from the hustings. His quarter-deck, on the contrary, is an egregious stage. Is Ishmael, on the other hand, with his quietly profound humor, one of "the choice hidden handful of the Divine Inert"? We need not take his own words to be so self-serving. But we should notice that his conclusion to these observations in "The Specksynder" – remember that this term refers to the one who cuts through the fat – shrewdly and gently deconstructs Ahab the histrio:

> But Ahab, my Captain, still moves before me in all his Nantucket grimness and shagginess; and in this episode touching Emperors and Kings, I must not conceal that I have only to do with a poor old whale-hunter like him; and, therefore, all outward majestical trappings and housings are denied me. Oh, Ahab! what shall be grand in thee, it must needs be plucked at from the skies, and dived for in the deep, and featured in the unbodied air!

In this tricky world of masks and other base "external arts," Ishmael at least will "not conceal" the truth as it appears to him, namely, that Ahab is really "a poor old whale-hunter" who has tricked himself out in "outward majestical trappings and housings." That is not Ishmael's way, though he undoubtedly enjoys a good performance ("I, Ishmael, was one of that crew; my shouts had gone up with the rest"). What is grand in Ahab, Ishmael effectively says – himself parodically echoing Hotspur's hyperbolic speech about honor in *Henry IV, Part I* – must be plucked out of thin air: It is essentially something made out of nothing. But the deflationary thrust of Ishmael's thoughts on Ahab's posturing will not keep Melville from allowing his majestical captain to speak again with all the trappings of the histrio. For how can an actor stand a ghost of a chance of being "featured in the unbodied air"?[14]

3

Though it may seem arch-heresy to suggest that Ahab is a kind of Nantucket Junius Brutus Booth, stamping the boards of the quarter-deck with a loony high-seriousness that is at once darkly powerful and over-blown, the idea is very old in criticism of *Moby-Dick* and, indeed, may be said to originate with George Duyckinck's review in *The Literary World* in November 1851. Despite the fact that Melville was his friend and a member of his own circle, Duyckinck criticized "the intense Captain Ahab" for being "too long drawn out; something more of *him* might, we think, be left to the reader's imagination. The value of this kind of writing can only be through the personal consciousness of the reader, what he brings to the book; and all this is sufficiently evoked by a dramatic trait or suggestion. If we had as much of Hamlet or Macbeth as Mr. Melville gives us of Ahab, we should be tired even of their sublime company." These shrewd observations may consciously hark back to Melville's own reflections on Shakespeare in his Hawthorne piece (published, after all, in the same journal), for George Duyckinck was only

seconding the notion that a truly great dramatic creation is most effectively presented through insinuation and "cunning glimpses," as Melville had said, rather than through excessive mouthing and posturing.
Duyckinck wants his "personal consciousness" to be engaged (what
could be more Melvillean?), rather than to be battered into submission
by sheer rhetorical energy.

Surely Melville knew well enough – knew as well as George
Duyckinck – that truly discriminating Americans were tired of the
ubiquitous and perennial scenes and speeches from Shakespeare that had
been played for their violence and bombast since the earliest days of
American theatricals. "Shakespeare was America's favourite play-
wright," Larzer Ziff notes (as had Constance Rourke before him),
"peculiarly dear to the frontier as well as to more civilized regions.
Performances of his plays appeared to mean equal value given to each
roared-out line, with little if any regard for proportion, symmetry, or
interpretation of the whole. The frontier enthusiasm for spread-eagle
screaming and violent action seems to have been well nourished by
America's barn-storming Richards."[15] Ziff adds – and we have seen – that
Melville was contemptuous of this kind of "rant," and he himself insists
that "Ahab's soliloquies are at the opposite extreme from such bombast
for its own sake." Still, he goes on, "they do partake of the prevailing
American habit of coupling scenes of natural vastness and terrifying peril
with vaunting characters." It was easy for an intelligent auditor to tire
even of Hamlet and Macbeth when they were played with unrelieved
intensity and spasmodic lurching (that might be a debasement of Ishmael's interest in "a bold and nervous lofty language," but the dividing
line could sometimes be perilously thin). Emerging perhaps from such
experiences, indeed, from the very nineteenth-century American Southwest that nurtured Mark Twain's King and Duke and their ludicrous
Shakespearean antics, T. S. Eliot would come to condemn *Hamlet* mainly, one suspects, because it had become little more than a vehicle for the
performer's "personality." Eliot did not need to be reminded about the
near total appropriation of certain parts by popular actors – Joseph
Jefferson's Rip Van Winkle or the elder O'Neill's Count of Monte
Cristo, for example. The cult of the actor in the nineteenth century not
only frequently made a mockery of Shakespeare but also stifled the
creation of serious drama. The prodigious Edwin Forrest had proved,
after all, that such a wretched imitation of Shakespeare's Roman plays as
R. M. Bird's *The Gladiator* was good enough for an audience that came
to hear Forrest as Spartacus, not immortal lines of blank verse. Individual
thespians were the lords of the American theater as Ahab was lord over
the Pequod, and ranting and roaring were all too often the order of the
day.

It is possible to reconstruct a context suggesting Melville's awareness of this situation and thus to shed a further complicating light on Ahab's performances. I refer to the tragic (the word is used advisedly) rivalry between the "silk-stockinged" English actor William Macready and America's true-blue Edwin Forrest himself, culminating in the Astor Place Riot of May 10, 1849, in which almost two dozen people were killed and more than one hundred wounded. The story is a long one and has been told before,[16] but we may at least pay particular attention to the central issue: dramatic interpretation. Macready, who had toured the United States since the 1820s, considered himself too intelligent and refined for crude American audiences nurtured on the obvious and overblown performances of their native sons. As he noted in 1843, "the audiences of the United States have been accustomed to exaggeration in all its forms, and have applauded what has been most extravagant; it is not therefore surprising that they should bestow such little applause on me, not having their accustomed cues." Those cues, of course, in Macready's view, were easily given by his popular rival, Forrest, whom Macready pronounced, *"not an artist."* "Let him," he went on, "be an American actor – and a great American actor – but keep him on this side of the Atlantic, and no one will gainsay his comparative excellence." When Forrest did venture across the ocean for his second English tour in 1845, the notices were interestingly mixed. Some charitable journals felt that he had learned to temper his exuberance and perform in a manner "more chaste than heretofore," but others, taking up a familiar line, spoke of his "spasms of rage" and "lack of study." One of Macready's associates, Richard Moody reports, described Forrest's "Macbeth as a 'caricature' and his Lear as a 'roaring pantaloon.' " Those with a taste for Western barbarians, however, were capable of imagining Forrest as a child of nature who had "shot up like the wild mountain pine and prairie sycamore, amid the free life and spontaneous growths of the west, not rolled in the garden-bed of cities to a dead-level, nor clipped of all proportion by too careful husbandry." That might do as a momentary indulgence in New World mythology, especially for Romantic Englishmen three thousand miles from the wild mountains and prairies, but it was hardly adequate as drama criticism, and Macready, certainly, had no patience with such talk.

The same can be said for discriminating reviewers in New York City concerned for the improvement of American performances and critical standards. When Forrest played in the city during the spring of 1849, one paper in particular, the *Herald,* kept at him, lamenting his "horribly disfigured throat and face, and . . . final death gasp and gurgle" in one play and, in another, the way he "gesticulates and pauses, emphasizes and looks aghast, treads the stage heavily and stops suddenly," with his climax reached "by a series of jerks." Though the *Herald* did not neglect to make due note of Forrest's large audiences and the "high estimation" in which they held him, it observed of his Richard III that the bursts of "vehement passion . . . seemed to be too uniform when they occurred, and to be saved and hoarded up, as it were, to bring out the telling parts, while all the rest of the character was played carelessly and negligently." Perhaps that passed as effective playing for the majority of Forrest's audience, but the *Herald* was obviously concerned with fine discriminations and not with crowd pleasing. Such was equally the case for Melville's friends the Duyckincks and their *Literary World*. Though they *were* the voice of Young America, as Perry Miller has demonstrated, and thus were fundamentally committed to the cause of fostering a genuine native spirit in the arts, they balked at the extravagance and exaggeration of a Forrest, whose voice, as a fellow actor reported, "surged and roared like the angry sea, 'Till, as it reached its boiling, seething climax, in which the serpent hiss of hate was heard, at intervals, amidst its louder, deeper, hoarser tones, it was like the falls of Niagara.' " Such Ahab-like carryings on were not, apparently, to Young America's taste. " 'He tramps and staggers,' said Duyckinck, 'and is convulsed like an ox in the shambles. If a bull could act, he would act like Forrest.' "[17]

We may safely assume, I think, that Melville – who reported to Evert Duyckinck in February 1849 that he had just begun making "close acquaintance" with the "divine William" – had a sharpened interest in Shakespearean performance and knew what the Duyckincks thought of Forrest. He was surely paying attention to the *Literary World,* where he reviewed Parkman's *California and Oregon Trail* in March, so he must have noticed that his friends were carrying on a steady campaign in favor of Macready and effectively against Forrest. In January the *Literary World* picked up an item from the London *Times* reporting on Forrest's engagement at the Princess's Theater. "He was tolerably successful in several parts," they noted, "but signally failed in *Othello* and *Macbeth*, the latter of which excited a great deal of honest merriment. On the whole, he was considered an actor of great physical power, and with the smallest *quantum* of intellectuality in his performances. He came, was seen, and . . . was forgotten." Forrest was thus viewed as a bull in the Shakespearean china-shop and a boorish and broken-down Caesar to boot. Even worse, said the *Times,* the placard Forrest published attacking Macready was "one of the very lowest productions in the English language," an example of pure "grossness." Finally, the Duyckincks reprinted from the *London Chronicle* a letter from Macready absolving himself of any culpability or misconduct in the feud with Forrest. Such extracts were intended to make the position of the *Literary World* perfectly clear, and if it was not, their notice of a benefit performance at which

Forrest read in the February 17 issue took pains to damn him with faint praise. "Where the good humor of the audience and the success of the object of the evening were so apparent, it is unnecessary to be very critical. The applause was ample if not discriminating," which was about the best that could be said of an American audience when Forrest was treading the boards. Though his style *was* "quieter" than usual, "Mr. Forrest's performance of Macbeth is too well known to require much remark." But Macready was another matter! In its March 10 number the *Literary World* reprinted an item from the *New Orleans Picayune* praising Forrest's rival for his handling of the role of Cardinal Richelieu in the tragedy by John Howard Payne. He "drew another brilliant house last evening," they noted

> and no audience was ever moved to a higher pitch of admiration than by the matchless personation of the old Cardinal. The decrepitude of tottering age was so skilfully caught that the actor was completely lost sight of in the character. The same temperance which we took occasion to note in Hamlet reigned throughout Richelieu, and those bursts of passion which escape the old man at the prospect of the loss of power, at the taunting of his hated rival, at the sudden conception or consummation of his plots – it matters not where they occur, nor do we pause to recall them – they were all delivered with that subdued manner which made the energy more terrible. In this we have a striking characteristic of this actor. The great scenes written by modern playwrights for the purpose of affording to the actor "points," or whatever else they may be technically termed, are not neglected by Macready, but they are not hurried through, as if but for the purpose of reaching a climax, when all the energies of mortal man are thrown into one word or phrase which is made to burst on the ear with the effect of a dying effort.

Suppression of self, temperance, a subdued manner, the refusal to make "points" and play for the climax – all of the things so markedly un-characteristic of Ahab, with his "terrific, loud, animal sob, like that of a heart-stricken moose" and his burning determination to "burst his hot heart's shell" upon the white whale's hump – these things, we may be sure, were duly noted by Melville, for they were to find their way into a curious sketch entitled "The Two Temples" written just a few years later. Macready would come to cut a very pale figure indeed on the ultimate quarter-deck of Melville's imagination.

The events of the spring of 1849, however, were hurrying toward their own tragic climax. Both Macready and Forrest were back playing in New York, and there was a good deal of skirmishing between them in the public press. As the second week of May began, three different theaters advertised performances of *Macbeth* (this gives us some sense of the passion for Shakespeare at the time), including Macready at the highly fashionable Astor Place Opera House and Forrest at the somewhat more plebeian Broadway Theater. Though some said their feud was heating up, and causing the city to follow suit, others made light of it; but when Macready opened on Monday, May 7, the gallery of the Astor, which had foolishly been oversold, was packed with pro-Forrest forces. The evening went very badly, though without actual riot, and a shaken Macready decided to cancel the rest of his engagement and return to England. Respectable elements in the city, even those who were not Anglophiles, including the *Literary World,* were outraged because they knew that much of the anti-Macready agitation was being organized by a group called the Order of United Americans, a proto-Know-Nothing party with a xenophobic America-for-Americans point of view. Such mindless ruffians (led by Elmo Z. C. Judson, known as "Ned Buntline," the man who was to invent "Buffalo Bill") did not represent Young America in the eyes of the Duyckincks and their associates. So a letter was drafted urging Macready to reconsider his decision to curtail the engagement and assuring him that "good sense and respect for order" would prevail. Among the forty-seven signers was Herman Melville.

As we know, pandemonium and not good sense unfortunately prevailed on that fatal Thursday night, May 10, with the casualties and loss of life already noted, but nothing further has been recorded about Melville's interest or involvement in the affair. My own guess would be that Melville signed the letter to Macready largely out of loyalty to the Duyckincks and perhaps also as an expression of his political opposition to the Know-Nothings, but I suspect that he nourished a secret enthusiasm for Forrest, as well as some sympathy for a mob which, however misguidedly, was rooting for Shakespeare in feathers and war paint. They were the *demos,* after all, and though (in Ishmael's language) they might seem "detestable" in the mass – "knaves, fools, and murderers" with "mean and meager faces" – man the glowing ideal was somehow buried in that mob, too, and "over any ignorant blemish in him all his fellows should run to throw their costliest robes." Was that not what Forrest, with all his crudities, had attempted to do – to cast the mantle of poetry over the vulgarities of American Life, to make Shakespeare speak in the New World even if (as Whitman would soon say) with an "American rude tongue"? Ishmael, in a particular mood, might have stood with that crowd in Astor Place, just as he gave himself up "to the abandonment of the time and place" and cheered Ahab's rhetoric with all the rest. Were American thespians bound to do no more than ape the chaste and temperate manners of their English models? "Let us boldly contemn all imitation," Melville would proclaim in his Hawthorne essay, "though it comes to us graceful and fragrant as the morning; and foster all originality, though, at first, it be crabbed and ugly as our own pine knots." It might even be justifiable for Americans to "turn bullies" in the service of fostering native products. Melville's association of a reserved and careful Hawthorne with "the smell of young beeches and hemlocks," the "broad praries," and the roaring Niagara, was close to absurd – like clothing Macready in a buffalo-robe and suggesting that he take some lessons from Forrest. *Forrest!* Duyckinck might snort at an autodidact Shakespearean with a voice "like the falls of Niagara," but how could he account for the fact that even some of the English reviewers, as we have seen, cheered this spontaneous growth of the western wilderness? Melville loved his newly discovered "divine William" and would have him as subtle as he could get him, but, as he wrote Evert Duyckinck, he could only wish that Shakespeare "had lived later, and promenaded in Broadway," so that he might shake off the Elizabethan muzzle and speak in a freer and franker voice. "The Declaration of Independence," Melville concludes, "makes a difference." The problem, therefore, was that despite all his reverence for the English Shakespeare tradition as nurtured and transmitted, say, by a Macready, Melville refused to believe that Shakespeare was "absolutely unapproachable," either in terms of comparable depth of thought or of the possibility of his being equaled or surpassed by a modern author. If the Declaration of Independence was licensing Melville to make free with the Shakespearean mode, why might it not do the same for an American player determined to strut the boards in his own rough and ready fashion? Macready was a model of education and restraint, Forrest an exemplar of the wilder genius of the New World, and Melville might well have felt his head and heart tugging in different directions.

At all events, five months after the Astor Place Riot Melville set sail for England, carrying with him, we may assume, some memory of the Macready–Forrest brouhaha and a set of opposed images of the Shakespearean histrio. As things turned out, about two weeks after his arrival in London Melville had a chance to refresh his memory when he observed the distinguished English player at the Haymarket Theater. Here is his journal entry: "Macready panted [painted?] hideously. Didn't like him very much upon the whole – bad voice, it seemed. James Wallack, Iago, very good. Miss Reynolds, Desdemona – very pretty. Horrible Roderigo. Stayed out the first farce – 'Alarming Sacrifice' by Buckstone the great commedian, who played the principal part – Bob Ticket. Very funny."[18] Whether Macready "panted" or was "painted" does not seem to make much difference, for Melville's comment on Forrest's great rival seems simply dismissive and leads one to wonder (as Melville might have been led to reconsider) what all the fuss was about in New York. In certain moods, indeed, Melville could appear to weary of the high tragic mode altogether, with its pantings and paintings, in favor of a good farce. Perhaps this represents the nascent posture of an Ishmael, capable of being caught up in a strong heroic performance but also aware of the pasteboard folly of it all and content therefore to fall back on the "free and easy sort of genial, desperado philosophy" that stimulates his risibilities. His special brand of wry humor reduces the world from serious theater to private joke, enabling him to roll with the punches and avoid breaking up on the hard rocks of experience. He would neither crow like a cock nor write an ode to dejection – just sit quietly on the fence and chuckle as he watched the world go by.

When Melville reimagined his experience at the Haymarket Theater in the sketch "Temple Second," written some two years after the publication of *Moby-Dick*, he did so unmistakably in terms of a posthumous whaling voyage by one Ishmael. "Dismally cut adrift in Fleet Street without a solitary shilling," this now familiar Melville narrator figures "great London" as a "Leviathan" in whose "maw" he finds himself caught. Being in the belly of this whale of a city is like a Babylonian exile, and he even wishes he might "perish mid myriad sharks in mid Atlantic" rather than "die a penniless stranger . . . forlorn, outcast, without a friend," in this "pitiless and pitiable" Tartarean scene. But our Jonah redivivus is about to be cast up onto a kind of "oasis of tranquility." Receiving a ticket to the theater from a kind soul, he gratefully enters this seeming temple of salvation when he learns the "stately Macready" is about to enact his celebrated role as Cardinal Richelieu. He climbs high up to the top of the gallery and feels himself to be "at the very main-mast-head of all the interior edifice" looking down at the quarter-deck stage below. But this is no wild *Pequod* with a savage crew and a ranting Captain Ahab: "Such was the decorum of this special theatre, that nothing objectionable was admitted within its walls. With an unhurt eye of perfect love, I sat serenely in the gallery, gazing upon the pleasing scene, around me and below. Neither did it abate from my satisfaction, to remember, that Mr Macready, the chief actor of the night, was an amiable gentleman, combining the finest qualities of social and Christian respectability, with the highest excellence in his particular profession; for which last he had conscientiously done much, in many ways, to refine, elevate, and chasten."[19]

Ishmael has been resurrected into what amounts to the heaven of all good whalers, a kind of parodic fulfillment of Father Mapple's promises, a top-gallant world of perfect theatrical delight where decorum reigns, sans burning corpse and mad captain spouting bombastic apostrophes to hell and damnation as if he were some demonic Edwin Forrest. No, the chief actor in this performance is not only an "amiable gentleman" who is a respectable Christian but a "mimic priest," a Christian impersonating a Christian in a theater turned temple that, to this Ishmaelian narrator, seems the apotheosis of a whaling ship. What a set of illusions! "And hath mere mimicry done this?" he asks. "What is it then to act a part?" Is Mr. Macready's decorous Christian dramaturgy any more credible than Ahab's imitation of a demon? Perhaps Ahab, after all, is just a poor old devil of a whale hunter uttering mere sounds, full of Leviathanism and signifying little more than that he needs to work off an inherited theological dyspepsia first born, as Ishmael opines, "on an undigested apple-dumpling." Macready's performance, in any case, certainly appears less exciting than Ahab's on his quarter-deck and will give birth to no *Moby-Dicks*, only to a modest sketch in the ironic mode spoken by an ex-sailor who might well be feeling nostalgic for the high old crazy times with Ahab. Folly and fustian it might have been, Romantic cock-and-bull, but it was still a pretty good show. Yes, the world's a ship on its voyage out, but it is also, as the man said, a stage, and Ishmael has a taste for all sorts of players. He is an ideal audience, a good critic, and a bit of a ham to boot. Perhaps, when the drama's done, that is what we remember best.

EPILOGUE

It will not do to bring down the curtain on *Moby-Dick*, however, without a word about Queequeg, Melville's magnificent response to Cooper's Chingachgook and perhaps also to Edwin Forrest's all too familiar portrayal of King Philip in *Metamora, or the Last of the Wampanoags*, a lugubriously heroic concoction put together by John Augustus Stone for Forrest in 1829. Washington Irving had tried to lay King Philip to rest in 1820 in *The Sketch Book*, but Forrest resurrected him and caused him to die a thousand pathetic deaths in the decades following Stone's capture of first prize in a contest sponsored by Forrest for the best tragedy with an American aboriginal hero. Indeed, the night before the Astor Place Riot, Forrest was still at it, playing Metamora at the Broadway (perhaps that was one reason why Irving himself signed the letter urging Macready not to abandon the field). But Melville's "noble trump" of a savage is not some cigar-store Indian wheeled on stage to thunder dark prophecy or indulge in interminable lamentation about being the last of his race. He speaks little (though much to the point when he does), being more notable for prompt, generous, and graceful action. Queequeg is a redemptive figure, as Ishmael first learns in Chapter 10, "A Bosom Friend." This serene, self-contented, equable creature, with his "simple honest heart," is frequently shown saving others from their folly or the vagaries of fate. On the packet schooner from New Bedford to Nantucket, for example, when a sudden storm tears the mainsail boom from the sheet, setting it free to sweep the deck like "the lower jaw of an exasperated whale" and petrify all aboard with fear, Queequeg deftly secures it before jumping overboard into the freezing sea to rescue one of the boorish bumpkins who had been jeering at him only a moment before. "From that hour," Ishmael declares, "I clove to Queequeg like a barnacle," for he knows a good thing when he sees it. But Queequeg does not act like a hero or expect "a medal from the Humane and Magnanimous Societies." Unlike Chingachgook, he carries no Washington medallion to certify that he has done the state some service, for Queequeg needs no such medal, being a living incarnation of the great white patriarch in the form of a noble western savage. "Queequeg was George Washington cannibalistically developed," says Ishmael – *developed*, be it noted, suggesting that this child of nature is not a lower form of life but rather the perfection of uncorrupted humanity.

It is quite possible that Melville had Cooper's *The Pioneers* and Chingachgook in mind when he inserted a church service and sermon in the early chapters of his book as Cooper had done before him. In this case, as in Cooper's, the Natty Bumppo figure is present with his sidekick and an explicit contrast is provided between the white man's religion and the pagan's, though Melville wisely does not allow *his* Chingachgook to engage the minister in debate. For one thing, Father Mapple is a far nobler figure than the Reverend Mr. Grant – no mere bookish divine preaching from the study and by rule, but a former harpooner and repentant Jonah who prays as if from "the bottom of the sea." Melville has no intention of undercutting the virtue and wisdom of Father Mapple and his message by suggesting verbal casuistry or providing an ironic confrontation between the Christian Gospel and the voice of the wilderness. He simply offers an alternative by setting chapter against chapter, one way against the other. When Ishmael returns to the Spouter-Inn from the chapel in Chapter 10, he finds Queequeg, who had "left the Chapel before the benediction some time," sitting alone whittling away at his idol. We do not know how much of Father Mapple's sermon Queequeg has heard, but it does not matter, for Ishmael has heard it, as we have, and the contrast is being made for his benefit and for ours, not for Queequeg's; he is not interested in religious controversy. He understands perfectly that standard conceptions of God, whether Judaeo-Christian or pagan, figure Him as omnipotent and just but severe. The Father whom Mapple addresses is chiefly known by his "rod," through his righteous castigation, and Queequeg is well versed in notions of divine ferocity: "Queequeg no care what god made him shark . . . wedder Fejee god or Nantucket god; but de god wat made shark must be one dam Ingin."

Instead, Queequeg shapes his own god, a little black phallic divinity
"with a hunch on its back" which is clearly presented as a kind of
humorous antitype to Moby-Dick – or rather, to Moby-Dick viewed as
the vengeful god of the Shakers or, in Ahab's conception, as the destructive agent of a vicious supernatural "principal." Queequeg's god is
manageable in size, portable, seemingly amiable – at least in terms of
being satisfied with small sacrifices. At its eucharistic feast it presides
over the communion shared between Queequeg and Ishmael that seems
to consecrate their mock marriage. It is a human and humane creature,
the spirit of brotherhood and sperm-squeezing as opposed to the spirit of
phallic aggression that Ahab perceives in Moby-Dick and answers with
his own. *That* spirit, imaged in the figure of a man striking a whale and
embodied in Ahab's need and desire to drive through the pasteboard
mask of reality to the ultimate Being or Nothingness beyond, is precisely
what Queequeg will have nothing to do with; he is a harpooner by
profession, not on account of metaphysical rage. As Daniel Hoffman has
pointed out, Queequeg removes the "papered fireboard representing a
man striking a whale" which he finds in front of the empty fireplace in
the Spouter-Inn and simply places Yojo there. The fact that there seems
to be "naught beyond" or behind the pasteboard does not appear to
disturb him. He quietly posits his own divinity, places his own loved and
loving idol in the empty space. To cite Hoffman, "the pasteboard mask
conceals nothing that man has not put there."[20] We make our own gods
and devils, and Queequeg chooses to be the high priest of a divinity and
religion of fellowship and good cheer. Father Mapple's divinity, at least
in the context of Queequeg's religion, is abstract and withdrawn – the
principle or *principal* of a promised deliverance that we must take on faith.
But Queequeg enacts his own kind of "deliverance" when he delivers
Tashtego from the head of the whale in a true redemptive gesture that
humorously compares this opportunity for an actual second chance with
both physical and spiritual rebirth. "Midwifery should be taught in the
same course with fencing and boxing, riding and rowing," Ishmael
observes, suggesting that the so-called manly arts and sports do not
provide an adequate description of all the human skills that round out
Queequeg's capacious personality.

As I have noted, Queequeg does not speak much; his mode is not that
of self-dramatization; he is not a figure for the stage. The friendship
between him and Ishmael is well on the way to becoming a sort of
Hemingway relationship in which knowing glances and silent accords
take the place of a presumptively insincere rhetoric. Melville, like Hemingway, seems to enjoy putting himself sometimes in the posture of an
author who mistrusts his own trade and would gladly drown his book in
the silent tides of understated or unstatable truth. Indeed, the "pale

Usher" whom we meet in the introductory paragraph entitled "Etymology" may be intended as a pathetically humorous emblem of the futility
of bookishness, for though he loves to "dust his old grammars," they
remind him of his mortality by making him cough, and they may well
have hastened his demise. He would clearly have done better to get a
good dose of fresh air, perhaps at sea (though Moby-Dick would have
given him rather more forceful intimations of his mortality). Queequeg,
however, is an exemplar of the healthy analphabetic soul. Though he
does show some interest in the voluminousness of a book he finds at the
Spouter-Inn (is it the Bible?), he finally puts it aside, for Queequeg
represents the unlettered wisdom of a prelapsarian consciousness uncon-
taminated by book learning. Or rather we should say that Queequeg has
no need of books because his very body, as Ishmael notes, "is a
wondrous work in one volume," tattooed as it is with those "hieroglyphic marks" containing "a complete theory of the heavens and the
earth, and a mystical treatise on the art of attaining truth." Though
Ishmael goes on to lament that not even Queequeg could decipher these
mysteries and that they were "therefore destined in the end to moulder
away with the living parchment whereon they were inscribed, and so be
unsolved to the last," Queequeg is hardly in a worse fix than Ishmael
himself and many another would-be scholar who swims through great
libraries but cannot quite puzzle out what he finds there. Books molder
as well as the hieroglyphical inscriptions on the parchment of the body.
Neither they nor their wisdom is any more durable, or necessarily
comprehensible, than the body and its wisdom. But Queequeg does in
fact at least once "read" the meaning of his body when he compares the
cabalistics on the doubloon to his own genitals in Chapter 99. "What
Queequeg recognizes," as Daniel Hoffman observes, "is the identity of
his own sexual vitality with the supernal potency of Moby Dick. This is
his intuitive acknowledgment that fertility is sacred."[21] If that is what
Queequeg learns about his corporeal "work in one volume" it is certainly as much worth crossing seas to find as Moby-Dick. He has created the
creative without benefit of pen and ink, for the body is a sufficient test
and witness of its own truth.

As for Ishmael, he too seems rather suspicious of book learning, as
when he suggests that his little encyclopedia of whale-lore extracts at the
beginning of *Moby-Dick* should not be taken for "veritable gospel cetology." How about his own "Cetology"? "What then remains?" to cite his
very words. "Nothing but to take hold of . . . whales bodily, in their
entire liberal volume," and such precisely does Ishmael attempt to do,
most notably in the chapter entitled "A Bower in the Arsacides," where
he describes his physical encounter with a great sperm whale's skeleton at
Pupella in the isle of Tranque. What Ishmael experiences in "the green,

life-restless loom of that Arsacidean wood" is the very tapestry of creation itself: "Life folded Death; Death trellised Life." So impressed is he with this ever-verdant never-dying skeleton that he determines to have its dimensions tattooed on his right arm, leaving the other parts of his body unmarked "to remain a blank page for a poem [he is] then composing." This may well be Ishmael's best joke, for though he thus appears to carry the key to all cetological mythologies on his own body, he insists in "The Prairie" that he is unable to decipher the hieroglyphics on the sperm whale's brow because of his lack of learning. Compared to "Sir William Jones, who read in thirty languages" but "could not read the simplest peasant's face in its profounder and more subtle meanings, how may unlettered Ishmael hope to read the awful Chaldee of the Sperm Whale's brow? I but put that brow before you. Read it if you can." Well, we might respond, we are trying, Ishmael, in this devilish whale of a book. But what do you mean by calling yourself *unlettered*, you who have not only run through so many whale books to make this one but also have a body *lettered* with the whale's dimensions? Why, you are almost as tattooed as Queequeg and may be as much "a mystical treatise on the art of attaining truth" as he is. What *is* the meaning of your inscriptions – or are you simply telling another cock-and-bull story?

Chapter 8

Douglass and Stowe: Scriptures of the Redeemed Self

===

1

In the last chapter of his *Narrative*, Frederick Douglass relates how surprised he was to find a thriving black community in New Bedford, Massachusetts, when he arrived there in 1838:

> The most astonishing as well as the most interesting thing to me was the condition of the colored people, a great many of whom, like myself, had escaped thither as a refuge from the hunters of men. I found many, who had not been seven years out of their chains, living in finer houses, and evidently enjoying more of the comforts of life, than the average of slaveholders in Maryland.[1]

So much, Douglass seems to suggest, for the vaunted economic advantages of the slaveholding system! Douglass also believed the former slaves were more alive morally than their erstwhile masters. The black community, he notes, was remarkably "spirited."

Perhaps this characterization helps to explain an incident in Chapter 2 of *Moby-Dick* when Ishmael, just arrived in New Bedford at a time, presumably, when he might have rubbed shoulders with Douglass, wanders into a prayer meeting:

> It seemed the great Black Parliament sitting in Tophet. A hundred black faces turned round in their rows to peer; and beyond, a black Angel of Doom was beating a book in a pulpit. It was a negro church; and the preacher's text was about the blackness of darkness, and the weeping and wailing and teeth-gnashing there.

Backing away from this "wretched entertainment," Ishmael, who clearly has a lot to learn, mistakes the black congregation for a convocation of devils, providing us with an ominous adumbration of that massive inversion of color values that will form the substance both of Ishmael's

213

education and of the book at large. In other words, we ourselves are about to be read a long sermon on the blackness of whiteness.

In Chapter 96, "The Try-Works," for example, we come upon a powerful counterstatement to Ishmael's initial misreading of the values inherent in the Christianity of New Bedford's black community. Now, it is the Pequod, owned by Quakers and commanded by a despotic white master, that seems a truer image of Tophet:

> . . . as the wind howled on, and the sea leaped, and the ship groaned and dived, and yet steadfastly shot her red hell further and further into the blackness of the sea and the night, and scornfully champed the white bone in her mouth, and viciously spat round her on all sides; then the rushing Pequod, freighted with savages, and laden with fire, and burning a corpse, and plunging into that blackness of darkness, seemed the material counterpart of her monomaniac commander's soul.

Such, clearly, does not represent the fulfillment of Ishmael's liberating "ocean reveries" in the first chapter of *Moby-Dick,* when he and other landsmen ("of week days pent up in lath and plaster – tied to counters, nailed to benches, clinched to desks") spend the sabbath looking out over the waters surrounding Manhattan Island and dream of deliverance from wage slavery. They would all be romantic voyagers to the perpetually undiscovered land of spiritual redemption.

So, too, the actual slave, Frederick Douglass. Rousing himself on a Sabbath morning from the "beast-like stupor" imposed by his condition, he casts his eyes over a Chesapeake Bay "whose broad bosom was ever white with sails from every quarter of the habitable globe." But "those beautiful vessels, robed in purest white, so delightful to the eye of freeman, were to me so many shrouded ghosts, to terrify and torment me with thoughts of my wretched condition." In an eloquent set-piece representing one of the most celebrated moments in his *Narrative,* Douglass underscores the ironies inherent in his vision:

> "You are loosed from your moorings, and are free; I am fast in my chains, and am a slave! You move merrily before the gentle gale, and I sadly before the bloody whip! You are freedom's swift-winged angels, that fly round the world; I am confined in bands of iron! O that I were free! O, that I were on one of your gallant decks, and under your protecting wing! Alas! betwixt me and you, the turbid waters roll. Go on, go on. O that I could also go! Could I but swim! If I could fly! O, why was I born a man, of whom to

make a brute! The glad ship is gone; she hides in the dim distance. I am left in the hottest hell of unending slavery. O God, save me! God, deliver me! Let me be free! Is there any God? Why am I a slave?"

Burning under the theology of slavery, Douglass is carried to the brink of nonbelief. These seemingly "swift-winged angels" are in effect "shrouded ghosts," a terror and a torment to Douglass, because they are unwittingly the minions of that very white commerce that has forged his chains. Only a freeman can truly enjoy "those beautiful vessels, robed in purest white." For Douglass, the vision serves but to mock him, since, implicitly, the black man's ships are not these but rather the slave-ships, like the San Dominick of Melville's "Benito Cereno," described ironically as "a white-washed monastery" with its freight of enslaved "Black Friars." The slave-ship is the vicious shadow, the demonic double, that lurks behind and vitiates Douglass's vision and renders absurd the professed religious values of white Christian America.

Here is Henry Thoreau's description of the archetypal American ship, drawn from the speech on John Brown that Thoreau delivered in Boston in 1859 as a substitute speaker when Frederick Douglass himself was unable to appear:

The slave-ship is on her way, crowded with its dying victims; new cargoes are being added in mid ocean; a small crew of slaveholders, countenanced by a large body of passengers, is smothering four millions under the hatches, and yet the politician asserts that the only proper way by which deliverance is to be obtained, is by "the quiet diffusion of the sentiments of humanity," without any "outbreak." As if the sentiments of humanity were ever found unaccompanied by its deeds, and you could disperse them, all finished to order, the pure article, as easily as water with a watering-pot, and so lay the dust. What is that that I hear cast overboard? The bodies of the dead that have found deliverance. That is the way we are "diffusing" humanity, and its sentiments with it.[2]

White America itself, Thoreau argues, is a slave-ship, fueled by the hypocritical religious values of a government, as he puts it, "that pretends to be Christian and crucifies a million Christs every day!"

Thoreau's view echoes Douglass's own, whereby, as he tells us in the Appendix to his *Narrative*, the official religion of America is a travesty of "the pure, peaceable, and impartial Christianity of Christ." *That* Douglass professes to love, and therefore, he says,

I . . . hate the corrupt, slaveholding, women-whipping, cradle-plundering, partial and hypocritical Christianity of this land. Indeed, I can see no reason, but the most deceitful one, for calling the religion of this land Christianity. I look upon it as the climax of all misnomers, the boldest of all frauds, and the grossest of all libels. Never was there a clearer case of "stealing the livery of the court of heaven to serve the devil in." . . . Revivals of religion and revivals in the slave-trade go hand in hand together. The slave prison and the church stand near each other. The clanking of fetters and the rattling of chains in the prison, and the pious psalm and solemn prayer in the church, may be heard at the same time. The dealers in the bodies and souls of men erect their stand in the presence of the pulpit, and they mutually help each other. The dealer gives his blood-stained gold to support the pulpit, and the pulpit, in return, covers his infernal business with the garb of Christianity. Here we have religion and robbery the allies of each other – devils dressed in angels' robes, and hell presenting the semblance of paradise.

Drawing his text, with heavy irony, from the eleventh chapter of Luke, Douglass likens Anglo-Saxon Protestant Americans to "whited sepulchers," asserting that *that* is the truly "dark and terrible" picture of the nation's spiritual life.

Douglass's principal literary strategy throughout his *Narrative* consists in his ironically appropriating and inverting traditional Judaeo-Christian images, figures, and values.[3] Though eating the fruit of the tree of knowledge is commonly thought to have brought death into the world and all our woe, it is the withholding of "the means of knowing" that constitutes Douglass's most profound bondage and affliction. He comes to learn that the "bread of knowledge" is truly the bread of life. Douglass's journey to salvation begins on Colonel Lloyd's plantation, with its "large and finely cultivated garden" filled with "excellent fruit" that was "quite a temptation to the hungry swarms of boys." This was a garden from which they were excluded – paradise unknown. Moving on to Baltimore, however, Douglass finds a more serious and important temptation held out to him by the seemingly humane and indeed "heavenly" wife of his new master. "She at first lacked the depravity indispensable to shutting me up in mental darkness," he relates; but, reproved by her husband for teaching a slave to read, she takes "the first step in her downward course" – effectively proving herself a fallen creature – and becomes "even more violent in her opposition than her husband himself," transforming herself into a demon in Douglass's eyes. He learns from her example that salvation lies not in mindless obedience but rather in defiance for the sake of acquiring knowledge. This, and not his master's putative Christianity, was the "new and special revelation" that explained "dark and mysterious things." Douglass sees that the *only* reprehensible darkness is ignorance; he comes to understand that ignorance *is* slavery, and knowledge "the pathway from slavery to freedom."

Along that path, Douglass meets a veritable nineteenth-century Satan in the person of the slave-breaker Covey. Called "the snake" by Douglass and his fellow slaves, Covey spies on the workers, crawling through the cornfield "on his hands and knees to avoid detection." His comings, Douglass tells us, "were like a thief in the night" – whereby the diabolical overseer is parodically compared to the returning Messiah. This formidable adversary almost succeeds in breaking Douglass's body and spirit, thus forcing him back into "the dark night of slavery." But Douglass, like a black Jacob wrestling with a demonic angel, bests him in a two-hour fight and finds himself again on the road to salvation. "It was," he concludes, "a glorious resurrection, from the tomb of slavery, to the heaven of freedom."

Douglass's "resurrection," achieved through his struggle, figures him as a self-engendered Christ rising to the beatific state of liberation. Appropriately, then, he leaves Covey's service on Christmas day, 1833, and moves on to the plantation of a Mr. Freeland, whose name becomes emblematic of Douglass's newly awakened aspiration, the need to exist not simply as an adjunct of the white man but as a self-determining and even dominating figure in his own right. After a year, he tells us, "I began to want to live *upon free land* as well as *with Freeland.*" He plans, accordingly, to lead himself and his fellow slaves to freedom on the Saturday before Easter, but they are "betrayed" and delivered over to "so many fiends from perdition." As we should expect, however, the story does not end in despair. As we know, Douglass fights his way to freedom and becomes the voice and literary savior of his people.

Douglass's *Narrative* is offered as an alternative gospel for a race that has been systematically degraded by a perverted use of the Christian Gospel – "devils dressed in angels' robes and hell presenting the semblance of paradise." Douglass himself, "sincerely and earnestly hoping that this little book may do something toward throwing light on the American slave system, and hastening the glad day of deliverance to the millions of my brethren in bonds," insists that salvation lies, not in ritual and the rote recital of scripture, but rather in intellectual enlightenment and authentic speech. His revelation consists simply of opening up the dark places of the earth, whereby the theology of slavery is made to yield to a true Romantic theology of the Word. As Thoreau argues in the "Reading" chapter of *Walden:*

There are probably words addressed to our condition exactly, which, if we could really hear and understand, would be more salutary than the morning or the spring to our lives, and possibly put a new aspect on the face of things for us. How many a man has dated a new era in his life from the reading of a book.

For readers of his book, then, as well as for its author in the writing, the new era, A.D., would effectively mean *After Douglass*, at least in a political sense. As Wendell Phillips suggests in his "Letter," Douglass's *Narrative* amounts to a second Declaration of Independence truly fulfilling the first and designed to free New England, at least, from "a blood-stained union" and impel it to consecrate "anew the soil of the Puritans." The *Narrative* is not only a jeremiad,[4] reminding America to take up again its holy errand into the wilderness, but also a reenactment of that sacred political document that is the proof-text of America's secular mission.

2

Having said thus much about Douglass's *Narrative,* one is still left not quite satisfied, wanting to account more fully for the extraordinary myth-making power of this nineteenth-century black *Pilgrim's Progress* or *Odyssey.* The slave narrative, of course, was already a well-established genre by the time Douglass wrote his own version, and its links with – among others – the Puritan captivity have not gone unnoticed.[5] Douglass, too, is writing a kind of providential autobiography, as when he remarks that going to live in Baltimore was the "first plain manifestation of that kind providence which has ever since attended me, and marked my life with so many favors." It is, in fact, a "remarkable" providence, Douglass says, using the term made popular in Puritan tracts. He regards himself as having been singled out, or elected, to receive divine favor, and he therefore is careful to "offer thanksgiving and praise." He is a kind of black Everyman in an emblematic tableau, who passes through "the bloodstained gate, the entrance to the hell of slavery," when he sees Aunt Hester whipped but is on his way to the "gateway" of prosperity in Baltimore, though "at every gate through which [he was] to pass" there was a grim "watchman" seeming to bar the way. Staging his tableau artfully, Douglass sets himself between – "on the one hand" – "slavery, a stern reality, glaring frightfully . . . its robes already crimsoned with the blood of millions," and, "on the other hand, away back in the dim distance, under the flickering light of the north star, behind some craggy hill or snow-covered mountain . . . a doubtful freedom – half frozen – beckoning us to come and share its hospitality." That northern freedom, still white and clothed in the New England chill and therefore "doubtful" to this beleaguered child of the South, causes him to pause motionless between the terrible past and the uncertain future. Like Bunyan's Christian pilgrim,[6] Douglass moves through what is virtually an allegorical landscape, beset by creatures whose names, though presumably real, are also appropriately symbolic, as Douglass himself notes, from the "rightly named" Mr. Severe and Mr. Gore to the vicious Covey (whose name clearly points to his ability to hide), and on through Mr. Freeland, who, as Douglass remarks, "was exceedingly free from those degrading vices to which Mr. Covey was constantly addicted. The one was open and frank, and we always knew where to find him. The other was a most artful deceiver." Douglass thus sees *himself* as a representative figure negotiating a world of pitfalls, snares, temptations, and false hopes on the way to true, if elusive, goals.

It is not hard to account for Douglass's knowledge of some of the narrative structures paradigmatic for his own effort. Bunyan, as already noted, was as well known in America as the Bible, and Douglass hardly needed to be instructed in the methods and materials of moralizing parable. It is, however, more difficult to make explicit claims for Douglass's awareness of some of the more sophisticated mythological matter that seems clearly to be embedded in his work, though it may not be necessary to do so. Melville became one of the most dazzling myth users and mythmakers in modern literary history without, as he boasts, ever having gone to Harvard or Yale. We lack precise knowledge of Douglass's reading, especially before he wrote the first version of his *Narrative*. But we must not overlook the possible influence of a substratum of folklore and fable, perhaps part of his African heritage, that could have provided sources or analogues for mythic material known to us mainly through familiar literary versions.

I have referred to Douglass's adventures as an odyssey, for example, not only because of the general resemblance of Douglass's *Narrative* to that of the wily and much-beset hero who leads himself and his men through a series of trials as a means of reconstructing his identity and reestablishing domestic order, but also because of a particular incident that argues for the universality of Homer's folk material: the story about Sandy Jenkins and the magic plant. In this episode, Douglass finds himself cast under a spell by the enchanter-deceiver Covey, who "transformed" – that is Douglass's word – "a man . . . into a brute." Covey is a kind of Circe figure (we note the rhyming names) who further degrades slaves by unmanning them and turning them into beasts. In order to combat this spell, Douglass-Odysseus must depend on the clever Sandy, who plays the part of Hermes and gives him that "certain *root*" – called "moly" in the *Odyssey* – that has a peculiar "virtue."[7] Indeed, the root *is* Douglass's *virtue* because it returns him to manhood. Let us recall that Hermes, besides being general factotum and psychopomp, is also a fertility god, one of whose forms is the *herme* or phallic lingam. We might also recall that Homer's plant is described as a black root with a white flower: It represents the mysterious union of these two seemingly opposed forces. Now Douglass himself, as a mulatto, the unacknowledged son of a white man begotten on a black woman, is both ambiguously white and demiblack (Betsy Freeland calls him a "yellow devil"). He has, we may say, a white root that has been cut off and is therefore useless to him. He is a not quite white, not entirely black flower, without a well-defined root. His root – or *roots*, in our common use of the term – can thus be viewed as his black manhood, which he must repossess or really create for himself.[8] Sandy's plant is the emblem of Douglass's willingness to assert his black identity as a man in his crucial confrontation with Covey, for as he himself asserts, "This battle with Mr. Covey was the turning-point in my career as a slave. It rekindled the few expiring embers of freedom, and revived within me a sense of my own manhood."

This imbruted slave, faced with the threatened nullification of his own sense of self through the agency of the slave-breaker, is depicted as undergoing an odyssey that, as in Homer's version, concerns the reconstruction of an identity. He has *no name* (compare Odysseus's description of himself to Polyphemus as *Outis,* "nobody"), or rather, a variety of assumed names – Bailey, Stanley, Johnson (and we should add the two middle names he drops, Augustus and Washington: heroic titles, indeed, but not appropriate for *this* hero) – until his friend Johnson teaches Frederick out of Walter Scott that he should call himself Douglass, the name of the legendary Highlander that, as John Seelye tells us, means "the black one."[9] Thus does this black Jacob obtain his blessing, the definition of himself as the exemplar of his race, as Jacob is renamed Israel. The final stage in the odyssey occurs when Douglass, now possessed of a name and nominal freedom, reads Garrison's *Liberator* – for reading, as we have seen, is the true instrument of his liberation – and as a result attends a meeting of the antislavery convention at Nantucket, where he attempts to speak, "reluctantly," to a white audience but still feels himself to be "a slave." He does speak though, and then experiences "a degree of freedom." We might say it *is* his degree, or diploma, in freedom, for utterance is true freedom and manhood in Douglass's eyes. This once benighted slave now becomes a writer, the equal of any white man, who is proud to remind us repeatedly in his book that it is *he* indeed who is writing his narrative. Perhaps the most touching and powerful moment in the book occurs when, in Chapter 5, recalling his own sufferings as a boy, Douglass remembers the gashes in his feet and asserts "that the pen with which I am writing might be laid in the gashes." It *is*, for he in effect dips his pen in his own youthful blood, joining hands with his childhood and thus writing himself fully into existence as a man.[10]

One other aspect of the conscious or unconscious myth-making force of Douglass's *Narrative* deserves attention, especially in a Romantic context. This man is a titan (indeed, the title of a recent study links Douglass and Du Bois as "Two Bronze Titans"[11]). Son of a white "Master" and a shadowy very black mother associated with the dark (of Day and Night, as it were), Douglass presents himself as a black Prometheus whose most serious crime, in the eyes of his masters, was stealing the fire of knowledge, learning to read, without which he and his race were truly locked in mental darkness.[12] Like Aeschylus's hero, Douglass comes to understand that "not by power, nor by strength . . . / but by craft the victors should prevail. . . ."[13] He becomes a trickster in order to learn his letters and then undertakes to transmit his knowledge to his companions after "creating in them a strong desire to learn how to read." At one point, Douglass reports, he had "over forty scholars," and he remembers those days as "great" ones to his soul: "The work of instructing my dear fellow-slaves was the sweetest engagement with which I was ever blessed."

The Promethean essence of the figure Douglass describes in his *Narrative* is that he learns to read in order to think clearly. Since, typically, blacks were presented in white formulations as being merely creatures of feeling and passion, Douglass effectively combats this demeaning mythology by demonstrating that the black's capacity to take thought is limited only by his opportunities. By definition, a slave is a creature without the means of reflecting on his or her condition. And as with Prometheus in his enchained state, the ability to reflect without the power to act seems a kind of vulture devouring Douglass's innards:

> I would at times feel that learning to read had been a curse rather than a blessing. It had given me a view of my wretched condition, without the remedy. It opened my eyes to the horrible pit, but to no ladder upon which to get out. In moments of agony, I envied my fellow-slaves for their stupidity. . . . Anything, no matter what, to get rid of thinking! It was this everlasting thinking of my condition that tormented me.

But, of course, this inner torture and divine discontent distinguishes Douglass and prepares the way for his salvation. He knows that only a "thoughtless" slave is a "contented" one, but it is a false contentment, and he can remain thus only through the enforced darkening of "his moral and mental vision." Douglass's last master, Master Thomas, exhorted him to content himself

> and be obedient. He told me, if I would be happy, I must lay out no plans for the future. . . . He advised me to complete thoughtlessness of the future. . . . He seemed to see fully the pressing necessity of setting aside my intellectual nature, in order to contentment in slavery.

Douglass *thinks,* however, that this is true slavery: "In spite of him, and even in spite of myself, I continued to think and to think about the injustice of my enslavement, and the means of escape." Douglass's narrative self *is* Prometheus, for the willingness to take thought beforehand, and to persevere in this painful path, is the true measure of his heroism.

We may note in addition that just as Douglass functions as a veritable Prometheus for himself and his companions, he is also, ironically, a kind of negative Prometheus to the masters:

> I would keep the merciless slaveholder profoundly ignorant of the means of flight adopted by the slave. . . . Let him be left to feel his way in the dark; let darkness commensurate with his crime hover over him. . . . Let us render the tyrant no aid; let us not hold the light by which he can trace the footprints of our flying brother.

Douglass's Prometheus both holds out the light that enables the slave to find his way to freedom and puts out the light for the evil tyrant. Moreover, many of Douglass's readers, as Garrison seems to suggest in his preface to the *Narrative,* themselves are in need of Douglass's Promethean spirit, for they are

> so profoundly ignorant of the nature of slavery . . . that they are stubbornly incredulous whenever they read or listen to any recital of the cruelties which are daily inflicted on its victims. . . . [T]heir incredulity arises from a want of reflection; but, generally, it indicates a hatred of the light.

White resistance to such narratives as Douglass's, Garrison implies, is as much mental darkness as the benighted world of slavery itself. Both constituencies lack the power of thought and the ability to read with full comprehension. But the white world in particular must resist the impulse to reject Douglass's *Narrative* as the fabrication of a mere literary trickster. Douglass's words are true gospel slavelore designed to release from bondage those who are "scripturally enslaved" – not just the sons and daughters of Ham, but equally those white Christians whose understanding of the Word is sadly limited.

3

Harriet Beecher Stowe's *Uncle Tom's Cabin* was also designed to remind white America of its sacred mission, but not so much by providing a new revelation as by reinscribing the ancient one. Her book was primarily addressed both to those whose nominal Christianity coexisted comfortably with the abomination of slavery and to the presumably more enlightened segment of society that put its faith in a purely secular mode of redemption – those, as she complained in the original serial version of her book, who had "outgrown the old myths of past centuries" and were content to hug the essays of Emerson or Carlyle to their bosoms.[14] Thoreau could have been a particularly pertinent example. As an ardent reader of both Emerson and Carlyle, he was not only blatantly skeptical in his religious views; he was also standoffish about abolition. Thoreau, it is true, did help an occasional fugitive slave on the way to Canada, but he tended, at least before he was stirred up by John Brown, to undercut criticism of what, in "Economy," he describes as "the gross but somewhat foreign form of servitude called Negro Slavery" by subsuming it in the larger question of his neighbors' subjection to their own materialistic goals and self-esteem. Thoreau's voluntary assumption of poverty and a lowly existence in his hut – call it Brother Henry's Cabin – in what was essentially the old black quarter of Walden woods might have been intended as a kind of penance for the sins of his neighbors, but it was also markedly individual both in its spiritual underpinnings and in its social character. Frederick Douglass's pathetic description of the cruel treatment accorded his noble old grandmother – who, like Faulkner's Dilsey to come, had "seen the beginning and the end of all of them" – stresses the horror of being detached from the family unit:

> They took her to the woods, built her a little hut, put up a little mud-chimney, and then made her welcome to the privilege of supporting herself there in perfect loneliness. . . . Instead of the voices of her children, she hears by day the moans of the dove, and by night the screams of the hideous owl.

Such sounds might be music to Thoreau's ears, as was the song of the solitary loon with which he was happy to identify, but Douglass considers this kind of isolation no better than a living death, and Mrs. Stowe undoubtedly agreed. Her famous book – less a novel than a tract, and less a tract than a sermon – reaffirms the social covenant by preaching the gospel of the Christian family.[15]

William Lloyd Garrison comments with bitter sarcasm on "the humanizing influence of THE DOMESTIC INSTITUTION" in his preface to Douglass's *Narrative,* scornfully employing a popular euphemism for slavery. Mrs. Stowe's book amounts to an implicit critique of such jargon, for her profoundest belief was that the only "domestic institution" worth preserving was the Christian family, the redemptive tabernacle of the home. *Uncle Tom's Cabin* might be called a tale of (at least) four houses, moving as it does from its "lowly" eponymous epicenter up to a well-managed and pious New England farmhouse, then to St. Clare's romantic home in New Orleans, with its strange garden and preternatural child, and then down – ever down – to Simon Legree's habitation of cruelty on the Red River. In her carefully composed descriptions, Stowe sets order against disorder, piety against impiety, divinely inspired decorum and beauty against devilish slovenliness and decay.[16] Uncle Tom's Cabin itself is a microcosm of decency, patriotism, and faith, with its "neat garden-patch" flourishing "under careful tending," its bed-sofa "covered neatly with a snowy spread," its "very brilliant scriptural prints," and its portrait of George Washington in blackface.[17] Though this is the lowly home of slaves, it is presented as a model of self-respect and dignity.

Similarly, the New England farmhouse of Ophelia St. Clare, though austere, exudes the pure atmosphere of high thinking and right living, an "air of order and stillness," from its "clean-swept grassy yard," where nothing was "lost, or out of order," to its "wide, clean" interior "where everything is once and forever rigidly in place" and "the staid, respectable old book-case" displays copies of *Paradise Lost, Pilgrim's Progress,* and Scott's *Family Bible* "side by side in decorous order, with multitudes of other books, equally solemn and respectable." Though Stowe's description directs a touch of humor at the everlasting respectability and unbending decorousness of Miss Ophelia's dwelling, there is nothing derisive in it. And her next sentence, "There are no servants in the house," is deadly serious, for servitude is banished from this moral universe (except for the excusable fact that "Miss Ophelia was the absolute bond-slave of the '*ought*' "), and Stowe's language burns with approval.[18] In essence she is describing the stern splendor of the New England conscience, especially as exemplified by its women: "It is the granite formation, which lies deepest, and rises out, even to the tops of the highest mountains."

The New Orleans mansion of Miss Ophelia's Southern cousin, Augustine St. Clare, *seems* a very different story – at least in the eyes of the New England conscience. Augustine, despite his stern name, is presented as a "poetical voluptuary" in the manner of Poe, as we have noted before, and his "luxurious and romantic" homestead presumably follows suit. " 'Tis a pretty place," Miss Ophelia concedes in Chapter 15, though it strikes her as "rather old and heathenish." Ancient indeed, as ancient as the Bible itself, is the "picturesque and voluptuous ideality" of its mystical garden, but "heathenish" it is not, since it prefigures the heavenly little evangelist who dwells within:

In the middle of the court, a fountain threw high its silvery water, falling in a never-ceasing spray into a marble basin, fringed with a deep border of fragrant violets. The water in the fountain, pellucid as crystal, was alive with myriads of gold and silver fishes, twinkling and darting through it like so many living jewels. . . . Two large orange-trees, now fragrant with blossoms, threw a delicious shade; and, ranged in a circle round upon the turf, were marble vases of arabesque sculpture, containing the choicest flowering plants of the tropics. Huge pomegranate trees, with their glossy leaves and flame-colored flowers, dark-leaved Arabian jessamines, with their silvery stars, geraniums, luxuriant roses bending beneath their heavy abundance of flowers, golden jessamines, lemon-scented verbenum, all united their bloom and fragrance, while here and there a mystic old aloe, with its strange, massive leaves, sat looking like some hoary old enchanter, sitting in weird grandeur among the more perishable bloom and fragrance around it.

Here, too, is order, though not the rock-ribbed austerity of Miss Ophelia's New England. Rather, this seeming Bower of Bliss, or Garden of Adonis (or even of Rappaccini), exudes the levantine odors and mysterious symbolism of the Bible, most particularly, the Song of Songs:

A garden enclosed is my sister, my spouse;
A spring shut up, a fountain sealed.
Thy plants are an orchard of pomegranates, with pleasant fruits;
Camphire with spikenard,
Spikenard and saffron;
Calamus and cinnamon, with all trees of frankincense;
Myrrh and aloes, with all the chief spices;
A fountain of gardens, a well of living waters . . .

This is the language not so much of nineteenth-century flowery sentiment as of biblical prophecy, but Mrs. Stowe knowingly draws on both worlds of discourse. The garden-fountain, which is virginal sister-

spouse, with its "myrrh and aloes" and "well of living waters," is also a
type of Christ (Nicodemus brings the same "myrrh and aloes" to em-
balm the burial clothes of Jesus in John 19, and Christ himself is the "well
of living waters" in John 4). Mrs. Stowe uses it to introduce her own
messenger of the Gospel, the pathetic and prodigious little Eva.

After the sacrificial death of this most divinely sentimental of all
nineteenth-century child martyrs, Stowe makes explicit the connections
among garden-fountain, little Eva, and the Christian message, when she
depicts Uncle Tom sitting on the veranda, "watching the rising and
falling spray of the fountain, and listening to its murmur," which seems
to hint of his freedom. His thoughts turn to "the beautiful Eva," now
among the angels, and he almost fancies "that that bright face and golden
hair were looking upon him, out of the spray of the fountain. And, so
musing, he fell asleep, and dreamed he saw her coming bounding towards him, just as she used to come, with a wreath of jessamine in her
hair," her eyes filled with "divine radiance," and "a golden halo . . .
around her head." She is indeed the "fair star" of her dwelling – the
redemptive center of its faith and seemingly the direct emissary of her
Lord. Christ, in the "solemn words" quoted by Stowe from the last
chapter of Revelation (and wryly echoed by Thoreau at the end of
Walden), is "the root and offspring of David, and the bright and morning
star." And it is the radiance of Christ – "the angelic glory of the morning
star" – that the spirit of little Eva brings to Tom as he lies preparing for
death at the hands of the fiendish Simon Legree. Christ's emblem is also
"the morning star of liberty" for George and Eliza Harris, as well as a
judgment on "the man of sin," Legree, who greets that "holy eye of
light" with "an oath and a curse" on his lips and a tumblerful of brandy
in his hand. The merged figures of Eva and Christ are the touchstone of
all virtue in this deeply pious book and a constant measure of the
degradation of slavery and the slaveholders.

Which brings us to the total inversion of Mrs. Stowe's regenerating
"domestic institution," Simon Legree's decaying estate, the emblem of a
rotting and corrupt system that is the offspring of Satan. Stowe's description of Legree's place is set in clear opposition to the other, positive
domestic images in the book[19]:

> What was once a smooth-shaven lawn before the house, dotted
> here and there with ornamental shrubs, was now covered with
> frowsy tangled grass, with horse-posts set up, here and there, in it,
> where the turf was stamped away, and the ground littered with
> broken pails, cobs of corn, and other slovenly remains. Here and
> there, a mildewed jessamine or honeysuckle hung raggedly from
> some ornamental support, which had been pushed to one side by
> being used as a horse-post.

This is not simply an image of disorder but, as we note from the "mildewed jessamine," a type of Eva's – which is to say the Lord's – garden defaced. Legree has neglected not only his plants but his Christian faith and duties. This vile habitation, as Edmund Wilson notes, represents the lowest circle of Dante's Hell: "the nightmare plantation . . . a prison and a place of torture, with its Negroes set to flog other Negroes and its tensions of venomous hatred between Simon Legree and his mistress – where, amidst the black moss and the broken stumps of the muddy and rank Red River, the intractable New England soul is delivered to its deepest damnation."[20] That last detail, so often overlooked, deserves to be underlined: Legree is by origin a Yankee. Mrs. Stowe had no intention in her book of setting a self-righteously virtuous North against a sinful South, but rather of depicting the collective soul of her presumably Christian nation locked in the toils of its own inner anguish. The fact that her most vicious southerner is actually a transplanted northerner only emphasizes how thin is the Mason–Dixon line of the spirit.[21] *Corruptio optimi pessimum.*

Though there is a significant political theme in *Uncle Tom's Cabin*, represented mainly by George Harris – the strong and aggressive black (a sort of Byronic Frederick Douglass, whose Promethean "adroitness and ingenuity" enables him to invent a machine for cleaning hemp) – who heads north to freedom as Tom descends southward to his martyrdom, Mrs. Stowe's real proof-text is not so much the Declaration of Independence as it is the Bible. Her tale is a jeremiad,[22] the wail of the matriarch Rachel weeping for her lost Israel, as Stowe indicates in the epigraph to Chapter 12. The text is the same used by Melville in Chapter 128 of *Moby-Dick*. Unlike Ishmael, however, the wandering orphan here does not find an earthly haven but rather must look to the bosom of Abraham and the New Jerusalem. Heaven, finally, "is better than Kentuck."

As we have noticed, *Uncle Tom's Cabin* leans heavily on the Book of Revelation: in a minor way for its political theme, as when Augustine St. Clare speaks of "a mustering of the masses, the world over," that will usher in a millennium of freedom; in a major way for its evangelical hope.[23] Allusions to the Book of Revelation are threaded throughout Stowe's novel, especially in relation to the divine spirit of motherhood and domestic love, incarnated in the actual mothers of St. Clare and Legree, as well as in the pure female-child as heavenly mother, little Evangeline (whose scriptural interests center in Revelation and "the Prophecies"). Mrs. Stowe believed little more than Douglass did in the hope of political union. It is "reunion" in a home beyond this world that Augustine St. Clare achieves, as did his namesake before him, through the agency of his sainted mother as well as through the beatified child-Christ.

Uncle Tom, who ends up being called "Father," is not intended, I believe, to be a normative portrait of the black man as passified and passive weakling, but rather a prime example of the true *domestic* Christian spirit, which tempers male power by conjoining it to the feminine-divine.[24] He is a black Christ, as Eva and St. Clare are white ones, no less notable for his self-respect and endurance than is Frederick Douglass, but dependent for his redemption on a Book not of his own making. In contrast, as a true Romantic hero, Douglass re-creates himself by shaping the very scripture that redeems him. He thus achieves a dignity beyond Uncle Tom's by demonstrating that the greatest force for manumission lies squarely in one's own hands. That, to cite Thoreau once again, "in respect to egotism, is the main difference."

Chapter 9

Whitman: "Take Me as I Am or Not at All. . . ."

1

In 1868, thirteen years after the debut of *Leaves of Grass* in America, William Michael Rossetti presented the first selection of Whitman's poems for an English audience. The edition had been achieved after much negotiation, for Whitman's sense of the integrity of his work was strong, and he insisted at first on an unexpurgated text in England as in America. But a strong antipornography law (known as Lord Campbell's Act) had been passed in 1857, and both Rossetti and the publisher, a strange character named John Camden Hotten, were unwilling to risk prosecution. (I call Hotten strange because he was himself a collector and publisher of erotica and would attempt, within five years, to capitalize on the initial, tantalizingly truncated version of Whitman's work by bringing out a complete pirated edition of *Leaves of Grass* with a forged American imprint.) Whitman's eagerness to develop an English following unfortunately prevailed over his better instincts as a poet, and he allowed the work to go forward, though he would later come to regret deeply this systematic emasculation of his beloved book: "I should have said, take me as I am or not at all. . . ." That statement might serve as Whitman's slogan, first or last, though his desire for a wider, indeed, a "refined," audience would sometimes lead him to tone down language that seemed to promote him as the raunchy Romantic barbarian of the New World.[1]

Rossetti's selection duly appeared as *Poems by Walt Whitman*, with an epigraph on the title page drawn from Michelangelo:

Or si sa il nome, o per tristo o per buono,
E si sa pure al mondo ch'io ci sono

[And now, for good or ill, my name rings clear,
At least the world can see that I am here.]

What, precisely, was this English audience allowed to see and hear? "Whitman is a poet who bears and needs to be read as a whole," Rossetti insisted in his preface, but his own practice belied such a bold statement. Though he announced: "I have not in a single instance excised any *parts* of poems: to do so would have been, I conceive, no less wrongful towards the illustrious American than repugnant, and indeed unendurable, to myself, who aspire to no Bowdlerian honours," Rossetti systematically distorted the central thrust of Whitman's book by removing its center – "Song of Myself" and almost all the "Children of Adam" and "Calamus" poems. It was *Hamlet* without the troubled prince, the soul without the body, the human form divine without its baser parts. Those were the *parts* (Whitman himself called it a *dismemberment*) that Rossetti excised from Whitman's volume, though he tried to reassure the suspicious poet in advance of publication that his preface contained "a longish passage affirming that, if such freedom of speech as you adopt were denied to others, all the great literature of the whole world would be castrated or condemned."

The passage in question did indeed dissociate Rossetti from the "mealy mouthed" Victorian prudishness that insisted on draping every statue and suppressing all frank talk about the functions of the body. He pronounced himself far "from indignantly condemning Whitman for every startling allusion or expression which he has admitted into his book" and which he, Rossetti, "from motives of policy," had excluded from his selection, but he did "think many of [Whitman's] tabooed passages . . . extremely raw and ugly on the ground of poetic or literary art, whatever aspect they may bear in morals." One wonders, however, about both the taste and the morals of an editor in 1868 who thought that Whitman's speaking of "the sweet milk of the nipples of the breasts of the mother of many children" was all right only sans *nipples,* which were excised. That sort of perfect particularity could have seemed pornographic to Rossetti – and, by extension, to the readership whose surrogate he was – only if the physical act of a baby suckling seemed repulsive. Whitman's unerring sense of poetic rightness led him to see that his inclusion of the nipples turned a sentimentally clichéd image into a bodily presence. The poetry lay in the power of those exact words to reproduce an actual experience on a leaf of paper. (In his *American Primer* Whitman argued that "a perfect user of words uses things – they exude in power and beauty from him – miracles from his hands – miracles from his mouth. . . . A perfect writer would make words sing, dance, kiss, do the male and female act, bear children, weep, bleed, rage . . . or do anything, that man or woman or the natural powers can do."?) The same is true of Whitman's allusion to "one goodshaped or wellhung man" – though in this case the word Rossetti excised, *wellhung,* is only a humorous euphemism. It also serves, however, to bring alive the aptness of that "goodshaped" male body for sexual congress. It is repugnant to the refined because it is slang and thus conveys meaning with a directness that would be blunted by more genteel terminology.

In Whitman's 1855 preface "clean and vigorous children are jetted and conceived" – *jetted* (which was removed by Rossetti) as well as conceived because undoubtedly for Whitman *conceived* was too abstract a term, serving for intellectual acts as well as sexual ones. Conception is not only a blessing but a physical process that Whitman was determined to get down on paper so as to celebrate the actual intersexual energy that makes creation possible – jetting on one side, conceiving on the other. Whitman insisted on saying that "men beget children upon women" as he did on saying a poet is born "out of his mother's womb," because the processes of conception and birth are transactions requiring the full participation of male and female. The mentality that would excise both these phrases – *upon women* and *out of his mother's womb* – as Rossetti did not only denies both female sexuality and the female body but also effectively removes women as active partners in the work of procreation. It is, we might say, the force of repression masquerading as gallantry (precisely the "gallantry" that Whitman claimed in 1856 was "enough to make a man vomit"), pretending to protect its women by keeping them out of sight. It represents a world that refuses to take itself as it is, for whom poetic language is the fig leaf of propriety and not the transparent medium of self-revelation. *That* leaf, as many of Whitman's contemporaries noted either sniggeringly or despairingly, was the one leaf missing from *Leaves of Grass* by design because Whitman's intent was not to whimper shamefully but to celebrate his body. He may well have found Rossetti's deceitfully exculpatory preface at least as offensive as the actual bowdlerization of his text. In both cases, Whitman's "semitic muscle" had been relegated to a literary ghetto.

One other aspect of Rossetti's edition deserves attention both as a reflection of Victorian taste and as an indicator of Whitman's own concerns as the poetic entrepreneur of his bodily self. To serve as the frontispiece for his volume, Rossetti had reengraved a portion of the almost full-length portrait that Whitman had used in the 1855 *Leaves*. It displays the poet from about the diaphragm up, the whole being enclosed or circumscribed by an oval rule that serves to render the portrait a kind of cameo. Whitman was decidedly not pleased by this presentation and wrote Hotten immediately on receipt of the volume complaining about the portrait as a "marked blemish" on the whole. He then offered to procure for Hotten the original 1855 plate at a cost of forty dollars, or eight pounds, so that he might print "a frontispiece more creditable – as per impression enclosed." Since we do not know what "impression"

Whitman enclosed, it is impossible to be certain about the nature of his objection. It seems likely, though, that Whitman simply wanted Hotten to reproduce the 1855 frontispiece, which would then, as he said, "coincide entirely with the text in note & preface, as they now stand." The portion of the 1855 engraving that Rossetti reproduced was not ill done, only partial, presenting a man without limbs instead of a full-sized poet. Perhaps Whitman was ashamed to say, "I want *all* of me shown," hence the "impression" he enclosed, which was probably cut out from one of the 1855 volumes.

When it became clear that Hotten had no intention of sending the eight pounds (he had already spent five on the existing frontispiece), Whitman agreed to Hotten's suggestion (which, again, Hotten had no intention of carrying through) that a certain photograph in the possession of Whitman's London agent, his friend and disciple Moncure Conway, be used, saying: "I am glad to hear you are having Mr. Conway's photograph engraved in place of the bad print now in the book. If a faithful presentation of that photograph can be given it will satisfy me well – of course it should be reproduced with all its shaggy, dappled, rough-skinned character & not attempted to be smoothed or prettyfied." Whitman then added some details about the costume, the shaping of the "fine free angle below the chin," the delineation of the shirt-collar, and – especially – the eyes. "I hope you have a good artist about the work," he went on. "It is perhaps worth your taking special pains about, both to achieve a successful picture & likeness, something characteristic, & as certain to be a marked help to your edition of the book. Send me an early *proof of the engraving.*" Hotten undoubtedly sent nothing, because the frontispiece was never changed, but we may notice at least the extent of Whitman's concern about his visual presentation. That part of the 1868 *Poems,* as Morton Paley observes, "appears to have become the aspect . . . that most interested him."

It was indeed an aspect of Whitman's project that had interested him intensely from the beginning.[3] "Writing and talk do not prove me," he announced in the long autobiographical poem that was to be called "Song of Myself"; "I carry the plenum of proof and everything else in my face" – but not just in his face, as we shall see.[4] Whitman had an obsessive need to present himself as a fully equipped, powerful male animal – hence, when Hotten seemed uninterested in paying for the full 1855 portrait, Whitman's insistence on having the Conway photograph left in its "shaggy, dappled, rough-skinned character & not attempted to be smoothed or prettyfied." Rossetti had cited in his own preface to the selections an apocryphal story that reported President Lincoln as having said, after catching a glimpse of the poet, "Well, *he* looks like a man." That was precisely Whitman's goal: to look not only like *a* man, but like *the* man who had written such outrageously spermatic things. Whitman wanted Hotten to reproduce the full 1855 portrait, I believe, because it was the perfect emblem of his poetic self as originally conceived and was intended to go with that first preface that Rossetti included long after Whitman himself had abandoned it (but we must keep in mind that since "Song of Myself" was not included in Rossetti's volume, the 1855 portrait was the only remaining evidence, along with the preface, of Whitman's original intent; it was, to paraphrase "Song," the essential "vision" of the poet, of which "speech" was only a "twin" that could not hope "to measure itself").

2

I want to return shortly to a fuller consideration of the 1855 portrait as an integral, in fact essential, part of Whitman's initial project, but it is worth pursuing a bit Whitman's interest in portraiture generally, especially as exemplified in the face of Lincoln. Whitman, as we know, was strongly attracted to Lincoln, almost in a sense exchanging identities with him. Apart from the intense affinity witnessed by his great Lincoln elegy, "When Lilacs Last . . . ," Whitman lectured more or less regularly on his idol – perhaps some dozen times – on the anniversary of Lincoln's death, beginning in 1879. If we go back to Whitman's comments on Lincoln in the 1860s, before his death, we notice how entranced Whitman was by Lincoln's appearance, by that tragic face that seemed the complete emblem of the man's inner being and destiny. Here is Whitman's comment on August 12, 1863:

> I see the President almost every day. . . . I see very plainly
> A B R A H A M   L I N C O L N's dark brown face, with the deep-cut
> lines, the eyes, always to me with a deep latent sadness in the
> expression. We have got so that we exchange bows, and very
> cordial ones. . . . They pass'd me once very close, and I saw the
> President in the face fully, as they were moving slowly, and his
> look, though abstracted, happen'd to be directed steadily in my
> eye. He bow'd and smiled, but far beneath his smile I noticed well
> the expression I have alluded to. None of the artists or pictures has
> caught the deep, though subtle and indirect expression of this
> man's face. There is something else there. One of the great portrait
> painters of two or three centuries ago is needed.[5]

Whitman's suggestion of a silent, almost secret acknowledgment between the president and himself turns on the ability of each to read the other's form perfectly, to breach the normal decorum of looks given and received so as to be able to perceive physiognomy in a transcendent sense. The key here is Whitman's use of the phrase "indirect expression"

to describe what he sees in Lincoln's face, for it echoes a passage in the
1855 preface in which Whitman announces that "the expression of the
American poet is to be transcendant and new. It is to be indirect and not
direct or descriptive or epic." *Expression* here must be taken in a double
sense, not simply alluding to what the paradigmatic poet, Whitman
himself, says, but to what his body expresses (as in the frontispiece): the
innerness of being, the essential privacy without which a public figure is
simply a hollow shell. The *expression* of each of these men betokens not
only a capacity for personal engagement but also a fund of human
meaning not yet articulated, layers of the self still to be uncovered and
disclosed: "There is something else there." This is a president whose
right to govern resides in his rich humanity and not in his position, as the
great poet commands respect because his voice is ours raised to a higher
power, not because it is superior or grandly epical. It is a personal voice
that is also representative. Whitman had stated in the 1855 preface that
the presidents of the United States would not be the "common referee"
of the people "so much as their poets shall," but in Lincoln he found a
different sort of presidential figure, one to whom all could refer themselves because he was only a simple separate person to whom authority
had been delegated, not a demigod lording it over his subjects. He is the
perfect president of a democracy because of his intense concern for the
individual among the "En-Masse." His ability to perceive the complete-
ness of Whitman's physiognomy – to perceive that "*he* looks like a
man" – proves that he himself is a poet as well as a president. One of
Whitman's Calamus poems, "Among the Multitude," first published in
1860, seems to generalize the sort of interchange Whitman felt taking
place between himself and Lincoln and as it were enacts the phrase *e
pluribus unum* as a personal imperative:

> Among the men and women the multitude,
> I perceive one picking me out by secret and divine signs,
> Acknowledging none else, not parent, wife, husband, brother,
>   child, any nearer than I am,
> Some are baffled, but that one is not – that one knows me.
>
> Ah lover and perfect equal,
> I meant that you should discover me so by faint indirections,
> And I when I meet you mean to discover you by the like in
>   you.

The poet is chosen and the poet chooses one, out of many, to be
celebrated as "lover and perfect equal." The democratic mass here finds
its true individual identity in a single face that corresponds to the poet's
own – like acknowledging like in their ability to read the "divine signs"
inscribed, however indirectly, in the ordinary human form.

It is clear that Whitman's need to find something intensely private in the face of Lincoln the public man reflected his own desire to be read accurately as a complex figure who had not sacrificed a rich interior life in the act of performing as a representative man. Here is Whitman's comment on Lincoln at the inauguration in March 1865:

> I saw him on his return, at three o'clock, after the performance was over. He was in his plain two-horse barouche, and look'd very much worn and tired; the lines, indeed, of vast responsibilities, intricate questions, and demands of life and death, cut deeper than ever upon his dark brown face; yet all the old goodness, tenderness, sadness, and canny shrewdness, underneath the furrows. (I never see that man without feeling that he is one to become personally attach'd to, for his combination of purest, heartiest tenderness, and native western form of manliness.)[6]

Whitman portrays Lincoln as a man wearied to exhaustion by the need to perform his public role, indeed physically marked by the demands of that role, who nevertheless maintains his native good humor and simplicity under it all. His face is a palimpsest in which experience is inscribed over innocence, public responsibility over private concern, intricate designs over the broader, freer strokes of a character lacking guile or sophistication. Lincoln's figure is that of a great statesman superimposed on that of a humble backwoodsman. Most important of all, perhaps, for Whitman is his perception of Lincoln's "tenderness" (mentioned twice for emphasis) being copresent with his "manliness" (looking forward, we may note, to William Carlos Williams's portrait of Lincoln walking up and down carrying a neighbor's baby "sleeping inside his cape upon his shoulder" – Lincoln as "a woman in an old shawl, with a great bearded face and a towering black hat above it'"[7]). Whitman figures Lincoln, that is, like himself, as the great androgyne, uniting opposites, marked for death but exuding and conferring life.

As Whitman continues his description, he renders Lincoln's visage as the very essence of poetry exfoliating out of prose, a rare essence at once undeniably there and tantalizingly elusive:

> Probably the reader has seen such physiognomies (often old farmers, sea-captains, and such) that, behind their homeliness, or even ugliness, held superior points so subtle, yet so palpable, making the real life of their faces almost as impossible to depict as a wild perfume or fruit-taste, or a passionate tone of the living voice – and such was Lincoln's face, the peculiar color, the lines of it, the eyes, mouth, expression. Of technical beauty it had nothing – but to the eye of a great artist it furnished a rare study, a feast and fascination. The current portraits are all failures – most of them caricatures.[8]

Whitman's meditation on Lincoln's face, beginning with the absolute plainness or ordinariness of it, moves to the level almost of pure abstraction, transforming itself into a consideration of the fundamental operations of the artistic imagination. That hauntingly elemental physiognomy provides a feast for all the senses as the vision of one representative American face stimulates the poet to smell wild perfume, to taste fruit, to hear the passion in a living voice. Whitman's Lincoln is a provocation to the imagination because the "indirect" life of every human form is essentially poetic. In the hands of this great democratic artist ugly or undistinguished faces are rendered not as Dickensian caricatures but as Romantic rhapsodies. Whitman could describe Lincoln as "a Hoosier Michael Angelo"[9] because, to paraphrase a quip of Ellery Channing's that pleased Emerson, the nineteenth-century American Midwest was only Renaissance Italy turned upside-down – the sublime inverted or masquerading as country boorishness or bluff.[10]

"In the faces of men and women I see God," Whitman insists in "Song of Myself" – "and in my own face in the glass." Whitman's own physiognomy was as much the emblem of divinity as Lincoln's and both were equally important as the necessary antecedent to poetic expression, for to Whitman the human form was the matrix of all literature. He could no more write poetry without an image of that form before his eye than a painter or sculptor could work effectively without a model. In this regard, Whitman's remarks about seeing Lincoln and then buying a likeness of the very view he had had are pertinent:

> It was endors'd by every one to whom I show'd it. Though hundreds of portraits have been made, by painters and photographers, (many to pass on, by copies, to future times,) I have never seen one yet that in my opinion deserv'd to be called a perfectly *good likeness;* nor do I believe there is really such a one in existence. May I not say too, that, as there is no entirely competent and emblematic likeness of Abraham Lincoln in picture or statue, there is not – perhaps cannot be – any fully appropriate literary statement or summing-up of him yet in existence?[11]

If the face is not available to be read, Whitman implies, the spirit cannot be set down on paper, for the two modes of representation are interdependent, mutually provoking and ratifying each other.

But how can one expect to find an "entirely competent and emblematic likeness" of Abraham Lincoln or anyone else, including Whitman himself? Such a likeness would need to be a *perfect* representation in order to be adequately "emblematic," but no artistic medium is sufficiently transparent to be adequate in this way; a "likeness" remains just that –

visual metaphor and not equivalence. Photographs or engravings or paintings or statues only point to the body thus represented as any system of signifiers points to the things signified. But Whitman knew all this perfectly well:

> My words are words of a questioning, and to indicate reality;
> This printed and bound book . . . . but the printer and the
>   printing-office boy?
> The marriage estate and settlement . . . . but the body and
>   mind of the bridegroom? also those of the bride?
> The panorama of the sea . . . . but the sea itself?
> The well-taken photographs . . . . but your wife or friend close
>   and solid in your arms?

Whitman's desire for a perfectly emblematic representation of himself to serve as the frontispiece of the 1855 *Leaves* (or Rossetti's selections, for that matter) was necessarily thwarted of satisfaction by the very difficulty he articulates so well. The book was not the body, though he wished it was. Through his *Leaves* he attempted to put himself in the hands of his readers, promising and demanding an intimacy born of frustration – but ironically leading only to the same. The second poem of the 1855 *Leaves* issued an invitation to a private rendezvous that Whitman would periodically repeat without ever indicating how it might truly be accepted:

> Come closer to me,
> Push close my lovers and take the best I possess,
> Yield closer and closer and give me the best you possess.
>
> This is unfinished business with me . . . . How is it with you?
> I was chilled with the cold types and cylinder and wet paper
>   between us.
>
> I pass so poorly with paper and types . . . . I must pass with
>   the contact of bodies and souls.

The business of writing as an embodiment of physical presence and amorous contact must perforce remain unfinished business, a romantic provocation and not a realistic fulfillment, despite the poet's insistence that "this is no book, / Who touches this touches a man." Perhaps the implicit coyness of Whitman's invitation, the fact that it is a sexual promissory note that can never be cashed in, is indeed the emblem of a love that not only dared not speak its name but feared even more the possibility of its being acted out. Whitman's book may be said to

represent both a bond and a boundary, in that it at once celebrates the
union of writer and reader and yet also marks the eternal separation
between word and deed, complaining of the inadequacy of its own
performance. The very vehemence of his insistence on *contact* can only
serve to remind us that this is a verbal love affair – semiotic sex, or the
comic coitus interruptus of every purely literary exchange of hearts.
Nevertheless one must still admire the boldness of Whitman's attempt to
provide a large degree of physical intimacy, no matter how illusive its
premises, for an age that was as skittish in its reading as in its actual
practice. The extent to which we are now capable of accepting Whitman
as he was without extenuation or embarrassment is also a gauge of the
extent to which the outrageousness of his sexual promises and pretensions no longer seems as important as the more durable and finer extravagance of his language and total vision.

3

Thy body permanent,
The body lurking there within thy body,
The only purport of the form thou art, the real I myself,
An image, an eidólon.

By the time Whitman published these lines in 1876, he seems to have
drifted into a rather conventional notion that the permanent self, the real
self lurking within the physical frame, was a kind of spiritual essence,
representation rather than presence. In this sense, the "entirely competent and emblematic likeness" he speaks of in connection with portraits
of Lincoln would be no more than a perfect *image* that stands for the inner
essence of its subject. But the relative bloodlessness of this idea, a
reflection perhaps of Whitman's need, in his later years, to cover his
openly sexual and bodily language with a mantle of quasi-religious
respectability, clearly misrepresents the thrust of Whitman's project as
articulated at least in the first decade following his appearance as the
brazen bard of *Leaves of Grass*. There can be no doubt about the strength
of Whitman's initial belief that the naked self, the carnal body in its
Adamic birthday suit, was the true and only matrix of poetry, and that
every body was potentially a great poem. In his preface to the 1855
edition, Whitman assumed the posture of a Christlike teacher and delivered a sort of latter-day Sermon on the Mount pointing the way by
which all his readers could achieve a resurrected poetic body:

This is what you shall do: Love the earth and sun and the animals,
despise riches, give alms to every one that asks, stand up for the

stupid and crazy, devote your income and labor to others, hate
tyrants, argue not concerning God, have patience and indulgence
toward the people, take off your hat to nothing known or unknown or to any man or number of men, go freely with powerful
uneducated persons and with the young and with the mothers of
families, read these leaves in the open air every season of every year
of your life, re-examine all you have been told at school or church
or in any book, dismiss whatever insults your own soul, and your
very flesh shall be a great poem and have the richest fluency not
only in its words but in the silent lines of its lips and face and
between the lashes of your eyes and in every motion and joint of
your body.

That these were precepts he himself observed readers would discover
in reading *his* lines – not just the ones to follow in *Leaves* but the "silent
lines" he had already provided in the frontispiece as an earnest of his
premises. Anyone could see that his hat was firmly on his head, and the
engraving also showed precisely that "richest fluency" in its lines, motions, and joints that the poet-master promised to his disciples. The
engraving was intended to render the writer physically present for the
reader not simply as a face but as a full human form, decently clothed yet
indicative of the supple male strength and potential lurking within.
These two points, the totality of the self presented and the suggestion of
an active body beneath the informal costume, are important and deserve
amplification. The figure is the emblem of a real body standing expec-
tantly and perhaps even provocatively before us, just such a figure as will
say in the opening long poem that became "Song of Myself":

Who need be afraid of the merge?
Undrape . . . . you are not guilty to me, nor stale nor
     discarded,
I see through the broadcloth and gingham whether or no,
And am around, tenacious, acquisitive, tireless . . . . and can
     never be shaken away.

That challenge is one we may ourselves be expected not only to take up
but to throw back at the figure standing before us. We, too, may be
expected to see through the broadcloth to the spontaneous creature who
awaits our response and will not be denied.
     The importance of presenting the full human form, what Whitman
calls the "physiology" and not just the "physiognomy," is suggested by
lines included in the fifth poem of the 1855 *Leaves*:

The expression of a wellmade man appears not only in his face,
It is in his limbs and joints also . . . . it is curiously in the
   joints of his hips and wrists,
It is in his walk . . the carriage of his neck . . the flex of
   his waist and knees . . . . dress does not hide him,
The strong sweet supple quality he has strikes through the
   cotton and flannel;
To see him pass conveys as much as the best poem . .
   perhaps more,
You linger to see his back and the back of his neck and
   shoulderside.

In the prose "Notes for Lectures" that essentially replicate these lines Whitman adds: "Great is the body!"[12] The full body, then, with its expressive movements and postures, is the naked poem that strikes through the garments in which it is clothed as Whitman's sexual urge palpitates beneath language that is no more than a covering for that ineffable impulse. Whitman's frontispiece accordingly is the model of an almost perfect poem – almost perfect because it is still clothed, although the clothing depicted is simple and, to use the language of the preface, without ornament: "Of the human form especially it is so great it must never be made ridiculous. Of ornaments to a work nothing can be allowed . . but those ornaments can be allowed that conform to the perfect facts of the open air and that flow out of the nature of the work and come irrepressibly from and are necessary to the completion of the work. Most works are most beautiful without ornament." The work of the body is most beautiful unadorned, but Whitman is not allowed to present it that way. He therefore provides clothing that follows the contours and nature of that work and thus functions as an almost transparent medium. The engraving-poem well represents the poet's physical energy and thus can serve as the model of a natural form that will provoke the jetting and conceiving of "clean and vigorous children."

    Perhaps the clearest and best articulation of Whitman's intent in his poetic project is to be found in an introduction to his book dated December 23, 1864, and marked "*good – & must be used*" (it was in fact not used by Whitman but first saw the light of day in Clifton Furness's *Walt Whitman's Workshop*, published in 1928).[13] In this piece Whitman declares that his American song must "hold up at all hazards . . . the divine pride of man in himself. It must pierce through the shifting envelope of costumes & formulas, and strike perennial born qualities and organs." Whitman insists that "the genius of America" cannot listen to poems in "which natural humanity bends low, humiliated," but wants chants that are "erect & haughty." This sort of language, calling for phallic pride instead of shame and humiliation, is of course familiar to readers of Whitman. What is of particular interest, though, is Whitman's figuration of piercing through *costumes,* as well as formulas, to the *organs* within, re-evoking as it does that primary visual emblem we have already been examining as in itself the central text and test of Whitman's work. As he goes on in this important essay to make the distinction between "physiognomy" and "physiology" to which I have alluded, Whitman seems in fact to echo language in the 1855 preface that redirects our attention (as does so much in the book) to the frontispiece: "You shall stand by my side and look in the mirror with me." Now he attempts to provide a more complete theory of what we were supposed to see in that *reflection* of the poet (his thought and image, body and soul, intertwined):

> Prevalent poems cast back only a facial physiognomy, a part. In the following chant, the apparition of the whole form, as of one unclothed before a mirror is cast back. The teachers of the day teach (and stop there) that the unclothed face is divine. It is indeed; but I say that only the unclothed body, diviner still, is fully divine. These Leaves image that physiology – not apologising for it, but exulting openly in it and taking it to myself, I know the rectitude of my intentions & appeal to the future. I seek, by singing these to behold & exhibit what I am, as specimen to all – these material, aesthetic and spiritual relations & tally the same in you, whoever you are, I am.

Conventional poetry, Whitman argues, offers reflections only of the "facial physiognomy," that is, provides a means for judging human nature that is partial, based as it is on a displacement upward, a soul-picture, of the body's creative shape and energy. Whitman's poem, by contrast, offers a reflection of human "physiology," the total organism, which includes all its parts. It attempts to embody the naked organism, to provide an image of that, to take it to itself, and in that image we are to see ourselves, to embrace ourselves, and equally to embrace the poet, who is what we are. In the act of looking at the poet in frontispiece and poem we are invited to undrape every human figure in reflection and to reflect on the union of "material, aesthetic and spiritual relations" represented by the human form. *This* seems to be the "entirely competent and emblematic likeness" Whitman was seeking; as he goes on to say, "the Body merged with & in the soul & the soul merged in the Body," a "tantalizing wonder . . . not as it might be or as it is fancied in conventional literature to be, but as it actually is, good and bad, as maturity and passions, youth, sex, experience and the world turn it out."

We are now in a position, perhaps, to understand more completely Whitman's theory of the entirely competent and emblematic likeness. There could be no such likeness of Lincoln because Whitman conceived of that revered figure *only* as a physiognomy, a face without a body. In "When Lilacs Last in the Dooryard Bloom'd" Whitman felt compelled to image the fallen father as fully apotheosized and abstract: "the lustrous and drooping star with the countenance full of woe." When he thinks of adorning the chamber walls with appropriate images, these images are derived from notions of Lincoln as the representative of a generalized land and its people: the principle of growth in the spring, homes, an April evening, sunset, herbage and leaves of trees, a river, hills, the city, scenes of life and workmen returning home. The father, in fact, is conceived as part of a supernal "trinity" ("lilac blooming perennial," "drooping star," and "thought of him I love"). But the poet embodies a different sort of universality; he is, as we know, a "kosmos" that comprehensively encloses and represents all physical and spiritual things.

Whitman's emblem of himself – the 1855 frontispiece, say – can be seen as an entirely competent likeness when we take his advice and regard it in a dual fashion: envision the union of self clothed and unclothed, soul and body, physiognomy and physiology, spirit and sexuality, *and* consent to behold ourselves in that figure and process, thereby realizing that Whitman's emblem points to a living body, our own, although his image is only a leaf in a book. *We* are competent to complete Whitman's theory of likeness when we acknowledge that we are made in his image. It is a mistake, I believe, to read Whitman's book as representing only *his* body. The "man, nude & abysmal," as he puts it in the 1864 introduction, who is "supreme and above these pictures and plays," is ourselves. To take Whitman as he is is thus to take ourselves in the same fashion. "I am a man who, sauntering along without fully stopping, turns a casual look upon you and then averts his face," he notes,

> Leaving it to you to prove and define it,
> Expecting the main things from you.[14]

Whitman *leaves* his image for us, and we are enjoined not simply to leave it at that.

Walt and Emily

Of all the now seemingly inevitable pairings in nineteenth-century American literature, Whitman and Dickinson still may strike us as the strangest.[1] Unlike, say, Henry James and Edith Wharton (good friends, master and disciple), Whitman and Dickinson were not bound by ties of personal relation or influence. So far as the other was concerned, each of these two might have lived on the moon (and mid-nineteenth-century Amherst probably would have struck Whitman as sufficiently lunatic; ditto New York for Dickinson). This is the same epoch in our literature when Whitman and Melville, exact contemporaries and both living and working for a time in New York, seem to have been almost completely oblivious of each other. But Melville, of course, did discover Hawthorne, Thoreau sought out Whitman, and Emerson, one way or another, came upon or was pounced upon by almost everybody. Which is to say that the crucial middle term, culturally and literarily speaking, between Whitman and Dickinson was the improbable Brahma-Bacchus-Buddha of Concord, and that mutual influence quite naturally continues to engage critical interest. But we do not link Whitman and Dickinson only because of Emerson; put simply, in stunning contradistinction to what their own age would have believed, they have turned out to be the major poets of their time. "She and Walt Whitman," writes one literary historian, "represent the farthest pioneerings of the nineteenth-century American mind in the trackless regions of spirit, in so far as they are reflected in poetry."[2]

What they both seemed to represent, however, to received, or establishment, literary opinion when they appeared on the scene was disorder and the breaching of decorum. It is interesting and amusing to note how exactly the criticisms of the first Dickinson publications in the 1890s replicate what genteel opinion had to say about Whitman in the fifties and beyond. "His language is too frequently reckless and indecent," wrote Charles A. Dana in Horace Greeley's New York *Tribune*.[3] Harvard's Charles Eliot Norton was equally perplexed and put off by Whitman's "scorn for the wonted usages of good writing," but also captivated by "this gross yet elevated, this superficial yet profound, this preposterous yet somehow fascinating book."[4] The young Henry James, reviewing *Drum-Taps* in 1865, was – alas – condescending and correct (he would come a long way later on): "There is," he wrote, "fortunately, but one attempt at rhyme. We say fortunately, for if the inequality of Mr. Whitman's lines were self-registering, as it would be in the case of an anticipated syllable at their close, the effect would be painful in the extreme."[5]

So, too, Dickinson. When her poems first appeared in 1890, even her editor and supporter, Colonel Thomas Wentworth Higginson, felt obliged to apologize: "Wayward and unconventional in the last degree; defiant of form, measure, rhyme, and even grammar; she yet had an exacting standard of her own." Higginson insisted that when "a thought takes one's breath away, who cares to count the syllables?"[6] Well, sniffed one genteel reviewer, "having one's breath taken away is a very agreeable sensation, but it is not the finest sensation of which we are susceptible."[7] Dickinson was castigated, like Whitman before her, for "technical imperfection": "The author was as unlearned in the technical side of art as if she had written when the forms of verse had not yet been invented."[8] By a kind of tacit agreement, hostile critics who harped away at propriety implicitly or explicitly linked Dickinson with Whitman. The London *Daily News*, lambasting "this farrago of illiterate and uneducated sentiment," noted that "many uneducated and incompetent persons get pleasure out of scribbling incoherences."[9] A man who was to become professor of English at the Massachusetts Institute of Technology spoke of Dickinson, clearly with Whitman in mind, as having "a certain rude and half barbaric naivete in many of the poems."[10] Incredibly, an English critic insisted that "compared with her, Walt Whitman is a sturdy poetical conservative"[11] (but we remember that by 1890 Whitman, who had a substantial following in England as well as in America, had somewhat tempered his barbaric yawp). The reviewer for *Scribner's* magazine – the same who objected to having his breath taken away – once again linked Dickinson and Whitman as practitioners of a decidedly "new" kind of poetry by saying: "it is curious to note how prone are all apologists for formlessness, including Mr. Higginson in the present instance, and the admirers of Walt Whitman, *passim*, for example, to insist that what to the convention-steeped sense appears amorphous is in reality the very acme of form."[12] Exactly, we say: the world is still learning how to read Whitman and Dickinson. "She stands as a precursor of the modern mind," George Frisbie Whicher wrote in 1947, "whom we have not yet fully overtaken."[13]

In a curious way, then, Whitman and Dickinson have long been linked in critical opinion, and it is worthwhile extending the implications of that linkage. Both writers were eccentric autodidacts – great though unsystematic readers and self-formed practitioners of a new art of poetry.

Both were introspective voyagers who took themselves as their fundamental, inescapable subjects. But we must quickly add that they did not
speak naively in the first-person singular. "When I state myself, as the
Representative of the Verse," Dickinson wrote Higginson (perhaps at
least half in terror), "it does not mean – me – but a supposed person."[14]
Whitman, too, though he insisted that his poetry was "an attempt, from
first to last, to put *a Person*, a human being (myself, in the latter half of
the Nineteenth Century, in America,) freely, fully and truly on record,"
was nevertheless not being merely personal. " 'Leaves of Grass,' already
publish'd," he wrote in 1872, "is, in its intentions, the song of a great
composite *democratic individual,* male or female."[15] Most importantly,
Whitman and Dickinson were unprecedented poetic experimenters who,
in an age – with the possible exception of Emerson – largely confined to
literary convention, achieved greatness by extending once and for all the
range of lyric expression. R. P. Blackmur's observation is still pertinent:

> We can say, amiably enough, that the verse-language of mid-
> nineteenth century America was relatively nerveless, unsupple, flat
> in pattern, had very little absorptive power and showed no self-
> luxuriating power whatever. The mounting vitality that shows
> itself as formal experiment and the matured vitality that shows
> itself as the masterly penetration of accepted form . . . were equally
> absent. The great estate of poetry as an available condition of
> language lay flat in a kind of desiccated hibernation, and the clue to
> resurrection was unknown. It is not for nothing that our poets
> never mastered form in language. Poe and Longfellow accepted the
> desiccation, contributing a personal music which perhaps redeemed
> but never transfigured their talents. Whitman and Emily Dickin-
> son, with more genius, or . . . with more favorable cultural situa-
> tions, were unable to accept the desiccation and drove forward on
> the élan of their natural aptitudes for language, resorting regardless
> to whatever props, scaffolds, obsessive symbols, or intellectual
> mechanisms came to hand . . .[16]

including, we might note, Watts's *Hymnal*, the King James Bible, the
dictionaries of Webster and Worcester, Italian opera, oratory, the ocean,
the lonely waste of the pine woods, riddles and jokes and paradoxes and
puns . . .

Longfellow, as Blackmur suggests, was certainly the test case, and it
can still be highly instructive to set his example and performance next to
the seemingly eccentric new work that was designed – consciously, I
would say – to supplant him. But one must insist first that the "clue to
resurrection" was in fact *not* "unknown." Emerson the poet at his best

(in his prose as well as his verse), with his subtle manipulations of traditional rhythms, extravagant tropes, vernacular intonations, and sometimes mystifying excursions into new spiritual postures, not only functioned as a direct provocation to Whitman and Dickinson but also helped to establish an atmosphere in which bold experimentation could be welcomed as well as practiced. Whitman and Dickinson responded to Emerson at once as two unique poetic geniuses *and* as egregious examples of a larger audience (larger than two, even if not massive) capable of setting out from Emersonian premises for a wilder world of thought and expression. The most startling example, brought to our attention recently by Eleanor Tilton, may be too good to be true, but – until he is proven a fraud – the thirty-five year old woodchopper from Winchester, Massachusetts, named Simeon Carter who wrote an ebullient fan-letter to Emerson in 1860 can serve as a significant sign of the times.[17]

My dear Old Friend, he was tempted to address the exalted Sage, because Emerson's essays had become his familiar companions. Carter called them not only perpetually surprising and fresh as the Bible but also "*concentrated* Poetry, or a cargo of Poetry in bulk," which – though "rather *too rich* diet" for ordinary times and readers – was just the ticket for a healthy, nature-loving woodsman. "O how free the *Soul* is!" exclaimed this Emersonian wielder of the broad axe, as he went on to praise the master for the "*brown* thing" he did in "Brahma." Twenty-five years later Oliver Wendell Holmes would still be scratching his head with the average reader at this "nearest approach to a Torricellian vacuum of intelligibility that language can pump out of itself,"[18] but Simeon Carter on first acquaintance thought it "contained the *whole law & the gospel*," preferring it thenceforth to attendance at meeting. The strangeness of the writing seemed not to bother this new kind of reader because his taste had not been formed, or deformed, by textbook rules. "One of my friends says she wishes she knew how you'd *parse* the first verse – but I can give her no light on that for I know nothing of grammar. If I can only pass the *last* verse through my daily life, Id ask no more." In the light of such a reaction, Carter's next remark is hardly a surprise:

> I have lately got hold of a book with which I am delighted, viz. "Leaves of Grass" by Walt. Whitman, and I must just whisper, Ralph, look well to your laurels or this uncouth bawler will slide them off your brows. He is a new man, he is fresh, he has been in the *real presence;* he has embraced the Goddess naked, while the others have only knelt at her feet, kissed the tips of her fingers, & some few, her lips. His Egotism is admirable, equal to that of Jesus, hear him, "I sound my barbaric yawp *over* the *roofs of the world.*" "*My* voice is Orotund *sweeping* & final!" Could anything beat that?

we are all groping in shadows, he takes hold of *reals*. God bless him! I should like to hug & kiss him. As a Poet Philosopher, & Christian, he is at the top of the heap, ancient or modern.

Whether real or not himself, Simeon Carter is very *ben trovato* – a guileless or artful indication that Emersonian premises could easily slide into Whitmanian extravagance. Inferentially, if "Ralph" was in danger of losing his laurels, "Henry Wadsworth" was at even greater peril. And, indeed, the "new man" largely responsible for such a shift in taste was well aware that he was really competing, not with the writer he acknowledged publicly as Master, but with the popular poet who "strikes a splendid average, and does not sing exceptional passions, or humanity's jagged escapades." Longfellow, Whitman said years later, "is not revolutionary, brings nothing offensive or new, does not deal hard blows." These postmortem observations were presumably meant to pass as praise, but Whitman's defense of Longfellow's "want of racy nativity and special originality" is transparently a retrospective justification of his own crucial mission.[19] Like Dickinson when faced with the conventional criticisms of a Higginson (the complaint about her "spasmodic" gait, for example), Whitman knew well enough how to imitate Longfellow, and we may easily observe the manner in which he performs his momentous swerve from the Longfellow idiom (we shall shortly glance at parallel examples in Dickinson). "The Bridge," a Longfellow composition dating from the mid-1840s, anticipates in form Dickinson's appropriation of the version of hymn-meter known as *sixes* (compare Poem 306: "The Soul's Superior instants / Occur to Her – alone – / When friend – and Earth's occasion / Have infinite withdrawn – "), as it clearly also points the way, however banally, to "Crossing Brooklyn Ferry" (with Hart Crane in the farther distance):

I stood on the bridge at midnight,
  As the clocks were striking the hour,
And the moon rose o'er the city,
  Behind the dark church-tower

I saw her bright reflection
  In the waters under me,
Like a golden goblet falling
  And sinking into the sea.

And far in the hazy distance
  Of that lovely night in June,
The blaze of the flaming furnace
  Gleamed redder than the moon.

Among the long, black rafters
  The wavering shadows lay,
And the current that came from the ocean
  Seemed to lift and bear them away;

As, sweeping and eddying through them,
  Rose the belated tide,
And, streaming into the moonlight,
  The seaweed floated wide.

And like those waters rushing
  Among the wooden piers,
A flood of thoughts came o'er me
  That filled my eyes with tears.

How often, oh how often,
  In the days that had gone by,
I had stood on that bridge at midnight
  And gazed on that wave and sky!

How often, oh how often,
  I had wished that the ebbing tide
Would bear me away on its bosom
  O'er the ocean wild and wide!

For my heart was hot and restless,
  And my life was full of care,
And the burden laid upon me
  Seemed greater than I could bear.

But now it has fallen from me,
  It is buried in the sea;
And only the sorrow of others
  Throws its shadow over me.

Yet whenever I cross the river
  On its bridge with wooden piers,
Like the odor of brine from the ocean
  Comes the thought of other years.

And I think how many thousands
  Of care-encumbered men,
Each bearing his burden of sorrow,
  Have crossed the bridge since then.

I see the long procession
  Still passing to and fro,
The young heart hot and restless,
  And the old subdued and slow!

And forever and forever,
  As long as the river flows,
As long as the heart has passions,
  As long as life has woes;

The moon and its broken reflection
  And its shadows shall appear,
As the symbol of love in heaven,
  And its wavering image here.

That last stanza might easily bring Poe to mind ("For the moon never beams, without bringing me dreams / Of the beautiful Annabel Lee. . . ."), but Whitman is more to the point. Instead of writing, as he did,

Flood-tide below me! I see you face to face!
Clouds of the west – sun there half an hour high – I see you
  also face to face.
Crowds of men and women attired in the usual costumes, how
  curious you are to me!
On the ferry-boats the hundreds and hundreds that cross,
  returning home, are more curious to me than you
  suppose,
And you that shall cross from shore to shore years hence are
  more to me, and more in my meditations, than you might
  suppose . . .

Whitman *could* have settled into the rut Longfellow had provided:

I stood on the Brooklyn Ferry,
  As the sun was sinking low,
Face to face with the flooding ocean,
  And the western clouds aglow.

And I thought of the hundreds and hundreds,
  That shall cross in years to come,
The curious men and women,
  Whose voices yet are dumb. . . .

But some profound instinct warned him, as it did Dickinson, away from what he was to call that "sickness . . . of verbal melody" and the banality of sentiment (Huck Finn's "tears and flapdoodle") of which it was the too-perfect medium.[20] Whitman knew he was born to "deal hard blows," not to hold the "trivial harp" Emerson complained of in the very year in which Longfellow published "The Bridge," as he called for chords that ring "Free, peremptory, clear." It was a challenge from Waldo to Walt, and the reverberations were to shake Emily even more profoundly than they did Simeon Carter.

Chapter 10

Dickinson's "Celestial Vail"

Snowbound in Self-Consciousness

Any attempt to link Emily Dickinson securely with the dominant literary tradition in which she grew up, in particular the American literary scene in the mid-nineteenth century, seems always to founder on the absolute singularity of her vision and craft; but the filaments that attached her to the public writers of her time, though thin, are plainly visible. We *know* that she read Emerson and Hawthorne and Thoreau, as well as Bryant and Longfellow and Lowell and – not to be forgotten – Thomas Wentworth Higginson (one can add James and Howells, but that is part of a later and somewhat different story). Even in some of her earliest allusions to this cast of characters (early, that is, in the sense of Dickinson's formative period, when she might be said to have been reading these worthies more or less "straight," without unsheathing the surgeon's knife that we later see flashing so often), we observe her whetting the critical edge, as in Poem 131[1]:

> Besides the Autumn poets sing
> A few prosaic days
> A little this side of the snow
> And that side of the Haze –
>
> A few incisive Mornings –
> A few Ascetic Eves –
> Gone – Mr. Bryant's "Golden Rod" –
> And Mr. Thomson's "sheaves."
>
> Still, is the bustle in the Brook –
> Sealed are the spicy valves –
> Mesmeric fingers softly touch
> The Eyes of many Elves –
>
> Perhaps a squirrel may remain –
> My sentiments to share –
> Grant me, Oh Lord, a sunny mind –
> Thy windy will to bear![2]

The poem is essentially a rewriting of Bryant's "The Death of the Flowers" ("The melancholy days are come, the saddest of the year, / Of wailing winds, and naked woods, and meadows brown and sere. . . . "), without the sentimental – indeed, lugubrious – moralizing that insists on joining every natural event to its pathetic human counterpart. As Dickinson dismisses "Mr. Bryant's 'Golden Rod' " (itself a symbol in his poem of the "autumn beauty" wiped out by the frost that fell "as falls the plague on men"), she seems simply to be turning away from the mode of his singing. Her "prosaic days" represent a more rigorous view of autumn – a hard glance at sharper mornings and sparer evenings that tilts the mind in the direction of winter, without the sighs and lamentations that displace our attention, in Bryant's poem, from the natural scene to the poet's sensibilities. As Dickinson's brook thickens with chill and her flowers (only alluded to obliquely in the metonomy "spicy valves") seal shut and sleep descends from mysterious fingers, the natural world prepares to celebrate its own funeral – that is all. When the voice of the poet enters it does so only to conclude with a mock appeal that mimics the pious turn one might normally expect from a New England speaker who catches herself being querulous about the Lord's "windy will."[3] She implies that her wish will not be granted, not only because it is not in her nature to be "sunny" about sinister things but also because the changeful divinity whose vagaries include the afflictions of autumn is unlikely to respond to such an appeal. But Dickinson's conclusion is itself sufficiently breezy, quickly turning off what is clearly meant to be an exercise in tweaking the tradition, not a serious metaphysical meditation.

One can see a similar mildly irreverent attitude toward Longfellow in some of Dickinson's very frequent allusions, early in her career, to his old chestnut, "The Rainy Day":

The day is cold, and dark, and dreary;
It rains, and the wind is never weary;
The vine still clings to the mouldering wall,
But at every gust the dead leaves fall,
    And the day is dark and dreary.

My life is cold, and dark, and dreary;
It rains, and the wind is never weary;
My thoughts still cling to the mouldering Past,
But the hopes of youth fall thick in the blast,
    And the days are dark and dreary.

Be still, sad heart! and cease repining;
Behind the clouds is the sun still shining;
Thy fate is the common fate of all,
Into each life some rain must fall,
    Some days must be dark and dreary.

Though this may now strike us as the very quintessential moralizing balladic bromide that renders so much of Longfellow unappealing to serious readers today, it epitomizes, to use Whitman's phrase, precisely that "splendid average" that helped form the taste of nineteenth-century America (compare, for example, the last pages of *Little Women*) and against which both Whitman and Dickinson (especially Dickinson) formed themselves. At about age twenty-two Emily Dickinson was a sentimental, as well as a sportive, young woman, manifestly not the poet we know (Whitman at the same age was composing bad patriotic verse and bathetic temperance stories), capable of writing as follows to a friend (also named Emily):

> I have wanted to come and see you – I have tried earnestly to come, but always have been detained by some ungenerous care, and now this falling snow, sternly, and silently, lifts up its hand between.
> How glad I am affection can always leave and go – How glad that drifts of snow pause at the outer door, and go no farther, and it is as warm within as if no winter came! Dear Emily, do not sorrow, upon this stormy day – "into each life some *'flakes'* must fall, some days must be dark and dreary." Let us think of the pleasant summer whose gardens are far away, and whose Robins are singing always![4]

Dickinson's slight revision of Longfellow's familiar line seems merely to reflect the fact that snowflakes were a greater affliction than raindrops in her long rural winters, but her cheerful melancholy matches his own and exhibits her at a point of balance between the maudlin and the morbid, preparing to abandon all clichés, except by way of parody or mock appropriation. Indeed, we may notice that Dickinson, approximately balanced here also in time between Emerson's "Snow-Storm" and Whittier's "Snow-Bound," depends at least partly for her comforting aphorisms about the winter upon the commonplace notion that the wilder it gets outside, the cozier it seems within.[5] To cite her favorite line from Emerson's poem, she feels safely enclosed "in a tumultuous privacy of storm." Even Longfellow, when he turns his thoughts from rain to snow, though he does not render the storm a domestic companion, sees it as another sad human heart whispering its secrets to a sympathetic listener:

> Out of the bosom of the Air,
>   Out of the cloud-folds of her garments shaken,
> Over the woodlands brown and bare,
>   Over the harvest-fields forsaken,
>   Silent, and soft, and slow
>   Descends the snow.

Even as our cloudy fancies take
  Suddenly shape in some divine expression,
Even as the troubled heart doth make
  In the white countenance confession,
    The troubled sky reveals
    The grief it feels.

This is the poem of the air,
  Slowly in silent syllables recorded;
This is the secret of despair,
  Long in its cloudy bosom hoarded,
    Now whispered and revealed
    To wood and field.

There is surely more art in Longfellow's "Snow-Flakes" than in his "Rainy-Day," but the hint of terror or ultimate secrecy in the silent "poem of the air" is not developed. Instead, as in the other verses, the "troubled heart" of nature is laid bare and reveals only that it occasionally needs to have a good cry – interchangeably, it seems, in liquid or in crystalline form.

Emily Dickinson was well aware of this New England tradition that tamed the natural sublime through sentimentalization and aesthetic appropriation and was capable of both enjoying it in its own terms and of turning it to her peculiar uses. In 1869, for example, she observed of a minor masterpiece in the genre, James Russell Lowell's "A Good Word For Winter," that "one does not often meet anything so perfect."[6] In a highly literary treatment of its subject, Lowell's essay, inter alia, made the by then obligatory gesture of respectful appreciation toward Emerson's poem and cited the line about "tumultuous privacy" that Dickinson would herself still be sending to correspondents as late as 1884. But a more intriguing example of Dickinson's interest in such genial exercises concerns that sturdy, if subaltern, American littérateur who figured so largely in Dickinson's destiny, the much-maligned Colonel Higginson. We know, of course, that it was Higginson's "Letter to a Young Contributor" in the *Atlantic Monthly* for April 1862 that prompted the more momentous Letter to a Distinguished Editor beginning, "Mr. Higginson, Are you too deeply occupied to say if my Verse is alive?" But it is also worth paying attention to other pieces from Higginson's pen in that crucial spring of 1862 (as Anna Mary Wells points out, in her second letter to Higginson, Dickinson made reference to his "*Chapters* in the Atlantic"). It is clear that Dickinson was an avid reader of this journal throughout the period, and one can hardly doubt that she saw his essay "Snow" in the February number.[8] In both pieces, Dickinson found not only clichés and commonplaces against which she could measure the originality she already knew she possessed, but also cultured pearls, or near-pearls, which she could burnish and restring to her own purposes.

In the "Letter," for example, she might well have overlooked such banal middlebrowisms as that one must write "for the average eye . . . and submit to its verdict" or that one must be sure to send each "composition in such a shape that it shall not need the slightest literary revision before printing" and be certain to be "agreeable," avoiding "conundrums" and "mannerisms" (as well as excess dashes!) – when she could also find her own beliefs echoed in a defense of "the magnificent mystery of words" as against "the perfection of the pure and colorless" (including a very Dickinsonian recommendation of "Worcester's Unabridged") and further welcome praise of laconicism, such as that "a phrase may outweigh a library. . . . [A] single word may be a window from which one may perceive all the kingdoms of the earth and the glory of them. . . . [T]here may be years of crowded passion in a word, and half a life in a sentence." Dickinson also found in Higginson's "Letter" much approving mention of Emerson and an allusion to Wordsworth's injunction (the same that stirred Whitman) that would prove prophetic for her: "Remember how many great writers have created the taste by which they were enjoyed, and do not be in a hurry." Though one may question, as Karl Keller has,[9] the degree of Higginson's personal investment in these notions, they spoke to her directly at an important watershed in her career and as a result carried a force that would far outweigh Higginson's presumed palterings and perfidies. The man, in any case, was not a fool, though he may have been more a knave than a knight, and Dickinson found what she needed in him and his writings despite his shortcomings as her friend or critic.[10]

Thus we may speculate about the extent to which Higginson's "Snow" could have helped to crystallize Dickinson's own magnificent meditation on the subject, "It sifts from Leaden Sieves – " (Poem 311). Higginson's essay, like Lowell's after it, offers a curious compendium of attitudes toward, associations with, and aspects of this perennial New England subject. Principally, of course, like any true *Atlantic* essay, it strove to be genial and good-humored, balancing sun against shade, the picturesque against the profound, the odd against the ordinary.[11] His winter woods are bracing, though they are bone-cold, and preach divine benevolence and the renewal of life, though the leafless trees seem to tell a tragic tale. The woodland "is not dead, but sleepeth; and each [tree] bears a future summer of buds safe nestled on its bosom, as a mother reposes with her baby at her breast." Such creatures as are killed by frost or fatigue are neatly buried in the snow, for "with what a cleanly purity does Nature strive to withdraw all unsightly objects into her cemetery!" Higginson turns "amidst so much that seems like death" to "study life." Yet notwithstanding all this piety and decorous sentiment, which would have been as familiar to Dickinson as Longfellow's homilies and the prayer-book on the stand in her room, Higginson managed to strike some stranger notes. He pays particular attention to the "sky of lead" that threatens snow and the "fine powder which can sift through wherever dust can, or descend in large woolly masses"; paraphrasing Emerson, he likens the "agriculture" of winter to work done "with a pencil, instead of a plough"; he observes that "every grass-blade and flowerstalk is a mausoleum of vanished summer"; he figures the whitened hemlocks as "a congress of ermined kings"; he speaks of the "terror" of "the glaring days of pitiless cold," adding that "the sensations of such days almost make us associate their clearness and whiteness with something malignant and evil," but he attempts to overbalance this sinister view by concluding his piece with a long summary of a sermon by Increase Mather on the text "He giveth snow like wool" from Psalm 147, wherein the snow is likened to fleece.

The possible relevance of all these details to Dickinson's own performance would be hard to overlook:

It sifts from Leaden Sieves –
It powders all the Wood.
It fills with Alabaster Wool
The Wrinkles of the Road –

It makes an Even Face
Of Mountain, and of Plain –
Unbroken Forehead from the East
Unto the East again –

It reaches to the Fence –
It wraps it Rail by Rail
Till it is lost in Fleeces –
It deals Celestial Vail

To Stump, and Stack – and Stem –
A Summer's empty Room –
Acres of Joints, where Harvests were,
Recordless, but for them –

It Ruffles Wrists of Posts
As Ankles of a Queen –
Then stills its Artisans – like Ghosts –
Denying they have been –[12]

Throughout her poem Dickinson seems to seize on the weirdest of Higginson's observations in order to build up her own essay on "Snow" to very different effect. The face that *her* winter draws on the landscape is

the characterless face of an infinite and eternal age – age without beginning or end. The body that is being depicted – wrinkles, face, forehead,
joints, wrists, ankles – is also being buried; the "Celestial Vail" is its
shroud. All parts, equalized as the indistinguishable records of their own
dismemberment, are pressed into service as the sculptors of a negating,
disorganic art (this, perhaps, as a grim commentary on the "frolic
architecture" of Emerson's notably organic force that builds up forms
instead of taking them apart). There is no domestic refuge in Dickinson's
poem: this creature is simply lost in the drifts that have filled "Summer's
empty Room" and made it a wintry mausoleum. The "tumultuous
privacy" of Emerson's room is stilled here. Higginson himself had
alluded twice in his essay to Emerson's Divinity School Address, referring to the "beautiful meteor of the snow" and to the reality of the storm
as compared to the frigidity of Emerson's preacher, but here everything
seems equally drained of reality – a ghostly storm making a ghost of
whatever it touches. Dickinson's kosmos – to use Emerson's word from
Nature – is not so much beauty as universal blankness.[13]

It is worth noting that "It sifts from Leaden Sieves – " has the form
(not unusual in Dickinson's work, of course) of a riddle, since neither
snow nor *white* is mentioned.[14] Although we assume that "it" refers to
snow, that most mysterious of Dickinson's pronouns, or expletives,
stands only for the unnamed something that sifts, powders, fills, makes,
reaches, wraps, deals, ruffles, and – finally – stills. Most disconcertingly,
perhaps, in the third stanza ("It reaches to the Fence – / It wraps it Rail by
Rail / Till it is lost in Fleeces – ") the "it" that reaches and wraps is itself
confounded with the "it" it acts upon, as both become one and are "lost
in Fleeces." Whatever this "it" is, it has the power to make all things
over in its own empty image. We may choose to say that "it" is snow,
but it is equally plausible to view the snow as no more than the agent of
which "it" remains the inscrutable principal. Ultimately, the "it" here is
hardly more specifiable than it is in another sinister riddle poem of about
the same period (Poem 510) that seems curiously linked to "It sifts from
Leaden Sieves – ":

> It was not Death, for I stood up,
> And all the Dead, lie down –
> It was not Night, for all the Bells
> Put out their Tongues, for Noon.
>
> It was not Frost, for on my Flesh
> I felt Siroccos – crawl –
> Nor Fire – for just my Marble feet
> Could keep a Chancel, cool –

And yet, it tasted, like them all,
The Figures I have seen
Set orderly, for Burial,
Reminded me, of mine –

As if my life were shaven,
And fitted to a frame,
And could not breathe without a key,
And 'twas like Midnight, some –

When everything that ticked – has stopped –
And Space stares all around –
Or Grisly frosts – first Autumn morns,
Repeal the Beating Ground –

But, most like Chaos – Stopless – cool –
Without a Chance, or Spar –
Or even a Report of Land –
To justify – Despair.

Though the mystery seems evenly balanced between fire and ice, ice finally does appear to suffice as the poem ends with a grisly frost that seems like cool stopless Chaos, another featureless infinity of blank. We should also pay attention to Dickinson's use of *like*, for the terrible thing she is trying without clear success to specify can only be described analogically,[15] as the unseen force that causes the snow in Poem 311 can be observed only in its effects, which are, in any case, represented by a nonrepresentation, a silent void without character. This "poem of air," to use Longfellow's language, "slowly in silent syllables" records nothing but rather obliterates all records. What is "whispered and revealed / To wood and field" is only the quiet work of negation.

In view of the fact that Higginson ends his essay with a report of Increase Mather's dissertation on the text from Psalm 147, we may be tempted to view Dickinson's effort as an antisermon of her own, perhaps on the same text. If her "it" is a divinity, "lost in Fleeces" and dealing "Celestial Vail," it appears to be a divinity of negative apocalypse, since it obscures rather than reveals, and of negative creation, since it is the spirit that denies. The *eschatos* being celebrated in this Book of Non-Revelation is a nonmarriage, since the "Queen" is dead, her bridal gown a burial garment, and the Bridegroom arrayed in his own white is equivalent to the grim reaper. If Dickinson looked up Mather's text, as she might well have done, she would have noticed that the "snow like wool" that God gives seems intended by the psalmist to stand for His commandment:

He giveth snow like wool:
He scattereth the hoarfrost like ashes.
He casteth forth his ice like morsels:
Who can stand before his cold?
He sendeth out his word, and melteth them. . . .

If God's word is a cold that melts, Dickinson could well have appreciated
the paradox without sharing its hope as a saving ordinance. The freezing
Word, in her rendition, turns beings into nonbeings: All do indeed lie
down before this cold. In fact, the Word, in her version, is the voice of
silence, stilling as it descends. But it may be that the divinity whom
Dickinson is thus fearfully depicting is not the God of Love but the harsh
Jehovah of the Calvinists, if she actually intended her poem to be a
response to Higginson's rendition of Mather's sermon, for Mather is
reported as saying that "if God speaks the word, the Earth is covered
with snow in a few Minutes' time," whence "Atheists will be left
Eternally Inexcusable." Believers, however, seem to fare not much
better at the hands of such a deity. All are equally denied their being by
that chilling word. The minister's veil, in this case, is white, not black,
but it appalls nevertheless. Is that the sort of comment Dickinson intended to make on what Higginson himself calls "the grim theology of the
Mathers"? We can only speculate, but it is interesting to note that when
she sent a copy of this poem to a correspondent in 1881, she wrote: "will
you . . . accept a View of *my* House, which Nature painted White,
without consulting me – but Nature is 'old fashioned,' perhaps a Puritan – "[16] Does that represent a good word either for winter *or* for the old-
time religion?

"It sifts from Leaden Sieves – " is, I believe, a central text in Dickinson's work and radiates curiously to other poems in her canon. When
Dickinson sent another copy of the poem[17] to the publisher Thomas
Niles in 1883 in response to his gift of a life of George Eliot, she included
with it Poem 1068, "Further in Summer than the Birds," along with this
message: "Dear friend. I bring you a chill Gift – my Cricket and the
Snow. A base return indeed, for the delightful Book . . . but an earnest
one."[18] Did she deem her poems an inadequate return for the gift of
Eliot's life, not simply out of humility, but because the life depicted in
them, though "earnest," was a deprived and frigid one? The Cricket, in
fact, may well be "slant" autobiography:

Further in Summer than the Birds
Pathetic from the Grass
A minor Nation celebrates
Its unobtrusive Mass.

No Ordinance be seen
So gradual the Grace
A pensive Custom it becomes
Enlarging Loneliness.

Antiquest felt at Noon
When August burning low
Arise this spectral Canticle
Repose to typify

Remit as yet no Grace
No Furrow on the Glow
Yet a Druidic Difference
Enhances Nature now

Dickinson seems clearly to identify with this "minor Nation" which celebrates its small size pathetically in a scarcely observable "spectral Canticle" that represents the liturgy of loneliness and death. I am reminded of Poem 486:

I was the slightest in the House –
I took the smallest Room –
At night, my little Lamp, and Book –
And one Geranium –

. . .

I never spoke – unless addressed –
And then, 'twas brief and low –
I could not bear to live – aloud –
The Racket shamed me so –

And if it had not been so far –
And any one I knew
Were going – I had often thought
How noteless – I could die –

This timorous creature, so shy of utterance that she appears unable to initiate conversation (or perhaps can bear to speak only in her letters – when "addressed"), presents herself as diminished and obscure and consequently capable of decamping silently and without notice, as soundless, perhaps, as a dot on a disk of snow (the notation of quiescence). As a Druid she is the priestess, sometimes at least, of *quiet* despair. Niles, in fact, wanted very much to publish Dickinson's poetry and asked for a manuscript – a request that she simply ignored. Had she not already observed (Poem 709):

Publication – is the Auction
Of the Mind of Man –
Poverty – be justifying
For so foul a thing

Possibly – but We – would rather
From our Garret go
White – Unto the White Creator –
Than invest – Our Snow. . . .

Her gift was "chill," then, because it was indeed an earnest version of her
life. She refused to publish because she envisioned it as a form of
prostitution. Her virginity and her public silence were equivalent. Dickinson was the Snow White of her own immaculate fantasy, made white
by the "White Creator" and determined to remain that way – snow
created by snow and wedded to snow.[19] The Queen bedded and buried in
her bridal shroud is Dickinson herself, as she puts it superbly in Poem
1072:

Title divine – is mine!
The Wife – without the Sign!
Acute Degree – conferred on me –
Empress of Calvary!
Royal – all but the Crown!
Betrothed – without the swoon
God sends us Women –
When you – hold – Garnet to Garnet –
Gold – to Gold –
Born – Bridalled – Shrouded –
In a Day. . . .

Dickinson's voluntary assumption of the "Celestial Vail" – her
"White Election" (#528) or wearing of white – dates from the spring of
1862 and seems to have reference to the departure for San Francisco
(Calvary Church) of one of her hopeless loves, the Reverend Charles
Wadsworth, but we may conjecture that it had deeper sources in her
psychic economy.[20] The expression of sexuality may normally be considered a definition of life (for Whitman, say), but for *her*, "Life is over
there – / Behind the Shelf" (#640). She seems to have felt safer in her alabaster chamber, "Untouched by Morning – / And untouched by Noon"
(#216). Dickinson lived much of her life in an ecstasy of negation. "Dont
you know," she wrote Judge Lord, "you are happiest while I withhold
and not confer – dont you know that 'No' is the wildest word we

consign to Language?"[21] Dickinson's language is, frequently, precisely, a no – a riddle, a puzzle, a denial of meaning. That also would be too easy a yielding. Though she argues, in Poem 210,

The thought beneath so slight a film –
Is more distinctly seen –
As laces just reveal the surge –
Or Mists – the Apennine

those laces reveal only by means of velation. The thought may be more distinctly *seen*, but it must remain untouched; the surge of that virgin bosom is perceivable but forever covered by the lace. Dickinson's strategy, in fact, seems to be that of a woman who feels herself to be "small," and is therefore shy of exposure, but comes to believe that the physical withholding of herself will enable her to swell in other ways:

A solemn thing – it was – I said –
A woman – white – to be –
And wear – if God should count me fit –
Her blameless mystery –

. . .

I pondered how the bliss would look –
And would it feel as big –
When I could take it in my hand –
As hovering – seen – through fog –

And then – the size of this "small" life –
The Sages – call it small –
Swelled – like Horizons – in my vest –
And I sneered – softly – "small"!   (Poem 271)

Keeping her snow intact, as she says, "in Everlasting flake" (#275), makes her feel at once regal and reduced, something less than adult and more than human: "A Mien to move a Queen – / Half Child – Half Heroine – " Consequently she has

A Voice that Alters – Low
And on the Ear can go
Like Let of Snow –
Or shift supreme –
As tone of Realm
On Subjects Diadem –

and views herself, paradoxically, as

> Too small – to fear –
> Too distant – to endear –
> And so Men Compromise –
> And just – revere –   (Poem 283)

Dickinson evidently liked to be revered rather than possessed, and such a posture tempted her, in her writing at least, to play the roles, alternately, of virgin–child–martyr. "If you doubted my Snow – for a moment – you never will – again – I know – " she wrote her friend Samuel Bowles, followed by Poem 792:

> Through the strait pass of suffering –
> The Martyrs – even – trod.
> Their feet – upon Temptation –
> Their faces – upon God –
>
> A stately – shriven – Company –
> Convulsion – playing round –
> Harmless – as streaks of Meteor –
> Upon a Planet's Bond –
>
> Their faith – the everlasting troth –
> Their Expectation – fair –
> The Needle – to the North Degree –
> Wades – so – thro' polar Air!

Such quasi-religious self-dramatization could easily appear overdone, could even strike Dickinson's brother Austin as a kind of insincere posing,[22] as when she told Higginson portentously that her "Business is Circumference," meaning, if we are to use Poem 1620 as a gloss, that she was the "Bride of Awe," only to be possessed by hallowed knights who dared to covet such an exalted creature. She was as royal as Higginson's ermined hemlocks and perhaps as austere:

> I think the Hemlock likes to stand
> Upon the Marge of Snow –
> It suits his own Austerity –
> And satisfies an awe
>
> That men, must slake in Wilderness –
> And in the Desert – cloy –
> An instinct for the Hoar, the Bald –
> Lapland's – necessity –

The Hemlock's nature thrives – on cold –
The Gnash of Northern winds
Is sweetest nutriment – to him –
His best Norwegian Wines. . . .   (Poem 525)

She would therefore choose to live in an exalted society of one that
simulated the noble solitude of a Queen:

The soul selects her own Society –
Then – shuts the Door –
To her divine Majority –
Present no more –

Unmoved – she notes the Chariots – pausing –
At her low Gate –
Unmoved – an Emperor be kneeling
Upon her Mat –

I've known her – from an ample nation –
Choose One –
Then – close the Valves of her attention –
Like Stone –   (Poem 303)

To be a rare flower thus shut up – was that the apogee of a sublime life or
the nearest thing to living death? Had she in fact been touched only by
the "Visitor in Marl"?

Who influences Flowers –
Till they are orderly as Busts –
And Elegant – as Glass –

Who visits in the Night –
And just before the Sun –
Concludes his glistening interview –
Caresses – and is gone –

But whom his fingers touched –
And where his feet have run –
And whatsoever Mouth he kissed –
Is as it had not been –   (Poem 391)

Had this fantasy Snow Maiden[23] allowed herself to be kissed only by the
noble courtier whose gift is that of nonbeing? If so, it had left her heart
frozen, almost dead, a "Pendulum of snow," as she says in Poem 287.
She had been marked, it seems, by "Tribulation,"

Denoted by the White –
The Spangled Gowns, a lesser Rank
Of Victors – designate –

All these – did conquer –
But the ones who overcame most times –
Wear nothing commoner than Snow. . . .   (Poem 325)

To put it simply, this noble reclusiveness, lofty detachment, or chilly sublimity, represented the only mode of queenliness available to a nineteenth-century provincial American poet who, through an accident of birth and culture, came to "see – New Englandly – ," which meant that "the Snow's Tableau" was radically a part of her being (#285). "My House is a House of Snow," she said in 1875, after her father's death,[24] but the sentence might be taken in a wider sense (compare the 1881 letter cited above, in which "It sifts from Leaden Sieves – " is described as "a view of *my* House, which Nature painted White"). The drifts of that perpetual winter storm in which she found herself seeped steadily into her soul. Like nature, she had attempted to squander love but more and more could only squander rigor:

It came at last but prompter Death
Had occupied the House –
His pallid Furniture arranged
And his metallic Peace –

Oh faithful Frost that kept the Date
Had Love as punctual been
Delight had aggrandized the Gate
And blocked the coming in.   (Poem 1230)

She did, in fact, dream of living in the fullest sense, imagining endless

. . . Certainties of Sun –
Midsummer – in the Mind –
A steadfast South – upon the Soul –
Her Polar time – behind. . . .

That vision, "pondered long – ," as she goes on,

So plausible becomes
That I esteem the fiction – real –
The Real – fictitious seems. . . .   (Poem 646)

Such a fiction proved to be no more durable than Dickinson's fantasy that she was a rose, when in truth God had made her "a little Gentian." It was laughable to try to force the condition of summer on a flower destined for another season, a different splendor. "But just before the Snows":

There rose a Purple Creature –
That ravished all the Hill –
And Summer hid her Forehead –
And Mockery – was still –

The Frosts were her condition –
The Tyrian would not come
Until the North – invoke it –
Creator – Shall I – bloom?   (Poem 442)

Bloom, of course, she did, but most splendidly and terribly in crystals of ice. Dickinson's finest performances are the fruit of tribulation – "the fine hammered steel of woe," in Melville's phrase – and are firmly and unmistakably linked to that unending snowstorm that was seated on the throne of her soul:

After great pain, a formal feeling comes –
The Nerves sit ceremonious, like Tombs –
The stiff Heart questions was it He, that bore,
And Yesterday, or Centuries before?

The Feet, mechanical, go round –
Of Ground, or Air, or Ought –
A Wooden way
Regardless grown,
A Quartz contentment, like a stone –

This is the Hour of Lead –
Remembered, if outlived,
As Freezing persons, recollect the Snow –
First – Chill – then Stupor – then the letting go –   (Poem 341)

This may seem as far from Emerson as it is from Longfellow, for Dickinson's all but affectless description of the aftermath of a storm of "great pain" does not allow for any cathartic release of passion and a return to normalcy and geniality. Dickinson's feeling is so "formal" that she quite uncharacteristically dignifies it with the marmoreal heroic couplets that open and conclude the poem. Both friends *and* housemates appear to be shut out of the quiet privacy enforced by suffering. The speaker is enclosed in a chilled body that represents her own sepulcher. That is the sort of masonry provided by the fierce artificer of human experience: "A Quartz contentment, like a stone – " She feels *her* hours to be numbered, or at least reduced or frozen to one horrific "Hour of Lead" from whose oppressive horizon sifts the entombing alabaster. Dickinson's fiercely precise art can only mimic, in the stumbling gait of the final line ("First – Chill – then Stupor – then the letting go – ") this process by which unbearable pain lays the heart to rest, since detailed memory is thwarted by the mind's being on the brink of its own oblivion. We must deny that such experience has been if we are to go on living, but that denial becomes part of our loss – "the letting go" of dead parts of the self that slowly and steadily dis(re)members us. The departing storm of feeling leaves the speaker fearfully diminished and she utters her lines almost posthumously, from behind the "Celestial Vail," out of her uncertain awareness of an impending dissolution. Her poem, to paraphrase Frost, is an icy crystal that rides on its own melting and ends in nothing.[25]

I do not intend to suggest any absolute opposition between Dickinson and Emerson; indeed, "After great pain . . ." might easily be seen as issuing from the same empty affect (lethargy, sleepiness, numbness) that prompted Emerson's bleak meditations on suffering after his son's death in "Experience." Dickinson remains always and inescapably the poetic child of Emerson, as they are both offspring of the larger Romantic movement. Like Emerson, Dickinson is a connoisseur of polarities, oppositions, and contradictions. She, too, is "always insincere, as always knowing there are other moods."[26] She, too, could feel glad to the brink of fear and experience despair as a total blankness that obliterates pain. She had read her Keats, along with Emerson, and knew that veiled melancholy keeps her shrine in the very temple of delight, that pleasure can turn to poison as the bee mouth sips.[27] In her utter isolation, Dickinson represents an Emersonian consciousness, the Romantic Me, bound in breathless horror to its own imaginings, trapped in its own being but fearful of a release that would tumble it into madness or the gulf beyond:

Me from Myself – to banish –
Had I Art –
Impregnable my Fortress
Unto All Heart –

But since Myself – assault Me –
How have I peace
Except by subjugating
Consciousness?

And since We're mutual Monarch
How this be
Except by Abdication –
Me – of Me?   (Poem 642)

Where Dickinson differs from Emerson is not in the way she conceived of existence but rather in the *intensity* with which she felt squeezed by the antinomies of experience. Emerson's own sense of the fragility and doubleness of things was strong, but his corresponding cycles of mood and expectation were longer; perhaps he had more patience than Dickinson. He *can* remain hopeful in the spring – even, or at least, through a poem of many hundred lines ("May Day," for example). But a half-dozen lines are sufficient room for Dickinson to turn around in:

A Pang is more conspicuous in Spring
In contrast with the things that sing
Not Birds entirely – but Minds –
Minute Effulgencies and Winds –
When what they sing for is undone
Who cares about a Blue Bird's Tune. . . .   (Poem 1530)

Her pleasures rarely make it to the end of the page; and her pains seem more durable.

* * * * *

I began this book with a rather duplex view of the great Romantic discovery and celebration of consciousness and its apocalyptic marriage with nature. For Wordsworth and Emerson the age of the first-person singular was largely a time for expanding the self in its potentially joyful relationship with both the natural world and others. But Brockden Brown, we remember, sounded a darker note with respect to egotism: "Consciousness itself is the malady, the pest, of which he only is cured who ceases to think." Three-quarters of a century later Emily Dickinson had shaken off Brown's residual Calvinism but not his nagging concern. Her life in nature was a "smart Misery" (#376), heaven no more than a condition of removal – an "ablative estate" (#1741) – the promise of resurrection a riddle (#89). She knew the soul was condemned to "Adventure most unto itself" (#822), attended ineluctably by an identity, "That awful stranger Consciousness" (#1323), that was at once her glory and her torment.[28] She was therefore forced to celebrate, in a voice that is close to our own, her belief that freedom is no less an option for the modern self than is constriction and containment:

The Eagle of his Nest
No easier divest –
And gain the Sky
Than mayest Thou –

Except thyself may be
Thine Enemy –
Captivity is Consciousness –
So's Liberty.   (Poem 384)

Though Dickinson does not specify the ways in which we may be inimical to ourselves, she does suggest, with her ambiguous word order, that "Captivity" and "Liberty" are themselves modalities of self-awareness: The necessary circumscription of the self within its own circle is as enabling as "one's grand flights" (Stevens).[29] Perhaps she was thinking of Hamlet: "O God, I could be bounded in a nutshell, and count myself a king of infinite space, were it not that I have bad dreams."[30] It is precisely the nature of our "dreams" that defines the condition of consciousness. What is in fact not an option, though it is conventionally and traditionally considered one, is to get "beyond egotism." The appeal to selflessness or self-abnegation as a presumed antidote to Romantic self-involvement resonates strongly in western culture (whether owing to the continuing influence of Classicism or Christianity), as when Santayana says eloquently, "the best things that come into a man's consciousness are the things that take him out of it – the rational things that are independent of his personal perception and of his personal existence."[31] Such a dictum, reinforced by the advent of Modernism (we hear Eliot's "Tradition and the Individual Talent" waiting in the wings), will always carry great weight.[32] But we should not overlook the fact that getting "out" of one's consciousness is possible only figurally (we might recall that "alienation," the nineteenth-century term for madness, also implies going "out" of one's mind). In truth, we remain wedded to our consciousness whether we like it or not and must make the best of it. As Thoreau remarks pertinently in the "Monday" section of *A Week on the Concord and Merrimack Rivers*, "If I am not I, who will be?"

The dilemma of consciousness as Dickinson presents it finds its subtlest and most searching exponent today in John Ashbery. Meditating on Parmigianino's "Self-Portrait in a Convex Mirror," Ashbery apprehends the "point" it makes[33]:

That the soul is a captive, treated humanely, kept
In suspension. . . .

The soul, suspended in Parmigianino's frame (and equally in Ashbery's stanza), must remain in its room,

. . . has to stay where it is,
Even though restless, hearing raindrops at the pane,
The sighing of autumn leaves thrashed by the wind,
Longing to be free, outside, but it must stay
Posing in this place. It must move
As little as possible. This is what the portrait says.

Ashbery thus seems to stress the "captivity" side of Dickinson's dilemma, wherein the soul remains trapped and "posing" (movement would spoil the portrait) in the space of its own artistic self-display, representing "the enchantment of self with self." But there is nonetheless nourishment for us here:

Why be unhappy with this arrangement, since
Dreams prolong us as they are absorbed?
Something like living occurs, a movement
Out of the dream into its codification.

The soul, framed in its portrait, the victim of its own "arrangement," nevertheless moves toward us, offering us an imaginative paradigm – a dream, "like living," that encodes our own experience. Parmigianino's face is, and is not, our "reflection":

. . . Since it is a metaphor
Made to include us, we are part of it and
Can live in it as in fact we have done. . . .

So we may say finally that we have escaped from the circle of Parmigianino's subjectivity by means he himself provides: a magic globe of self-reflection that, unlike Ahab's doubloon, does not devour others and the world but rather moves both (to cite Philippe Lacoue-Labarthe and Jean-Luc Nancy again) to "the very limit of exemplarity and figuration."[34] When we speak in this manner in "respect" to egotism, we are looking back, with Ashbery, to the best of the Romantic tradition.

Notes

PREFACE

1 On this point my understanding has been enriched by Albert J. Von Frank's *The Sacred Game: Provincialism and Frontier Consciousness in American Literature, 1630–1860* (Cambridge: Cambridge University Press, 1985).
2 Gertrude Stein, *What Are Masterpieces?* (New York: Pitman, 1970), p. 62.

INTRODUCTION: WRITING, READING, ROMANTICISM

1 See, for example, James Franklin Beard's review of three books on Cooper in *Studies in Romanticism* 18 (1979): 482, as well as his Historical Introduction to *The Pioneers* (Albany: SUNY Press, 1980).
2 J. Lyndon Shanley, *The Making of Walden* (Chicago: University of Chicago Press, 1957).
3 Though I am not suggesting that Phillips and Garrison had a hand in the actual composition of Douglass's *Narrative* (so far as I know there is no evidence to support such an allegation), a persistent strain in recent commentary on Douglass argues that abolitionist sponsorship of his, and other ex-slaves', work amounts to an interference that calls into question the absolute authenticity of such work. Thus Henry Louis Gates, Jr., observes that "many ex-slave narrators confess that their printed texts are structured formal revisions of their spoken words organized and promoted by anti-slavery organizations" (*The Slave's Narrative*, ed. Charles T. Davis and Henry Louis Gates, Jr. [New York: Oxford University Press, 1985], p. xvi). Gates also cites Ulrich B. Phillips in 1929: "[E]x-slave narratives in general . . . were issued with so much abolitionist editing that as a class their authenticity is doubtful" (p. xxxii). See especially James Olney, " 'I Was Born': Slave Narratives, Their Status as Autobiography and as Literature," in ibid., pp. 148–75, who argues that the imposition of prescribed, conventional forms kept many ex-slave narrators "captive to the abolitionist intentions." Similar arguments are framed in various contributions to *Frederick Douglass's Narrative of the Life of Frederick Douglass*, ed. Harold Bloom (New York: Chelsea House, 1988). Thus Houston A. Baker, Jr. (pp. 105, 107): "[W]hile autobiographical conventions forced him [Douglass] to portray as accurately as possible the existentiality of his original condition, the light of abolitionism is always implicitly present, guiding the

narrator into calm, Christian, and publicly accessible harbors. . . . The voice of the unwritten self, once it is subjected to the linguistic codes, literary conventions, and audience expectations of a literate population, is perhaps never again the authentic voice of black American slavery." So, too, Annette Niemtzow (p. 121): "Douglass's autobiography then, by virtue of its genre, unconsciously pays tribute to a definition of self created by whites." Also John Sekora (p. 156): "As author he [Douglass] was . . . caught in a genuine dilemma. He was indeed an individual human being with a particular story to tell, but if he were to discover personalizing words for his life, he must do so within the language of abolition." See additionally John Sekora, "The Dilemma of Frederick Douglass: The Slave Narrative as Literary Institution," *Essays in Literature* 10 (1983): 219–26; Eric J. Sundquist, "Frederick Douglass: Literacy and Paternalism," *Raritan* 6 (1986): 108–24.

4   See the epigraph to "Heroism."

5   *Walden*, "Economy."

6   See *A Critique of Modern Textual Criticism* (Chicago: University of Chicago Press, 1983). For a spirited attack on the prevailing principles of textual editing, as well as a new view of "authorial intention," see Hershel Parker, *Flawed Texts and Verbal Icons: Literary Authority in American Fiction* (Evanston: Northwestern University Press, 1984).

7   Cited in Jonathan Culler, *Structuralist Poetics* (Ithaca: Cornell University Press, 1975), p. 131.

8   Ibid., p. 131.

9   Ibid., p. 130.

10   Ibid., p. 116.

11   Ibid., p. 255.

12   Ibid., p. 247.

13   Ibid., pp. 259–63.

14   Ibid., p. 252.

15   Relevant here is the work of Jerome J. McGann, especially his introduction to *Historical Studies and Literary Criticism* (Madison: University of Wisconsin Press, 1985) and *The Beauty of Inflections: Literary Investigations in Historical Method and Theory* (Oxford: Clarendon Press, 1988).

16   This and all following quotations from *Historicism Once More* (Princeton: Princeton University Press, 1969), Chapters 1 and 2. Pearce has recently extended his views on the historical and humanistic approach to literature in *Gesta Humanorum: Studies in the Historicist Mode* (Columbia: University of Missouri Press, 1987). See also Warner Berthoff, "The Study of Literature and the Recovery of the Historical," in *Fictions and Events* (New York: Dutton, 1971), pp. 15–29.

17   "The American Scholar," in *Essays and Lectures,* ed. Joel Porte (New York: Library of America, 1983), p. 59.

18   Michel Foucault, *The Archaeology of Knowledge* (New York: Pantheon Books, 1971), p. 140.

19   Ibid., pp. 138–9. A cogent recent critique of the "call to history," especially as regards Foucault, is to be found in Jonathan Culler, *Framing the Sign* (Norman: University of Oklahoma Press, 1988), pp. 57–68.

20 Reprinted in *Essays in the History of Ideas* (New York: G. P. Putnam's Sons, 1960).

21 Though the subject is vast, several items in particular might be singled out. In addition to works cited below, such as René Wellek's *Concepts of Criticism*, and to Lovejoy's *Essays in the History of Ideas*, as well as to his "The Meaning of Romanticism for the Historian of Ideas" (*Journal of the History of Ideas*, 2 [1941]: 257–78), *Romanticism: Points of View*, ed. Robert F. Gleckner and Gerald E. Enscoe (Englewood Cliffs, N.J.: Prentice-Hall, 1962) is still useful, as is *Romanticism Reconsidered*, ed. Northrop Frye (New York: Columbia University Press, 1963). Two stimulating recent studies are Philippe Lacoue-Labarthe and Jean-Luc Nancy, *The Literary Absolute: The Theory of Literature in German Romanticism* (Albany: SUNY Press, 1988), and Vergil Nemoianu, *The Taming of Romanticism: European Literature and the Age of Biedermeier* (Cambridge, Mass.: Harvard University Press, 1984). See also Paul de Man's brief but provocative Introduction to *Studies in Romanticism* 18 (1979) and Maurice Blanchot, "The Atheneum," *Studies in Romanticism* 22 (1983): 163–72.

22 See Arthur O. Lovejoy, "The Meaning of 'Romantic' in Early German Romanticism," *Essays in the History of Ideas* (New York: G. P. Putnam's Sons, 1960), pp. 183–206.

23 René Wellek, *Concepts of Criticism* (New Haven: Yale University Press, 1963), p. 130.

24 Ibid., p. 133.

25 Ibid., p. 141.

26 Ibid., p. 140.

27 Cited in Lilian R. Furst, *Romanticism* (London: Methuen, 1969), pp. 41–3.

28 The question of whether or not the Schlegels' "*romantisch*," as defined especially in the famous *Atheneum* fragment 116, refers specifically to the modern "*roman*" has been hotly debated for a long time. In 1916 Lovejoy argued (in "The Meaning of 'Romantic' in Early German Romanticism") that the Schlegels' intent should not be so narrowly delimited. Lacoue-Labarthe and Nancy, *The Literary Absolute*, especially pp. 86–93, and p. 143, note 25, essentially agree with Lovejoy, insisting that the privileged "literary Genre is Literature itself, the *Literary Absolute* . . . a sort of beyond of literature itself." But in a review of Madame de Staël's *Corinne* published in 1807, A. W. Schlegel argued for an understanding of the "true criterion" that would discover in the modern "romanesque" novel "more poetry and above all more Romanticism." See *Cahiers Staëliens: Nouvelle Série* 16 (1973): 57–71. Cf. Blanchot, "The Atheneum," p. 171.

29 Alfred North Whitehead, *Science and the Modern World* (New York: Free Press, 1967), p. 94.

30 James Engell, *The Creative Imagination* (Cambridge, Mass.: Harvard University Press, 1981), pp. 200–5.

31 M. H. Abrams, *The Mirror and the Lamp* (New York: W. W. Norton, 1958), p. 141.

32 Ibid., p. 193.

33 Ibid., p. 172.

34 Ibid., p. 191.

35 See *The Journals and Miscellaneous Notebooks of Ralph Waldo Emerson*, vol. 9, ed. Ralph H. Orth and Alfred R. Ferguson (Cambridge, Mass.: Belknap Press of Harvard University Press, 1971), p. 72. Emerson removed the word "oestrum" when he used this passage in "The Poet."

36 Cited in *The Mirror and the Lamp*, p. 213.

37 In his 1807 review of *Corinne*, A. W. Schlegel observes that "if the Romantic character derives above all from the confrontation between ideal enthusiasm and prosaic reality, then it is reasonable to consider love, which animates the contradictions in the nature of man and his destiny, as the Romantic passion par excellence."

38 See William K. Wimsatt, "Organic Form: Some Questions About a Metaphor," in *Romanticism: Vistas, Instances, Continuities*, ed. David Thorburn and Geoffrey Hartman (Ithaca: Cornell University Press, 1973), pp. 13–37.

39 Vladimir Nabokov, *Lolita* (New York: G. P. Putnam's, 1955), p. 167.

40 From Edgar Allan Poe, *Essays and Reviews*, ed. G. R. Thompson (New York: Library of America, 1984), p. 1341.

41 See Simms's "Daniel Boon; The First Hunter of Kentucky," in *Views and Reviews in American Literature, History and Fiction*, ed. C. Hugh Holman (Cambridge, Mass.: Harvard University Press, 1962), pp. 148–77. The intensity of Boone's love of the wilderness is underscored by William Carlos Williams's portrait of him as a "great voluptuary" in *In The American Grain* (New York: New Directions, 1956), p. 130.

42 Jean Béranger and Maurice Gonnaud, *La Littérature Americaine Jusqu'en 1865* (Paris: Librairie Armand Colin, 1974), pp. 54–5.

43 Perry Miller cites Alfred North Whitehead on America's "lack" of an eighteenth century in "New England's Transcendentalism: Native or Imported?" in *Critical Essays on American Transcendentalism*, ed. Philip F. Gura and Joel Myerson (Boston: G. K. Hall, 1982), p. 396. In "Washington Irving: Nonsense, the Fat of the Land and the Dream of Indolence," in *The Chief Glory of Every People*, ed. Matthew J. Bruccoli (Carbondale: Southern Illinois University Press, 1973), pp. 143–4, William L. Hedges observes: "Between 1800 and 1810, or even 1820, American intellectual life, caught in the conservative reaction to revolution and terror in France and general war in Europe, stultified considerably. The widespread fear of anarchy and atheism that swept the country at the turn of the century brought in its wake suspicion of new ideas generally. The early work of the English romantics, as we know, was very coolly received for the better part of a generation. Official culture tended to retreat into ponderous 'truths.' This was particularly the case in Federalist New England."

44 Explored at large in Howard Mumford Jones, *Revolution and Romanticism* (Cambridge, Mass.: Belknap Press of Harvard University Press, 1974). For a stimulating recent discussion, see David Brion Davis, *Revolutions* (Cambridge, Mass.: Harvard University Press, 1990).

45 M. H. Abrams, "English Romanticism: The Spirit of the Age," in *Romanticism Reconsidered*, ed. Northrop Frye (New York: Columbia University Press, 1963), p. 33.

46 V. L. Parrington, *Main Currents in American Thought*, vol. 2: *The Romantic Revolution in America* (New York: Harcourt, Brace, 1959), p. x.

47 In *Revolution and Romanticism* Jones suggests that unlike the American Revolution, which was conceived in terms of the Enlightenment, the French Revolution was essentially Romantic in its glorification of the individual ego: "[T]he climate of opinion in Europe in 1789 differed radically from the climate of opinion in North America in 1763. God was remote, the universe was malleable, the future of mankind depended upon humanity itself, the world was what the ego made of it, and French revolutionary egoists were entirely prepared to assert that they and they alone, taken collectively or individually, were capable of interpreting the present wishes and probable future of mankind in terms they themselves laid down with a personal passion not evident in American patriots or the American founding fathers. The disappearance of the Christian order from French revolutionary thought turned Man into an enlarged surrogate for deity. Victory and remorse were here and now; the development of advanced thought, if it isolated the individual revolutionary leader, also permitted him to picture a perfected society and a rational future as an enlarged image of himself. This is not, of course, the whole story of the French revolution, but it is an image sufficiently cogent to illuminate the profound psychological difference between a Jefferson and a Marat, a George Washington and a Robespierre" (p. 243).

48 On this subject generally, see Michael Kammen, *A Season of Youth: The American Revolution and the Historical Imagination* (New York: Knopf, 1978).

49 Geoffrey Hartman, "Reflections on Romanticism in France," in *Romanticism: Vistas, Instances, Continuities*, ed. David Thorburn and Geoffrey Hartman (Ithaca: Cornell University Press, 1973), p. 44.

50 See Larry Reynolds, *European Revolutions and the American Literary Renaissance* (New Haven: Yale University Press, 1988).

51 In *Essays and Lectures*, p. 68.

52 *Margaret Fuller: American Romantic*, ed. Perry Miller (New York: Anchor Books, 1963), p. 279.

53 Ibid., pp. 279–80.

54 Cf. ibid., p. 294.

55 On European influence in the American Renaissance generally, see Leon Chai, *The Romantic Foundations of the American Renaissance* (Ithaca: Cornell University Press, 1987).

56 *Journals and Miscellaneous Notebooks of Ralph Waldo Emerson*, vol. 3, ed. William H. Gilman and Alfred R. Ferguson (Cambridge, Mass.: Belknap Press of Harvard University Press, 1963), p. 70.

57 "Historic Notes of Life and Letters in New England," cited in *The American Transcendentalists*, ed. Perry Miller (New York: Anchor Books, 1957), p. 5.

58 "The Lord's Supper," in *Essays and Lectures*, p. 1140.

59 Wallace Stevens, *Collected Poems* (New York: Knopf, 1957), pp. 36–7.

60 Cited in Wellek, *Concepts of Criticism*, p. 174.

61 *Essays and Lectures*, pp. 672–3.

62 Cited in Wellek, *Concepts of Criticism*, p. 177.

63 In *Selected Writings of the American Transcendentalists*, ed. George Hochfield (New York: New American Library, 1966), p. 74.

64 Ibid., p. 77.
65 Cited in M. H. Abrams, *Natural Supernaturalism* (New York: Norton, 1971), pp. 467–8.
66 Ibid., pp. 14, 28.
67 "The Eye and Ear," in *The Early Lectures of Ralph Waldo Emerson*, vol. 2, ed. Stephen E. Whicher, Robert E. Spiller, and Wallace E. Williams (Cambridge, Mass.: Belknap Press of Harvard University Press, 1964), p. 273.
68 In the Houghton Library, Harvard. Quoted by permission.
69 *Concepts of Criticism*, p. 138.
70 Baroness Staël Holstein, *Germany* (London: John Murray, 1813), vol. 1, p. 306.
71 Ibid., p. 307.
72 Cited in *The American Transcendentalists*, p. 7.
73 *Germany*, vol. 2, p. 323.
74 Ibid., p. 372.
75 *Germany*, vol. 3, p. 81.
76 Ibid., p. 109.
77 Ibid., pp. 14–15.
78 *Essays and Lectures*, p. 403.
79 *Germany*, vol. 3, p. 111.
80 Ibid., p. 112.
81 *Essays and Lectures*, p. 41.
82 *Germany*, vol. 3, p. 120.
83 Ibid., p. 388.
84 On "enthusiasm," see Abrams, *The Mirror and the Lamp*, pp. 188–90, and Daniele Fortezza, "La nozione di 'entusiasmo' nella cultura riformata anglo-americana," in *Rivista di Studi Americani* 2 (1982): 218–27. A comprehensive recent study is David S. Lovejoy, *Religious Enthusiasm in the New World* (Cambridge, Mass.: Harvard University Press, 1985).
85 Cf. Madelyn Gutwirth, *Madame de Staël, Novelist* (Urbana: University of Illinois Press, 1978), pp. 279–80. This book provides a full assessment of the impact and influence of *Corinne*.
86 Miller, *Margaret Fuller*, p. xxi.
87 Cf. Gutwirth, *Madame de Staël*, p. 210: "Italy represents Romantic fullness as against the 'masculine' linearity of Enlightenment England."
88 *Germany*, vol. 1, p. 283.
89 Ibid., pp. 258–9.
90 *Corinne; or, Italy*, transl. Isabel Hill (New York, 1858), pp. 78–9.
91 *Germany*, vol. 3, p. 133.
92 In "Rome and Its Romantic Significance" (*The Beauty of Inflections*, p. 324) Jerome J. McGann observes that, for Byron, "the history of Rome becomes an emblem of his heart." This useful essay also explores the meaning of Rome for Goethe, Chateaubriand, Madame de Staël, and Stendhal.
93 All quotations in this paragraph are from Book 5, Chapter 3 of *Corinne*.
94 *Corinne*, p. 124.
95 Ibid., p. 100.
96 Ibid., p. 102.

97 In *The World of Washington Irving* (Philadelphia: Blakiston, 1944), p. 326, Van Wyck Brooks claims that Madame de Staël herself named the South Carolinian John Izard Middleton, whom she knew both at Coppet and in Rome, as the model for Lord Nevil. It is true in any case that, initially through her father, M. Necker, and continuing on her own after his death, Madame de Staël came to possess large tracts of land in New York State. Interestingly, some of this land was sold to James Fenimore Cooper's father, Judge William Cooper, in 1804, at which time Madame de Staël herself wrote him in English. These American holdings remained an imaginative, as well as a financial, resource for Madame de Staël, for she spoke frequently about her desire to emigrate to America in quest of freedom and a new life – or at least to send her son (as she wrote to Jefferson in 1816) on a New World pilgrimage "towards reason and liberty." In her family, she insisted, "Franklin, Washington, and Jefferson are revered as in their own country." See Richmond Laurin Hawkins, *Madame de Staël and the United States* (Cambridge, Mass.: Harvard University Press, 1930).

98 *Memoirs of Margaret Fuller Ossoli*, vol. 1 (Boston, 1852), p. 215.

99 Ibid., p. 228.

100 *Journals and Miscellaneous Notebooks of Ralph Waldo Emerson*, vol. 10, ed. Merton M. Sealts, Jr. (Cambridge, Mass.: Belknap Press of Harvard University Press, 1973), p. 69.

101 *Memoirs of Margaret Fuller Ossoli*, vol. 1, p. 289.

102 *Romanticism and Consciousness*, ed. Harold Bloom (New York: Norton, 1970), p. 56.

103 Thomas Pfau, "Rhetoric and the Existential: Romantic Studies and the Question of the Subject," *Studies in Romanticism* 26 (1987): 511. See also Jeffrey Steele, *The Representation of the Self in The American Renaissance* (Chapel Hill: University of North Carolina Press, 1987), esp. "The Question of the Subject," pp. 172–85. Steele observes that "Transcendentalist 'rhetorics of regeneration' . . . encourage their readers to accept the transformative power of language; they assume that unconscious 'spirit' can be incarnated and made present in their texts. . . . Participation lies at the center of this process. Rhetorics of regeneration work if readers participate in them as models of potential being. . . . Emerson, Thoreau, Whitman, and Fuller base their rhetorical practices upon faith in a collective ideality located in the depths of both author and reader."

104 Lacoue-Labarthe and Nancy, *The Literary Absolute*, p. 70. They go on to describe, by means of Friedrich Schlegel's *Ideas*, this "absolute mediator" in terms that bring to mind Emerson's notion of the "representative" figure, he who " 'perceives the divinity within himself' – who perceives himself as divine or as 'the God within us' – and who is charged with 'revealing,' 'communicating,' and 'presenting this divinity to all mankind in his conduct and actions, in his words and works.' " "Fundamentally," they explain, "the exemplarity of the absolute Subject (of the artist), absolute exemplarity, is auto-sacrifice" (p. 78). "The author, in order to reach his 'second power,' must take on literary character; he . . . must become *gedichtet*, composed, invented, written" (p. 118).

105 In an early *Dial* essay, "Thoughts on Modern Literature" (reprinted in

Essays and Lectures, pp. 1147–68), which it is likely Thoreau read, Emerson meditated on the radical *subjectiveness* of modern literature, worrying over "a pernicious ambiguity in the use of the term." Praising, on the one hand, the "single soul" that "sit[s] in judgment on history and literature" and "summon[s] all facts and parties before its tribunal," he rejected, on the other, those who have "no interest in anything but its relation to their personality" and who behold everything in the "partial light or darkness of intense selfishness." Then he adds, significantly, "nor is the distinction between these two habits to be found in the circumstance of using the first person singular, or reciting facts and feelings of personal history. A man may say *I,* and never refer to himself as an individual; and a man may recite passages of his life with no feeling of egotism." A useful discussion of "The First Person" in Transcendentalist writing is Lawrence Buell, *Literary Transcendentalism: Style and Vision in the American Renaissance* (Ithaca: Cornell University Press, 1973), pp. 263–330; also, Buell's treatment of the relationship, in Emerson, between the "first person superlative" and the "first person particular" in "First Person Superlative: the Speaker in Emerson's Essays," *American Transcendental Quarterly,* Part 1, no. 9 (1971): 28–34. Warner Berthoff reflects on the difference in Emerson between "mean egotism" and "*virtuous* conversion" in *Fictions and Events,* pp. 210–11.

1. "WHERE . . . IS THIS SINGULAR CAREER TO TERMINATE?"

1   I discuss the nature of Godwin's and Brown's "Gothicism" in "In the Hands of an Angry God: Religious Terror in Gothic Fiction," in *The Gothic Imagination: Essays in Dark Romanticism,* ed. G. R. Thompson (Pullman: Washington State University Press, 1974), pp. 42–64. In *La Tentazione della Chimera: Charles Brockden Brown e le Origini del Romanzo Americano* (Rome: Edizioni di Storia e Letteratura, 1965), p. 77, Marisa Bulgheroni observes that "while in Europe *le roman noir* fed the tortuous and invasive progress of eroticism and decadence, in America, through the filter of Brown's work, it provided an impulse toward the definition of a narrative sensibility that was metaphysical and moral, speculative." My understanding of Brown generally, and of his relation to the Gothic tradition, is indebted to this excellent study. See also Cathy N. Davidson, *Revolution and the Word: The Rise of the Novel in America* (New York: Oxford University Press, 1986), esp. pp. 212–53, "Early American Gothic: The Limits of Individualism." I find it hard to understand Henri Petter's claim that Brown "was taking first steps in psychological realism within a more or less distracting Gothic framework" (*The Early American Novel* [Columbus: Ohio State University Press, 1971], p. 371.)

2   In *Margaret Fuller: American Romantic,* ed. Perry Miller (New York: Anchor Books, 1963), p. 224.

3   William Spengemann, *The Adventurous Muse: The Poetics of American Fiction, 1789–1900* (New Haven: Yale University Press, 1977), p. 93.

4   See Roger Stein, "Pulled Out of the Bay: American Fiction in the Eighteenth Century," *Studies in American Fiction* 2 (1974): 13–36.

5   Robert Adams, *The New York Review of Books,* September 28, 1978, p. 8.

6   John Kirtland Wright, *Human Nature in Geography* (Cambridge, Mass.: Harvard University Press, 1966), p. 253.

7   Cited by Emerson in his journal for 1849. See *Journals and Miscellaneous Notebooks,* vol. 11, ed. A. W. Plumstead, William H. Gilman, and Ruth H. Bennett (Cambridge, Mass.: Belknap Press of Harvard University Press, 1975), pp. 130–1. For an eloquent discussion of Emerson's own "equation of landscape and redemptive history" see Sacvan Bercovitch, *The Puritan Origins of the American Self* (New Haven: Yale University Press, 1975).

8   Cited in ibid., p. 148.

9   Cited in Spengemann, *The Adventurous Muse,* p. 16.

10 Ibid., p. 16.

11 Ibid., p. 30.

12 Ibid., p. 31. On the opposition of the redemptive and geodemonic views of the New World, see also Howard Mumford Jones, *O Strange New World* (New York: Viking, 1964), and Leslie A. Fiedler, *The Return of the Vanishing American* (New York: Stein and Day, 1968).

13 Jones, *O Strange New World,* p. 70.

14 Walt Whitman, *Leaves of Grass,* ed. Harold W. Blodgett and Sculley Bradley (New York: Norton, 1968), pp. 417, 421, 423.

15 *Moby-Dick,* Chap. 127.

16 *Edgar Huntly,* Chap. 27.

17 *Frontier: American Literature and the American West* (Princeton: Princeton University Press, 1965), p. 9.

18 *Edgar Huntly,* "To the Public."

19 Ibid., Chap. 18.

20 Ibid., Chap. 10.

21 In "Charles Brockden Brown's *Edgar Huntly*: The Picturesque Traveler as Sleepwalker," *Studies in American Fiction* 15 (1987), 25–42, Beth Lueck suggests that Edgar is "naively ignorant of the real dangers of the American wilderness" because he has carried the standard categories of the European picturesque into a threatening new environment.

22 *Edgar Huntly,* Chaps. 9, 10.

23 Larzer Ziff has aligned Brown with Edwards in "A Reading of *Wieland,*" *PMLA* 77 (1962): 51–7. See also my "In the Hands of an Angry God: Religious Terror in Gothic Fiction."

24 *The Adventurous Muse,* p. 121.

25 Alden T. Vaughn and Edward W. Clark observe that the captivity genre "fused the prominent features of spiritual autobiography, lay sermon, and jeremiad with those of the secular adventure story." Such a "secular adventure story" as *Edgar Huntly* suggests that the proposition is reversible, that these stories themselves fused the captivity, the sermon, and the jeremiad. See *Puritans Among the Indians: Accounts of Captivity and Redemption* (Cambridge, Mass.: The Belknap Press of Harvard University Press, 1981).

26 *The Adventurous Muse,* pp. 87–8. Spengemann, of course, recognizes the

"poetics of adventure" as a unique American contribution to prose narrative, but he tends to view travel writing and the novel (seen in "domestic" terms) as "two genealogical lines [that] constitute two antagonistic literary traditions" (p. 68).

27 Ibid., p. 38.

28 Richard Slotkin, *Regeneration Through Violence: The Mythology of the American Frontier, 1600–1860* (Middletown: Wesleyan University Press, 1973), p. 256. In "Turning the Lens on 'The Panther Captivity': A Feminist Exercise in Practical Criticism," *Critical Inquiry* 8 (1981): 329–45, Annette Kolodny provides a female-centered reading of the narrative that stresses that archetypal American treatments of what Poe was to call "life in the wilderness" are not inevitably male oriented.

29 *Regeneration Through Violence,* p. 101.

30 Ibid., p. 107.

31 Cited in Stein, "Pulled Out of the Bay." All quotes from Stein are drawn from this article.

32 Joseph Dennie, "On Gothicism," *The Port Folio,* vol. 3 (1803). Reprinted in *Literature of the Early Republic,* ed. Edwin H. Cady (New York: Rinehart, 1950), pp. 474–7.

33 Reprinted in *The American Literary Revolution, 1788–1837,* ed. Robert E. Spiller (New York: Anchor Books, 1967), p. 22.

34 *Edgar Huntly,* "To the Public."

35 *Margaret Fuller: American Romantic,* p. 225.

36 Herman Melville, "Hawthorne and His Mosses," in *The Shock of Recognition,* ed. Edmund Wilson (New York: Modern Library, 1955), p. 192.

37 Leslie Fiedler observes that, in Brown's hands, the "novel of terror . . . is well on the way to becoming a Calvinist exposé of natural human corruption." See *Love and Death in the American Novel* (New York: Meridian Books, 1960), p. 148. Bulgheroni observes that Brown inherited "the Puritan sense of evil without being able to accept its metaphysical explanations" (*La Tentazione della Chimera,* p. 54).

38 This motif is explored at length by Norman S. Grabo in *The Coincidental Art of Charles Brockden Brown* (Chapel Hill: University of North Carolina Press, 1981). See also Sydney J. Krause's "Historical Essay" in the Kent State edition of *Edgar Huntly* (1984).

39 *Edgar Huntly,* Chap. 23.

40 In "Charting the Hidden Landscape: *Edgar Huntly,*" *Early American Literature* 16 (1981): 133–53, George Toles argues that "the 'country' that emerges in the . . . narrative is a spectral forest, receding ever further into a twilight gloom where objects shed both form and feature, and 'the conditions' that are revealed relate solely to the psychic disorder of the narrator."

41 See David Stineback, Introduction to *Edgar Huntly* (New Haven: College & University Press, 1973), p. 7.

42 Cf. Bulgheroni, *La Tentazione della Chimera,* p. 68: "Like perhaps no other figure in his time, the young Brown reflects the contradictions in an America moving from the eighteenth to the nineteenth century." On this subject generally, see Leon Howard, "The Late Eighteenth Century: An Age of

Contradictions," in *Transitions in American Literary History*, ed. Harry Hayden Clarke (Durham: Duke University Press, 1954), 51–89.

43 W. H. Prescott, "Charles Brockden Brown," in *Library of American Biography*, ed. Jared Sparks (Boston, 1839), 117–80.

44 See Basil Willey, *The Seventeenth Century Background* (New York: Anchor Books, 1955), p. 277.

45 Line 6 of *An Essay on Man* (1733).

46 See the beginning of *Natural Theology* (1802).

47 See his Introduction to *Arthur Mervyn* (New York: Holt, Rinehart, and Winston, 1962), p. xviii.

48 From *Stephen Calvert*, cited by Berthoff, p. xvi.

49 *Ormond*, Chap. 16.

50 *Arthur Mervyn*, Chap. 3.

51 Cited in *The Age of Enlightenment*, ed. Isaiah Berlin (New York: New American Library, 1956), p. 274.

52 *Arthur Mervyn*, Chap. 8.

53 *Edgar Huntly*, Chap. 16.

54 This and the following quotations from *Edgar Huntly*, Chap. 12.

55 Cf. Beverly R. Voloshin, "*Edgar Huntly* and the Coherence of the Self," *Early American Literature* 23 (1988): 276.

56 *Edgar Huntly*, Chap. 27.

57 Ibid., Conclusion, Letter 3.

58 *Moby-Dick*, Chap. 110.

59 Ibid., "Epilogue."

60 Reprinted in *The American Literary Revolution*, pp. 226–8.

61 Irving's influence on later American writers is detailed in William L. Hedges, *Washington Irving: An American Study, 1802–1832* (Baltimore: Johns Hopkins University Press, 1965).

62 On the origins of the concept of "be-wilderment," see John R. Stilgoe, *Common Landscape of America, 1580 to 1845* (New Haven: Yale University Press, 1982), pp. 7ff.

63 Cf. Jeffrey Rubin-Dorsky, *Adrift in the Old World: The Psychological Pilgrimage of Washington Irving* (Chicago: University of Chicago Press, 1988), pp. 75, 95–8.

64 Terence Martin, "Rip, Ichabod, and the American Imagination," in *A Century of Commentary on the Works of Washington Irving*, ed. Andrew B. Meyers (Tarrytown: Sleepy Hollow Restorations, 1976), p. 336.

65 Since "A History of Witchcraft" (or "History of New England Witchcraft" as it is called earlier in the tale) does not correspond to any of Mather's publications, it is not clear to what Irving is referring, whether to *Memorable Providences* (1689) or *Late Memorable Providences* (1691) or *Wonders of the Invisible World* (1693) or the *Magnalia* (1702). It *is* clear in any case that Irving is invoking Mather's obsession with witchcraft rather than his filiopietistic celebrations of seventeenth-century New England's great theocratic leaders. Albert J. von Frank observes that "as the allusions to Cotton Mather suggest, Ichabod's superstitiousness is the vestige of a decadent Puritanism from which God and glory have departed equally." See "The Man That

Corrupted Sleepy Hollow," *Studies in American Fiction* 15 (1987): 132. See also Lloyd M. Daigrepont, "Ichabod Crane: Inglorious Man of Letters," *Early American Literature* 19 (1984): 68–81.

66 Cf. Daniel Hoffman, *Form and Fable in American Fiction* (New York: Oxford University Press, 1965), p. 94.

67 Cotton Mather's father, Increase Mather, in fact delivered a sermon in 1702 entitled "Ichabod, or, a Discourse Shewing what Cause there is to Fear that the Glory of the Lord, is Departing from New England" that Perry Miller characterizes as "a jeremiad-to-end-all-jeremiads." See *The New England Mind: From Colony to Province* (Boston: Beacon Press, 1961), p. 247. The tradition lasted at least until John Greenleaf Whittier's "Ichabod," an indictment of Daniel Webster for his support of the Compromise of 1850.

68 *Emerson in His Journals,* ed. Joel Porte (Cambridge, Mass.: Belknap Press of Harvard University Press, 1982), pp. 260–9.

69 Reprinted from "Weeds and Wildings" (1890) in *A Century of Commentary,* pp. 75–84.

70 William Carlos Williams, *In the American Grain* (New York: New Directions, 1956), p. 130.

2. "WHERE THERE IS NO VISION, THE PEOPLE PERISH. . . ."

1 Susan Fenimore Cooper, *The Cooper Gallery; or, Pages and Pictures from the Writings of James Fenimore Cooper* (New York, 1865), pp. 129–31.

2 In "Sketches from Memory" (part of *Mosses from an Old Manse*), cited in Lee Clark Mitchell, *Witnesses to a Vanishing America* (Princeton: Princeton University Press, 1981), p. 113. Since the author claims to be quoting from "the portfolio of a friend," we must be a little wary of taking this remark as strictly confessional. Here and elsewhere Hawthorne does touch on Indian legends, and he retells a famous captivity story in "The Duston Family."

3 Sydney J. Krause provides a comprehensive survey of Brown's knowledge of and attitude toward the American Indian in his "Historical Essay" appended to the Kent State Edition of *Edgar Huntly,* concluding that for Huntly "the Indian and cougar are yet other selves."

4 Mitchell observes in *Witnesses to a Vanishing America* (p. 47) that "at the heart of [Cooper's] mythic interpretation of America, regret intensifies to tragic loss."

5 Leslie Fiedler explores the "vision of love and reconciliation between the races whose actual history is oppression and hate" in *The Return of the Vanishing American* (New York: Stein and Day, 1968). For more comprehensive surveys of white–red relations, see Roy Harvey Pearce, *The Savages of America: A Study of the Indian and the Idea of Civilization* (Baltimore: Johns Hopkins Press, 1953), and Elémire Zolla, *The Writer and the Shaman: A Morphology of the American Indian* (New York: Harcourt Brace Jovanovich, 1973).

6 In McGuffey's *Eclectic Fourth Reader* (1838). See Richard D. Mosier, *Making the American Mind: Social and Moral Ideas in the McGuffey Readers* (New York: Columbia University Press, 1947), p. 149; also, Edward D. Seeber, "Critical Views of Logan's Speech," *Journal of American Folklore* 60 (1947): 130–46.

7 Thomas Jefferson, *Notes on the State of Virginia*, ed. William Peden (Chapel Hill: University of North Carolina Press, 1955), p. 63.

8 According to Fiedler, *Return of the Vanishing American*, p. 79, but the actual sources are more ambiguous. Thus a certain Père Chonelec wrote in the year of her death: "[A]s soon as she died her appearance changed completely. She seemed so joyous and devoted that everyone was astounded." Cited in Henri Bechard, S.J., *Kateri Tekakwitha* (Ottawa: Editions Fides, 1967), p. 190. Daniel Sargent observes: "Before the darkness came a transformation took place in Catherine's visage. A kind of glorification of this Indian girl was enacted before the Indians. It seemed not only as if her hood had at last been thrown back – as it was – but as if she had torn a pock-marked mask from her face. The pock-marks were still there. Yet she shone." *Catherine Tekakwitha* (New York: Longman, Green, 1940), p. 243.

9 Joyce Flynn, "Melting Plots: Patterns of Racial Amalgamation in American Drama Before Eugene O'Neill," *American Quarterly* 38 (1986): 422.

10 Cited in Marcel Clavel, *Fenimore Cooper: Sa vie et son oeuvre* (Aix-en-Provence, 1938), p. 383.

11 *The Pioneers*, Chap. 16.

12 Cf. R. W. B. Lewis, *The American Adam* (Chicago: University of Chicago Press, 1958), p. 108. James C. Bryant offers a convincing darkly Manichaean reading of *Nick* in "The Fallen World in *Nick of the Woods*," *American Literature* 38 (1966): 352–64.

13 *Nick of the Woods*, Chap. 4.

14 Ibid., Chap. 34.

15 Ibid., Chap. 30. As Robert P. Winston observes, "[I]n hunting the Indians who killed and scalped his family, Indians who are imaged as both demons and animals, Nathan Slaughter grows like them. . . . But he out-demons his demons." "Bird's Bloody Romance: *Nick of the Woods*," *Southern Studies* 23 (1984): 83.

16 *Views and Reviews in American Literature, History and Fiction*, ed. C. Hugh Holman (Cambridge, Mass.: Belknap Press of Harvard University Press, 1962), p. 139.

17 Ibid., p. 142.

18 According to C. Hugh Holman. See his Introduction to *The Yemassee* (Boston: Riverside Editions, 1961), p. xvii.

19 *The Yemassee*, Chap. 21. Annette Kolodny comments on Simms's use of snakes as "the fictive representation of the psychological dangers inherent in pastoral." *The Lay of the Land: Metaphor as Experience and History in American Life and Letters* (Chapel Hill: University of North Carolina Press, 1975). On the rattlesnake as religious totem, cf. the Legend of Atotarho in Francis Parkman, *The Conspiracy of Pontiac*, vol. 1 (Boston, 1880), p. 13. See also vol. 2, pp. 168ff, 248.

20 This and the following quotations from *The Yemassee*, Chap. 20.

21 *Views and Reviews*, p. 112.

22 *Pontiac*, vol. 1, p. x.

23 Ibid., vol. 1, pp. 217, 257.

24 Ibid., vol. 2, p. 247.

25 Ibid., vol. 2, p. 237.

26 Ibid., vol. 1, p. 39.

27 Ibid., vol. 1, pp. 204ff.

28 Parkman states that the "precise origin [of the legend] is not easy to determine." In Appendix C to the second volume of *Pontiac* he tells us that he
found an account of Pontiac's recitation of the Delaware legend in the
"Pontiac Manuscript" that he received from Lewis Cass. But in the chapter
in which he has Pontiac retell the legend he also refers back to John M'Cullough's narrative of his captivity (as printed in Joseph Pritts's *Incidents of
Border Life* [1841]), in which M'Cullough reports on the appearance of a
Delaware "prophet" in the early 1760s who received his message from the
"being that *thought* us into being." This account says nothing, however,
about the prophet's ascending a mountain. In *Pontiac and the Indian Uprising*
(Princeton: Princeton University Press, 1947), Howard H. Peckham describes the prophet as a "psychopathic Delaware" and offers a different
version, set down in 1762, suggesting "that the Prophet had learned a
smattering of Christianity, which after meditation and self-induced visions
he had adapted or misinterpreted for Indian consumption" (p. 100; see also
pp. 113–16). Parkman himself observes that the whole business "might have
been the offspring of Pontiac's heated imagination, during his period of
fasting and dreaming." Tales of vision quests, however, are a common
feature of Native American folklore. See, for example, W. Y. Evans-Wentz,
Cuchama and Sacred Mountains, ed. Frank Waters and Charles L. Adams
(Chicago: Swallow Press, 1981), pp. 147–53. A useful general treatment is in
Silvester John Brito, "Visions and Vision Quests," *Southwest Folklore* 4
(1980): 8–19. In *Thoreau and the American Indians* (Princeton: Princeton
University Press, 1977), Robert F. Sayre discusses Thoreau's *Walden* experience as a "vision quest," using a much broader definition of that category
than I employ here.

29 *Pontiac,* vol. 1, p. 208.

30 Ibid., vol. 1, p. 147.

31 Ibid., vol. 1, p. 160. Parkman's ambivalent attitude toward the opposition of
civilization and the wilderness, as well as toward the "progress" that was
leading to the despoliation of the forest and the extermination of its aborigines, is well analyzed by Howard Doughty in *Francis Parkman* (New York:
Macmillan, 1962), pp. 190–202. Robert Gale comments on Parkman's
"Manichean" oppositions in *Francis Parkman* (Boston: Twayne, 1973), p.
110. See also Angela Giannitrapani, *Francis Parkman e La Fleur de Lis* (Napoli:
Bibliopolis, 1984), and Brian Harding, *American Literature in Context,* vol. 2,
1830–1865 (London: Methuen, 1982), pp. 124–42. In *History as Romantic Art*
(New York: Harcourt, Brace & World, 1963) David Levin reads Parkman as
"consistently critical" of the Indians' habits and traits.

32 *Emerson: Essays and Lectures,* ed. Joel Porte (New York: Library of America,
1983), p. 130.

33 Proverbs, 29:18.

34 Since I believe it is likely Cooper had this verse in mind as he framed *The
Pioneers,* a book in which, as I shall argue, "the law" is frequently treated
with searing irony, it is important to note that "the Law" mentioned in

Proverbs 29:18 is *torah,* not civil law. Divine law and "vision" (the Hebrew term *chazon* includes the concept of prophecy) are thus conjoined in the verse as the twin pillars of religious faith.

35 Cooper has in fact been called an "apologist for the Episcopal Church" who believed that "the church is unquestionably, impeccably divine, the mother of noble sons and daughters . . . who dutifully proclaim to a provincial and benighted society the undoubted truths committed to them" (William S. Hogue, "The Novel as a Religious Tract: James Fenimore Cooper – Apologist for the Episcopal Church," *Historical Magazine of the Protestant Episcopal Church* 40 [1971]: 26). Even a cursory reading of *The Pioneers* undermines such a view. As E. Arthur Robinson observes, "Cooper's writing is ultimately religious," but "the religious arguments are assigned to Natty." See "Conservation in Cooper's 'The Pioneers,' " *PMLA* 82 (1967): 574–5. I shall argue the case, however, for Chingachgook's "religious" function, in line with Clavel's observation that Natty is sometimes subordinated to "Indian John" in *The Pioneers* (*Fenimore Cooper,* pp. 385–6). In *James Fenimore Cooper the Novelist* (London: Routledge & Kegan Paul, 1967), p. 50, George Dekker remarks that "even more than Leatherstocking, old John is a repository of the skills and wisdom of the primitive society which Judge Temple's settlers have displaced."

36 Lawrence's *Studies in Classic American Literature,* reprinted in *The Shock of Recognition,* ed. Edmund Wilson (New York: Modern Library, 1955), p. 938.

37 *The Pioneers,* Chap. 36.

38 Ibid., Chap. 33.

39 Ibid., Chap. 28.

40 Ibid., Chap. 12.

41 *Views and Reviews,* p. 54.

42 As Michael Clark observes in "Caves, Houses, and Temples in James Fenimore Cooper's *The Pioneers"* (*Modern Language Studies* 16 [1980]: 227), "Cooper seems to be toying with religious motifs . . . in contrasting the social system with nature. For example, the central object in the landscape is Mount Vision. The mountain not only overshadows the town, but its name suggests a spiritual perception." I find incomprehensible Peter Valenti's claim that " 'Mount Vision' carries modern, Babbitt-like connotations of the 'man of vision,' the businessman who can predict demand profitably." " 'The Ordering of God's Providence': Law and Landscape in *The Pioneers,"* *Studies in American Fiction* 7 (1979): 196.

43 *The Pioneers,* Chap. 21.

44 Ibid., Chap. 26.

45 *Paradise Lost,* ed. Merrit Y. Hughes (New York: Odyssey Press, 1935), p. 368.

46 *The Pioneers,* Chap. 29.

47 Ibid., Chap. 37.

48 *Paradise Lost,* p. 372.

49 *The Shock of Recognition,* p. 958.

50 *The Pioneers,* Chap. 13.

51   Ibid., Chap. 16.
52   *Emerson in His Journals,* ed. Joel Porte (Cambridge, Mass.: Belknap Press of Harvard University Press, 1982), p. 285.
53   *The Complete Poetical Works of William Wordsworth* (Boston: Houghton Mifflin, 1904), p. 450.
54   Ibid., p. 449.
55   *The Pioneers,* Chap. 36.
56   Ibid., Chap. 38.
57   Ibid., Chap. 36.
58   Ibid., Chap. 38.

3. POE: ROMANTIC CENTER, CRITICAL MARGIN

1   *Southern Literary Messenger* 16 (1850): 172–87.
2   *Edgar Allan Poe: Essays and Reviews,* ed. G. R. Thompson (New York: Library of America, 1984), p. 1418.
3   I have culled information about "The Raven" from *Collected Works of Edgar Allan Poe,* ed. Thomas Ollive Mabbott, vol. 1: *Poems* (Cambridge, Mass.: Belknap Press of Harvard University Press, 1969).
4   David S. Reynolds provides a helpful discussion of Poe's relationship to popular authors in *Beneath the American Renaissance* (New York: Knopf, 1988). See also William Charvat, *The Profession of Authorship in America, 1800–1870,* ed. Matthew J. Bruccoli (Columbus: Ohio State University Press, 1968), pp. 84–105.
5   James D. Hart, *The Popular Book* (New York: Oxford University Press, 1950), p. 89. I have depended on this book throughout my discussion.
6   *The Journal of Henry D. Thoreau,* ed. Bradford Torrey and Francis Allen, vol. 5 (Boston: Houghton Mifflin, 1906), p. 459.
7   *The Popular Book,* p. 92.
8   Charvat points out that *The Scarlet Letter* did relatively well (compared to *Moby-Dick*), selling 10,800 copies in its first five years and 25,200 in its first twenty. See *The Profession of Authorship,* p. 241.
9   *Nathaniel Hawthorne: The Letters, 1853–1856,* ed. Thomas Woodson et al. (Columbus: Ohio State University Press, 1987), pp. 304, 307–8.
10   Cited in Joseph Wood Krutch, *Edgar Allan Poe* (New York: Knopf, 1927), p. 143.
11   *Adventures of Huckleberry Finn,* Chap. 17.
12   *The Sketch Book,* "Rural Funerals."
13   In *The Recognition of Edgar Allan Poe,* ed. Eric W. Carlson (Ann Arbor: University of Michigan Press, 1966), pp. 75–6.
14   *Uncle Tom's Cabin,* Chap. 15.
15   *Miss Ravenel's Conversion,* Chap. 6.
16   *Walden,* "Sounds."
17   *Baudelaire on Poe,* trans. and ed. Lois and Francis E. Hyslop, Jr. (State College, Pa.: Bald Eagle Press, 1952), p. 40.
18   See John E. Reilly, "Ermina's Gales: The Poems Jane Locke Devoted to Poe," in *Papers on Poe,* ed. Richard P. Veler (Springfield, Ohio: Chantry Music Press, 1972), p. 214.

19 William Coyle, "An Attack on Poe in 1864," in *Papers on Poe*, pp. 161–4.
20 This material is drawn from William H. Gravely, Jr., "Poe and Thomas Dunn English: More Light on a Probable Reason for Poe's Failure to Receive a Custom-House Appointment," in *Papers on Poe*, ed. Richard P. Veler (Springfield, Ohio: Chantry Music Press, 1972), pp. 165–93.
21 "Thomas Dunn Brown," in *The Works of Edgar Allan Poe*, vol. 8, ed. Edmund Clark Stedman and George Woodberry (Chicago: Stone & Kimball, 1895), pp. 64–8.
22 *The Confidence-Man*, Chap. 36.
23 See G. R. Thompson, *Poe's Fiction: Romantic Irony in the Gothic Tales* (Madison: University of Wisconsin Press, 1973), pp. 32–4.
24 "Diddling Considered as One of the Exact Sciences," in *Edgar Allan Poe: Poetry and Tales*, ed. Patrick F. Quinn (New York: Library of America, 1984), pp. 607–17.
25 *The Works of Edgar Allan Poe*, vol. 6, p. xxv.
26 *The Recognition of Edgar Allan Poe*, p. 66.
27 *The Works of Edgar Allan Poe*, vol. 6, p. xii.
28 Poe's tendency to "call attention to his own performance" in his "self-distracting artifacts" is subtly anatomized by Louis A. Renza in "Poe's Secret Autobiography," in *The American Renaissance Reconsidered*, ed. Walter Benn Michaels and Donald E. Pease (New York: Columbia University Press, 1985), pp. 58–89.
29 *The Works of Edgar Allan Poe*, vol. 6, p. xxi.
30 *Poe: Essays and Reviews*, pp. 1309–11.
31 In "Op Writing: Derrida's Solicitation of Theoria," in *Displacement: Derrida and After*, ed. Mark Krupnick (Bloomington: Indiana University Press, 1983), pp. 43–52, Gregory Ulmer, citing the work of E. H. Gombrich, comments suggestively on "marginal writing" – surprisingly, without mentioning Poe – as a form of "grotesque" or "arabesque" literary "decoration" within a "zone of license" that allows for the droll, the monstrous, and the fantastic. Its interest in "everything having to do with borders rather than centers" provides a kind of "peripheral vision" that functions to displace attention from the *ergon* (text) to the *parergon* (frame or commentary). Poe's marginalia may thus be viewed as literary hors d'oeuvres that supplant the main meal, reducing "serious" writing to whimsical and self-promoting chatter.
32 *Poe: Essays and Reviews*, p. 687.
33 Ibid., p. 1464.
34 Ibid., p. 14.
35 Ibid., p. 573.
36 Ibid., p. 1340.
37 *The Works of Edgar Allan Poe*, vol. 6, p. xxiv.
38 This is a vexed subject that has occasioned much debate. Histories of the controversy and arguments for and against Poe's authorship of the "Outis" letter may be found in Burton Pollin, "Poe as Author of the 'Outis' Letter and 'The Bird of Dream,' " in *Poe Studies* 20 (1987): 10–15; Kent Ljungquist and Buford Jones, "The Identity of 'Outis': A Further Chapter in the Poe–Longfellow War," *American Literature* 60 (1988): 402–15. The "Outis" letter

and Poe's reply are conveniently reprinted in *Poe: Essays and Reviews*, pp. 709–59.

39 *The Works of Edgar Allan Poe*, vol. 6, p. xviii.

40 *Poe: Essays and Reviews*, p. 579.

41 *The Works of Edgar Allan Poe*, vol. 6, p. xix.

42 *Poe: Essays and Reviews*, p. 818.

43 Ibid., p. 833.

44 Ibid., p. 818.

45 Ibid., p. 1003.

46 Ibid., pp. 756–7.

47 Ibid., p. 31.

48 Ibid., p. 1171.

49 *Emerson: Essays and Lectures*, ed. Joel Porte (New York: Library of America, 1983), p. 465.

50 *Edgar Allan Poe: Essays and Reviews*, pp. 1178–79. Renza observes that "one can construe Poe's tales as autobiographical cryptograms" ("Poe's Secret Autobiography," p. 63).

51 T. S. Eliot, *To Criticize the Critic* (New York: Farrar, Straus & Giroux, 1965), p. 55.

52 Ibid., p. 27.

53 Ibid., p. 31.

54 *The Recognition of Edgar Allan Poe*, p. 65.

55 *To Criticize the Critic*, p. 31.

56 *The Recognition of Edgar Allan Poe*, p. 157.

57 *The Poems of Edgar Allan Poe* (New York: Dutton, 1927), p. xii.

58 *Poe: Essays and Reviews*, pp. 1383–4.

59 *Poe: Poetry and Tales*, pp. 1356, 1286, 1276. (Italics in the original.)

60 *The Pilot*, Chap. 5.

61 *Poe: Poetry and Tales*, p. 1275.

62 *Poe: Essays and Reviews*, p. 76. Published posthumously, "The Poetic Principle" consists probably of material formulated in the early 1840s. Compare, for example, this passage on the "efflorescence of language" with what Poe had written about "descending from metaphor" in his 1842 review of Longfellow (*Essays and Reviews*, p. 684).

63 *Poe: Poetry and Tales*, pp. 1300–1.

64 Ibid., p. 1272.

65 Ibid., pp. 1310–11, 1317.

66 *Poe: Essays and Reviews*, p. 685.

67 *Poe: Poetry and Tales*, p. 1349.

68 Ibid., p. 1353.

69 Ibid., p. 1297.

70 Ibid., p. 1287.

71 M. H. Abrams, *Natural Supernaturalism* (New York: Norton, 1971), pp. 146 ff., 224–5.

72 *Poe: Poetry and Tales*, p. 1353.

73 Ibid., p. 1353.

74 Daniel Hoffman conjoins the two works very briefly in *Poe Poe Poe Poe Poe*

Poe Poe (New York: Doubleday, 1972), p. 292. A more sustained comparison of *Eureka* and *Beyond the Pleasure Principle*, focusing, as does my treatment, on figurative language and *"fictive speculation,* a new form of fiction neither poem nor science nor philosophy," is Clive Bloom, *Reading Poe Reading Freud: The Romantic Imagination in Crisis* (New York: St. Martin's Press, 1988), pp. 44–61. Peter Brooks, in a stimulating discussion of "Freud's Masterplot," describes *Beyond the Pleasure Principle*, as a "radically figural . . . displaced argument that knows no literal terms" and an act of "mythopoesis." He does not mention Poe (though he Poesquely calls plot "a kind of arabesque or squiggle toward the end"). See *Reading for the Plot: Design and Intention in Narrative* (New York: Vintage, 1985), pp. 90–112.

75 *Beyond the Pleasure Principle*, trans. James Strachey (New York: Bantam, 1959), p. 93.

76 Ibid., pp. 69–70.

77 Santayana's "A Long Way Round to Nirvana; or, Much Ado About Dying," was originally published in *The Dial* in 1923. It is conveniently reprinted in *The Philosophy of Santayana*, ed. Irwin Edman (New York: Scribner's, 1953), pp. 563–71.

78 *Beyond the Pleasure Principle*, pp. 74–5, 97–8, 108.

79 Ibid., pp. 100ff.

80 *Poe: Poetry and Tales*, p. 1272.

81 *Philosophy of Santayana*, pp. 566, 161.

4. EMERSON: EXPERIMENTS IN SELF-CREATION

1 *Ralph Waldo Emerson: Essays and Lectures*, ed. Joel Porte (New York: Library of America, 1983), pp. 122–3.

2 George Santayana, *Interpretations of Poetry and Religion*, ed. William G. Holzberger and Herman J. Saatkamp, Jr., with an Introduction by Joel Porte (Cambridge, Mass.: MIT Press, 1989), p. 132.

3 *Essays and Lectures*, p. 47.

4 *Selections from Ralph Waldo Emerson*, ed. Stephen E. Whicher (Boston: Houghton Mifflin, 1957), p. 13.

5 *Essays and Lectures*, pp. 5, 7, 46.

6 Ibid., pp. 22–3, 25, 47, 32, 15.

7 Ibid., pp. 10, 47.

8 Ibid., pp. 392, 124.

9 *Interpretations*, p. 131.

10 *Essays and Lectures*, pp. 91, 63.

11 Ibid., pp. 57, 60, 61–2.

12 Ibid., pp. 84–5.

13 Ibid., pp. 85–6.

14 Ibid., pp. 69, 64–5.

15 *Emerson in His Journals*, ed. Joel Porte (Cambridge, Mass.: Belknap Press of Harvard University Press, 1982), p. 246.

16 Ibid., pp. 237, 235.

17 *Essays and Lectures*, pp. 344–5.

18 *Journals and Miscellaneous Notebooks of Ralph Waldo Emerson*, vol. 8, ed. William H. Gilman and J. E. Parsons (Cambridge, Mass.: Belknap Press of Harvard University Press, 1970), pp. 69–70.

19 *Essays and Lectures*, pp. 483, 587.

20 William H. Gass, *Habitations of the Word* (New York: Simon and Schuster, 1985), p. 21.

21 *Essays and Lectures*, pp. 412, 408–9.

22 Ibid., pp. 410, 406, 413.

23 *Habitations of the Word*, p. 21.

24 *Essays and Lectures*, p. 364.

25 *Habitations of the Word*, p. 25.

26 *Essays and Lectures*, pp. 425–6.

27 Gertrude Reif Hughes, *Emerson's Demanding Optimism* (Baton Rouge: Louisiana State University Press, 1984), explores the difference between what she terms "affirmation" and "confirmation" in Emerson's work.

28 *Essays and Lectures*, pp. 206, 316, 318.

29 Ibid., pp. 412, 411, 385, 343, 345, 414.

30 *Emerson in His Journals*, p. 240.

31 Ibid., p. 249.

32 Ibid., p. 221.

33 Ibid., p. 235.

34 Ibid., p. 298.

35 *Essays and Lectures*, pp. 457–8, 459, 463, 465, 466.

36 *Emerson in His Journals*, p. 322.

37 *Essays and Lectures*, pp. 466–7.

38 Harold Bloom, "Emerson: The Glory and the Sorrows of American Romanticism," *Virginia Quarterly Review* 47 (1971): 550.

39 *Essays and Lectures*, p. 463.

40 Ibid., pp. 471, 476, 479, 481.

41 Ibid., pp. 486–7.

42 Ibid., pp. 487, 490, 492. David W. Hill explores Emerson's use of the Aeschylean figure in "Emerson's Eumenides: Textual Evidence and the Interpretation of 'Experience,' " in *Emerson Centenary Essays*, ed. Joel Myerson (Carbondale: Southern Illinois University Press, 1982), pp. 107–21.

43 *Emerson in His Journals*, p. 283.

5. HAWTHORNE: "THE OBSCUREST MAN OF LETTERS IN AMERICA"

1 *Emerson in His Journals*, ed. Joel Porte (Cambridge, Mass.: Belknap Press of Harvard University Press, 1982), pp. 288–90, 522.

2 John S. Martin develops this point briefly in "The Other Side of Concord: A Critique of Emerson in Hawthorne's 'The Old Manse,' " *New England Quarterly* 58 (1985): 453–8.

3 I have used throughout the text of "The Old Manse" as printed in *Hawthorne: Tales and Sketches*, ed. Roy Harvey Pearce (New York: Library of America, 1982), pp. 1123–49.

4 *Emerson: Essays and Lectures,* ed. Joel Porte (New York: Library of America, 1983), pp. 33, 38.

5 Ibid., p. 48.

6 Ibid., p. 7.

7 Gustave Flaubert, *Extraits de la Correspondance,* ed. Genevieve Bolleme (Paris: Editions Du Seuil, 1963), p. 188.

8 Ibid., p. 233.

9 Henry James, *French Poets and Novelists* (New York: Grosset & Dunlap, 1964), p. 249.

10 *Essays and Lectures,* p. 22.

11 Ludwig Wittgenstein, *The Blue and Brown Books* (New York: Harper & Row, 1965), pp. 6, 28.

12 *Essays and Lectures,* p. 12.

13 *The Collected Poems of Wallace Stevens* (New York: Knopf, 1957), p. 10.

14 *Emerson in His Journals,* p. 522.

15 *Essays and Lectures,* pp. 37, 80, 89, 393, 394, 395, 397.

16 Ibid., p. 521.

17 *The Scarlet Letter,* Chap. 10.

18 F. O. Matthiessen, *American Renaissance* (New York: Oxford University Press, 1941), p. 359.

19 "Relation of Analytical Philosophy to Poetry," in *The Portable Jung,* ed. Joseph Campbell (New York: Viking Press, 1971), p. 316.

20 Nathaniel Hawthorne, *The Letters, 1813–1843,* ed. Thomas Woodson et al. (Columbus: Ohio State University Press, 1984), p. 462.

21 From preface to *The Snow-Image.*

22 Ibid.

23 *The Letters of Herman Melville,* ed. Merrell R. Davis and William H. Gilman (New Haven: Yale University Press, 1960), pp. 123–4.

24 Cited in George E. Woodberry, *Nathaniel Hawthorne* (Boston: Houghton Mifflin, 1902), pp. 150–1.

25 A useful survey of critical opinion on "The Minister's Black Veil" through 1979 is Lea Bertani Vozar Newman, *A Reader's Guide to the Short Stories of Nathaniel Hawthorne* (Boston: G. K. Hall, 1979), pp. 199–208. Studies focusing on the "theological" aspect of the tale that I have found most stimulating are William Bysshe Stein, "The Parable of the Antichrist in 'The Minister's Black Veil,' " *American Literature* 27 (1955): 386–92; W. B. Carnochan, " 'The Minister's Black Veil': Symbol, Meaning, and the Context of Hawthorne's Art," *Nineteenth-Century Fiction* 24 (1969): 182–92; Michael J. Colacurcio, *The Province of Piety* (Cambridge, Mass.: Harvard University Press, 1984), pp. 314–85; Rosemary F. Franklin, " 'The Minister's Black Veil': A Parable," *American Transcendental Quarterly* 56 (1985): 55–63; Judy McCarthy, " 'The Minister's Black Veil': Concealing Moses and the Holy of Holies," *Studies in Short Fiction* 24 (1987): 131–8. A provocative debate that uses "The Minister's Black Veil" itself as a "parable" testing the possibilities and limitations of determinative reading is conducted by J. Hillis Miller and D. A. Miller in *ADE Bulletin* 88 (1987): 42–58.

26 I have used the text of "The Minister's Black Veil" as presented in *Hawthorne: Tales and Sketches,* ed. Roy Harvey Pearce, pp. 371–84.

27 *Poe: Essays and Reviews*, ed. G. R. Thompson (New York: Library of America, 1984), pp. 574–5.

28 Commenting on the *Mona Lisa*, J. H. Van den Berg suggests that "her smile seals an inner self . . . the secret inner self, the inner world in which everything the world has to offer is shut away." See *Romanticism and Consciousness*, ed. Harold Bloom (New York: W. W. Norton, 1970), p. 60.

29 George Santayana, *The Life of Reason or The Phases of Human Progress*, revised by the author in collaboration with Daniel Cory (New York: Scribner's, 1954), p. 94.

30 On Hooper's ambivalence toward marriage, see Frederick C. Crews, *The Sins of the Fathers* (New York: Oxford University Press, 1966), pp. 108–9.

31 Cited in Woodberry, *Nathaniel Hawthorne*, p. 89.

32 *Pierre*, Book 5, Chap. 2.

33 Arlin Turner, *Nathaniel Hawthorne* (New York: Holt, Rinehart and Winston, 1961), pp. 98, 88. Once again I have used *Hawthorne: Tales and Sketches* for my text of "The Birth-mark" (pp. 764–80). A survey of criticism through 1979 may be found in Newman's *Reader's Guide*, pp. 29–37. Other discussions that I have found especially helpful are Judith Fetterley, *The Resisting Reader: A Feminist Approach to American Fiction* (Bloomington: Indiana University Press, 1977), pp. 22–33; James Quinn and Ross Baldessarini, " 'The Birth-Mark': A Deathmark," *University of Hartford Studies in Literature* 13 (1981): 91–8; Jules Zanger, "Speaking of the Unspeakable: Hawthorne's 'The Birthmark,' " *Modern Philology* 80 (1983): 364–71; Allen Gardner Lloyd-Smith, *Eve Tempted: Writing and Sexuality in Hawthorne's Fiction* (Totowa, N.J.: Barnes & Noble, 1983).

34 *Walden*, "Higher Laws."

35 *Essays and Lectures*, p. 334. On Emerson and "The Birth-mark," see Alfred S. Reid, "Hawthorne's Humanism: 'The Birthmark' and Sir Kenelm Digby," *American Literature* 38 (1966): 343.

36 The parallel between the infant's hand and Aylmer's own is made clear when, angry with Georgiana for entering his laboratory, he seizes "her arm with a gripe that left the print of his fingers upon it." Effectively, the true "blight" that destroys Georgiana's beauty is Aylmer's scientific grasp.

37 Robert Kiely, *The Romantic Novel in England* (Cambridge, Mass.: Harvard University Press, 1972), p. 164. Cf. Lloyd-Smith, *Eve Tempted*, p. 99.

38 *The Blue and Brown Books*, p. 1. In "The Obliquity of Signs: *The Scarlet Letter*," *Massachusetts Review* 23 (1982): 9–26, Millicent Bell meditates suggestively on *The Scarlet Letter* as "an essay in semiology" that thematizes the "indeterminacy of signs."

39 Cf. Luther H. Martin, "Hawthorne's *The Scarlet Letter*: A Is for Alchemy?" *American Transcendental Quarterly* 58 (1985): 31–42. See also Itala Vivan, "An Eye into the Occult in Hawthorne's Text: The Scar of the Letter," *Quaderni di Lingue e Letterature* 8 (1983): 71–107.

40 On this subject generally, see Carol M. Bensick, "His Folly, Her Weakness: Demystified Adultery in *The Scarlet Letter*," in *New Essays on The Scarlet Letter*, ed. Michael J. Colacurcio (Cambridge: Cambridge University Press, 1985), pp. 137–59. See also Donald J. Greiner, *Adultery in the American*

Novel: Updike, James, and Hawthorne (Columbia: University of South Carolina Press, 1985).

41 *The Journals and Miscellaneous Notebooks of Ralph Waldo Emerson*, vol. 3, ed. William H. Gilman and Alfred R. Ferguson (Cambridge, Mass.: The Belknap Press of Harvard University Press, 1963), p. 243.

42 Crews, in *The Sins of the Fathers*, p. 141, calls Chillingworth "the psychoanalyst *manqué*." Crews's reading of *The Scarlet Letter* remains the most cogent Freudian treatment of the book.

43 *The Portrait of a Lady*, ed. Robert D. Bamberg (New York: Norton, 1975), p. 46.

44 Keats, *Selected Poems and Letters*, ed. Douglas Bush (Boston: Houghton Mifflin, 1959), p. 257.

45 *The Collected Poems of Wallace Stevens* (New York: Knopf, 1957), p. 469.

46 *Emerson: Essays and Lectures*, p. 411.

6. THOREAU'S SELF-PERPETUATING ARTIFACTS

1 I have cited the texts of *Walden* and *A Week on the Concord and Merrimack Rivers* as presented in The Library of America volume of Thoreau's works, ed. Robert F. Sayre (New York, 1985). Recent studies of *A Week* that I have found especially stimulating are Eric J. Sundquist, *Home as Found: Authority and Genealogy in Nineteenth-Century American Literature* (Baltimore: Johns Hopkins University Press, 1979), pp. 41–85; John Carlos Rowe, *Through the Custom-House: Nineteenth-Century American Fiction and Modern Theory* (Baltimore: Johns Hopkins University Press, 1982), pp. 28–51; H. Daniel Peck, " 'Further Down the Stream of Time': Memory and Perspective in Thoreau's *A Week on the Concord and Merrimack Rivers*," *The Thoreau Quarterly* 16 (1984): 93–118; Yves Carlet, "Thoreau et le temps retrouvé: *A Week on the Concord and Merrimack Rivers*," in *Age d'or et Apocalypse*, ed. Robert Ellrodt and Bernard Brugiere (Paris: Pubs. de la Sorbonne, 1986), pp. 149–71. All students of *Walden* remain indebted to Stanley Cavell's *The Senses of Walden* (New York: Viking Press, 1972).

2 Thomas Carlyle, *Sartor Resartus*, ed. Kerry M. Sweeney and Peter Sabor (New York: Oxford University Press, 1987), p. 170.

3 From the penultimate paragraph of "Economy."

4 See Rainer Maria Rilke, *Duineser Elegien* (Frankfurt am Main: Insel Verlag, 1970), p. 38

5 *The Collected Poems of Wallace Stevens* (New York: Knopf, 1957), p. 477.

6 William Carlos Williams, *In the American Grain* (New York: New Directions, 1956), p. 39.

7 *The Scarlet Letter*, Chap. 17.

8 Thoreau's phrase, "some unimaginable point of time," may help strengthen the suggestion that the spirit of Wordsworth broods over this chapter – most particularly in his sonnet, "Mutability":

> From low to high doth dissolution climb,
> And sink from high to low, along a scale
> Of awful notes, whose concord shall not fail;

A musical but melancholy chime,
Which they can hear who meddle not with crime,
Nor avarice, nor over-anxious care.
Truth fails not; but her outward forms that bear
The longest date do melt like frosty rime,
That in the morning whitened hill and plain
And is no more; drop like the tower sublime
Of yesterday, which royally did wear
His crown of weeds, but could not even sustain
Some casual shout that broke the silent air,
Or the unimaginable touch of Time.

9   As Rowe observes, "*A Week* demonstrates how Thoreau struggles not to
    transcend the temporal but to enter it more authentically than either clocks
    or unreflective experience allow" (*Through the Custom-House*, p. 51).

10 *Emerson in His Journals*, ed. Joel Porte (Cambridge, Mass.: Belknap Press of
    Harvard University Press, 1982), p. 196.

11 On responses to Thoreau's "unsatisfactory parable," see Richard Bridgman,
    Dark Thoreau (Lincoln: University of Nebraska Press, 1982), pp. 154ff.

12 T. S. Eliot, *The Complete Poems and Plays* (New York: Harcourt, Brace &
    World, 1963), pp. 80-1.

13 *The Journal of Henry David Thoreau*, vol. 9, ed. Bradford Torrey and Francis
    H. Allen (Boston: Houghton Mifflin, 1906), pp. 115ff.

14 For the drawing, omitted by Torrey and Allen, see William Howarth, *The
    Book of Concord: Thoreau's Life as a Writer* (New York: Viking Press, 1982),
    p. 128.

15 That is how Emerson tells the story in his memorial address on Thoreau, but
    his journal reveals that he was talking about his own experience. See *Emerson
    in His Journals*, p. 391.

16 As Cavell observes, "[T]he boon of Walden is *Walden*" (*The Senses of
    Walden*, p. 117.)

17 Walt Whitman, *Leaves of Grass*, ed. Harold W. Blodgett and Sculley Bradley
    (New York: Norton, 1965), p. 87.

18 Victor W. Turner, *The Ritual Process* (Chicago: Aldine, 1969), pp. 94-5.

19 *Leaves of Grass*, p. 9.

20 "Whatever Thoreau was doing, he was always, ultimately, doing the same
    thing," observes Frederick Garber in *Thoreau's Redemptive Imagination* (New
    York: New York University Press, 1977), p. 48.

7. MELVILLE: ROMANTIC COCK-AND-BULL. . . .

1   I have used throughout the text of *Moby-Dick* as presented in the Library of
    America volume edited by G. Thomas Tanselle (New York, 1983).

2   Newton Arvin, *Herman Melville* (New York: Viking Press, 1957), p. 235.

3   The text of "Cock-A-Doodle-Doo!" used here is from the "Uncollected
    Tales" in the third volume of *Melville*, ed. Harrison Hayford (New York:
    Library of America, 1984).

4   *Great Short Works of Herman Melville*, ed. Warner Berthoff (New York:
    Harper & Row, 1969), p. 75.

5   This question is comprehensively treated by Allan Moore Emery, "The Cocks of Melville's 'Cock-A-Doodle-Doo!' " *ESQ* 28 (1982): 89–111.

6   *Ralph Waldo Emerson: Essays & Lectures,* ed. Joel Porte (New York: Library of America, 1983), p. 568.

7   *Emerson's Complete Works,* vol. 11 (Boston: Houghton Mifflin, 1883), pp. 329–30.

8   *Nick of the Woods,* ed. Curtis Dahl (New Haven: College & University Press, 1967), pp. 70–1.

9   Cited from the Library of America *Mardi,* ed. G. Thomas Tanselle (New York, 1982), Chap. 146.

10 Charles Olson, "Lear and Moby Dick," in *Herman Melville,* ed. Paul Gerhard Buchloh and Hartmut Kruger (Darmstadt: Wissenschaftliche Buchgesellschaft, 1974), p. 121. See also Olson's *Call Me Ishmael* (New York: Reynall & Hitchcock, 1947), where he elaborates on how Shakespeare gave Melville "a bag of tricks."

11 See F. O. Matthiessen, *American Renaissance* (New York: Oxford University Press, 1941), Chap. 10.

12 *Collected Works of Edgar Allan Poe,* vol. 1: *Poems,* ed. Thomas Ollive Mabbott (Cambridge, Mass.: Belknap Press of Harvard University Press, 1969), p. 286.

13 Brian Way, *Herman Melville: Moby Dick* (London: E. Arnold, 1978), p. 24. Martin Green argues that "Ahab is a figure purely of melodrama" who "casts an unreal theatrical light on whatever he comes in contact with" in *Re-Appraisals: Some Commonsense Readings in American Literature* (New York: Norton, 1965), p. 100. Although David Leverenz, *Manhood and the American Renaissance* (Ithaca: Cornell University Press, 1989), is not essentially concerned with Ahab's theatricality, he insistently points to it: "Ahab's grand, stagey voice bullies me into empathizing with his heroic mastery of pain"; he speaks "with an extravagantly artificial blending of gothic melodrama and Elizabethan soliloquy"; "His voice becomes a babble of poses, a gothic Lear on the outside"; Ahab's language "has climactic rhetorical intensity, but it looks like flimflam and hokum. Ahab sounds melodramatic, abstracted, incoherent, literary, and pretentious. . . . The whole affair has been staged by a verbal magician to manipulate his crew" (pp. 279–97).

14 Robert Zoellner discusses "the question of Ahab's *subtlety,* or lack of it," especially as regards Ishmael's remarks in "The Specksynder," in *The Salt-Sea Mastodon: A Reading of Moby-Dick* (Berkeley: University of California Press, 1973), pp. 105ff.

15 Larzer Ziff, "Shakespeare and Melville's America," in *New Perspectives on Melville,* ed. Faith Pullin (Kent, Ohio: Kent State University Press, 1978), p. 57. For a comprehensive assessment of the function of Shakespeare's plays in nineteenth-century American culture, see Lawrence W. Levine, "William Shakespeare and the American People: A Study in Cultural Transformation," *American Historical Review* 89 (1984): 34–66. Apart from noting that Melville signed the letter to William Macready (discussed below), Levine does not deal with Melville's part in the "high"/"low" ("aristocratic"/ "democratic") debate implicated in contemporary Shakespearean performances.

16 I depend mainly on Richard Moody, *The Astor Place Riot* (Bloomington: Indiana University Press, 1958). See, too, his *Edwin Forrest* (New York: Knopf, 1960), as well as David Grimsted's *Melodrama Unveiled* (Chicago: University of Chicago Press, 1968).

17 Perry Miller, *The Raven and the Whale* (New York: Harcourt, Brace & World, 1956), p. 164.

18 Herman Melville, *Journal of a Visit to London and the Continent,* ed. Eleanor Melville Metcalf (Cambridge: Harvard University Press, 1948), p. 38.

19 All quotations drawn from "Uncollected Tales" in the Library of America's third volume of *Melville*.

20 Daniel Hoffman, *Form and Fable in American Fiction* (New York: Oxford University Press, 1965), p. 270.

21 Ibid., p. 256.

8. DOUGLASS AND STOWE: SCRIPTURES OF THE REDEEMED SELF

1 I have used the Signet edition of Douglass's *Narrative* (New York, 1968).

2 Henry D. Thoreau, *Reform Papers,* ed. Wendell Glick (Princeton: Princeton University Press, 1973), p. 124.

3 Cf. Houston A. Baker, Jr., "Figurations for a New American Literary History," in *Ideology and Classic American Literature,* ed. Sacvan Bercovitch and Myra Jehlen (Cambridge: Cambridge University Press, 1986), pp. 163ff.

4 On Douglass's *Narrative* as jeremiad, see William L. Andrews, "The Performance of the *Narrative*," in *Frederick Douglass's Narrative of the Life of Frederick Douglass,* ed. Harold Bloom (New York: Chelsea House, 1988), pp. 165–82.

5 See, for example, Richard Slotkin, *Regeneration Through Violence* (Middletown: Wesleyan University Press, 1973), pp. 441ff. Cf. William L. Andrews, "The First 50 Years of the Slave Narrative, 1760–1810," in *The Art of the Slave Narratives: Original Essays in Criticism and Theory,* ed. John Sekora and Darwin T. Turner (Macomb: Western Illinois University Press, 1982), pp. 6–24; Lucinda H. MacKethan, "From Fugitive Slave to Man of Letters: The Conversion of Frederick Douglass," *Journal of Narrative Technique* 16 (1986): 57; Angelo Costanzo, *Surprizing Narrative: Olaudah Equiano and the Beginnings of Black Autobiography* (New York: Greenwood Press, 1987).

6 Cf. Andrews, "The Performance of the Narrative," p. 168.

7 For an engaging discussion of the *moly* episode and its possible sources and analogues, see Denys Page, *Folklore in Homer's Odyssey* (Cambridge, Mass.: Harvard University Press, 1973), pp. 51–69. Cf. *Margaret Fuller: American Romantic,* ed. Perry Miller (New York: Anchor Books, 1963), p. 213.

8 Cf. Annette Niemtzow, "The Problematic of Self in Autobiography: The Example of the Slave Narrative," in *Frederick Douglass's Narrative of the Life of Frederick Douglass,* (see n. 4 above) p. 123.

9 "The Clay Foot of the Climber: Richard M. Nixon in Perspective," in *Literary Romanticism in America,* ed. William L. Andrews (Baton Rouge: Louisiana State University Press, 1981), p. 131. On Douglass's names, see also MacKethan, "From Fugitive Slave to Man of Letters," pp. 66–7.

10 H. Bruce Franklin, *The Victim as Criminal and Artist* (New York: Oxford University Press, 1978), p. 12, observes: "The writer and the boy are brought into direct physical contact as the writer takes his pen and lays it in the frost-cracked gashes in the boy's feet." Cf. Lucinda MacKethan, in *The Art of the Slave Narrative,* p. 63: "The image becomes a metaphor of mastery over time itself, as retrospection and immediacy merge. . . ."

11 Logan Rayford Whittingham, *Two Bronze Titans: Frederick Douglass and William Edward Burghardt Dubois* (Washington, D.C.: Howard University, 1972).

12 Seelye, "The Clay Foot of the Climber," p. 128, calls Douglass "a black Faust, an enchained Prometheus stealing white fire." Cf. Andrews, ibid., pp. 48–9.

13 Henry D. Thoreau, *Translations,* ed. K. P. Van Anglen (Princeton: Princeton University Press, 1986), p. 13.

14 E. Bruce Kirkham, *The Building of Uncle Tom's Cabin* (Knoxville: University of Tennessee Press, 1977), p. 114.

15 On Stowe's belief in a renewed "corporate system" cf. Elizabeth Ammons, "Stowe's Dream of the Mother-Savior: *Uncle Tom's Cabin* and American Women Writers Before the 1920's," in *New Essays on Uncle Tom's Cabin,* ed. Eric J. Sundquist (Cambridge: Cambridge University Press, 1986), p. 157. See also Jane Tompkins, "Sentimental Power: *Uncle Tom's Cabin* and the Politics of Literary History," in *Ideology and Classic American Literature,* pp. 283–7.

16 For a discussion of the general issue of order/disorder in *Uncle Tom's Cabin* as an emblem of organic health versus decay, see Theodore R. Hovet, "Modernization and the American Fall into Slavery in *Uncle Tom's Cabin,*" *New England Quarterly* 54 (1981): 499–518.

17 I have used the text of *Uncle Tom's Cabin* edited by Kathryn Kish Sklar for the Library of America volume of Stowe's novels (New York, 1982).

18 Cf. Philip Fisher, *Hard Facts* (New York: Oxford University Press, 1985), pp. 124–5.

19 Cf. William R. Taylor, *Cavalier and Yankee* (New York: George Braziller, 1961), p. 310. See also Hovet, "Modernization and the American Fall," p. 515.

20 Edmund Wilson, *Patriotic Gore* (New York: Oxford University Press, 1966), p. 10.

21 As Cushing Strout observes, "[I]f [Mrs. Stowe] stacked the cards, she did not deal all the good ones to any one section or group, particularly not to her own." See "*Uncle Tom's Cabin* and the Portent of Millennium" in *The Veracious Imagination: Essays on American History, Literature, and Biography* (Middletown: Wesleyan University Press, 1985), p. 60.

22 Cf. Jean Fagin Yellin, "Doing It Herself: *Uncle Tom's Cabin* and Woman's

Role in the Slavery Crisis," in *New Essays on Uncle Tom's Cabin,* p. 99. See also Tompkins, "Sentimental Power," pp. 282–3.

23 On Mrs. Stowe's "millennial expectations" see Strout, *"Uncle Tom's Cabin* and the Portent of Millennium," passim.

24 Cf. Ammons, "Stowe's Dream of the Mother-Savior," pp. 163–4.

9. WHITMAN: "TAKE ME AS I AM OR NOT AT ALL. . . ."

1   For my knowledge of the circumstances surrounding the 1868 English edition and of Whitman's relations with Rossetti and Hotten, I have drawn heavily on Morton D. Paley's "John Camden Hotten and the First British Editions of Walt Whitman – 'A Nice Milky Cocoa-Nut,' " *Publishing History* 6 (1979): 5–35.

2   *An American Primer,* ed. Horace Traubel (Stevens Point, Wis.: Holy Cow! Press, 1987), pp. 14, 16. This is a reprint of Traubel's 1904 publication. A meticulously reedited version under Whitman's original title, "The Primer of Words," is to be found in *Walt Whitman: Daybooks and Notebooks,* vol. 3, ed. William White (New York: New York University Press, 1978), pp. 728–57. From this edition we learn that after "kiss" Whitman initially wrote, and then canceled, "copulate."

3   For a sensitive account of Whitman's investment in his daguerrean images, see Alan Trachtenberg, *Reading American Photographs* (New York: Hill and Wang, 1989), pp. 60–70. On the 1855 engraving as "a visual equivalent to the poem," creating *"presence* between reader and poem," see also Graham Clarke, " 'To Emanate a Look': Whitman, Photography, and the Spectacle of Self," in *American Literary Landscapes,* ed. Ian F. A. Bell and D. K. Adams (London: Vision Press, 1988), pp. 78–101.

4   I have drawn my Whitman texts, unless otherwise indicated, from *Complete Poetry and Collected Prose,* ed. Justin Kaplan (New York: Library of America, 1982).

5   From *Specimen Days,* in *Complete Poetry and Collected Prose,* pp. 734–5.

6   Ibid., p. 758.

7   William Carlos Williams, *In the American Grain* (New York: New Directions, 1956), p. 234.

8   *Complete Poetry and Collected Prose,* p. 765.

9   *Walt Whitman: The Correspondence,* vol. 1: *1842–67,* ed. Edwin Haviland Miller (New York: New York University Press, 1961), p. 82.

10 See *Emerson in His Journals,* ed. Joel Porte (Cambridge, Mass.: Belknap Press of Harvard University Press, 1982), p. 399.

11 *Complete Poetry and Collected Prose,* p. 1197.

12 In *Walt Whitman's Workshop,* ed. Clifton Joseph Furness (Cambridge, Mass.: Harvard University Press, 1928), p. 62.

13 Ibid., pp. 127–30.

14 *Collected Poetry and Prose,* p. 175.

INTERCHAPTER: WALT AND EMILY

1   After I drafted these pages, two essays appeared conjoining Whitman and
    Dickinson and treating more comprehensively than I do their relations with
    the more standard mid-nineteenth-century poets. These essays are Herbert
    Lindenberger, "Walt Whitman and Emily Dickinson," in *Erkennen und
    Deuten: Essays zur Literatur und Literaturtheorie,* ed. Martha Woodmansee and
    Walter F. W. Lohnes (Berlin: Erich Schmidt, 1983), pp. 213–27, and Sandra
    M. Gilbert, "The American Sexual Poetics of Walt Whitman and Emily
    Dickinson," in *Reconstructing American Literary History,* ed. Sacvan Ber-
    covitch (Cambridge, Mass.: Harvard University Press, 1986), pp. 123–54.
    Though I am happy to defer to these more fully developed treatments, I am
    letting my "interchapter" stand for the sake of the continuity of my argu-
    ment. For other comparisons of Whitman and Dickinson, see Albert Gelpi,
    The Tenth Muse (Cambridge, Mass.: Harvard University Press, 1975), esp.
    pp. 220–2, and Karl Keller, *The Only Kangaroo Among the Beauty* (Baltimore:
    John Hopkins University Press, 1979), pp. 251–93.
2   Stanley T. Williams, in *The Recognition of Emily Dickinson,* ed. Caesar R.
    Blake and Carlton F. Wells (Ann Arbor: The University of Michigan Press,
    1964), p. 251.
3   Cited in Gay Wilson Allen, *The Solitary Singer* (Chicago: University of
    Chicago Press, 1985), p. 169.
4   In *A Century of Whitman Criticism,* ed. Edwin Haviland Miller (Bloom-
    ington: Indiana University Press, 1969), pp. 2–3.
5   Ibid., p. 15.
6   *The Recognition of Emily Dickinson,* pp. 10, 7.
7   Ibid., p. 34.
8   Ibid., p. 13.
9   Ibid., p. 27.
10 Ibid., p. 13. This was Arlo Bates, who about a year later (in November
    1891) again commented on Dickinson, this time explicitly claiming that she
    and Whitman belonged "to the same class; or rather . . . they are both the
    result of the same tendency in American intellectual life." See *Emily Dickin-
    son's Reception in the 1890s,* ed. Willis J. Buckingham (Pittsburgh: University
    of Pittsburgh Press, 1989), p. 221.
11 *Emily Dickinson's Reception in the 1890s,* p. 204.
12 *The Recognition of Emily Dickinson,* p. 36.
13 Ibid., p. 250.
14 *Emily Dickinson: Selected Letters,* ed. Thomas H. Johnson (Cambridge,
    Mass.: Belknap Press of Harvard University Press, 1971), p. 176.
15 Whitman, *Complete Poetry and Collected Prose,* ed. Justin Kaplan (New York:
    Library of America, 1982), pp. 671, 1004.
16 *The Recognition of Emily Dickinson,* pp. 213–14.
17 See Eleanor M. Tilton, "*Leaves of Grass:* Four Letters to Emerson," *Harvard
    Library Bulletin* 27 (1979): 336–41.
18 *Ralph Waldo Emerson* (Boston: Houghton Mifflin, 1885), p. 397.

19 *Complete Poetry and Collected Prose,* p. 918.
20 Herbert Lindenberger, in "Walt Whitman and Emily Dickinson," undertakes a more detailed comparison of Longfellow and Whitman.

10. DICKINSON'S "CELESTIAL VAIL"

1 Sandra M. Gilbert, "The American Sexual Poetics of Walt Whitman and Emily Dickinson," in *Reconstructing American Literary History,* ed. Sacvan Bercovitch (Cambridge, Mass.: Harvard University Press, 1986), p. 132, observes that "though many of [Dickinson's] references to established writers – Shakespeare, Keats, and the Brownings, for instance – were far more reverential than Whitman's, Dickinson was capable of elliptical expressions of literary scorn." Citing Poem 131, Gilbert goes on to call it "a small, sly essay in criticism."
2 All citations are from *The Complete Poems of Emily Dickinson,* ed. Thomas H. Johnson (Boston: Little, Brown, 1960).
3 Years later (1881), commenting on the death of Horace Church, gardener and sexton of the First Church in Amherst, Dickinson remarked: "I remember he was at one time disinclined to gather the Winter Vegetables till they had frozen, and when Father demurred, he replied 'Squire, ef the Frost is the Lord's Will, I dont pospose [*sic*] to stan in the way of it.' I hope a nearer inspection of that 'Will' has left him with as ardent a bias in it's favor." See *Emily Dickinson: Selected Letters,* ed. Thomas H. Johnson (Cambridge, Mass.: Belknap Press of Harvard University Press, 1971), p. 271.
4 Ibid., p. 95.
5 Curiously, the same notion informs Poem 249, "Wild Nights – Wild Nights!" This poem seems to me one of the most frequently misread texts in the Dickinson canon. The "Wild Nights" refer, not to some sexual orgy, but to the weather. Dickinson is saying that the stormy winds outside are "futile" and cannot touch two people who have reached "port" in each other's love.
6 *Selected Letters,* p. 200. For an overview of the tradition, see Tim Armstrong, " 'A Good Word for Winter': The poetics of a season," *New England Quarterly* 60 (1987): 568–83. On Dickinson's use of winter generally as setting and trope, see L. Edwin Folsom, " 'The Souls That Snow': Winter in the Poetry of Emily Dickinson," *American Literature* 47 (1975): 361–76, and Wendy Barker, *Lunacy of Light: Emily Dickinson and the Experience of Metaphor* (Carbondale: Southern Illinois University Press, 1987), pp. 80–6.
7 Anna Mary Wells, *Dear Preceptor* (Boston: Houghton Mifflin, 1963), p. 149.
8 Wells observes that "in one of Emily Dickinson's letters appears an interesting hint that Samuel Bowles thought she had written [the essay "Snow"]." As I shall suggest below, Dickinson effectively rewrote it. "Snow" was gathered the following year in Higginson's *Out-Door Papers* (Boston: Ticknor and Fields, 1863), which Dickinson owned and cherished. In a letter to Higginson in 1876 she remarked that her opening of his first book was "still as distinct as Paradise. . . . It was Mansions – Nations – Kinsmen – too – to

me – ." See Jack L. Capps, *Emily Dickinson's Reading* (Cambridge, Mass.: Harvard University Press, 1966), pp. 126, 176.

9 Karl Keller, *The Only Kangaroo Among the Beauty* (Baltimore: Johns Hopkins University Press, 1979), p. 213.

10 R. Jackson Wilson provides a very helpful analysis both of Higginson's "Letter" and of his relations with Dickinson in *Figures of Speech: American Writers and the Literary Marketplace from Benjamin Franklin to Emily Dickinson* (New York: Knopf, 1989), pp. 221–75.

11 Wilson, ibid., p. 239, observes of Higginson's nature essays that "he managed to combine occasional strokes of concreteness reminiscent of Thoreau with complacent assurances that a genial Unitarian rightness saturated the world."

12 Until recently there has been little significant commentary on this poem. Charles R. Anderson, *Emily Dickinson's Poetry: Stairway of Surprise* (New York: Holt, Rinehart, Winston, 1960), pp. 159–62, prefers a later (and, to me, distinctly inferior) version of the poem, remarking imperceptively of 311 that "in an early version, she confined herself to the pictorial aspects of this wintry pantomine." Similarly, Wendy Barker, *Lunacy of Light,* pp. 83–4, somehow imagines that Dickinson is describing "a season of icy fruitfulness" in which "the snow *provides* a 'Celestial Vail,'" encouraging the poet's mental processes and keeping God's judgmental eye at bay. That the snow's artisans become silent after their work is done is another indication of how friendly this aspect of nature is for Dickinson." On the other hand, Cynthia Griffin Wolff, *Emily Dickinson* (New York: Knopf, 1986), pp. 434–8, in her incisive reading of the poem, observes that it is "ominous" and "the lines seem compelled to record an unrelenting process of annihilation." She also notes that the later, more playful version of the poem moves "in the direction of the merely scenic."

13 At a 1985 Harvard seminar in which this chapter was discussed, Barbara Johnson helpfully suggested that 311 be considered in the context of Paul de Man's "Autobiography As De-Facement" (*The Rhetoric of Romanticism* [New York: Columbia University Press, 1984], pp. 67–81), in which he deals "with the giving and taking away of faces, with face and deface, *figure, figuration* and disfiguration." De Man's conclusion ("Autobiography veils a defacement of the mind of which it is itself the cause") may help us to read "It sifts from Leaden Sieves – " as a "slant" version of Dickinson's predicament. In de Man's terms, Dickinson's "Celestial Vail" – her trope for the agency of defacement – is self-inflicted. The very act of inscribing herself as an obliterated snow-figure is itself antiapocalyptic, a *veiling* discourse that defaces the subject. The poem would then be read as an allegory of self-concealment – as a figure, that is, for Dickinson's self-concealing poetic identity (her strategy of self-obliteration). But, of course, Dickinson's play on the biblical trope of "revelation" suggests equally that the agency of this autobiographical "defacement" is external – an "imperial affliction," to borrow the language of Poem 258, sent her "of the Air."

14 Dolores Dyer Lucas, *Emily Dickinson and Riddle* (Dekalb: Northern Illinois

University Press, 1969), pp. 36–7, briefly comments on the later version of 311.

15 Vivian R. Pollak, *Dickinson: The Anxiety of Gender* (Ithaca: Cornell University Press, 1984), p. 216, remarks of "It was not Death . . ." that "as she seeks to explain herself to herself, negative definitions and imperfect analogies provide her with an approach to meaning."

16 *The Letters of Emily Dickinson,* ed. Thomas H. Johnson and Theodora Ward, vol. 3 (Cambridge, Mass.: Belknap Press of the Harvard University Press, 1958), p. 699.

17 This was the revised version. As Wolff shrewdly suggests, "[Dickinson] may have been moved by tact as much as anything else, for by 1883 the deep harmonic of religious implication that suffuses the earlier version would have seemed antique to the ear of a cosmopolitan publisher" (*Emily Dickinson,* p. 438).

18 *Letters,* vol. 3, p. 768.

19 Sandra M. Gilbert elaborates on the notion of Dickinson as "Snow White" in *The Madwoman in the Attic* (New Haven: Yale University Press, 1979), pp. 581–650.

20 On this point, see Sandra M. Gilbert, "The Wayward Nun Beneath the Hill: Emily Dickinson and the Mysteries of Womanhood," in *Feminist Critics Read Emily Dickinson,* ed. Suzanne Juhasz (Bloomington: Indiana University Press, 1983), pp. 22–44, as well as the chapter in *The Madwoman in the Attic,* cited in the preceding note.

21 In Jay Leyda, *The Years and Hours of Emily Dickinson,* vol. 3 (New Haven: Yale University Press, 1960), p. 305.

22 Cf. Wells, *Dear Preceptor,* p. 290, and Keller, *The Only Kangaroo Among the Beauty,* p. 213.

23 Cf. Gilbert, *Feminist Critics,* p. 33.

24 *Letters,* vol. 2, p. 537.

25 Cf. Thomas H. Johnson, *Final Harvest* (Boston: Little, Brown, 1961), p. x.

26 *Emerson: Essays and Lectures,* ed. Joel Porte (New York: Library of America, 1983), p. 587.

27 On Emily Dickinson, pain/pleasure, and Keats, see Joanne Feit Diehl, *Dickinson and the Romantic Imagination* (Princeton: Princeton University Press, 1981), esp. pp. 80–1.

28 On Dickinson and consciousness, see Albert J. Gelpi, *Emily Dickinson: The Mind of the Poet* (Cambridge, Mass.: Harvard University Press, 1965), p. 99ff. Cf. Gelpi's *The Tenth Muse: The Psyche of the American Poet* (Cambridge: Harvard University Press, 1975), pp. 263–4.

29 Wallace Stevens, *The Collected Poems* (New York: Knopf, 1957), p. 222.

30 *Hamlet,* II, ii, 250–2.

31 George Santayana, *Interpretations of Poetry and Religion,* ed. William G. Holzberger and Herman J. Saatkamp, Jr., with an Introduction by Joel Porte (Cambridge, Mass.: MIT Press, 1989), p. 129.

32 The case for the Modernists' movement "outward from the individual and local to the relational and universal" is made by Robert Kiely in his excellent

study of Joyce, Woolf, and Lawrence, *Beyond Egotism* (Cambridge, Mass.: Harvard University Press, 1980).

33 I have taken the text of "Self-Portrait in a Convex Mirror" from *The Harvard Book of Contemporary American Poetry,* ed. Helen Vendler (Cambridge, Mass.: Belknap Press of Harvard University Press, 1985), pp. 228–41.

34 Philippe Lacoue-Labarthe and Jean-Luc Nancy, *The Literary Absolute* (Albany: SUNY Press, 1988), p. 70.

Index

CAMBRIDGE STUDIES IN AMERICAN LITERATURE AND CULTURE

Continued from the front of the book

Printed in Great Britain
by Amazon